Memoirs of
Peasant Tolstoyans
in Soviet Russia

Memoirs of Peasant Tolstoyans *in* Soviet Russia

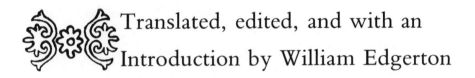Translated, edited, and with an Introduction by William Edgerton

Indiana University Press | BLOOMINGTON AND INDIANAPOLIS

This English-language edition is translated from
Vospominanija krest'jan-tolstovtsev 1910–1930-e gody,
compiled by A. B. Roginskij (Moscow: Kniga, 1989).

The paper used in this publication meets the minimum requirements of
American National Standard for Information Sciences—Permanence of Paper
for Printed Library Materials, ANSI Z39.48-1984.

MANUFACTURED IN THE UNITED STATES OF AMERICA

Library of Congress Cataloging-in-Publication Data

Vospominaniia krest'ian-tolstovtsev, 1910–1930-e gody. English.
   Memoirs of peasant tolstoyans in Soviet Russia / translated,
edited, and with an introduction by William Edgerton.
      p.   cm.—(Indiana-Michigan series in Russian and East
European studies)
   Includes bibliographical references and index.
   ISBN 0-253-31911-0 (cloth : alk. paper)
   1. Tolstoy, Leo, graf, 1828–1910—Appreciation—Soviet Union.
2. Peasantry—Russia—Biography. 3. Peasantry—Soviet Union—
Biography. I. Edgerton, William Benbow, 1914– . II. Title.
III. Series.
PG3409.5V613   1993
891.73'3—dc20   92-28608

1 2 3 4 5 97 96 95 94 93

PG
3409.5
.V613
1993

CONTENTS

LIST OF ILLUSTRATIONS

ACKNOWLEDGMENTS

The introduction to this book owes much to travel grants I have received from IREX and Indiana University for my research in Bulgaria and the Soviet Union on Tolstoy's worldwide social influence. I am also grateful to Indiana University for a whole series of faculty grants in aid of this research, and to the Hoover Institution for permission to publish one letter from its collection of Tolstoyan documents on microfilm.

I owe a great deal to the kindness of friends in Russia, notably to the late A. V. Khrabrovítsky for first putting me in contact with the surviving Tolstoyans; to A. B. Rogínsky, the editor of the original Russian edition of this book, who assisted me in obtaining the permission to translate it into English and gave me his own copy of the Russian page proofs, thus enabling me to begin translating it even before the Russian edition came off the press; and above all to Míra Iósifovna Pérper, a professional translator to and from English and the daughter of an associate of Tolstóy, for her unflagging helpfulness with my dozens of questions large and small about the Tolstoyans involved in these memoirs and the language in which they expressed themselves. I owe a special debt of gratitude to the late R. F. Zherlítsyn, his widow V. S. Zherlítsyna, and their daughter Olga Miloshúnas, who invited me to be their house guest in the summer of 1990 in the Siberian city of Novokuznétsk so that I could get personally acquainted with Borís Vasílyevich Mazúrin, whose memoirs form the centerpiece of this book. During each of my three days with them, the Zherlítsyns took me in their car to the nearby village of Tálzhino for conversations with Mazúrin, to whom I am likewise deeply grateful for his hospitality and for his continuing help and friendship.

The illustrations in this book call for a special note of appreciation. They are made from priceless photographs entrusted to me on loan by Borís Vasílyevich and by Míra Iósifovna from personal collections that were almost miraculously preserved through decades of turmoil and terror.

My final acknowledgment is to my wife, Jewell Conrad Edgerton, who has lighted my life for nearly six decades, and to whom this book is dedicated with love and gratitude.

This book tells the story of a confrontation between the rulers and the ruled that may possibly have no parallel in modern history. On the one side were the Bolshevik leaders who had seized power in Russia in October 1917. They were certain their blueprint for a socialist society could enable them to build a better paradise here on earth than the one the Church promised in heaven. On the other side were those whom the Bolsheviks' doctrine had led them to anticipate as the enemies of their new society, and whom they were prepared to handle: the dictatorship of the Communist Party in the name of the proletariat would take care of their opponents.

But one group of opponents did not fit neatly into the Bolsheviks' blueprint. They numbered in the thousands, most of them hard-working peasants, and they were known as Tolstoyans. They had come under the influence of Leo Tolstóy's writings during the last three decades of his life, when his study of the teachings of Jesus, particularly in the Sermon on the Mount, had led him to work out a kind of radical Christian anarchism, emphasizing truth, brotherly love, and the rejection of violence.

From the end of 1928 until September 1988, the fate of these Tolstoyans was so effectively blacked out by government censorship that several generations of Soviet citizens grew up unaware of the Tolstoyan movement during the 1920s or the fate of the thousands of peasant Tolstoyans during the forced collectivization of agriculture in the 1930s.

Tolstóy's Religious and Social Influence

Paradoxically, the story of Tolstóy's personal religious revolution at the end of the 1870s and the worldwide influence of his religious thought at the turn of the century have been as thoroughly forgotten in the West as they were distorted and suppressed (until 1988) in the Soviet Union. Tolstóy's *War and Peace* and *Anna Karénina* continue to be recognized among the classics of world literature, but few Americans now are aware of the excitement his religious and social message created a century ago. When Western readers suddenly discovered Russian literature in the mid-1880s, they telescoped some thirty years of Tolstóy's literary development, simultaneously coming to know the Tolstóy of the great novels and the Tolstóy of *A Confession, What I Believe,* and *What Then Must We Do?* For a reading public satiated with the nonmoral, materialistic scientism of the French Naturalists, Tolstóy's writings provided a refreshing change. His influence affected the lives of such distinguished public figures as the novelist and editor William Dean Howells in the United States, Mahatma Gandhi in India, and a host of less well known personages in Europe and America, as well as many ordinary people around the world whose response to his influence is reflected in the mass of letters from readers that are preserved in the Tolstóy archives in Moscow.

What was it that made Tolstóy's religious works have such an impact? Certainly one thing was the sheer drama of seeing Russia's leading writer turn his back on novels and address his readers in simple terms about such eternal questions as faith and doubt, good and evil, and the meaning of life and death. These works were all the more effective because they took the teachings of Jesus as their starting point, yet gave them a fresh interpretation. The heart of Tolstóy's message was what he called the Law of Love, as expressed in Jesus' commandments to love God with all one's heart and one's neighbor as oneself, and to "resist not him that is evil."

Starting from these commandments and proceeding with the kind of maximalist logic that the philosopher Berdyáev called a typically Russian trait,[1] Tolstóy built up a whole philosophy of Christian anarchism. He rejected all institutions based on coercion, including the state, the military forces, the law courts, and the police; and he condemned as immoral the ownership of private property and the use of money. His criticism of the Russian Orthodox Church for what he considered to be a distortion of Jesus' true teachings led the church first to censor his works and then to excommunicate the author. His acquaintance in the early 1880s with poverty and degradation in the Moscow slums strengthened his repulsion for city life and led to his cult of simplification and living by one's own physical labor on the land. His reading of Henry George's *Social Problems* and *Progress and Poverty* turned him into an enthusiastic supporter of the American writer's theories about land taxation. In time his nonviolence was extended to other forms of life and led him to renounce his old sport of hunting and adopt vegetarianism. He also came to give up alcohol and tobacco. In his later years, with the publication of his sensational short novel *The Kreutzer Sonata* and its Afterword, his moral maximalism drove him beyond the support of strict monogamy to the advocacy in theory of complete sexual continence—even though he frankly admitted his own failure to achieve that in practice.

In 1898 he published his book *What Is Art?*, which a prominent English critic called a liberating force because of Tolstóy's idea "that a work of art was not the record of beauty already existent elsewhere, but the expression of an emotion felt by the artist and conveyed to the spectator."[2] When Tolstóy went on, however, to present examples of what he considered good and bad art, his opinions were so wrong-headed that few readers have given his theoretical discussion the serious attention it deserves. His view of art is paralleled by a similar view of science. "True science," he asserts, "investigates and brings to human perception such truths and such knowledge as the people of a given time and society consider most important."[3]

The most controversial of these elements was Tolstóy's doctrine of nonresistance to evil by violence. This doctrine has been variously interpreted and misinterpreted, partly because "nonresistance" seems to imply mere passivity in the face of evil. In this respect it can be argued that Tolstóy's greatest disciple, Gandhi, spoke more wisely and clearly than the master. Gandhi believed not in nonresistance to evil by violence, but in *nonviolent resistance* to evil. He made it clear that he believed we are obligated to resist evil by the most effective means we know—but he also made clear his own conviction that the most effective means of resistance is nonviolent.

Aylmer Maude, Tolstóy's English translator and personal acquaintance, whose biography is arguably still the best one we have, always regretted that the writer's "mis-statement of the theory of Non-Resistance has served, more than anything else, to conceal from mankind his greatness as a thinker." Still, he insisted, "we need not let this permanently divert our attention from the many profound things he has said with admirable force and lucidity."[4] In a warm and appreciative letter written toward the end of Tolstóy's life, Maude gently hinted at a blind spot in his social vision. "You are definitely antipolitical," he said, "whereas it is bred in my bones to feel that the work done by Pym and Hampden, Washington and Abraham Lincoln, and in general the attempt the Western world has made at Constitutional Government—faulty and imperfect as it is, and slow as has been its progress—was not an ignoble effort and has not utterly failed; and that that path may yet lead on to a juster and kindlier society than the world has yet seen."[5]

Tolstoyism as a Movement

Tolstóy's revulsion against what he saw as the parasitic life of his own upper class and his belief in the moral value of physical labor for everyone inspired readers in Russia, England, Bulgaria, Holland, the United States, and even Chile and Japan to attempt to organize agricultural colonies on the basis of his principles. In Russia up to 1917 and in the other countries as well, these attempts were led by idealistic young landowners or city-bred intellectuals, innocent for the most part of any experience in farming and even of practical common sense. Instead of striving to live in the spirit of Tolstóy's Law of Love and working out its corollaries for themselves, they appeared to try to make a rigid new orthodoxy out of Tolstóy's own set of corollaries.[6]

Notwithstanding the failure of most of these agricultural ventures, Tolstóy's influence continued to spread. In Russia, his religious and social writings acquired a following among the peasants as a result of the organization by some of his associates in 1885 of the Posrédnik ("Intermediary") publishing house for the purpose of providing good literature to the masses at very low prices. In 1900 the Chief Procurator of the Holy Synod reported that Tolstoyism as a sect could now be found in eight provinces of the Russian

Empire as well as in the Caucasus. It was beginning to dominate other "sectarian false doctrines," he said, "which under its influence are losing their independence and originality," and was even making inroads into "the healthy part of the Russian people, the Orthodox population."[7]

The increasing censorship of Tolstóy's new religious works did not keep them from circulating in Russia. It merely encouraged alternative forms of distribution such as handwritten and hectographed copies. When two of Tolstóy's chief associates, Vladímir Chertkóv and Pável Biryukóv, were deported by the authorities in 1897, this only improved the circulation. Chertkóv settled in England and Biryukóv in Switzerland; and both of them began publishing uncensored Tolstoyan works for both the peasants and the intellectuals. As these illegal works found their way back into Russia, the number of Tolstóy's followers in all social classes steadily grew.

A turning point in the history of Russian Tolstoyism came in February 1909 when the writer's disciples founded the Moscow Vegetarian Society, whose humanitarian goals went considerably beyond mere dietary matters and have since been described by one of its members as "the establishment of love and peace among all living creatures." The society's headquarters in a two-story building at No. 12 Newspaper Lane[8] served for two decades as the unofficial center of the Tolstoyan movement and is mentioned frequently in these memoirs. It housed a vegetarian dining hall, a library and bookshop devoted to publications associated with Tolstoyan and vegetarian ideals, and a large meeting room for lectures, discussions, and performances. By the time of the October Revolution in 1917, the Tolstoyans were estimated to number between five and six thousand.[9]

Tolstoyism after the 1917 Revolutions

Between the February and October revolutions in 1917, the Tolstoyans took advantage of the eight months of freedom from censorship to get into print as many copies as possible of Tolstóy's religious works. In June of that year they founded the Society of True Freedom in Memory of Leo Tolstóy [Obshchestvo istinnoj svobody v pamjat' L. N. Tolstogo] in Moscow, which announced as its aim "to facilitate contacts among all who sympathize with the philosophy of life that Tolstóy represents, and also to assist in educational tasks." Within months there were branches of the new organization in Kíev, Sóchi, Tsarítsyn, Vítebsk, Vladímir, and many other towns and villages. The outbreak of the October Revolution soon gave the Society of True Freedom an opportunity to show how serious they were. During the armed uprising in Moscow, the Society printed a leaflet entitled "Stop the Fratricide!" ["Prekratite bratoubijstvo!"] and signed by two leading Tolstoyans whose names will appear often in this book, Vladímir Chertkóv and Ivan Gorbunóv-Posádov. Members of the organization went out in the streets and distributed it among fighters on both sides. In November 1918 they addressed a petition to the Council of People's Commissars proposing the abolition of the death penalty. In 1919 they published a brochure, *To All Friends and Like-minded People [Vsem druz'jam i edinomyshlennikam]*, recommending that the Society "raise its voice against war, the death penalty, pogroms, mob law, the torture of animals, and other deformities of society," and that it adopt as one of its highest priorities a campaign to persuade city dwellers to help build a better society by moving to the country, taking up farm work, and organizing agricultural colonies.

During the first years after the October Revolution, the Tolstoyans continued their vigorous publishing activity. The Intermediary publishing house issued sixty-three editions of Tolstóy's writings in 1917–18 alone, most of them small booklets for the masses. Provincial Tolstoyan publishing enterprises were also started in Samára, Vorónezh, Khárkov, and Yekaterinodár. In Moscow the Zádruga publishing house, which had no direct connection with Tolstoyism, published thirteen booklets in a series called Works of Leo Tolstóy Previously Forbidden by the Censorship; and in 1918 in Smolénsk Province, through some unexplained quirk of ideological inconsistency, six booklets of Tolstóy's works, including *The Gospel in Brief* and *The Teachings of Christ*, were published by no less an arm of the Soviet regime than the Commissariat of People's Education. Among the Tolstoyan periodicals appearing during the first years of the Soviet period were *The Voice of Tolstóy and Unity [Golos Tolstogo i edinenie]*; *The Renewal of Life [Obnovlenie zhizni]*, a monthly founded in the summer of 1917, only two issues of which were published; and *True Freedom [Istinnaja svoboda]*, whose eight issues, published between April 1920 and the spring of 1921, are considered the most important printed source of information we have about the Tolstoyan movement during the period of its most vigorous growth. The circulation of *True Freedom* reached about ten thousand copies. All these periodicals ceased publication by early 1921, and from then until 1929, the only Tolstoyan periodicals to appear were handwritten or mimeographed.

The Tolstoyans and War

The first serious problem confronting the Tolstoyans after the October Revolution was the same one they had faced under the tsarist government: their commitment to nonviolence and refusal to serve in the armed forces. At first the attitude of the new Soviet government was surprisingly conciliatory. On 4 January 1919, in the very midst of the Civil War, Lénin signed a decree of the Council of People's Commissars granting complete exemption from military service to any man who could demonstrate sincere objection on the basis of his religious convictions. Moreover, the power to determine each man's sincerity was placed in the hands of the United Council of Religious Communities and Groups, which had been formed in October 1918 on the initiative of Vladímir Chertkóv and was composed of representatives of the Tolstoyans, Mennonites, Baptists, Evangelical Christians, and other religious sects. Chertkóv's name carried so much weight that during the first ten months of 1918, even before Lénin's decree and the formation of the United Council, a written statement by Chertkóv attesting to the seriousness of a religious objector was accepted by the government as grounds for granting exemption from military service. During those ten months, between three hundred and four hundred exemptions were granted on the strength of Chertkóv's written testimony.[10]

With Chertkóv as its first chairman, the United Council of Religious Communities and Groups examined approximately ten thousand cases during 1919 and 1920.[11] As the Civil War dragged on, however, and desertions from the Red Army ran into the millions,[12] local authorities resorted to harsh measures in their recruiting, including the evasion of orders from Moscow granting exemption to religious objectors; and close to one hundred objectors were shot.[13]

Tolstoyan Agricultural Colonies

The end of the Civil War brought a respite in the Soviet persecution of Tolstoyan pacifists, and the economic and agricultural crisis that led to the New Economic Policy (NEP) in 1921 lifted the worst of the bureaucratic controls over agriculture and opened up opportunities for the peasants, including the Tolstoyans, to farm in relative freedom. The threat of widespread starvation led the new atheistic government to launch an appeal to the most energetic group of farmers in the country—the Old Believers and the religious sectarians,[14] including the Tolstoyans. On 5 October 1921, the People's Commissariat of Agriculture created a special commission for this purpose and issued the following proclamation:

> The sectarians and Old Believers of Russia, who for the most part belong to the peasant population, have behind them many centuries of experience in communal living. We know that there are many sects in Russia whose adherents have long aspired to a communal, communistic life, in conformity with their doctrines. They ordinarily take as the foundation for this aspiration the words from the "Acts of the Apostles": "Neither said any of them that any of the things which he possessed was his own; but they had all things common." . . . All governments, all authorities, all laws in the whole world and in all ages have been against such a life. . . . But now the time has come when all sectarians . . . can peacefully come out in the open, firmly confident that no one will ever persecute anyone among them for their beliefs. The Soviet Government of workers and peasants has proclaimed real freedom of conscience and absolutely does not interfere in any matters of religious belief, granting to everyone complete freedom of belief and unbelief.[15]

Great numbers of religious peasants took these assurances at face value, and enthusiastically set about organizing agricultural cooperatives, colonies, and communes. One source reports that when an All-Russian Congress of

Sectarian Agricultural and Manufacturing Cooperatives was held with the permission of the authorities in March 1921, it drew delegates from several hundred colonies in thirty-four provinces. By the following year the number of religious colonies was reported to have doubled, with at least a hundred of them organized by Tolstoyans.[16] This acceptance of collective living in independent agricultural colonies no doubt owed much to an old tradition among Russian peasants not generally known in the West. Even under serfdom they had lived in communities with a limited form of self-government known as the *mir,* which existed in Russia at least as early as the sixteenth century. The *mir* controlled the use of land set aside for peasant use, and periodically redistributed it among the peasant households according to the changing size and needs of the families. Several forms of organization will be found in the Tolstoyan colonies discussed in this book, ranging from cooperatives of one kind or another to communes in which members turned over all their money and property (except personal belongings) to the commune upon joining. The members then decided in their commune assemblies how they would organize their work and how they would share whatever income, food, or materials the commune earned or acquired.

The Tolstoyan colonies had a reasonably good life during the period of the New Economic Policy (NEP), from 1921 to the end of 1928. Even then, however, their religious orientation and their sturdy independence led the Soviet leaders to look on them as a potentially subversive element and to subject them to various forms of harassment. This period of relative freedom for the Tolstoyans, as well as for the whole Soviet population, came to a halt at the end of 1928 with the launching of the first Five Year Plan and the campaign to collectivize agriculture. Shortly after a week-long observance in September 1928 of the hundredth anniversary of Tolstóy's birth, organized by the Moscow Vegetarian Society and attended by hundreds of Tolstoyans from all over the country, the authorities arrested members of the Society's youth club, closed down the last of the Tolstoyan periodicals (the monthly *Newsletter of the Moscow Vegetarian Society*), and deprived the Society of its headquarters on Newspaper Lane by refusing to renew its lease.

As early as 1927, the government had begun using one pretext after another to close down the independent Tolstoyan agricultural colonies. The complete destruction of their colonies was forestalled for a few more years, however, when Vladímir Chertkóv helped them get permission from the Presidium of the All-Russian Central Executive Committee in February 1930 to resettle in Siberia. In May three peasant representatives, including one of the authors of these memoirs, Borís Mazúrin, went to Siberia as land scouts and found a suitable new location on the Tom River. They were followed in August by a working team of men from Tolstoyan colonies near Moscow and Stalingrad, who spent nearly a year building houses in preparation for the new settlers. As the authorities carried out their destruction of independent colonies all over the European territory, hundreds of Tolstoyans poured into the new settlement. By 1931 they numbered about one thousand.

Sixty Years of Cover-up: 1928–1988

The end of 1928 marked the beginning of a sixty-year period in which the authorities all but eliminated every mention of Tolstoyism in Soviet publications and closed off all public access to Tolstóy's religious works in the libraries. From then until 1983, *A Confession, What I Believe, What Then Must We Do?, On Life,* and *The Kingdom of God Is within You* were published only once, and then in a printing of only five thousand copies in the expensive ninety-volume scholarly edition of Tolstóy's complete works and letters. Tolstóy's place in Russian literary and cultural history was reinterpreted in line with Lénin's evaluation in his article "Leo Tolstóy as a Mirror of Russian Revolution," which became required reading for all Soviet schoolchildren. From Lénin's allegedly immortal words they learned that Tolstóy was "an artist of genius who created . . . first-class works of world literature," but that "as a prophet who has discovered new panaceas for the salvation of mankind, Tolstóy is ridiculous." Innocent schoolchildren also learned from Lénin that the typical Tolstoyan was "a haggard, hysterical sniveler" who "publicly beats his breast and says, 'I am vile, I am nasty, but I'm working on moral self-perfection.' "[17]

The memoirs and documents published in this book bear testimony not only to the distortion in Lénin's portrayal of the typical Tolstoyan but also to the Soviet failure to bury all traces of the Tolstoyan movement for good. Indeed, Tolstoyism in the Soviet Union today is by no means a dead issue. In May 1988 *Vaprósy literatúry,* the official journal of the Union of Soviet Writers, carried an article by the prominent literary critic (and long-time Party member) Vladímir Lakshín entitled "The Return of Tolstóy the Thinker." In it he called for an end to the suppression of Tolstóy's religious writings, specifically mentioning *What I Believe* and *On Life.* He even challenged Lénin's disparaging remark about Tolstóy's call for moral self-perfection and said: "We are understanding more and more clearly that we shall not attain any great social goal unless we succeed in getting all people to morally reconstruct themselves one by one"—significantly using the verbal form of the Russian word *perestroika.*[18]

During the 1960s, several of the surviving Tolstoyans began writing their memoirs, carefully preserving them from seizure and destruction at the hands of the authorities by distributing secret copies to trusted friends for concealment. The first news about these memoirs reached the West in 1977, when a dissident Soviet journalist, Mark Popóvsky, got acquainted with some of the Tolstoyans and was able to bring out more than three thousand pages of microfilmed Tolstoyan letters, diaries, and memoirs upon emigrating to the West later that year. He used this material as the basis for the first book published in any language about the fate of the Russian Tolstoyans in the Soviet Union, *Russian Peasants Tell Their Story: Followers of L. N. Tolstóy, 1918–1977,* published in Russian in London in 1983. (See above, note 9, for the Russian title and bibliographical information.) Following in the wake of Popóvsky, the young Leningrad historian Arsény Rogínsky edited the first

Tolstoyan document to be published in Russia in sixty years: Borís Mazúrin's memoirs about the Life and Labor Commune in Western Siberia, which appeared in September 1988 in the leading Soviet literary journal, *Nóvy Mir*.[19] The publication of these memoirs created a sensation. The eighty-seven-year-old Mazúrin, still living in the village of Tálzhino, not far from the site of the colony, was deluged with letters from readers all over the Soviet Union and besieged by journalists and even a television team, who made a documentary about the Tolstoyans. Highly favorable feature articles about him were published in *Izvéstia* and the *Teachers Gazette (Uchítelskaya gazéta)*. In April 1990 he was the principal speaker at a reunion of surviving members of the Life and Labor Commune held in one of the public libraries in Novokuznétsk—right across the river from the prison in which he had been arrested in 1936 and condemned to ten years in the labor camps.

The Memoirs

A year later, Mazúrin's memoirs, along with those of six other Tolstoyans, were published in Moscow in book form under the editorship of Rogínsky, along with twenty pages of his commentary on the various Tolstoyan organizations and publications during the first twenty years of this century and his biographical sketches of the seven authors. The present translation has been made from the text of this book, and much of the information in this introduction is drawn from Rogínsky's commentary, which will be indispensable for future researchers into the history of the Tolstoyan movement in Russia.[20]

The centerpiece of this book is Mazúrin's account of the Tolstoyan Life and Labor Commune under his leadership from the time of its organization in 1921 at Shestakóvka, on the edge of Moscow, to its relocation in Western Siberia in 1931, his arrest in 1936, and his sentence to ten years in the labor camps. All the memoirs published here are linked in one way or another through their associations with Mazúrin and that colony. After arresting all the leaders of the Life and Labor Commune in 1936, the Soviet authorities effectively destroyed it at the end of the 1930s by forcibly merging it with a state-controlled collective farm.

The principal value of these memoirs is twofold. First, they throw light on a long-suppressed chapter in the history of Tolstóy's religious and social influence in the Soviet Union. Second, they document the history of the Russian peasantry from what appears to be a unique source—the peasants themselves. The sickle never really carried equal weight with the hammer in the emblem of the Soviet Union, and this inequality of attention can be seen in the two-volume guide published in 1962–63 to personal papers in the state archives of the Soviet Union.[21] More than ten thousand names are listed in it, but only five of them are identified as peasants living in the period since 1850, and no memoirs or autobiographical materials are listed for any of the five.

The authors of the memoirs collected here were a remarkable group. Borís Mazúrin was educated as a geologist, but through his Tolstoyan convictions he deliberately became a peasant and was the leader of the largest and most successful Tolstoyan agricultural colony in history. Yeléna Shershenyóva was not a peasant at all but a member of the intelligentsia and the daughter of a close associate of Tolstóy. Her memoirs deserve their place here, however, as evidence of the attraction that Tolstóy's ideas about going back to the soil held for numerous city-bred intellectuals at that time. If Mazúrin was an intellectual turned peasant, Dmítry Morgachëv and Yákov Dragunóvsky were two farm boys with little formal education who through their own efforts became what can justly be called peasant intellectuals. Dragunóvsky's son Iván grew up under the strong Tolstoyan influence of his father, his older brothers, and his uncle Semyón, who sacrificed his life for his convictions.

It is evident that all these authors had a sense of history, an awareness that without their initiative this chapter of the truth about Russia was in danger of being forever buried through the efforts of the ideological myth-makers. Mazúrin wrote his memoirs between 1964 and 1967 and played an important role in encouraging other Tolstoyans to do likewise. The caution they felt about keeping these documents out of the hands of the security police was confirmed in the summer of 1977, when the KGB raided the home of Dmítry Morgachëv in the little town of Przheválsk, in Kirgízia,[22] and again at the end of the 1970s, after Iván Dragunóvsky had finished the memoirs from which his chapter in this book is taken. "Not long ago," he wrote, "a local schoolteacher borrowed my autobiography to read it. Through him it fell into the hands of 'the powers that be.' I was summoned and treated to a long 'chat,' during which I was told not to let anyone read my auto-biography. What was it that so disturbed the powers that be? After all, I'm not about to seize power from them!"[23]

The Tolstoyans were doubly persecuted, first because of their commitment to nonviolence and refusal of all support for war, and second because their hard work and success in farming exposed them to the charge of being "kuláks." After the Revolution, this old Russian word for "skinflint" was given a sinister new meaning. When the forced collectivization of agriculture was launched in 1929, the most innovative, independent-minded, and successful peasants were labeled "kuláks" and accused of enriching themselves by exploiting the poorest peasants. Under this regime of economic genocide, an accused kulák, along with his family and anyone else suspected of associating or sympathizing with him, had about the same chance of surviving the collectivization of agriculture as a Jewish family had of surviving Nazi Germany.

These memoirs contain many grim pages about the harassment, persecution, arrests, torture, and years of confinement in labor camps suffered by the Tolstoyans; but along with all that, they also contain scenes of a very different kind—descriptions of Russian village life before the Revolution, including the traditional matchmaking and wedding of one of the authors; scenes of the beautiful Siberian landscape in which the Tolstoyans relocated their

Life and Labor Commune; a fascinating account of the initiative and inge-
nuity they showed in developing a new type of farming in that region; and
a series of encounters with the authorities that at times reveal the self-con-
trolled courage of the Tolstoyans, occasionally some traces of humanity in
their rulers and oppressors, and now and then the utter absurdity of the whole
system.

For example, once when the local government resolved to liquidate the
Tolstoyans' commune and sent a representative out to collect their official
seal, they refused to hand it over. After a stormy session the representative
pounded the table and finally shouted:

> "For the last time I ask you—will you turn over the seal?"
> The answer was an unmistakable "No!"
> Then suddenly the representative turned to the chairman of the commune,
> quietly shook his hand, and said: "Well, if that's the way it is, then stick to it
> firmly—that's the only way you'll achieve anything."

On another occasion when the authorities padlocked the Tolstoyan school
and took the teachers to court for instructing the children in subversive religious doctrines, the whole court almost broke up in laughter when one witness declared that the school principal had taught the children to sing Tolstóy's religious song "The Kreutzer Sonata."

Still another example comes from 1936, when nearly a dozen leading
members of the commune were arrested and held in prison for seven months
for investigation before their trial took place. Among them was Yákov Dragunóvsky. He would go willingly whenever he was called out of prison to
be taken for an interrogation; but when he was taken back to the prison
gates, he would lie down and say: "I don't need to go in there." Two prison
guards would then have to pick him up and carry him in. Mazúrin recounts
this scene in his memoirs:

> I see it all as if it were today: a bright summer day, with the open cell win-
> dows looking out at the prison yard (at that time there were no shutters on them);
> and everybody's attention was attracted to the entrance checkpoint, where some
> sort of noise and movement could be heard. Then the procession would appear
> in the prison yard. Two guards . . . would carry in Dragunóvsky sitting on their
> crossed arms. Greetings and guffaws could be heard from all the windows above.
> Sitting in state like a tsar on the throne, with his arms around the shoulders of
> the guards and his beard fluttering in the wind, Yákov Deméntyevich would smile
> and answer their greetings with a wave. The guards too were smiling. All this
> somehow took place good-naturedly; Dragunóvsky was relaxed and not bitter,
> and the same mood infected those around him.

The absurdity of the whole system could scarcely be better illustrated
than in Mazúrin's account of what happened nearly four years after he and
eight other commune members had been put on trial and five of them sentenced to the labor camps. More than halfway through Mazúrin's five-year
sentence, all nine of them were suddenly rounded up, sent back to Stálinsk

for retrial, and given new sentences of five to ten years. Why? Because the authorities decided that the original sentences were too mild. The four who had been acquitted in 1936 were kept in prison for more than two years awaiting trial while the government tracked down the other five in the labor camps.

American readers may be surprised, and even puzzled, by the role that poetry plays in these memoirs. Russia is known abroad for its great novels, but at home Russia lives by its poetry. In what other country can one find football stadiums packed with people who have come to hear their favorite poets recite their verse? For these peasant Tolstoyans in prison and the labor camps, poetry was not a mere form of entertainment. It served as a form of spiritual nourishment in times of great suffering and anguish, just as poetry has traditionally served throughout human history. The same thing happened to at least some extent during the Vietnam War, when some ordinary American soldiers, including simple country boys, expressed their anguish and bewilderment in verse. The translations of poetry in this book do not adequately convey the force of the Russian because they fail to reflect the regular meter and rhyme of the original.

The Daring Experiment: Was It Worth the Cost?

The Tolstoyans themselves would probably answer that this question is not formulated correctly. An experiment is a way of testing a theory, on the assumption that if the theory is not confirmed, it will be discarded. To assume that the followers of Tolstóy, who faced torture and death, were engaged in a scientific experiment is a little like assuming that Jesus on the cross, Socrates drinking the hemlock, and John Huss burning at the stake were testing the validity of their convictions.

Moral principles—questions of right and wrong, good and evil—are not subject to scientific experiment. The authors of these memoirs and their like-minded friends looked on Tolstóy's doctrine of brotherly love as the basic moral law of the universe. They considered all their other beliefs—their rejection of violence, war, despotism, falsehood, exploitation—to be corollaries of that law.

Even though Tolstóy himself preached a kind of Christian anarchism, the Tolstoyans we observe in this book did not practice anarchism. The Life and Labor Commune governed itself according to the state's standard charter for agricultural communes, but with an additional provision in the article on membership requirements that Mazúrin persuaded the head of the government's land department to accept: ". . . and who share the views of L. N. Tolstóy and reject all killing not only of human beings but also of animals, and also reject the use of drugs—alcohol, tobacco, etc.—and of meat." The government official later thought better of it and tried in vain to get that charter back from the Tolstoyans. But Mazúrin recalls that "this charter lived on among us, and we used it as a trump card in court when we were accused of having an illegal commune."[24] In these memoirs the Tolstoyans demonstrated their willingness to observe all laws that did not conflict with their moral principles, but they were ready to die, if necessary, rather than obey those that did.

Regardless of the Tolstoyans' own attitude, outsiders can scarcely help looking on the experiences documented in these memoirs as one of the three great experiments in the use of nonviolence in the twentieth century. The first was the campaign for the liberation of India led by Gandhi—who corresponded with Tolstóy from South Africa during the last year of the Russian writer's life and always paid tribute to Tolstóy's influence on his own thinking. The second was Martin Luther King's campaign against segregation in the American South. The Russian Tolstoyans' experiment, however, differed in one important respect from the other two. Gandhi's and Martin Luther King's campaigns had a political goal: the liberation of India from the British and the liberation of American blacks from second-class citizenship. The Russian Tolstoyans in the 1920s and 1930s had only the dream of creating peaceful agricultural communities in which they could live out the nonviolent principles of Tolstóy. These memoirs will let readers judge for themselves just how close the Tolstoyans came to achieving their goal. They make it clear that the Tolstoyans were not without their human frailties, but it would be hard to come away from this book without admiration for what they attempted and a sense of awe for their courage.

In this connection it is appropriate to give the last word to young Semyón Dragunóvsky, a cousin of one of the contributors to this volume, who succeeded in throwing the following letter out the window of his prison cell:

23 December 1919

Dear parents, dear Father Abram Pímenovich, and dear Mother. I am writing to let you know that I am with Grigóry and others from the villages of Dekhteryóvo and Morkótovo. There are eight of us who have refused, and the Smolénsk military court has condemned all of us to be shot. They have let us live for 24 hours more; maybe they will set us free, and maybe they will shoot us. I beg you, dear parents, not to worry about me and not to grieve; I myself chose this path of Christ. When Christ was ordered to be put to death, He said: "Father, forgive them, for they know not what they do." The same with me—let them do what they want with me, but I forgive them and I will suffer in the name of Christ. I put my trust in what Christ said: "Not a single hair shall fall unless it be God's will." And He also said: "Fear not them that kill the body, but fear them that kill the soul." For the body is dust and it must perish all by itself, and just as it came from the earth, so it must return to the earth, but since the soul came from God, so must it return to God; it will not perish in vain unless it be God's will . . .

As I was writing these lines, I remembered all of you—my dear little sisters, my brothers, my nephews. I felt bitter and wept and could not go on writing for a long time. I felt sorry about leaving you all.

When they brought us to the prison, there were two more men here, deserters who had hidden for eleven months. They were condemned to death along with us. At court we were given the choice of working in a hospital for contagious

diseases or on the railroad; but we refused all of it, and they called us counterrevolutionaries and sentenced us to death.

Soon we will all be gone, since the 24 hours are passing. If they do not shoot
us this evening, maybe God will grant that we stay alive; but if they do shoot us,
we all ask you to beg the prison authorities to let you take our bodies and bury
them in our own villages. Dear parents in the flesh! Death is not terrible for me.
Forgive me if I ever offended and grieved anybody about anything, and I forgive
everybody.

Dear Father! Don't stay here around the prison—don't let yourself get upset.
If we happen to remain alive, then ask the Pýrikov brothers-in-the-spirit to say a
word for us to the United Council of Religious Communities and Groups.

The two deserters have been taken out to be shot, but we have been left here
for the time being, even though the 24 hours have already passed. We were told:
"Pray to God that a telegram about you has come from Moscow."

According to Iván Dragunóvsky's biography of his father, from which
this letter is translated, "Thanks to the intervention of V. G. Chertkóv and
the United Council of Religious Communities and Groups, a telegram can-
celing the execution was indeed sent from Moscow over Lénin's signature,
but it was deliberately held up, and on the evening of the 24th of December
1919 they were executed. When Semyón Dragunóvsky was shot, the bullet
did not hit his heart, and he was shoved into the pit and covered with dirt
while he was still half-alive. For a long time his groans could be heard coming from his dirt-covered grave. His father had been standing not far away
during the execution, and he ran up to the grave and heard his son's groans
just as they finished filling it with dirt. He reproached the executioners for
their evil deed, and they stood there hanging their heads in silence. But what
could they say? In a way they were not the ones directly guilty of this fratricide. It was the 'law' that condemned him to death, and they were only the
blind instruments of this 'law.' "[25]

NOTES

1. Nicolas Berdyaev, *The Origin of Russian Communism* (London: Geoffrey Bles,
The Centenary Press [1937]), pp. 131–132, 168.

2. Roger Fry, *Vision and Design* (London: Wm. Clowes and Son, 1920), p. 194.

3. Tolstoy, *What Is Art?* and *Essays on Art,* trans. Aylmer Maude (London: Oxford University Press, 1950 [1930]), p. 277.

4. Aylmer Maude, *The Life of Tolstoy,* Vol. II: *Later Years* (Oxford: Oxford University Press, 1930), pp. 223 and 258–259.

5. Ibid., p. 470.

6. See William B. Edgerton, "The Artist Turned Prophet: Leo Tolstoj after 1880,"
in *American Contributions to the Sixth International Congress of Slavists, Prague, 1968,
August 7–13,* Vol. II: *Literary Contributions* (The Hague: Mouton and Co., 1969), pp.
61–85.

7. Quoted from A. S. Prugavin, *O L've Tolstom i o tolstovtsakh* (Moscow, 1911), pp. 179, 192–195.

8. Gazetnyj pereulok, now ulitsa Ogarëva. The information given here and elsewhere in this Introduction is taken from the invaluable notes, bibliography, and biographical sketches of the contributors appended to the original Russian edition of this book, *Vospominanija krest'jan tolstovtsev*, pp. 459–478, which were prepared by its compiler and editor, A. B. Roginskij.

9. The estimate is given by Mark Popovskij in his book *Russkie muzhiki rasskazyvajut. Posledovateli L. N. Tolstogo v Sovetskom Sojuze 1918–1977* (London, 1983), pp. 21 and 41, which was the first full-length book to discuss the fate of the Tolstoyans in the Soviet Union and is based in part on some of the Tolstoyan documents now published here.

10. A detailed account of the decree of 4 January 1919 on exemption from military service, including the text of the decree, is given in A. I. Klibanov, "Sektantstvo i stroitel'stvo vooruzhennykh sil Sovetskoj respubliki (1918–1921 gg.)," in *Religioznoe sektantstvo i sovremennost'* (Moscow: Nauka, 1969), pp. 188–208.

11. See Roginskij, pp. 465–467.

12. S. Olikov in his book *Dezertirstvo v Krasnoj armii i bor'ba s nim* [Desertion in the Red Army and the struggle against it] (Leningrad: Izdanie Voennoj tipografii upravlenija delami Narkomvoenmor i RVS SSSR 1926), p. 11, refers in passing to desertions from the Red Army running into seven figures ("millionnaja tsifra dezertirstva iz Krasnoj armii"), and on pp. 30–35 gives detailed statistics by regions.

13. Val[entin] Bulgakov, "Kak umirajut za veru," *Sovremennye zapiski (Paris), 38 (1929), pp. 189–223.*

14. The Russian word for "sectarian" is used for any religious group other than the Orthodox Church, and in this sense—except as part of an organizational name—it can often best be translated into English by "religious." Otherwise, I have translated it with the English "sectarian," trusting that the context will make its meaning at least as clear as the Russian word.

15. Quoted by Popovskij, *Russkie muzhiki rasskazyvajut*, pp. 83–84, from a document found in the Central State Archive of the October Revolution in Moscow, fund 2077, file 11, page 2–2: "RSFSR. Narkomzem. Glavsovkolkhoz. Komissija po zaseleniju pustykh zemel' i byvshikh imenij sektantami i staroobrjadtsami." Moskva, 2 oktjabrja 1921 goda. 'K SEKTANTAM I STAROOBRJADTSAM, ZHIVUSHCHIM V ROSSII I ZA GRANITSEJ.' " (The Biblical quotation is from Acts 4:32.)

16. These figures come from Popovskij, p. 85, who gives no source for them.

17. V. I. Lenin, "Lev Tolstoj, kak zerkalo russkoj revoljutsii," *Polnoe sobranie sochinenij*, 5th edition, vol. 7 (Moscow, 1961), pp. 209–210.

18. V. Lakshin, "Vozvrashchenie Tolstogo-myslitelja," *Voprosy literatury*, No. 5 (May 1988), pp. 109, 115.

19. Seven years earlier, on 4 December 1981, Arsény Rogínsky had been condemned to four years of imprisonment in the labor camps for "the publication of archival documents in foreign editions." For details see M. H., "L'historien soviétique Arsenij Roginskij," *Cahiers du Monde Russe et Soviétique*, vol. 23, no. 1 (Paris: January–March 1982), pp. 119–121.

20. *Vospominanija krest'jan-tolstovtsev. 1910–1930-e gody* [Edited and with a commentary by A. B. Roginskij] (Moscow: "Kniga," 1989), 480 pp. Published in a printing of 75,000 copies.

21. *Lichnye arkhivnye fondy v gosudarstvennykh khranilishchakh SSSR: ukazatel'*, 2 vols. (Moscow, 1962–1963).

22. Popovskij, p. 21.

23. Roginskij, p. 477.

24. The complete Russian text of the charter, filling ten pages, is printed in the original Russian edition of this book.

25. Translated from the Mark Popovskij microfilm collection of materials from Tolstoyans in the Soviet Union, now deposited in the Hoover Institution Archives, Reel No. 15, Part 2: Ivan Dragunovskij, "Biografija Jakova Dement'evicha Dragunovskogo," pp. 40–41.

A NOTE FROM THE TRANSLATOR AND EDITOR

About the Translation

This translation is focused upon the story of the Tolstoyans who were associated with the Life and Labor Commune in Western Siberia. Consequently, of the eight chapters in the Russian edition, the following three have been omitted:

1. "The Spiritual Journey of a Russian Peasant Tolstoyan," by Vasíly Yánov, was omitted because he had no association with the Life and Labor Commune or any other Tolstoyan colonies. His story is one of the most interesting in the Russian edition, and it will very likely be published as a separate book.

2. "One Year Out of Ten Just Like It," by Borís Mazúrin, is a gripping account of his ten years of imprisonment in the labor camps. It was omitted because it partly overlaps with Morgachëv's prison experiences and because of the great number of accounts already available in English about experiences in Soviet prisons and labor camps.

3. "Three Communes," by Mikhaíl Gorbunóv-Posádov, an eight-page memoir published as a supplement to the Russian edition, deals only with the author's brief visits to three Tolstoyan communes, two of which are described in other chapters of the English edition.

Three of the five chapters translated in this book represent essentially the complete text of the Russian original. The two exceptions are Borís Mazúrin's chapter "The Life and Labor Commune," which I have translated from the slightly abridged version that was published in *Nóvy Mir,* and "From the Papers of Yákov Dragunóvsky," which represents 77 of the 111 pages of the Russian text. In a very few places I have omitted lists of names of victims of the terror—important information for Russian readers anxious about the fate of friends or relatives but not immediately pertinent to most foreign readers. In each case I have noted the omission with a sentence such as "Twenty-four of them never came back alive" or "My list includes twenty-five of them who I know were arrested in 1937, and almost all of whom lost their lives." The five chapters translated here represent 307 of the 340 pages they occupy in the Russian edition.

As a convenience to the reader, I have inserted subheads in the long chapter by Morgachëv. The subheads in the chapters by Mazúrin and Yákov Dragunóvsky are taken from the Russian edition.

Russian Weights and Measures

The traditional Russian system of weights and measures was replaced by the metric system on 14 September 1918, so during the transitional period covered in these memoirs it is not surprising to find the authors using both systems. In this translation, the terms used in the older system—*pud, arshín, sázhen, desyatína, verstá,* etc.—are recalculated in pounds, feet, yards, acres, miles, etc. The weights and measures given in the metric system remain unchanged.

Reading Russian Names

The Russian spelling system, with its thirty-two-letter alphabet, is so simple and regular that it offers almost no problems in reading or writing for Russian schoolchildren. It is only when we try to convey the sounds of Russian in our chaotic English spelling system that we run into problems. These problems are so vexing that three different transliteration systems are in common use among English-speaking specialists on Russian studies.

With one exception, the system used for proper names throughout this book is the one that is closest to English spelling. Most consonants are given approximately the same sound as in English, except that *g* is always pronounced hard, as in *get,* not as in *general,* and *s* is always voiceless, as in *sit,* never like the voiced *s* in *easy.* The digraph *zh* is pronounced like the *s* in *pleasure,* and *kh* in words such as *Chékhov* takes approximately the same sound as the German *ch* in *Reich* or the Spanish *j* in *Jaime. Sh* and *ch* are pronounced about the same as in English, but don't be surprised to find them also used together to represent a single letter in the Russian alphabet. If you can say "fresh cheese" in English, you can say "Shcherbátsky" in Russian.

Vowels are pronounced approximately like the *a* in *father,* the *e* in *met,* the *i* in *machine,* the *o* in *note,* and the *u* in *lunar.* The letter *y* is used in two different ways. Between consonants or at the end of a word, it normally represents the sound of the short *i* in *bit* (Býkov, *Nóvy Mir*). But when it is preceded or followed by a vowel, the *y* normally represents the semiconsonantal sound of *y* in the English words *boy* or *yard (Nóvoye Vrémya).* It is *never* used with another vowel in Russian to form part of such a diphthong as the *ay* in *day* or the *ey* in *hey.* The Russian name Nikoláy is pronounced "Nee-ko-lie," not "Nee-ko-lay." When two vowels occur together in transliteration, each is given its own value. For example, Gorbachev's first name, Mikhaíl, is pronounced "mee-kha-eel," not "mee-khale," regardless of what the television journalists may call it. And incidentally, all Russians know that the *e* in his last name really should be written with two dots over it (Gorbachëv) to show that it is pronounced *o* rather than *e;* but since all Russians know this, they don't usually bother to add the two dots. In this book, however, whenever *e* is pronounced *o,* we shall tell you by writing it *ë,* as in Mor-gachëv.

This so-called Popular system of transliteration is used everywhere in this book except for bibliographical information about Russian sources, which will be useful only to readers who know the Russian language. That information is given in a more accurate modification of the Library of Congress system than the one commonly used in American publications in the social sciences. The system used here substitutes a *j* for the *i* plus ligatures and diacritical marks that are otherwise required for accurate transcription in the Library of Congress system.

One final word about Russian pronunciation: the hardest thing in Russian, as in English, is knowing which syllable to stress, especially in proper names. With the help of numerous modern Russian reference works, where the accent is regularly marked, and above all with the generous help of Míra Iósifovna Pérper in Moscow, a professional translator to and from English who is also the daughter of an associate of Tolstóy, I have attempted to provide accents for every proper name in this book, including even those of obscure villages in Siberia that are found in no atlases.

Russian Personal Names

Russians have their own special ways of addressing and referring to one another, and a translation that failed to reflect this would lose something important. Prerevolutionary forms of address such as Mr., Mrs., and Miss (replaced after the Revolution by Citizen) are little used in Russian social life. The politest way to address Russians is by using their first name and patronymic, a special form of their father's first name, which usually ends in -ovich or -evich for men and -ovna or -evna for women. For example, the polite way to address Borís Mazúrin, the son of Vasíly, is Borís Vasílyevich. Yeléna Shershenyóva, whose father was Fyódor Strákhov, was addressed as Yeléna Fyódorovna. Most Russian family names come in a feminine as well as a masculine form. The wife of Pyotr Shershenyóv is Yeléna Shershenyóva, and the wife of Iván Dragunóvsky is Frósya Dragunóvskaya.

Just as many English given names have various familiar or affectionate forms (Thomas—Tom, Tommy; Elizabeth—Beth, Betty, Liz, Liza, Lizzie), Russian has an even larger array; and a translation that failed to take them into account would be impoverished. The most common endings of these forms are -ya, -sha, -zha, and -ka. To help you keep track of persons mentioned in this book by more than one form of their names, here is an alphabetical list of frequently occurring familiar names along with their formal equivalents:

Álechka, Álya—Yeléna
Bórya—Borís
Fédya—Fyódor
Gítya—Gyúnter
Gútya—Gústav
Ilyúsha—Ilyá
Kátya—Yekaterína
Kólya—Nikoláy
Kóstya—Konstantín
Lyóva—Lev
Mánya—Maríya, Márya
Maryánka—Maryána

Mísha, Míshka—Mikhaíl
Mítya—Dmítry, Dimítry
Nádya—Nadézhda
Ólya—Ólga
Pétya—Pyotr
Sásha—Aleksándr, Aleksándra
Seryózha—Sergéy
Shúra—Aleksándr, Aleksándra
Tánya—Tatyána
Ványa—Iván
Vásya—Vasíly

Memoirs of
Peasant Tolstoyans
in Soviet Russia

Mikhaíl Gorbunóv-Posádov

Mikhaíl Gorbunóv-Posádov's father, Iván *(seated)*, with Vladímir Chertkóv and his wife, Anna Konstantínovna Chertkóva (1924).

Mikhaíl Ivánovich Gorbunóv-Posádov (1908–1991) died in January 1991, a little over a year after the original Russian edition of this book was published. While remaining faithful to the Tolstoyan convictions of his family, in his chosen profession he became a highly respected authority on technical problems of laying foundations for large-scale construction. He was a Doctor of Technical Sciences, held the rank of Professor, and won several awards for his work in the technical sciences, including a State Prize of the USSR and the title of Honored Worker in Science and Technology of the RSFSR.

FOR MANY YEARS I have felt that I ought to write down my memoirs. Many friends have told me the same thing. I am the son of Iván Ivánovich Gorbunóv-Posádov and Yeléna Yevgényevna Gorbunóva. They were followers and friends of Leo Nikoláyevich Tolstóy and were the founders and editors of the Intermediary Publishing House for the masses, which lasted for half a century, from 1885 to 1935. I spent my childhood and youth in the world of Tolstóy, among the participants in the Tolstoyan movement in Russia.

Tolstóy and his cause have always been present in my life. My cradle, made of iron and covered with netting, was given to my parents by Leo Nikoláyevich. (It was the cradle of his especially beloved youngest son, Ványechka, who died very early. It has since been returned to the Tolstóy museum established in his Moscow home.) The brightest memories of my childhood were Yásnaya Polyána and Ovsyánniki, the estate of Tolstóy's eldest daughter, Tatyána, eight kilometers from Yásnaya, where our family lived every summer and where Leo Nikoláyevich would come almost every day on his stallion Délire to see my father and bring him manuscripts and proofs. During my schoolboy and student days, I worked diligently for the Intermediary Publishing House, translating children's books from the English, binding books, and delivering them to the bookshops. (After the Revolution it became a cooperative, and my mother was the chairman of its board of directors.) During the 1920s the monthly *Letters of the Moscow Vegetarian Society* were typeset and printed in our apartment. That was the last periodical publication of the Tolstoyans; I would type articles on the typewriter, run off the pages on my father's duplicating machine, put them into envelopes, write the addresses, and take them around to the mailboxes. . . .

All during my childhood and youth, I wanted to continue the work of my parents. In order to carry on the cause of the Intermediary, nothing was needed but willingness and love of work, and I had plenty of both. But history decided otherwise. In 1929 the Moscow Vegetarian Society was closed down; all cooperative and private publishing houses, including the Intermediary, were closed down; and my life followed another course. I devoted myself to the natural sciences.

But I always considered, and still do, that the life and work of Tolstóy's friends and like-minded people represented the most important aspect of the spiritual history of Russia (and not only of Russia) from the 1880s till the 1930s (when Tolstoyism as an organized movement was destroyed), and every effort must be made to resurrect it from the darkness of that compulsory silence. The history of the Tolstoyan movement deserves a scholarly study in many volumes.

Even in former years, while my mother was still alive, she and I wanted to write such a history, making use of printed and archival materials and surviving correspondence and photographs. Now I no longer have either the time or the strength for such an enormous task. But I am confident that such a book will be written. The story of the Tolstoyan publishing houses and journals, the Societies of True Freedom in Memory of Tolstóy that were founded in 1917 in almost every corner of Russia, the vegetarian movement, the antiwar activity of the Tolstoyans during the First World War, the international contacts, the struggle of the United Council of Religious Communities and Groups (organized by Vladímir Chertkóv in 1918) for freedom of conscience, the Tolstoyan Academy (courses about free religious ideas) that functioned in Moscow during the famine years of 1918–19, the Yásnaya Polyána museum and school that were directed until 1929 by Tolstóy's favorite daughter, Aleksándra Lvóvna—for all this, the future scholar will find a wealth of material in the libraries and archives (he will find my memoirs there too).

But there was another very interesting and powerful branch of the Tolstoyan movement during the first decades of the Soviet regime, and that was the life of the Tolstoyan farmers. Inspired by Leo Nikoláyevich's ideas about the great moral significance of productive labor, thousands of Tolstóy's followers—intellectuals and peasants, workers and former soldiers—began to implement Tolstóy's long-cherished dream of peaceful, fraternal life on the land—of free, nonviolent agricultural labor as the ideal form of human society. The majority of the Tolstoyan farmers joined together in agricultural cooperatives and communes; some worked the land individually. But they all believed their life and labor would help to achieve the goals proclaimed by the Russian revolution—the building of a worldwide brotherly, stateless society, free of violence and exploitation. Severe ordeals awaited them. Deeply opposed as they were to all violence, the twentieth century brought that violence down upon them in unprecedentedly cruel forms—two world wars, civil war, Stalinist terror. Many hundreds of Tolstóy's followers perished. But those who lived through it while remaining true to their convictions, those who were able to hold fast to Tolstóy's living truth, to the light of goodness and love, all through the hell of prisons and labor camps, have earned the right to love and respect from their contemporaries and descendants. The book that you hold in your hands contains their recollections about their life. I knew many of these authors very well, and I remember the communes about which they wrote.

I am happy that at last our readers will learn about their lives, so filled with active goodness and love toward everything living.

Yeléna Shershenyóva

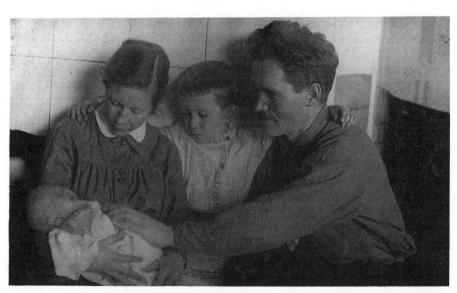

Yeléna and Vasíly (Vásya) Shershenyóv and their son Fédya and daughter Asya in 1934.

1.

The New Jerusalem Tolstóy Commune

YELÉNA SHERSHENYÓVA

Yeléna Fyódorovna Shershenyóva (1905–1979) was the daughter of a close associate of Tolstóy, Fyódor Alekséyevich Strákhov, who had grown up in a family of landowners not far from Tolstóy's estate at Yásnaya Polyána. Her lively chapter describes a largely youthful agricultural colony some thirty miles northwest of Moscow in which about half the members were of peasant origin and the other half were intellectuals with no previous experience in farming. Nevertheless, they threw themselves into the work so energetically that in 1926–27 at the All-Union Agricultural Exhibition, their farm products won first place.[1] In 1929, when collectivization began, the New Jerusalem Commune was forced to merge with a state-controlled collective farm, and the Tolstoyans who were unwilling to submit to the new controls were obliged to leave. Many of them joined the Life and Labor Commune at Shestakóvka and resettled with it in Siberia two years later.

IN 1923 AN AGRICULTURAL colony named for Leo Tolstóy was organized near the New Jerusalem station on the railway line between Moscow and Vindáva.

Land and buildings that had formerly belonged to the landowner Shvetsóv were turned over to a group of persons who wished to live and work on the soil. The chief initiator and inspiration was Mitrofán Nechësov, and his principal helpers were a group of young men who were followers of Leo Tolstóy. At that time the children's colony at Snegirí had been liquidated because the steadily growing Tolstoyan spirit within it had aroused the opposition of the district department of public education. The first ones to leave

---

1. This information, not in Shershenyóva's memoirs, comes from K. Petrus [pseud.], *Religious Communes in the U.S.S.R.* (in Russian), Research Program on the U.S.S.R., Mimeographed Series No. 44 (New York City, 1953), p. 62.

the children's colony and come over to New Jerusalem were Mitrofán Nechësov, Vásya and Pétya Shershenyóv, Kólya Lyubímov, Geórgy Vasílyev, and Pyotr Nikítich Lepyókhin. For all those who joined it at one time or another, who lived there for a while, or who merely visited it occasionally, it remained forever in their memory as the best and brightest time of their lives.

The farm on the former estate of Shvetsóv had fallen into utter neglect. We had no equipment, no seeds, no money, and nowhere to get any. We had no clothing and no shoes. We had only our unity of convictions, our confidence in one another, our love of work and devotion to our common cause, and our youth with its endurance and optimism. It mattered not at all that we had only one pair of boots for five men and had to decide every evening who would need them the most the next morning, and who would most need our most presentable jacket.

How we twisted and turned in our efforts to get the farm going again! We had several half-starved animals on it, staggering from weakness, which we had to bring back to health no matter what. But skillful hands, self-confidence, an enterprising spirit, and inexhaustible initiative did their work. We dug, plowed, weeded, and mowed; we got up with the sun, kept going, held up under everything—and we saved the animals. In the summer we rented accommodations to Geórgy Khristofórovich Táde, a lovable man who sympathized with our undertaking. He generously supported the commune members at that time and became their friend and counselor for many years. We sold that year's crop of hay, repaired our equipment, bought some cows, put our neglected young orchard in order, and mended our hotbeds. We raised a wonderful stallion. All this did not happen at once, of course, and it was by no means easy. There were disappointments, mistakes, and blunders; but in general the farm developed vigorously, and soon it attracted the attention of the district land department.

New members began flocking to the commune. The first chairman was Mitrofán Fyódorovich Nechësov. Vásya Shershenyóv assisted him in administrative matters and also worked in the fields, along with Ványa Svinobúrko (who later took the name of his wife, Rutkóvsky). Ványa knew farming very well. He loved horses and was an expert on them. Seryózha Alekséyev was in charge of the vegetable garden; Kólya Lyubímov gladly applied his skill to every kind of work. Administrative affairs and the supervision of the work and behavior of our inexperienced young teenagers fell to the lot of the staid, mature, and sometimes—or so it seemed to us—too sober-minded Pyotr Nikítich Lepyókhin, who had formerly worked as a teacher in a children's colony. Geórgy Konstantínovich Vasílyev took charge of beekeeping. Some time later, Pyotr Yákovlevich Tolkách and his family arrived, and he turned out to be experienced in stock raising. Up to the liquidation of our commune (and later in the Altái region), he continued to look after that generally unappealing work.

Women joined us. The first one to arrive was Mánya Savítskaya, who was given the task of looking after the meager, impoverished household of the unmarried commune members. Needless to say, they had neither sauce-pans nor dishes; and Mánya's greatest worry was about their linen, which none of them possessed. Almost every day she would have to sew a sleeve back on, or piece together two worn-out shirts to make one, or make a sleeveless blouse. Later came Ólya Brem, who subsequently became the wife of Kólya Lyubímov; and then, as I remember, Ólya Déyeva; in 1924 I left the Chertkóvs and joined the commune for good. Pyotr Tolkách, along with his wife, Márta, and their children, came much later; and Yúliya Frántsevna Rutkóvskaya arrived from a children's colony. Up to the very end of our commune's existence she stayed aloof, unlike Ványa Svinobúrko, the former inhabitant of a children's colony, who later became her husband. Ványa was uncommonly obliging, open, good-humored, and peaceable. A broad-shoul-dered, semiliterate, good-hearted, hard-working fellow, he was completely nonpolitical and never troubled his mind with social questions.

I do not remember where Prokópy Pávlovich Kuvshínov and his wife, Nína Lapáyeva, came from. She was a good worker but an extremely diffi-cult character, subject to hysterical outbursts and constantly dissatisfied with other people.

One of the first to join the commune was Ványa Zúyev, a quiet, remark-ably levelheaded person, and an ardent vegetarian.

Depth and goodness were evident in almost everyone who lived in the commune. Almost all showed their worth in some special way. Breaking out of the usual pattern, they each tended to seek something better in their own fashion, according to their own lights and desires—thinking, searching, and involving themselves in life as best they knew how. Ványa Zúyev tempered his body by sleeping in winter on the balcony, eating raw vegetables and seeds, and using absolutely no cooked food. He thought that was more healthful and convenient. Seryózha Alekséyev did not cut his hair; and once he suddenly decided to go around completely without clothes, believing that the natural state would strengthen chastity and cultivate a healthy view of sexual difference. A few of us—Kóstya Blagovéshchensky, Seryózha Alek-séyev and Ványa Zúyev, Pétya Shershenyóv, Zhénya Antonóvich, and for a while I, too—did not use milk, wishing to have no part in cattle raising, and consequently in the killing of young bulls and old cows that were good for nothing but their meat. Except for me, all the others just mentioned would not wear leather boots for the same reason, that is, because they wanted to be consistent vegetarians all the way. Nobody made fun of anybody else; we respected each other's views. We only teased Seryózha for his "nakedism" (as he called it). And not only teased him but got indignant about it (espe-cially Pyotr Nikítich) and struggled against it (especially Vásya). "Now, what's the meaning of all this?" Nádya Khorúzhaya would exclaim when she came across Seryózha naked on her way to the brook. Nádya was frail and slender, always unsettled and distressed about one disorder or another, which did crop up among us but never took deep root. Vásya and Mitrofán would jokingly call her "the universal mourner" and "Nadézhda Squeakovna Troubleton." She did not take offense (or perhaps only did not show it), and

The barn at the New Jerusalem Tolstóy Commune (about 1926–27).

continued to bustle around, worrying about somebody, getting distressed about something, or trying to prevail on someone in her thin little squeaky voice.

I remember Tánya Vishnévskaya, who had come to us from a children's home. She was an orphan, a foundling, as I remember—a stubborn little creature, with a deep scar on her cheek. She and Kátya Dorónina studied with Yevgény Ivánovich Popóv, improving their knowledge of grammar and arithmetic, learning shorthand and very likely other things too, profiting by the all-round education of that remarkable man.[2] Tánya Vishnévskaya grew up to be a serious, strong-willed person. She became a pediatrician. Kátya Dorónina was a radiant little blonde, a good, kind, modest friend of mine. Working together for weeks at a time (we always did household service as a pair), sometimes in the kitchen, sometimes in the garden, or in the fields or the cattle-yard—how many days of our youth we spent together!

Our good-hearted Vásya Dyómin was a versifier and a clever lad who would celebrate our Sundays by making fluffy rolls and sweet buns. Vásya Ptítsyn was a master at cabinetmaking. The locksmith Mísha Dyachkóv was a merry joker, a clown, and something of a grumbler. The clumsy Pávlo Chepúrny, a Ukrainian, was one of the very few who never found a place for himself in the commune. Seryózha Sínev was a self-taught draftsman, mediocre but self-confident. There were also the Blagovéshchensky brothers—Kóstya and Mísha. Kóstya was an ascetic with a philosophical turn of mind, who was then studying theosophy and managed to convince me that

2. Yevgény Ivánovich Popóv (1864–1938)—a follower of Tolstóy who was associated with him for many years. He published a number of books and articles on education and on gardening and spent his last years in the Life and Labor Commune in Western Siberia.

Setting out plants raised in the New Jerusalem Tolstóy Commune's greenhouse (about 1926–27).

The New Jerusalem Commune, 1922 or 1923. The bearded man in the center is Iván Gorbunóv-Posádov, the father of Mikhaíl.

I was a second Annie Besant,[3] destined to bring light and understanding to the world, rather than create my own personal happiness by starting an ordinary family. He swept me off my feet with karmas, otherworlds, and retribution in the next life (after death) for sins in this one. My infatuation with Kóstya's fantasies caused a lot of suffering for all three of us—me, Vásya Shershenyóv, and Kóstya. It became strongly interwoven with an aspiration implanted in my childhood for complete chastity and unwavering devotion to a life of service to others. I did not know how to put this aspiration into practice, and the first thing I did was to refuse Vásya, who at that time was asking me to marry him. Mísha Blagovéshchensky, Kóstya's brother, a thin, sickly fellow with a jovial disposition, did not share Kóstya's philosophizing. Both brothers were very musical. Kóstya, who had not finished his studies at the conservatory, was a virtuoso on the mandolin, as Mísha was on the balalaika. Vásya sometimes accompanied them on the guitar. There was a time when Mísha and I sang duets together. Kóstya directed us and accompanied us.

During the winter, Mísha's task was to repair the communal footwear and resole everybody's felt boots.

Among those who lived with us for a while were Mítya and Várya Filíppov. Zóya Grigóryevna Rubán would come on visits along with her sister Nadézhda Grigóryevna and little son Lyósik. One person who had also lived at "Beryózki"[4] and was very close to us in spirit was the intelligent and affectionate Véra Ippolítovna Alekséyeva and her children, who all helped with the general work according to their strength. Among those who lived off and on in the commune were Dúnya Trífonova, a former member of the children's colony, with whom I was destined later to sleep on the same prison bunk in the Voskresénsk Prison; Pelagéya Konstantínovna (I do not remember her family name), who was the friend of a man from Khersón; and Mísha Salýkin and his wife. Mísha performed classical works in a powerful baritone voice. Many of us remember to this day how seriously and with what feeling he sang "Do not weep, my child, do not weep in vain," from Chaykóvsky's "Demon," and also "Sail boldly ahead, o sailor, sing a song, sing. . . ." I remember the powerful, reticent blond Kleménty Yemelyánovich Kraskóvsky, who had gone through a lot in his time, and who had lived with us at the Pýrikovs' in Smolénsk Province; and Bórya Nepómnyashchy, who was always distressed about his ideological differences with his wife.

A particularly colorful personality was Seryózha Bulýgin, whose father

3. Annie Besant (1847–1933) was an English social reformer who left Christianity and her Protestant clergyman husband to take up a series of various causes, finally embracing theosophy in 1889 and becoming a disciple and later the biographer of the Russian theosophist and occultist Helena Blavátsky.

4. Beryózki—a Tolstoyan commune near Moscow, made up largely of intellectuals, including Shershenyóva's father, Fyódor Alekséyevich Strákhov, one of Tolstóy's closest friends, her mother, and her older sister Natálya. During the famine years immediately following the October Revolution, the Strákhov family had taken refuge in Smolénsk Province in the home of the Tolstoyan peasant family of Iván Pýrikov, and Natálya married his son Yelizár, who exerted an important influence on Yákov Dragunóvsky (see Dragunóvsky's chapter in this book).

was a contemporary of Tolstóy's and wrote and published memoirs about him. Seryózha and Vásya formed a lasting friendship, despite certain disagreements in their views. Seryózha believed in the divinity of Christ. Along with his exceptional mind, there lived within him a special kind of mysticism, close to the mysticism of the Evangelical Christians,[5] whose sectarian religion he had far outgrown. Good-looking and restless in spirit, a tall man with black curly hair and dark eyes who was filled with an inward glow, he burned with a desire to bring about world brotherhood at once. He believed in this as a practical possibility, and thought it could be achieved through a special agrarian reform, the land-tenure system advocated by Henry George.[6] Seryózha meditated long and hard about this, and drew up a project for it. As late as the 1930s, against the advice of his friends, he took his materials to the Central Committee of the All-Union Communist Party. I do not know whether they got acquainted there with the details of his project; but they gave him a package with a wax seal on it and suggested that he take it to an agency (perhaps the Land Department) at his place of residence, in the Siberian Territory. Later we learned through his wife, whom he managed to visit briefly, that after they read the package Seryózha himself had brought to them, they arrested him, and he never regained his freedom. Some ten years later, it was rumored that while sailing with a shipload of other liberated convicts, he lost his life along with all the rest of the passengers when their ship went down. Incidentally, the affair for which my Vásya received his last conviction (in 1951) was for some unknown reason connected with the case of Seryózha, who had been arrested many years before, and also with the case of Pyotr Nikítich Lepyókhin, who was taken "in the Bulýgin affair" (very likely only because he had Seryózha's suitcase with his papers in his room). Later, when the case of Vásya and Pétya Shershenyóv was examined, Seryózha's case was reviewed too. His wife was called in and told that her husband had been rehabilitated—posthumously, of course. Vásya was rehabilitated too; but as for Pyotr Nikítich, we know that he died during the war from starvation and cold in the logging camps. There was no one to help him.

Ilyúsha Kolpáchnikov also lived among us for a while. On the instructions of Vladímir Chertkóv, I visited him in the Moscow prison where he was confined for his refusal of military service; after his release he joined us, and suddenly, for some incomprehensible reason (presumably of a romantic nature), he took his own life. As I remember, that was the first tragic event among us during that time.

The second sad event to disturb our sunny life was the arrest of Faddéy

<hr/>

5. Evangelical Christians—a Russian religious sect originally known as Pashkovites, from Colonel V. A. Páshkov, who had become a follower of the English Lord Radstock during Radstock's evangelistic visits to Petersburg in the mid-1870s. Their relative freedom came to an end in 1929. After being severely persecuted in the 1930s, they united with the Baptists in 1944 during the wartime relaxation of the government's antireligious campaign.

6. Henry George (1839–1897) was an American economist whose single-tax theories, particularly as set forth in his book *Progress and Poverty* (1879), aroused great enthusiasm in Tolstóy and had considerable influence on tax legislation in various countries.

Ivánovich Zablótsky. I remember that day, in June 1928. The meadows were flourishing, haymaking was in progress, the air was filled with the pungent smell of dry hay and freshly mown grass. We felt young, happy, and independent. Suddenly our independence was invaded by an alien will—Faddéy was arrested. Wishing to be consistent to the end in his antimilitarism, he had refused to contribute money to a military loan. He was put into a wagon between two armed militiamen and taken away. All of us then living in the commune followed along behind the wagon. We went through the farmyard, down the drive lined with honeysuckle, and into the highway. Faddéy sat with his back to the horses and meekly, calmly smiled at us, while we wept and waved to him until the wagon disappeared from sight.

Here I want to quote a recent letter I received from Yúlik Yegúdin in which he tells about Faddéy's second arrest, when he had settled in the commune in Siberia after serving out his first sentence. Here is what Yúlik wrote:

> I remember the trial in our dining hall in the Altái region. Faddéy Ivánovich was among those on trial. His words before the court were reminiscent of Socrates' last words to his judges, they resounded so truthfully, so solemnly and fearlessly. In conclusion he said, almost like Socrates: "I have finished. Judge me and do with me what you will." Almost all his friends shed tears of compassion.

It was probably in reference to this same event that one of our Altái friends told us the following: at a meeting where government representatives were present, Faddéy said he could not take part in the elections to the Supreme Soviet because the government acted on the basis of violence, and he was against violence. The government representatives started calling him an enemy of the people, saying that he was a "wolf in sheep's clothing," and men like him were very bad for the people. Lyóva Alekséyev said in defense of Faddéy that he was a most peace-loving man, that he wouldn't hurt a fly. They made a note of Lyóva's name. Afterwards they collected signatures from those present on a statement claiming that Faddéy was an enemy of the people. Lyóva refused to sign. And so he was arrested along with Faddéy. Faddéy never came back, but Lyóva returned after long years of hardship in prisons and exile. Still, how many there were like him who never came back at all!

Where are you, dear brothers! Probably the grass on your graves has long since grown, withered, and grown again, and of course life still goes on for a few people of your age. Why were you fated to leave us so early? You had so much vitality, truth, and energy! Without any doubt you were among the best of the many people living on this earth.

I return now to our life together in the New Jerusalem Commune. With the addition of new commune members, and especially with the coming of whole families, the organization of work, the distribution of our money income, and the solution of many farming problems became much more complicated. Some people grew dissatisfied. Some, like Pétya Shershenyóv, wanted more free time for painting; others wanted to satisfy the not exactly modest requirements of their family members (in comparison with those of the early settlers). Both their requirements and their capacity for work varied widely. Mitrofán, as the chairman, wanted at all costs to preserve the spirit of simplicity and brotherhood that had originally existed in the commune. He was completely repelled by what were in his eyes the vulgar bourgeois traditions of family life, and by any appearance of personal egoism. He demanded subordination, and his term as chairman began to take on an air of despotism. Our meetings became stormy, and our multiplying problems found no solution. Mitrofán was asked to resign his duties as chairman, and Vásya Shershenyóv was elected in his place. By that time Vásya had already become my husband. He had to take over the leadership of a mixed crowd of people who were already highly upset. There was dissatisfaction with the mothers, who were the targets of many complaints. Vásya's situation was complicated by the fact that by then we too had a little baby, and I was passionately devoted to motherhood and in my own heart had broken away from communal life. In the first place, my baby gave me no opportunity to take part in group work, or to be present at the general meetings and evening entertainment. In the second place, I probably romanticized my own motherhood too much. And then my baby required a great deal of care, both because he was weak and sickly and because I brought him up without anyone to help me. I relied on the guidance of books and the advice of doctors at the clinic—absolutely pure and undiluted, according to all the rules and without any exceptions. To a certain extent motherhood cut me off from the joys of brotherhood in work within our communal family. I did not have enough strength and skill to combine the two. I would often sit up all night with Fédya when he was sick and then get up at four in the morning to do the milking. It was not easy, but what could I do? "In the conditions of communal life, you can't spend so much time on a baby," Seryózha Sínev would say. "I have no child, but I still want time for my sketching." Some members thought it was unjust for the mothers to work less than the bachelors but still receive just as much as they. In our general meetings the question arose how we could arrange things so that the babies would get adequate care without encroaching on the material situation of the bachelors. The amounts of time and resources necessary for their care were reckoned differently. My desires appeared exaggerated to people like Márta Tolkách, who brought up her children more simply and criticized me. Yúliya Rutkóvskaya was also criticized because she once flatly refused on account of her little Vitúsya to share in the general work, and also refused to entrust him to anyone else (except Dúnya Trífonova). But everything gradually got straightened out, a solution was found, and eventually everyone calmed down and became reconciled. Much of this was due to the gentleness and peaceable nature of Kólya Lyubímov (he too had little children) and to the fairness and levelheadedness of Ványa Rutkóvsky, who had never defended his wife Yúliya's selfishness. The decision was made to give the mothers an extra day off each week to take care of their children, to relieve women with rheumatism in their arms from the milking, and to give Várya Filíppova and me the task of looking after all the children in the collective. After objecting at first, Yúliya later entrusted Vitúsya to us, and she herself joined us in sharing the duty of looking after all the children. The men wove together a large playpen for us out of slender withes, and we would carry it out to a meadow and keep our tiny children in it.

We met our artists halfway. At a special meeting we decided to recognize Pétya's special abilities in painting and give him two hours a day. Prokófy Pávlovich said at the meeting: "The instant that an artist catches for us in nature is unrepeatable; it is something to be valued." Pétya Shershenyóv began to work a lot on his painting. As I remember, we also granted the same possibility to Sínev in order not to offend him, although his artistic talent was very weak. In those days Pétya, tanned, well-built, and wearing a turban, was a real child of nature. Geórgy called him a "sunny fellow." Many years later I ran across somebody's poem that Yevgény Popóv had sent to Pétya, evidently associating it with his way of life in that period:

> Goodness is not in the world;
> It appears at times in your soul.
> And it is not the harmony of nature
> That resounds in the woods and waters,
> But rather the sound of your heart
> Singing within your breast in a pure moment of freedom.

In those days we lived in the free expanse of nature, our hearts were pure, and we were filled with a desire to think and live freely and justly. That is how Vásya, who was then only twenty-five years old, was able to handle his complicated duties as our chairman. It must be said, though, that he had great tact and self-control along with the kind of decisiveness that helped him to be the leader and guiding spirit of our organization, in which we had common ownership and a common budget, and observed the principle of "from each according to his abilities, and to each according to his needs." We had to discover and develop our abilities and not let ourselves be carried away by our needs. We had to keep from letting personal advantage stifle brotherhood and joy in our work. To be sure, we made our blunders, but just the same the life of the commune at that time was filled with enthusiasm, trust, a spirit of give-and-take, and genuine joy in our work. Individual notes of dissatisfaction were balanced out by the general spirit of good nature, gaiety, and the happiness of youth.

Our life began at three or four o'clock in the morning, and sometimes even as early as two. First the person on duty would wake up whoever was supposed to send our milk off in a freight car from the railway station to Moscow, and then he would wake up those who were to milk the cows and go out to the fields to plow or mow. Some would jump up at the first call, others would wake up by themselves, and some had a hard time waking up, but nobody shirked their duties. Our evenings, especially during the early years, were invariably a time of merriment—merriment to the point of exhaustion. In spite of our fatigue, we would play *laptá* or *gorélki*;[7] and in the winter we would stage theatrical performances, sing, joke, and simply laugh and clown around till we dropped. Vásya and Mitrofán were the ringleaders in our merriment—which, I should add, involved everybody. In summer our holiday visitors would also take part—Natálya Strákhova and her husband and son, the Kurákins, the Dobrolyúbovs; and people would also come to visit us from the Armand colony. No one felt shy, and no one put on airs. Nadézhda Grigóryevna Dobrolyúbova brought us a great deal of pleasure with her remarkably gentle, heartfelt, and melodious singing. She formed the habit of "dedicating" to each of us in turn some song from her repertory that she considered to have some special association with us. She dedicated Rakhmáninov's song "The Lilac" to me and Glínka's "The Lark" to Vásya. Throughout our lives, both Vásya and I associated the sweet song of that little inhabitant of the fields with the period of our youth.

One of our buildings was occupied in the summer by a children's home, a center that the Vegetarian Society had organized for homeless waifs. We called the children our "centrists" and supplied them with milk and vegetables. At that time the leader of the center was Sásha Známenskaya. She also had a melodic voice and a gracious manner all her own of singing Russian folksongs and ancient lyrics. At the end of our working day, we would gather somewhere in the moonlight or on the terrace steps, and somebody would say: "Come on, Sáshka, strike up 'Nóchenka' for us." Someone would sing a second part, and somebody else would join in. We could not know then that those were the best days of our lives—unique as well as the best. Vásya and Mitrofán were inexhaustible storytellers. They always had new material for a colorful portrayal of somebody. They would improvise their act as they went along, each of them cleverly supporting the other with striking details.

Our commune members also had another repertory, which consisted of almost no content but called forth so much laughter and merriment that I still remember it. They once used this repertory for a performance in winter before the railroad colony at Zheléznikovo (or Dubráva—I no longer remember). They went over there accompanied by just about all of us in sleighs—not just one but a whole train of them. It was a freezing day, and the snow crunched and sparkled under the runners. The men jumped out of the sleighs and ran along with the horses to warm themselves. They performed an old song, "Three beauties from heaven went along the streets of Madrid, Donna Clara, Donna Res, and the beautiful Pepita." The "beauties" were Vásya, Pétya, and Kólya Lyubímov. They dressed up in our bright-colored dresses, skirts, and kerchiefs. Mitrofán was the beggar who kissed Pepita, and Geórgy Vasílyev was the rose seller. They portrayed it all with such phenomenal seriousness and such comical grace that it was hard to keep from rolling on

7. *Laptá*—a kind of Russian ball game; *gorélki*—a Russian game of tag.

the floor with laughter. Mitrofán presented Pepita with a bare twig broom. The most comical of all was Kólyashka Lyubímov, wearing a very low-cut dress and a kerchief tied on the back of his head.

Sometimes after supper on long winter evenings, suddenly as if by a signal, and to the horror of the leaders, some grown-up pranksters would grab saucepans, pot lids, and frying pans from the stove or wherever they found them, and out of the kitchen would come the ear-splitting sound of a percussion orchestra. Mísha Blagovéshchensky and a few others would dance the *trepák*.

Naturally we also put on plays in winter. I remember Tolstóy's *Living Corpse*. Vásya played Fédya Protásov, Mitrofán was Karénin, Nádya or Sónya Nikítina was Líza, and Kóstya was the producer. Guests would come out from Moscow. Pyotr Nikítich organized the reading of literary works in the kitchen, and tried to arrange the regular reading of Tolstóy's *Circle of Reading* and *For Every Day;*[8] but for some reason that did not catch on, although discussions of serious matters—about the meaning of life, the different manifestations of morality, its various stages, and other serious questions—would sometimes continue far beyond midnight.

Vásya had the virtues of straightforwardness and good will. These traits enabled him to talk frankly to people about their errors and still remain on good terms with them. That is the way it was with Mitrofán. Vásya had occasion to argue with him, correct him, and give him reprimands. He once had to inform him about the decision of the general assembly to remove him from the chairmanship, and afterwards he had to take over that responsibility himself. With all that, he remained to the end of his days on the best of terms with him. Mitrofán was offended by his dismissal, of course; but he later said that he accepted it solely because the one who took his place was Vásya—the only one he could trust with the commune. At the same time, Mitrofán knew that it was Vásya alone who had raised the question of removing him—Mitrofán—from the position.

In September 1928, Vásya was offered the job of managing the vegetarian dining hall in Moscow during the winter season. He went to try it out and get acquainted with the work, but after a time he came back convinced that he could not shut his eyes to the employees' abuses, which they had become accustomed to, and that he would have had to hire a whole new staff of workers in order to introduce his own system of work. That would have been a huge task, requiring a great deal of time, whereas Vásya would have been working there only during the winter season, when he could get away from the commune. As I remember, at that time Vásya was elected chairman of the Vegetarian Society, and thereafter he often went to Moscow.

In 1924 Vásya was a member of a delegation of peaceful antimilitarists who were received by Stálin. They requested legalization and noninterference

---

8. Two collections of daily readings for a whole year, compiled by Tolstóy during the last decade of his life from his own writings and those of others to reflect his religious philosophy.

in their life and work. I do not remember the specific points of their declaration, but I remember that Stálin received them well and said: "In military
matters you are no help to us, but in peaceful construction we know you as
honest and hard-working people."

As the official representative of the commune, Vásya knew how to get
along well with the local authorities. Our commune was foremost in the
district in farming matters. All the surrounding population took a liking to
us. Many of them used our seeds, which incidentally had been developed by
Ványa Zúyev, who took part in no other work. The local population would
come to our commune for advice on farming, and we helped some of the
women who were living alone with their physical labor. We had set up a
milk collection point for those who had cows, and of course this was very
convenient for the peasants. We became popular, and people talked about us
and pointed to us as an example for other farms. But our ideology was alien
to the local authorities. We in no way tried to impose our convictions on
anyone else, and we did not carry on any kind of propaganda. But our very
popularity and the great sympathy for us among the local people made the
officials suspicious of us, and they eventually proposed that we accept the
surrounding population as members of our commune along with everybody
else the officials might want to send to us. That marked the beginning of the
end for us.

By that time our commune had grown. At least thirty to thirty-five persons gathered around our table. We did not want to add to the collective,
especially not with people who were alien to us. We were all vegetarians;
none of us drank, smoked, or used foul language. We understood very well
that the harmony of our social structure was maintained thanks to the community of convictions among the majority and our mutual confidence and
respect for one another. We understood that we could not sustain our
Leo Tolstóy Commune, that is, maintain its free and peaceful spirit, if people poured into the commune who not only did not share our convictions
but tried in every way to oppose them. At first the authorities proposed
only that we change the character of our collective, but afterwards they delivered an ultimatum to us. Representatives of the local government came
to visit our general assemblies. Vásya presided, and he said outright that
without our community of feeling and inner unity, our life could not
continue on its smooth course. Even our labor productivity would be
affected.

No common language or common decision could be found with the government representatives. They accused us of living too much to ourselves.
"You dangle between heaven and earth," they told us. "You're neither a
candle for God nor a scourge for the devil." Finally they announced that we
must get ready for the commune to be reorganized as a state farm and be
merged with another organization, taking the new name "Red October."
The state farm that was to be merged with us already had its charter, which
we too would have to accept. They set a date by which we would have to
accept the new members of "Red October."

Unrest and discussions followed. Some families, such as the Tolkáches, had come to us from a distance after liquidating their whole farm and turning their property over to the commune—cows and some equipment. It was not easy to pull up stakes suddenly and move—and besides, where could they go? Some could leave without luggage and wanted to do so at once; others felt sure that somewhere else we could revive the project that meant so much to us; still others proposed to remain for a time in the new collective. We could not avoid handing over our farm to the new organization. Many planned to transfer to the Shestakóvka Commune, which was ready to welcome us. The day and hour were set for the arrival of representatives of the district center, the land administration, and the newly merged collective. (Some of them had already arrived and been put up in our houses.)

At that moment something happened that probably none of us will ever forget. It decided the fate of many of us before we had a chance to collect ourselves.

Our little son, Fédya, was then two years old. I am reminded about how it all happened by a note in a diary that I kept for Fédya over many years, addressing him directly. I jotted down this note in Khóvrino, where we settled temporarily in the summer of 1929:

Almost a month has passed since I last wrote in this diary. A fateful month! It seems to me like several months—so much happened during that time. About two o'clock in the afternoon of 29 April, our house caught on fire. On that day the liquidation commission was to come and take over our farm. All the horses were in use transporting the belongings of the commune members; there was no way to haul water, and—what had never happened—there was no supply of water anywhere. Evidently, the chimney had spewed out hot ashes onto the shingles of the roof, which had thoroughly dried out under the spring sun. The wind quickly fanned the flames. Fire extinguishers were not effective in the open air. The burning house was where we—the Rutkóvskys, Ványa Zúyev, Dúnya Trífonova, and some of the new members of the "Red October"—all lived. You were asleep in only your nightshirt and were awakened by some sort of racket on the stairway. Amid all this racket and clatter, Vásya ran out and shouted to me: "Quick, dress Fédya, our house is on fire!" Then everybody and everything began spinning, flashing, running, shrieking. I could not get your legs into your pants; your clothes had suddenly disappeared. I handed you to Márta Tolkách and ran in to carry out our things. Márta held you there right in front of the fire, then handed you to Ilyúsha Alekséyev, who for some reason sat down on a chair that happened to be at his feet and sat there in front of the blazing house. I kept running in and out of the house and then suddenly realized you might be terrified. And so, pretending to be calm, I went up to you and said: "What are you looking at? At that nice fire? It's a fine, big fire, isn't it?" I could not imagine that someone would be listening to me, that I was being followed, that they would give my words an entirely different meaning and write them down, and that they would provide grounds for suspecting us of arson. Among the commune members rushing about with belongings and buckets there appeared men with red borders on their caps, from the Criminal Investigation Department. I looked around for your father and saw him first pulling the roof off a shed next door which had also begun to burn, then giving some orders, then with a bucket of water in his hands. Later, when a fire brigade finally came from Voskresénsk, he was continuously pumping water out of the pond. He ran up to me for a moment and said: "They are probably going to arrest me."

"Why?"

"They will accuse me of arson."

The cows had been let out of the cattle barn and were quietly wandering about the yard. They set to work munching grass just as if nothing had happened. Men on horseback from the Criminal Investigation Department foolishly and futilely tried to drive them off somewhere.

When they found out I was the wife of the chairman, they began to bustle around and ask me questions: "Don't you know how the fire got started?" and so on.

Peasant women who had hastened over from the village were helping to carry things into another house while they talked complete nonsense to one another, for example: "Just look how they took it into their heads to drive out the commune members! How is that possible? They're such good people, been living and working so many years. A fire was bound to break out here!"

Somebody threw our furniture out from the second floor, and naturally it was smashed to pieces. Urchins from the village rummaged through a pile of trifles. The piano belonging to my father, who at that time was with us in the commune, had been taken by the commune members to my sister in Moscow a few days before the fire. "Now they will certainly suspect us of arson," our women said. I tried to reason with them, and tried to calm down Nína Lapáyeva, who was sobbing. I told her not to despair, never suspecting that those words too would be held against me as evidence of arson. I sat you down with Ilyúsha in a room of the house that was still intact and put your feet in some felt boots that had turned up from somewhere. The fire had almost burned out. Your father, Ványa Zúyev, and Ványa Rutkóvsky had been placed in separate rooms and were being called up one by one for questioning. Ilyúsha handed you over to Nína, who had lost her head and started to weep and wail. You were crying in her arms. I had nothing for you to eat; you had not eaten all day. But I had no chance to take care of you. Your father came into the room and said to me: "Get my things together—underwear and a few other things. Find my documents—I gave them to somebody." That was a hard task. You had developed diarrhea. Somehow I found everything your papa had asked for, and I cooked something for you, but no sooner had I begun to feed you than I was called for interrogation. "Social origin? Education? What were you doing before the fire started? When were you married? When did you register your marriage? When, in plain Russian, did you actually get married?" I didn't know how to break it off and stop him!

"Are you a Tolstoyan?"

"I share Tolstóy's views."

"Not from childhood, not from conviction, but just by chance?"

"No, deliberately."

"But why did you ask to read the protocol before you signed it? Tolstóyans are supposed to believe everybody!"

I had been given only ten minutes to get ready for a trip to Voskresénsk "for a little talk," but the young guard still detained me: "But Leo Tolstóy preached that you had to love everybody and believe everybody, and here you don't believe them! Your Zúyev too is not a real Tolstóyan—he wouldn't believe the agent either, and he too read the protocol . . ."

When I went back to the room, my poor little Fédya, you were asleep. Your papa came up to say farewell to me, but I told him happily that I was going with him.

"They're taking you too?"

"Yes, we're going together."

"I will keep him, please don't worry, Álechka," said Dúnya Trífonova. We could entrust the child to her care. We kissed each other.

"Trífonova, you too get ready to go," said the same guard, glancing at us.

Ványa Rutkóvsky had changed his boots after the fire, and nothing else of his turned up. Everything was soaked, and it was impossible to find any dry things. I too could find none of my things in all the chaos. Some of our people handed Ványa and me some kerchiefs, socks, and shawls. Softly touching you with my lips, I got ready for the journey.

"We won't leave Fédya, don't worry," said Kólya Lyubímov. He gave me an especially anxious, affectionate kiss. Márta asked in nervous astonishment: "Are they really being arrested?"

"What do you think we're doing," retorted the guard, "taking them to a party?"

Prokófy Pávlovich was still sitting on a bundle where he had sat down after the fire was put out. He sat in silence, with his head on his knees.

We went out on the porch and plunged into the darkness, snow, spring slush, and water. Someone accompanied us along the lane. I remember only Kólya's dear face and his almost guilty smile. His eyes said: "What will all of you do without me? Why am I staying here?"

The guards offered to let Dúnya and me sit with them on the cart. "Special respect for the women," they said, "but you men will trot along on your feet." We wanted to be with our own, with Vásya, and not in the company of the militiamen; and in spite of Vásya's and Ványa's insistence that we conserve our strength, Dúnya and I went along on foot and did not regret it. The agents drove off, leaving us in the charge of the guard. The night was warm, the sky was clear, and the stars had come out. It seemed as if we could hear the last snow melting as we dragged our feet through the mud and the wheels of the guards' cart behind us sloshed through the puddles of water. Soon the guard himself evidently got tired of it all, and he very politely begged us to go on by ourselves to the Voskresénsk militia station. Vásya promised to do this, also very politely, and repeated the address after him. We were left alone. The road to the highway was very bad, and time and again Vásya gave me a hand, helping me to pick my way through the mud. When we got to the highway, we started walking single file. I walked between Ványa Svinobúrko and Vásya. The five of us were united in our consciousness of our innocence, our inner freedom, and our readiness to meet the new form of life cheerfully, even though it was hard to comprehend why all this had so suddenly fallen on our shoulders. "It's some kind of dream!" said Ványa. "It's so strange that it's really hard to believe it's not a dream." It was indeed truly hard to take in all that had happened. The fire would have to break out just when it was so natural to suspect us of arson! We were prepared for a long separation from our children, our families, and each other. "I've just thought how good it is," said Ványa Zúyev, "to be honest and to adhere to this principle always and without exception. I know that whatever they may ask me,

I will always tell only the truth, and for that reason I have nothing to worry about." All of us agreed with him completely. May you, my child, always be honest, in big matters as well as little ones.

We arrived at the militia station at 11:30 at night. While we were being interrogated, some drunks in the next room were spoiling for a fight, cursing loudly.

"How old are you?" I was asked.

"Twenty-four."

"Just my age!" shouted a drunken voice with a coarse oath. Vásya shuddered and for some reason sat me down at his side. The guard who had waited for us at the militia station was sent home. "Strange people," someone said. "Five persons, and they came alone, without a guard."

"Let's go!" We were taken by an armed guard, but a different one, across the courtyard to the Voskresénsk jail house, set up in the former New Jerusalem Monastery. While they were taking us, Vásya said: "This is no accident! There is some kind of significance in this." I too believed that nothing in life was accidental.

Then the stinking cell, the latrine bucket, the sound of the locks snapping shut, and my sound youthful sleep the first night, alongside Dúnya on the stone floor. The next day, we were given a place for two on a bunk.

I tried with all my might to kill time so as not to think about you, and suddenly—a familiar cough! Was Vásya in the next cell? Then a parcel from the commune, thanks to friends—Kólya Lyubímov, of course. My refusal to eat meat, and the dry, horribly oversalted wheat kasha, which we managed to throw out on the roof for the pigeons. An unexpected meeting with our people (in the corridor), just for a second. Our overseers were not harsh; they seemed to show some sympathy, and I was grateful to them. In the same cell with Dúnya and me were women arrested for prostitution. They sang something, and we joined in with them for the sake of unity. We wanted to show that we did not look down on them; we felt like having a conversation. Perhaps we would be with them, or others like them, for many long years. Readiness for everything, animation, the strength of youthful years. Belief in the triumph of truth and goodness everywhere. Readiness for everything, but fear and horror at the possible execution of Vásya. At that time there were many executions. Time and again the newspapers would publish: "Execution for arson on a collective farm." Can we prove that we did not commit arson? Will Vásya remain alive? I wanted us to go through everything, everything together. If only we could be together!

I slipped a note into the cell where I had heard Vásya's cough. The result was something horrible: in the hole between our cells was another note—perhaps pushed in by someone else long before—and I pushed it all the way through with my note, but mine got stuck between the walls. Vásya took the note. In it someone had expressed complete despair and the intention to commit suicide. The handwriting was not mine, but Vásya thought it had changed because of my state of mind. Everything was explained when I pushed my next note through.

Our good friend and a great friend of Seryózha Bulýgin, Nadézhda Varfoloméyevna Vinográdova, worked at the time in the Voskresénsk Prison as a psychoneurological physician, and evidently she had some kind of connections that enabled her as a doctor to get permission to meet us—first with Vásya and then with me. She said that Kólya Lyubímov was trying to get a commission of fire experts to come out to the commune from Moscow, that all our friends were worried about what had happened to us, that you were with my sister Natásha and were alive, well, and safe, and that Iván Ivánovich Gorbunóv was seeking permission to get all of us out on bail until the trial. I was called up a time or two for questioning. I was asked why I had talked during the fire with my child about the "nice fire," why I had cut short all the talk of our people about possible suspicions of arson, and where I was when the house caught on fire. Ten days later, Dúnya and I were released. My sister Natásha and Kólya Lyubímov met us at the prison gate. Kólya rented space in a room in Voskresénsk, carried messages for us, got in touch with Gorbunóv, and made efforts to arrange for the visit by the commission of experts. As secretary of the commune, he was busy with the disposal of the commune's property.

Natásha took me to her apartment in Moscow. When we got there, Fédya was asleep. Yelizár Ivánovich had laid him in the cradle beside Natásha's bed. When he saw me, he got very excited, his lips began to tremble, he stretched out his little arms first toward Natásha and then toward me, and he whimpered for a long time and would not let me go.

Afterwards I started looking for a lawyer. Iván Ivánovich and I went to see N. K. Muravyóv (an attorney), and he and I drew up a declaration. I met our friends, and my heart was filled with anxiety about the fate of Vásya and both Ványas. Iván Ivánovich went to see the investigator in Voskresénsk and personally requested that those who were still under arrest be released to him on bail. They were released until the trial.

Thus ended the New Jerusalem period.

My sister Natásha and her husband, Yelizár Ivánovich Pýrikov, invited us to live at their dacha in Khóvrino until the trial, when the verdict was expected to clarify our further situation in life. We moved in with them, and soon afterwards Ványa Zúyev joined us.

Finally the trial was set. The Moscow commission of fire experts went out to the charred remains of our property and concluded that there was a crack in the brick chimney, which had survived the fire, through which it was quite possible for a spark to reach the dry shingles of the roof—all the more so because it was ascertained that the stove warming both the ground floor and the upper floor of the house had been in use almost constantly, serving two big groups. On the day of the fire, two successive batches of bread had been baked in it.

Vásya, as chairman of the commune, was accused of a negligent attitude toward state property (he did not see the crack in the chimney). He was condemned to work for several months and pay his salary to the state. That was the best we could have hoped for. What saved us was the crack in the chimney, that is, its discovery by the fire commission that Kólya Lyubímov had summoned.

Vásya had to start work at once. We moved into a service room in Tolstóy's house at Khamóvniki that Klávdiya Dmítrievna Platónova made available to us. Vásya went to Vorónezh to look for work. We and Ványa Zúyev had made plans to go to either Vorónezh or the Caucasus and begin building a new life together. But Vásya found nothing suitable in Vorónezh and got work as a stone crusher that paid well but was terribly hard physically. He was joined by Sergéy Bulýgin, who was then in serious financial difficulty. They would go every day to some highway on the outskirts of Moscow that was being rebuilt, and there they would crush and haul stones. Their hands were covered with bloody blisters, and their bodies ached. When he got home, that is, to Khamóvniki, Vásya could barely make it to bed, he was so tired. But the court garnisheed a large part of his salary, and much of what we owned had disappeared in the fire, so Vásya decided to endure it. He still remained in good spirits. Despondency was not in his nature.

After a time we had to give up the room we occupied. Vásya took Fédya and me to the Life and Labor Commune at Shestakóvka, in the Krásnaya Pakhrá district. A few of our New Jerusalem Commune members were already living there.

At the beginning I was in low spirits at Shestakóvka. I greatly missed Vásya, who would walk out to see us (the distance from Moscow to the commune was nearly seven miles). It had its own rules, its own cohesiveness, its own way of life, which we had to get accustomed to. I encountered the great inner culture of Mazúrin, the gentle character of Aleksándr Nikoláyevich Ganusévich and a few others; but both qualities were lacking in the general atmosphere of that life. Besides that, difficulties arose for me once again in bringing up our child. Fédya, who was then a little over two years old, kept me tied down. The children of commune members loitered about wherever they pleased, dirty and without any supervision. The rest of the mothers had somehow gotten used to that and made their adjustment to it. I could not get used to it, and for the sake of our child I stuck to our routine and to our perhaps exaggerated cleanliness. I did not try to organize a children's center such as we had at Jerusalem, since I lacked any feeling of unity with some of the mothers, who in their turn probably considered me arrogant. I was unable to fully grasp the situation, which involved self-esteem and required a greater understanding of the interests of our common cause. And nobody there understood me. When Vásya came home on his free days, he could find no peace and quiet, because he saw that things were not going well with us. When his seasonal work on the highway was over, he decided to join an artel[9] to produce graphite for a new type of flooring. Fédya and I moved to a temporary rented room on Plyushchíkha Street in Moscow.

The graphite work was also very hard and very dirty. Vásya and Yelizár Ivánovich Pýrikov, who had also joined the artel, washed themselves off every day in the bath, but even there they could not scrub off the deeply ingrained graphite dust.

Vásya often visited the Chertkóv home, attended meetings at the Vegetarian Society, and participated in its affairs. The graphite work in the artel did not suit Vásya. The business was organized on an unethical basis, and its organizer proved to be a dishonorable man. Vásya found it intolerable to associate with him, and we went back to Shestakóvka. Vásya tried to support

---

9. Artél—a cooperative association of workmen or peasants.

me, spoke at our general meetings, and was aroused and distressed by the lack of understanding on the part of some members. But gradually the tension subsided. In the autumn, when it turned cold and the children continued to run around in the dirt and rain without supervision, not only I but other mothers too began to have difficulties, especially because the children caught cold and became ill. Again help came from Kólya Lyubímov, who had also moved back to Shestakóvka. At that time he was in poor health and was unable to take part in heavy labor, and at our assembly he offered to take turns with me in looking after all the children. The children loved him for his gentleness and a kind of feminine quality in his character; and he, I remember, treated all the little tykes—his own as well as others'—with wonderful kindness and care. At that time Yevgény Ivánovich Popóv was again living with us in the commune. He brought a certain warmth and coziness to our life in common. Life was settling down well. Then suddenly Vásya fell ill. At first we thought he just had some sort of chronic stomach disorder, but he kept getting worse and worse. A doctor was called in, and he diagnosed it as typhoid fever. I took Vásya in a cart, lying flat on his back, to Kalúzhskaya Street, to the same hospital where his sister Lyudmíla worked, and where their mother and younger sister Mánya lived with her near the hospital. The hospital orderlies lifted him off the cart. He was almost unconscious. His illness was long and serious. Finally he came back. He had grown very weak, and walked with difficulty using a cane. His legs pained him. By that time we were completely accustomed to the commune. Everything had settled down. I had begun to serve often on kitchen duty. Yevgény Ivánovich often stayed with Fédya. Vásya recovered and began to take turns with Kólya hauling the milk to Moscow, at first in a wagon and then in a sleigh. That gave him a chance to visit his mother frequently. He helped her a little, carrying milk and vegetables. It seemed that everything had settled down, but that turned out to be wrong. The local government agencies had long been displeased with the commune's ideology, and the same clouds were gathering as at New Jerusalem.

The first steps were taken to abolish this Life and Labor Commune too. Vásya was in a delegation that went to Stálin requesting an allotment of land and the recognition of the people's right to life and labor. Their petition expressed the desires and possibilities of people who had their own views on life, their own religious and moral convictions, which did not allow them to participate in any form of violence and killing, and which channeled their lives in other ways as well. This was also an allusion to vegetarianism, which did not permit these people to engage in the raising of cattle, and to the impossibility of having their children taught in public schools, where military training was included. A great deal of thought had gone into the formulation of this petition. Many people had talked about it, argued about it, and become agitated about it. Several Moscow friends had also taken part in it. I do not remember on just which points the government met us halfway and on which it disagreed with the delegates' requests, but they did give us land in Siberia. We started preparing for resettlement. Every day in the kitchen, the women baked bread and dried rusks, vegetables, and potatoes. People started arriving in the Western Siberian territory from the Caucasus, Smolénsk Province, and other places. In March 1931, when talk had already begun about naming the day of our departure, Vásya was called to Moscow. Vladímir Grigóryevich Chertkóv, who by then had become very weak, needed a secretary and medical orderly; and his friends Nikoláy Sergéyevich Rodiónov and Alekséy Petróvich Sergéyenko, considering Vásya very well suited for that work, asked us not to leave, but to stay in Moscow and move into the Chertkóvs' home. Vásya felt he could not reject such a proposal; and in April 1931, when Fédya was almost four years old, instead of moving to Siberia we moved into the home of the Chertkóvs on Lefórtov Lane.

Borís Vasílyevich Mazúrin

2.

The Life and Labor Commune:

A HISTORY AND SOME REFLECTIONS

BORÍS MAZÚRIN

Boris Vasílyevich Mazúrin, born 13 (New Style 26) September 1901,[1] is the only one of the six contributors to this book who at the time of this writing is still alive. He lives in Western Siberia in the village of Tál-zhino, not far from the site of the Tolstoyan colony he describes in these memoirs. His father, Vasíly Petróvich Mazúrin, was a Tolstoyan schoolteacher of industrial arts and also a poet, whose work was first published in a slim volume in 1926 and has recently appeared in two new editions, published in the Western Siberian cities of Novokuznétsk in 1990 and Kémerovo in 1991.

Borís Mazúrin was educated as a geologist, but through his Tolstoyan convictions he went back to the soil and became the leader of the largest and most successful Tolstoyan agricultural colony in history. The centerpiece of this book is his account of the Life and Labor Commune from the time of its organization in 1921 at Shestakóvka, on the edge of Moscow, to its relocation in Western Siberia in 1931 and his arrest in 1936 and deportation for ten years of imprisonment in the labor camps. All the memoirs published here are linked in one way or another through their associations with Mazúrin and that colony. After arresting all the leaders of the commune in 1936, the Soviet authorities effectively destroyed it at the end of the 1930s by forcibly merging it with a state-controlled collective farm.

---

1. Mazúrin's birthday is sometimes listed as 27 September; but when I visited him in August 1990, he told me he was actually born on 13 (26) September, and his mother had the record changed to 14 (27) September because she felt that 13 was an unlucky number.

Mazúrin as a young man.

Part One: Near Moscow (1921–1931)

ON 31 DECEMBER 1921, several young people who had decided to start an agricultural commune signed a rental contract with the Moscow District Land Department for a small estate bearing the name of Shestakóvka. The area of all the usable land—fields, meadows, orchard, woodland, and pond—amounted to fifty hectares.

There were two large wooden houses in an old park of linden trees, and alongside a little old cattle-yard there was another building which had served as a sort of cook-house and dwelling for the workmen. The lower part was made of brick (one large room with a Russian stove); above it a ramshackle upper story had been built of logs, and a three-room outbuilding had been added onto the kitchen. This was the building into which the new occupants moved.

Shestakóvka was quite near Moscow, about twelve kilometers if you went straight through the woods by the country road, and about fifteen kilometers if you went by the Bórovsk highway, through the villages of Nikúlino and Troparyóvo. But despite its closeness to Moscow, the place was uncommonly quiet and isolated. It lay between the big fork of the Pávelets and Kíev railroad lines, and between the smaller fork of the Kalúga and Bórovsk highways. The fields lay on gently rolling land, covered with aspen trees and undergrowth. A small stream flowed through the bottom land. Beyond it was the village of Bogoródskoye (twenty households), and a little farther off to the side was the village of Troparyóvo. Judging by the names of the villages, these lands had once belonged to the church, and on the estate itself there was a little stone church of ancient architecture that was occasionally visited by tourist groups composed of amateur historians, who told us that it had been built during the reign of Ivan the Terrible. One of the wooden houses in the park—"the old summer house," as we called it—had been there for a hundred years. According to legend, Napoleon had stopped there in 1812. It stood on a good foundation of limestone blocks, and its logs were sheathed with boards. When we took it apart in 1928 to build a large communal house, the pine logs rang as if they were new. They were extraordinarily strong, and the butt ends had been cut with an ax. Evidently there were no saws when it was built.

The region was Moscow, the district was Tsarítsyn, the village soviet was Troparyóvo, and it was the fifth year after the Revolution.

A workers' detachment had lived there before us and evidently had done a bit of farming on the side, because when they left, they gave us a cow, Marúska, and two seventeen-year-old horses, Voróna and Lýska, who consisted of years and bones, with a bare hide covering the bones, since medicine to cure the mange had made all the hair fall out. There was also a two-wheel military cart. The workers' regiment also left us a silage pit of leafage from potato plants, a little over a ton of dried besom for fodder for the animals, and nearly nine tons of frozen potatoes. That was all. All over the country there was famine and ruin. We had to live and start farming. We had no money. We took apart one of the wooden houses in the park, sawed the wood up into blocks, split it into firewood, tied it into bundles, hitched up Voróna, and hauled it to Moscow. It took the whole day to go the twelve kilometers—the horses had no strength. Moscow was desperate for fuel, and we exchanged firewood for provisions—bread, hardtack, beans, millet, and so forth. We lived on that.

With the approach of spring, we got 250 pounds of oats, and with these 250 pounds we sowed about three hectares. We sowed them in rows, fifty centimeters apart, and the oats grew up as strong as reeds. After the first harvest, life got easier. We had plenty of potatoes, carrots, vegetables, and a little milk.

We named our colony "Life and Labor." That was suggested by Yefím Moiséyevich Serzhánov, the first pioneer of this whole business. He was a man of extraordinary energy and industry. After working all day long, he could lie down without undressing on the firewood behind the stove, sleep for two or three hours, and then start working again. His comrade and fellow believer Shvílpe (Shílpa, as we called him for short), like Yefím Moiséyevich, was the soul of our work. Both of them were anarchists and they had organized their own group, called "Ao," about which I will say more later. Shílpa enjoyed gardening and loved to tinker with machinery. He rummaged through the ruins of neighboring farms, scrounging broken parts of machines, and from them he put together a mowing machine, a harvester, a hand-turned threshing machine, and a seed drill. All this helped us a great deal in our work. Both of them were vegetarians, and from the very first days it was decided that our common meals would be vegetarian.

Among the commune members were the Zavádskys, a big peasant family consisting of the old people, father and mother, three grown sons, two daughters, and the wife of one of the sons. The old people were simple peasants, but all the children adhered more or less to the Communist ideology and were remarkably cultured workers, putting great love and energy into their work. I learned a lot from them in our peasant labor.

Two girls from Ryazán, Anísya and Alyóna, also worked in the commune. Famine and a lack of land had brought them to the outskirts of Moscow to seek work among the market gardeners. They came into the commune and just stayed. There were also two teenagers from a children's home— Fédya Sepp, an Estonian, and Antósha Krasnóv, a Chuvásh. In our close-knit, hard-working, sober collective, they too naturally grew up into good, hard-working men. My comrade Kótya Muravyóv, a Moscow schoolboy, and I also joined because of our longing for country life. Other people too would come and stay for a while. We lived happily and worked with great enthusiasm. We got up at daybreak and went to bed as soon as it was dark. Often we would agree among ourselves around the supper table on who should be on duty that night, who would feed the horses, clean up after the cows, bring in the milk, take it to Moscow, wake up the driver and help him hitch up the horse, wake up the milkmaids, and in general serve as night watchman, remaining on duty till morning and thus going without sleep for a whole twenty-four-hour period. After waking the milkmaids he would go to bed at four o'clock, and then at ten—without anybody waking him up— he would go out to start working. Once, I remember, this is what happened: After working all day, I was on duty that night. Yefím Moiséyevich was supposed to take the milk to town the next morning; but when I woke him up, he turned out to be sick with a high fever, so I decided to go myself. I delivered the milk to the Second City Hospital on Bolsháya Kalúzhskaya Street, to the day nursery at the Goznák Factory on Málaya Serpukhóvskaya Street, and then started home. I was sleepy, my eyes stuck together, and I kept nodding off. I kept thinking with pleasure about how I would fall into bed as soon as I got home. I got there and found everything upset: the colts had disappeared or else had run away by themselves, and they had to be found. I ran off to look for them too. After we found them, I dropped into the straw outside and fell asleep. Later I counted up: I had worked without sleep for thirty-six hours.

But all that was no burden then, and the farm did well. We had a going economy as early as the beginning of 1923. We supplied milk to the Second City Hospital and the day nursery at the Goznák factory. The milk was always of high quality and was delivered to the kitchens on time early every morning for more than seven years.

We would discuss all our work together around the table at breakfast, dinner, or supper. Nobody was the official leader. We tried to make sure that all members of the commune kept up with everything, and we decided that each one in turn, a day at a time, would be responsible for managing current affairs.

At the beginning, absolutely nobody bothered us. We knew nothing about residence permits, regulations, taxes, any kind of agricultural instructions, and so on. And our work went well. Our organization was not very large, but it was full of life, truly collective, hard-working, of high quality, and socially useful. Our expenses for administration, management, and office needs amounted to zero. Our only defect (as I now see it) was our excessive enthusiasm for work. Work swallowed up all our energy, all our attention. That, of course, was abnormal, but perhaps it was required by the times. Extraordinary effort was needed to save the country from famine and ruin.

Here I want to say something about the "Ao-ists" Serzhánov and Shvílpe, since they were the pioneers in this undertaking. At first they were anarchists, but later they went off in their own direction.

Serzhánov once said to me: "Strictly speaking, we are not anarchists but extarchists—that is, extragovernmentarians." Knowing my leaning toward Tolstóy, they said: "Now you Tolstoyans strive for what is natural, but we, on the other hand, consider that what is natural is wild chaos. We believe that everything, everything without exception in the realm of human life, needs to be perfected and contrived. We must contrive everything so that it will be reasonable and expedient. For example, take the language that people speak today—it is nonsensical chaos. Every word ought to have a connection with related words and concepts. Take 'nose,' for example. Why nose? Where does that come from? It must come from 'odor,' or 'smell.' So we logically should call it a smeller, not a nose, and so on." To be sure, I have taken only a crude example here, but they had invented their own language, "Ao." They spoke to each other in it. They gave themselves names that had their own meaning. Serzhánov was Biaelbi, something like "inventor of life," and Shvílpe was Biabi, something of the same kind. In Russian they called themselves universal inventors. They dreamed of creating artificial suns and setting up interplanetary communications. They wanted to make human life eternal. They had their own club on Tverskáya Street, and connected with it was a so-called "sociotechnicum," where they conducted various experiments on themselves. They said it was just plain stupid for people to waste one-third of their lives in sleep, and they practiced trying to sleep as little as possible, so as to save as much of that valuable time as they could. They said a man eats too much, that food burns up in his body, and as a result he wears out quickly. We need to invent some kind of concentrated food like pills—"pictons," they called them—so that a man could swallow them and get everything he needed for the life of his body, but at the same time this food would be nonexcremental, so his body would not wear out, but would last a long time. They conducted experiments of that sort; and one of our future commune members, Mísha Rogóvin, almost died as a result. They said nature was unfair: it made some people good-looking and others ugly. This needed to be corrected: everybody should wear masks. They thought the spruce was the most perfect tree in its structure. They considered Tolstóy to be the greatest inventor in the field of morality.

In our collective working life they were indispensable men—industrious, quick to learn, sociable, and always merry. They would not allow any tobacco, vodka, cursing, or debauchery, which, along with their vegetarianism, antimilitarism, and rejection of the state, paved the way for their closeness to us Tolstoyans in practical life. They loved farming, but it swallowed up all their time, and they wanted to work in their own way toward their own goals, so they left the commune around the end of 1923.

With the departure of Serzhánov and Shvílpe, we felt an acute shortage of people, not just of manpower but of people who were consciously striving toward a common life and a common goal.

We had to attract new forces. Very favorable circumstances arose for that. There existed in Moscow the Tolstóy Vegetarian Society, where lectures and discussions took place almost every day; but the largest and most important meetings were held on Saturday evenings, and then I would finish my working day a little early and run off to Moscow to Newspaper Lane. There I met a lot of people from various parts of the country. Many of them longed to live by their own labor on the land, but they did not have the wherewithal, neither money nor land. Suddenly they found out that land was available, work was under way, and comrades were already there, and so we started attracting people: A. N. Ganusévich and his family, S. V. Tróitsky and his family, Pólya Zhárova, Nádya Grinévich, A. V. Arbúzov, Alyósha Demídov, I. S. Rogózhin, and others.

But at this point the Zavádsky family separated from us. We did not wish to limit the number of applicants. On the other hand, the Zavádskys were in favor of a commune that was small but worked well together—almost like a family. So they left and found themselves a smaller plot of land, with a smaller number of participants. Without any argument, we gave them a share of our property corresponding to the proportion of labor time they had put into it, and what was left for us was a very poor farm. But we had a lot of energy as well as experience, and we were already organized.

By that time we had approved a charter and regulations for our commune and registered it with the land agency. We borrowed six hundred rubles from the bank, and Mísha Popóv and I went together to Tambóv Province, where he was born. The peasants there had good milk cows and fine horses. We bought some cows, took them back with us, and quickly completed and expanded our herd.

Our dairy was in good shape. We had hay from the meadows and clover fields. We had an abundance of root plants—turnips, beets, and rutabagas— and no end of oil cakes and bran for the livestock. We did not keep any cows that gave less than twenty-five liters of milk a day. We had some cows that gave thirty to thirty-five and even forty liters. This yield did not come immediately, however, but only after we had them on proper feed for a full year. We delivered our milk to the hospitals—they had money. We had livestock, and we had manure, for which we built proper storage pits, wetting them down every day with liquid dung from our settling tanks. We had good manure, and we spread it on the ground at the right time; we had mineral fertilizer, we had proper crop rotation and civilized soil cultivation, and so we had good harvests. We got more than twenty tons an acre of root crops, ten to fifteen tons an acre of potatoes, and about a ton an acre of rye. We would get two crops of clover a year.

By 1925 we were provided with everything we needed. Our meals were communal and free; so were our living quarters, lights, and heat; and for clothing and shoes everybody received twenty-five rubles a month to be spent as they thought best.

The commune flourished economically. We were well fed. Everybody had shoes and clothes. One cold, muddy fall day, I remember seeing Sergéy working near the cattle-yard in durable new boots, and this was so unusual it filled us with joy—we were used to seeing him plodding barefooted through the deep, sticky mud.

We got hold of a little spring wagon to haul our milk in. We started raising good horses. The neighboring peasants began flocking to us to get a good heifer for breeding. They started coming to borrow our two-bladed Sakk plow (at that time people around Moscow used mostly wooden plows), or they would borrow our winnowing machine (they winnowed with a shovel) or our threshing machine (they threshed by beating a barrel with a stick).

But one incident sticks in my mind as the clearest sign of our triumph. A good crop of wheat was ripe. We rented a binder from a state farm at Cheryómushki. Prokóp set it up. I hitched up three good horses and started around in a circle. Out came the neatly tied sheaves. I made them larger or smaller by adjusting the regulator as needed. On the other side of the road was a Troparyóvo field. Their sparse, stunted wheat could not compare to ours. Two Troparyóvo peasants stopped and watched my work. I stopped and we said hello. "Yes," said one of the old men, "your work is going up, and ours is going down"—and he pointed to his wheat.

Little by little we became acquainted with the people in the neighborhood; and we got along well with them, even though our way of life was entirely different from theirs. The people at Troparyóvo and Bogoródskoye were devoted to the church. They strictly observed all the church holidays, celebrating for two or three days at a time, while I in my youthful ardor would hitch up my horse every year on the first day of Easter and haul manure to the garden.

We got the idea somehow of organizing a discussion at Troparyóvo on Tolstóy and his world outlook. We went to the chairman of the village soviet, Rúblikov—a serious peasant, and a Communist. Rúblikov loved speeches, lectures, and discussions of all kinds. He gladly gave us permission and notified the peasants. The meeting was held in a tearoom. The tearoom was a sort of club in the village. Sitting around a pot full of cheap tea, the peasants would talk about their business, about the bazaar, and so on. Three of us went there—my father, Nikoláy Vasílyevich Tróitsky, and I. A lot of people had gathered, all of them peasants, and most of them old men, bearded and serious. My father talked about Tolstóy's gospel and read some passages. At first he was met with stern shouts: "Don't mix the spiritual and the worldly," and so forth; but afterwards they listened attentively, and at the end they asked us to come back and discuss some more.

Our commune grew in numbers. In addition to our steady core group, more and more people kept coming. There were relatives of commune members, some of whom would come for only a day or two and others for the whole summer. And there were guests, people who were interested in the commune and came to look around and see whether that kind of life was for them. We worked out an unwritten principle: anybody who wanted to could come, eat at the table with us, walk around and observe for three days; but beginning with the fourth day, even guests had to do their share of the work right along with everyone else. A lot of interesting people passed through the commune. Some of them became a part of the general family from the very first day, went right to work, and stayed in the commune for good. But there were others too. I remember a girl who came to us from Moscow. We knew nothing about her. We could tell only that she was a city girl and knew nothing about country life. For about two days she silently walked around and observed. She looked sad and withdrawn; something painful had taken place in her life. On the third day she asked for work. She was told to clean out the cow barn. Clumsily but diligently, she threw out the manure, put the stalls in order, cleaned the cows with a currycomb, and swept out the passageway with a broom. Having learned the joys of labor, she said when I came in: "How clean!" She worked like that for two more days; but when I came back to the cow barn, she asked: "Is it like this every day?"

"Yes."

"How dull!" she said, and left the commune for the same unknown from which she had come.

There were also guests like these: Two men arrived, one of them a curly-headed, thick-lipped, brown-haired fellow named Léitsner, and the other one younger and simpler—Shúra Póstnov. Everything would have been all right except that they turned out to be "strippers." They would go out to work and strip down to the way their mothers brought them into this world. They would settle down on a garden bed and pull weeds; and the women would turn their backs on them, bury their faces in the garden bed, and also pull weeds. Well! When they went to the dinner table, they did put on their shorts. We were a liberty-loving people; some would say, "Oh, let them be," and others: "Just the same, it's embarrassing." The further it went, the worse it got; the unrest grew till it came close to tragedy, and we finally just had to evict them.

There came to us a quiet, fair-haired fellow named Kleménty Kraskóvsky. For some reason he had been unable to settle down at the New Jerusalem Commune,[2] and among us he walked around depressed and apathetic.

---

2. New Jerusalem Commune—see the chapter by Yeléna Shershenyóva, "The New Jerusalem Tolstóy Commune," pp. 5–25.

Once I got into a conversation about him with one of the commune members. "What's the matter with Kleménty?" I asked. "He seems withdrawn and indifferent to everything." Kleménty was standing on the balcony above us and heard it all.

"Why do you say that?" he asked me.

"Well, isn't it so?" And we got into a conversation, without any harsh words but completely frank; and from that day on, Kleménty was like somebody else. The commune became something dear to him, like his own home, and all the more so because he himself had no family. He got completely absorbed in its life and concerns and remained that way until his tragic death in 1937. He came from a family of poor peasants in Smolénsk Province, as I remember. He finished elementary school, and for that reason he was sent to a school for ensigns when the war began in 1914. Shortly afterwards he was sent to the front. He naïvely believed whatever he was told at the village school and later at the military school. He believed that the Germans were enemies and that we had to defend our native land, the Tsar, and the Orthodox faith. He told me he had taken part in both combat and attacks during the war, but never had any fear of death. Everything was simple. Later, though, he began to have doubts. He met some Tolstoyans, and everything got turned upside down: the Germans were no longer enemies but victims just like them of deception, and the Tsar and the Orthodox faith turned out to be a cruel, empty hoax. His life acquired a new meaning. He no longer took up weapons.

Afterwards he (and many of our other commune members) had occasion to hear the reproach from representatives of the government: "Oh yes, you fought for the Tsar, but now you refuse to take up arms." Yes, they fought, and fought honorably, as long as they believed it was necessary. But the sufferings of war and revolution and the truthful, powerful message of Leo Tolstóy opened their eyes and awakened their consciousness, confirming what they had been faintly hearing from their consciences; and these people changed their way of life for good and gave up violence.

The most striking and tragic member of our commune was probably Sergéy Vasílyevich Tróitsky. The year 1917 found him in the ranks of the active army. He greeted the February Revolution in 1917 with joy, and then accepted the October Revolution in the same spirit. He seized the ideal of communism completely, without any reservations. He already knew about Tolstóy's ideas from his brother Nikoláy, a Tolstoyan. They talked and argued about that a great deal, but each of them went his own way. Sergéy finished the Red Military Academy; and not wishing to stay and work at staff headquarters, he went off to the army in the field. Sergéy fought, fought for his ideal; but evidently the seeds of Tolstóyism, once they had fallen into his consciousness, did not die out. They smoldered in his soul and suddenly flared up in a bright flame. This is what brought it about: two young boys of Chuvásh nationality in his unit, uprooted from their quiet working life and thrown into the incomprehensible hell of slaughter, decided to break out of it by shooting off each other's fingers. They were court-martialed and sentenced to death. The execution took place in the fall, at sunset. The troops were lined up on three sides of a small meadow, with the commanding officers in the middle. The sentence was read. The two boys were lined up side by side. Behind them was a golden field of ripe, unmown rye, lighted up by the rosy rays of the setting sun. A volley of shots rang out. The bullets shattered their skulls, and blood spurted forth in little fountains, even hotter and redder than the sun; and they stood there without falling for a longer time than was necessary. The next day, Sergéy went to regimental headquarters, put down his weapon, and said he could no longer wage war. He was also due to be court-martialed, and no doubt would have met the same fate as those two, but on the following day our army began to retreat. Everything became confused. Later Sergéy found himself in a psychiatric hospital.

Afterwards he turned up at our commune. Serious and not very talkative, he threw himself into his work. Sometimes when he felt a little more cheerful, he would take up a guitar and, closing his eyes and maintaining his serious expression, would sing some songs for us: "My unbridled steed through the swirling storm flies over the steppe like an arrow . . . ," or "Tánechka, my darling, my azure-blue flower, Let's take a seat in the buggy and go for a little ride," or some satire on Biblical legends: "Here comes Noah out of the ark, He sees God there before him . . . ," and so on.

Even though Sergéy had come to us out of a conviction he had reached after painful and frightful experiences in life, not everything within him was yet resolved. He was still in turmoil, like every serious, thoughtful person. Once he said to me: "Just the same, if the capitalists attack us, I will go and defend my country. "So what?" I answered. "That's your affair."

If only he had been alone—but he had a difficult handicap, his wife, Yelizavéta Ivánovna. I can't say that she was stupid, or spiteful, or too cantankerous—no—but she had no use whatsoever for the commune. She would have been far happier, of course, as the wife of an officer, especially one with a higher education, than she was as the wife of a barefooted worker, rooting around in the dirt and dung. He was drawn to the commune, and she held onto Moscow. So they lived in two homes. At times she would live and work for a while with us, and then he would go off to Moscow as a painter and earn a little extra for the family, because communal earnings were not enough for her and their two daughters in the city. But he did not want to abandon his family, and he bore this burden without complaining, patiently and quietly, trying to explain how he saw it. Still, she drew him toward Moscow. But he refused to be registered as an officer, and so he was forbidden to live in Moscow. Once more—life in two homes. He worked somewhere in road building. On rare occasions he would arrive illegally and spend a brief day with his family. On one of Sergéy's visits home, a neighbor in the apartment building told on him, and he was arrested. At that time our commune had moved to Siberia. Yelizavéta died, and our contacts were interrupted for a long time. Only by a miracle did I hear his voice coming to me in my solitary confinement when I was under arrest in 1936, in the pre-trial cell at the First House of the NKVD in the city of Stálinsk. The letters addressed to me at the commune were forwarded to my investigator; but once, through some misunderstanding, an unopened letter was brought to me in my cell. It turned out to be from Sergéy, who was in a labor camp in the distant Kómi Autonomous Republic. He wrote that he was still protesting against their having so inhumanely torn him away from his family, and that at various times he had gone on a total of 242 days of hunger strikes. That was the last letter I had from him. It pains me to think that he did not receive any answer from me and perhaps was offended, since he did not know that I too was no longer living in freedom.

There was a switchman at one of the Moscow railway junctions, a middle-aged man named Aleksándr Nikoláyevich Ganusévich, who came and took an interest in our commune. Then he came again. His job was such that he was on duty one day and then off for two days; and so, after his shift was over, he would come and work with us, then go back to his work in Moscow. He was of peasant origin, and he helped us a lot with his farm experience and knowledge. He had a family, a wife and small children, who all took to the commune and liked to participate in our work. Sometimes his sister and her little daughter, as well as his brothers—a whole big harmonious collective—would come to visit and work with us.

During the first years of the Revolution, Aleksándr Vasílyevich Arbúzov had been an investigator for the Cheká, the secret police. Then he came to know Tolstóy and resigned from the military service, and instead was assigned as an orderly in a hospital for venereal diseases. After that he came across us. He worked hard and well, but his agitated soul kept seeking something more, and he went off into extremes—began eating only raw foods, raw vegetables, whole grains, and so on. Then he took up with Julia (about whom I will say more later), and they went off on a pilgrimage in the south to the Malyóvannians.[3]

Two peasants from Tambóv, Mísha and Dásha Popóv, came to live and work at the commune. He had been a pupil of my father at a teachers' institute. Mísha loved Tolstóy and loved the soil, and this led him to the commune. Before his wife came to the commune, she had never been away from her own village. When they came out on the street from the Páveletsky railway station in Moscow and she saw an automobile for the first time in her life, she grabbed her husband by the arm and exclaimed: "Look, Mísha! Look! There goes a big black beetle on wheels!"

Yúliya Lápteva. During the Civil War she had worked in the Caucasus in the political section of the army. Their unit got into a difficult situation and was smashed by the Whites. The White officers took Yúliya prisoner, mortally beat her with ramrods, and threw her into a pit full of corpses; but she survived. She was saved by a woman passing by who heard her groaning,

3. Malyóvannians (Russian: Malyóvantsy)—followers of Kondráty Alekséyevich Malyóvanny (1845–1913), a wheelwright by trade, who was severely persecuted for his religious teachings, being confined in mental hospitals from 1893 till 1905. He visited Tolstóy in 1907, and Tolstóy showed some interest in his followers.

took her home, and finally nursed her back to health. This woman turned out to be a religious sectarian. Sometimes other women would come, and they would softly sing their hymns in the next room. The sound of these songs, some of them sad and some triumphant, reached Yúliya's ears and helped to soften her hardened, embittered soul. Yúliya began seeking some meaning in life, and this brought her to Vladímir Chertkóv, and then to us. She was a taciturn, skinny woman with short hair, wearing dark glasses, barefooted, a native of some place in the Kómi region. She said she had written a book about her experiences during the Civil War, published under the name Yúliya Slávskaya. She and Aleksándr Vasílyevich Arbúzov started living together, and they went off together on a pilgrimage. Subsequently, it seems, she went back to her Party way of life.

I also remember Iván Stepánovich Rogózhin, a peasant from near Yepifán. He could not explain his thoughts very clearly, but he worked hard and was always very deliberate and cool-headed. When the peasants got disturbed about something and he alone preserved his unruffled calm, they would say: "Iván Stepánovich, what's the matter? Doesn't this disturb you?" He would answer: "An excitable man always gets excited." He was arrested in 1937 and never came back.

Well, now, I'd better say something about myself, since I too was a member of the commune. Right from the school bench in 1918, I joined the Bolsheviks in my thinking. As a student at the Mining Academy, I split with them after a speech by Ársky in which he said we should give concessions to the foreign capitalists by exchanging our mineral resources for large mechanized farming.

In 1921 Pyotr Alekséyevich Kropótkin died.[4] There were some anarchist students in our academy, and they organized an evening meeting in memory of Kropótkin. I got acquainted with them and began to sympathize with them. At that same meeting I heard a speech by Seryózha Popóv, a Tolstoyan. During the question period after the talk, a note was passed up asking, "What is the difference between anarchists and Tolstoyans?" and one anarchist answered: "The difference is that the Tolstoyans are more consistent than we are." I started looking for somewhere to get acquainted with the Tolstoyans, and at last I found "The Vegetarian" (a dining hall on Newspaper Lane), where Tolstoyan meetings were held.

It was interesting that my father had long been attending these meetings. While Tolstóy was still alive, my father had visited him three times and talked with him about various matters. My father had tried to talk about Tolstóy's views with me; but at that time, in my enthusiasm for Bolshevism, they nauseated me. When my father said the word "love," I almost felt sick

---

4. Prince Peter Kropotkin (1842–1921), a highly respected philosophical anarchist who stopped using his title out of sympathy with the Russian peasants, escaped from Russia in the 1870s after two years of imprisonment for his beliefs, and spent most of his remaining life in England. In 1917 he returned to Russia, where he was held in high esteem despite his open disagreement with the Bolsheviks.

at my stomach. "How can you talk about love when enemies are attacking us on all sides?" I would shout. And so I found the Tolstoyans' meetings independently and met my father there and agreed with him in our understanding of life.

Seryózha Popóv in his talks would often quote poetry calling for a return to the soil: "Forsake the stifling city, friends . . . ," "Go out to the broad expanse, where the wheat fields without you have grown up in weeds and the flood plains are covered with sedge." He said that farm work was the most necessary, the purest, and the most worthwhile, and that everybody must bear his share of this labor, in order not to be a burden on anybody else, and to feel like a free human being.

I read the same thing in Tolstóy and Bóndarev,[5] and something close to it in Kropótkin; and even though I liked the profession of a geologist and prospector and was drawn to it, I left the Mining Academy, and I deliberately went back to the soil. As early as May 1919 I had joined a student gardening cooperative called "Cooperative Labor"; but I had been drawn into that by hunger and drawn out of it by a summons to the Red Army. In the spring of 1922 I came to the Tolstoyan commune and asked for land. They gave me half a hectare standing by itself in the bushes, so that we could live there and protect the commune's crops from damage by the village cattle. I expected to do hand-farming, that is, to work without the help of animals. I had gotten together with a young fellow named Kótya (Nikoláy) Muravyóv, a dropout from middle school—unusually taciturn and shy, but strong and burning with a desire to work. We built ourselves a little cabin and lived in it. We were joined by his brother and my younger brothers. My father visited us frequently, and sometimes our mothers, too. A little below us was another small cabin, where Nikoláy Vasílyevich Tróitsky lived. Sometimes Seryózha Popóv would come to visit him.

We lived there happy and free. We brought in a good harvest, helped families in that famine-ridden time, and—what was the main thing—grew stronger and felt that we were able to do something in life on our own. In the spring of 1923, Kótya and I entered the commune for good. Subsequently he became our cattle-breeder, and I must say that in spite of his youth he was very capable. Everything he did went well. He decided he wanted to study his specialty further, and he entered the Timiryázev Agricultural Academy, but there they somehow found out that he was from our Tolstoyan commune. They considered that a great sin and expelled him, almost made him lose his right to vote, and in general ruined the poor fellow's life.

Still more people passed through the commune.

If, as you might say, the first years of our communal life went along spontaneously, in time the commune members began to feel a need to think

5. Timoféy Mikháylovich Bóndarev (1820–1898)—a Russian peasant and writer whose book *Industry and Parasitism, or The Triumph of the Farmer* attracted the attention and admiration of Tolstóy.

through and clearly express just why and for what purpose we were living as a commune, and opinions were voiced that did not always agree with each other. On occasion the opinion was expressed among us that we should enter a commune for the sake of spiritual goals, for the sake of spiritual unity, and that a commune of like-minded people provided better conditions for spiritual improvement, that the desire for possessions tended to die out in a commune, and so on.

I did not agree with such views. This is what I thought:

(1) We can and should unite with all people in what is good always and everywhere, and not only in the commune. Unity only with the members of a commune is sectarianism, and that is not what will bring free people into a commune.

(2) We are not advocates of monasteries, of withdrawing from life with all its good and evil, its sufferings and joys. We should strive to be better, to be human beings, right in the midst of life, so that it is not the better conditions for self-improvement that draw us into the commune.

(3) Property, even though it belongs to the commune, still remains property, and entering a commune does not mean that we have gone beyond that boundary.

(4) I thought the idea of the commune was not a Christian idea—not in the sense that it contradicts Christianity, but rather that a human being remains the same regardless of whether or not he lives in a commune, with the same weaknesses and the same aspiration to be better; and the commune has no significance as far as spiritual life is concerned. That is not what brought us together. We joined together around land, around labor, around food.

The natural law of life is for each person to do his share of the hard but necessary physical work required to get our daily bread, build our dwellings, and obtain heat and clothing.

Kropótkin and others calculated that three or four hours of work a day would be enough to provide all these necessities for everybody, and people could devote the rest of their time to the sciences, the arts, sport, crafts, or whatever they wished, without such inequities as allowing one person to sit over a chess board or to write novels about labor without having any personal knowledge of labor, while another spends his entire life turning the soil or hauling logs, with no time left not only to play chess or read novels but even to get a decent night's rest. That is a great loss not only for those who spend their time on hard physical work, but also for those who do not know physical work at all.

I've already said that we had to work too much. That began to tell on us. We often heard voices raised against it:

"We didn't join together here for the sake of farming but for the sake of a life of brotherhood."

"Work like a horse, without even any time to read—what kind of life is that? You don't mean to say that's why we got together here?"

" 'The Life and Labor Commune'—there's labor all right, but where's the life?"

In reply to these just remarks, we would tell ourselves: "Yes, we joined together not just for labor but for life, but there is no life without labor—we have to work. Farming is necessary. And when we get things going right, under normal conditions, it won't take a lot of time and won't be a heavy burden."

Farming, especially along with organizing a commune (usually starting from nothing), requires a lot of strength and work. You don't want to see everything go badly, come unraveled, fall apart, grow up in weeds, and so you work instintingly, and things start going well. If you work without a bad temper, willingly and with love, that will lighten the burden of work.

And we worked unstintingly. That was clear to anybody. And of course that was what saved us.

The year 1927 got under way. The times began to change.

The Táyninskoye agricultural cooperative at Perlóvka was liquidated by a decree of the government agencies. The reason was supposedly its poor farming. But a reason will always be found. When talk started about liquidating the Tolstóy New Jerusalem Commune, it was attacked for not obtaining bank credits, for its "financial isolation"; and when they wanted to liquidate our commune, they accused us of getting bank credits to buy cattle. After Perlóvka was liquidated, we got several new members from there—Vásya Lapshín, a peasant from Yepifán, Mísha Dyachkóv, a former worker in the Túla arms factory. Some of their members went to the New Jerusalem Commune.

But in 1929 the New Jerusalem Commune was liquidated too. That was a good farm, but other reasons were found, in accord with the principle in Krylóv's fable about the wolf and the lamb. We got several more members from there—Prokóp Pávlovich Kuvshínov and his wife, Nína Lapáyeva, and their children; the Alekséyev brothers, Seryózha, Shúra, and Lyóva; Kátya Dorónina; Ványa Zúyev; Romásha Silvánovich; Pávlo Chepurnóy; Ványa Svinobúrko and his wife, Yúliya Rutkóvskaya, and their children; Mísha Blagovéshchensky; Vásya Ptítsyn; Pétya Shershenyóv; Faddéy Zablótsky; Vásya and Álya Shershenyóv;[6] Kólya Ulyánov; and along with them, Yevgény Ivánovich Popóv[7] also came to live with us. Life in the commune became fuller, with more people, more interests of all sorts, and more children.

About that time we built a large communal building with hot-water heat-

6. Vásya and Álya Shershenyóv—see the chapter "The New Jerusalem Tolstóy Commune," written by Yeléna ("Álya") Shershenyóva, pp. 5–25. Her husband Vasíly ("Vásya") Shershenyóv was the leader of that commune.

7. Yevgény Ivánovich Popóv (1864–1938) was a friend and follower of Tolstóy who wrote several works on farming and education. In the first decade of this century, he lived for a while among Russian émigrés in Switzerland, where he exerted an influence on young Bulgarian students who later became Tolstoyan leaders in their native land. He spent his last years in the Life and Labor Commune, moved with it when it resettled in Western Siberia, and is buried there in the commune's cemetery.

ing, a community kitchen and dining room, and ten rooms for living quarters, with two more rooms on the second floor for use in summer.

The food was good. We worked merrily and no longer so strenuously. So went our life until the complete collectivization began of the villages all around us. The cows bellowed when they were driven together in one place. The women bellowed too.

As chairman of our commune council, I was once summoned by the chairman of the district executive committee at Kúntsevo. I appeared. There were several other persons in the office along with Morózov, the chairman of the district executive committee.

"Well, tell us what kind of commune you have over there," said Morózov.

I briefly told about our charter, our farming, our milk production, our crop yield, and so on.

"Well, that's fine," said Morózov. "You have lived collectively for several years and gotten used to it, but now we are beginning to switch the whole countryside onto the collective track. We need experienced people as leaders. You will be the head of the neighboring villages and help them organize themselves into a collective farm."

I flatly refused.

"Why not? After all, you too are for collective labor."

"Yes, we are for collective labor, but for voluntarily collective labor, according to our own choice. But for them it's against their will. Besides, our way of life is very different from their way in regard to food, alcohol, bad language, recognizing the church and its holidays, and all kinds of rituals. Up to now we have lived as a commune, and we expect to keep on living that way; but as for merging into one collective, and even more, running the whole affair, we are not going to do it. Nothing would come out of that. As for our experience, we will be glad to share it with those who need it."

Morózov was very angry.

"It's long been high time for you to manage the district, but instead you are just messing around with your commune. Get going! And stop in to see the head of the militia."

I left, and even though I went past the militia, I preferred not to go in—I had an idea what that was all about.

Shortly afterwards, the district executive committee issued a decree disbanding our commune and handing over all our property and farm to a group of peasants from the village of Troparyóvo. From then on, events developed faster and became more strained. Once I was on my way back to the commune from Moscow. Walking down the long birch-lined lane, I came to our stable. The doors were wide open, and some unknown peasant woman was walking around. Across the road from our stable stood a neat pile of hay between four posts with a removable roof over it. The hay had been thrown down, and an unfamiliar nag was standing on it and eating it.

"Whose horse is that?" I asked.

"Ours," the woman answered.

"And what are you doing here?"

"We are going to live here. They've given everything to us."

"And where will we live?"

"I don't know."

I understood. I felt something hot rise in my heart. I went to the house. I had scarcely opened the door to our dining room when the smell of strong tobacco struck my nose. Acrid clouds of gray smoke floated about the room. A dozen peasants, some known to me, some unknown, were sitting around the table, talking animatedly. When I came in, they stopped and looked around at me. I stood in silence in the middle of the room. Everything within me was strained to the breaking point. The thought ran through my mind: "Why are these men here? What do they need? They are people, but we are people too! How can they do something like this—grab working people just like themselves by the throat?" I looked around. There was a stool nearby, and for a second my eyes stopped on it. Then I turned to the peasants and said just two words, in a low voice: "Get out!"

They all stood up in silence and one by one tiptoed out the door and into the street. Clouds of dark-blue tobacco smoke drifted after them through the open door. The empty dining hall began to fill as our commune members came out of their rooms. They told what had happened: "Some men came up and produced a paper from the Kúntsevo District Executive Committee ordering the breakup of our commune and turning over our whole farm to a new collective. They demanded our seal, and Prokóp gave it to them. Then they went through the house and assigned the rooms, telling each one where to live."

We decided to stand up for our rights.

In the reception room of M. I. Kalínin[8] I was received by the vice-chairman of the Presidium of the All-Russian Central Executive Committee, P. G. Smidóvich.[9] I told him everything. A few days later I went back for an answer. Smidóvich said that the order of the district executive committee had been canceled and our rights had been restored. He sealed up a paper to that effect in an envelope, wrote on it "To Morózov, Chairman of the Kúntsevo District Executive Committee," and gave it to me to deliver to him personally.

I went to Kúntsevo. Morózov was walking back and forth in his office, highly excited. "Well, what is it?" he asked stiffly when he saw me. I silently

8. Mikhaíl Ivánovich Kalínin (1875–1946) was chairman of the All-Russian Central Executive Committee from 1919 to 1937. His peasant origin and his approachable manner led the peasants to trust him and appeal to him as one of their own.

9. Mazúrin elsewhere describes Pyotr Germogénovich Smidóvich (1874–1935) as an old Bolshevik who "remained faithful to his convictions, but he was free of any narrow, sectarian impatience with those who had different opinions. Whenever we came to Smidóvich's office about something concerning the commune and our resettlement, he would listen, quickly make a decision, call in a secretary, have her type it up, and he himself would strike up a kind of philosophical argument with us—only he did all the talking" (*Vospominanija krest'jan-tolstovtsev,* pp. 180–181).

handed him the package. He looked at the seal of the All-Russian Central Executive Committee on the envelope, tore it open without a word, read it, muttered something, and again told me to go to see the head of the militia.

This time, for some reason, I decided to go. I went in and was arrested and put in the lockup. I demanded an explanation—what was the reason? But they gave me no answer. Then I said I would declare a hunger strike, and I went around the corner of the stove, where the orderly on duty could not see me, took a loaf of bread out of my pocket, and excitedly ate it with great appetite. That was my only hunger strike in all my life. Toward evening I heard the orderly telephone somewhere several times and ask what to do with me: "You see, he's declared a hunger strike. . . . I have no grounds at all for arresting him. . . ." And they let me go.

Our seal was still in the village soviet. They had already learned about the cancellation of the district executive committee's order, and when I got there and went up to the secretary, I said: "Give me the seal." He handed it over without a word. There were a lot of peasants in the room, including those I had driven out. "We lived it up for a while in the commune house," one of them said, with a good-humored chuckle.

Outwardly life in the commune went on as usual, but somehow there was a tense feeling that the whole thing was not yet over.

Soon after, legal action was brought against five of us—me, Kleménty, Kátya, Marúsya, and Aleksándr Ivánovich. There were no grounds for it, but that is what lawyers study for, to find a clause to fit anybody. We were tried in Kúntsevo. When they accused us of keeping no accounts, Kleménty (who did our accounting) lost his patience, jumped up from his seat, and raised over his head a stack of account books that he had prudently brought along with him.

"And what are these?" he shouted in the midst of laughter all over the room.

There were witnesses from among those I had driven out. One of them said: "Mazúrin drove us out of the house."

"How did he drive you out?" asked the judge.

"He just did—he said, 'Get out,' and we left."

"And how many of you were there?"

"Twelve."

"And Mazúrin?"

"One."

The judge and the public started laughing.

Our defender was a member of the Public Defenders' Office, Kropótkin—a nephew, it seems, of Pyotr Kropótkin. He said: "Why put them on trial? After all, they really did live as a commune and did not talk big about it, the way some people do."

"Who are those 'some people'?" snapped the judge, and the court issued a special ruling that resulted later in Kropótkin's being dismissed from the Public Defenders' Office.

They convicted us on the basis of some completely insignificant and vague article, something about negligence. Two of us got two years, and the rest of us got shorter sentences. The whole point was not guilt or sentences, but rather the need to get us out of the neighborhood. To this day I fail to understand what made us a disturbance, how our commune could have disturbed anybody else. The provincial court refused our appeal. But even though we remained at liberty, there was a question about how much longer our commune could survive. However innocent the lamb may be, the wolf will still eat it because he wants to.

Here the question arose about resettling.

There were followers of Tolstóy in all corners of the country. Almost all of them lived on the land, some working collectively and some as individuals. And almost all of them came into conflict with representatives of the local government. Some would ask to join a collective farm and be refused because they were Tolstoans. Others did not want to go into a collective farm, but they were dragged into it. Some went in but came up against various aspects of collective-farm life that ran counter to their convictions.

And then this idea arose: that all the followers of Tolstóy who wanted to till the soil should join together and resettle in one place for collective life and work. Vladímir Grigóryevich Chertkóv[10] suggested this idea to us. We felt that in our old location we would no longer have a life but only a struggle. Our own commune became the organizational core of the resettlement.

An application was submitted to the All-Russian Central Executive Committee in the name of V. G. Chertkóv. Then on 28 February 1930, a decree was issued by the Presidium of the Committee, Protocol 41, Paragraph 5, about "the resettlement of Tolstoan communes and cooperatives."

Along with other commune members, I frequently had occasion to go to see Smidóvich on resettlement business, to talk a time or two with Mikhaíl Ivánovich Kalínin, and to visit with V. D. Bonch-Bruyévich,[11] and everywhere we met with a good reception and a tolerant attitude toward our beliefs. In my very first conversation with Smidóvich, I said that for the success of our resettlement, some kind of instructions needed to be drawn up for the local government officials about certain peculiarities of our convictions, so that we would not be looked on with suspicion but would be given serious

---

10. Vladímir Grigóryevich Chertkóv (1854–1936), Tolstóy's most famous and influential disciple, played a controversial role in the writer's stormy family life for more than two decades. After the Bolsheviks came to power in 1917, he was generally recognized and respected, even by the new rulers, as the leading representative of the Tolstoans. He was especially active in behalf of religious objectors to military service and was instrumental in the negotiations leading to the decree signed by Lénin on 4 January 1919 granting exemption to sincere religious objectors.

11. Vladímir Dmítrievich Bonch-Bruyévich (1873–1955)—a leading prerevolutionary Bolshevik who was the executive director of the Council of People's Commissars from 1917 to 1920 and who had an active scholarly interest in the various religious sects in Russia throughout his life.

consideration. Smidóvich asked me to write out approximately what we considered necessary.

Here is what I wrote out and presented to him:

1. The settlers cannot take part in any kind of duties, campaigns, or loans connected with military aims, and—what is the most important—they refuse to take up arms.

2. The settlers are vegetarians and cannot take part in state meat procurement, the supplying of cattle for meat, or any activities connected with the slaughter of livestock.

3. Because of their convictions, the settlers cannot take part in the agencies of state government or in the election of representatives to them.

4. The resettled collectives can enter a system of agricultural cooperative federations on the condition of noninterference with the settlers' internal affairs and way of life.

5. The settlers shall not be hindered in organizing independent schools for teaching reading and writing to their children.

6. The settlers consider their collective to be vital only when all members share the same views, and for this reason any administrative enlargement or merging with people of other views is not admissible. Likewise inadmissible is any administrative interference in the internal structure of life in the collectives.

7. The policy and manner of running the farm shall be determined by a general meeting of each collective.

Smidóvich sat at a big table in a leather-upholstered armchair and read this note of mine; he read it to himself, saying "hm" from time to time and repeating under his breath:

". . . will not take up arms . . . we will judge . . . we will set free . . . no state meat procurement . . . can substitute something else . . . take no part in elections . . . So, you won't have any Soviet power?"

"We have a commune soviet," I said.[12]

"A school? Yes, a school," he said doubtfully. "If you don't send them to state schools, we will fine the parents . . . We'll think about it," he concluded.

Evidently some sort of directives unknown to us had been sent out to the provinces about this matter, but there were no complete, official instructions of any kind—at least as far as we knew. The matter went from the Central Executive Committee to the People's Commissariat of Agriculture, which was charged with the practical organization of our resettlement within the framework of general resettlement plans. The first step was to select and reserve a plot of land. The Commissariat of Agriculture gave us a land-scouting ticket. At that time in underpopulated areas, where free land was available, there were still resettlement agencies which would welcome peasant land scouts, supply them with shelter and provisions, give them addresses

---

12. A play on words: the Russian word *soviet* means "council."

and maps of available plots of land, and reserve the plots chosen by the scouts according to their scouting tickets.

They pointed out a big area to us—Kazakhstán and Western Siberia. We also could have gone to Eastern Siberia, but we somehow could not make up our minds to go there—it was very far away.

Ványa Zúyev and I were chosen as land scouts from our commune, and Ioánn Dobrotolyúbov from the "World Brotherhood" colony in Stalingrad Province. We set out in May 1930, and we traveled at least fifteen thousand kilometers. We went to Tashként, Auliyé-Atá, Frúnze, Almá-Atá, Semipalátinsk, Ust-Kamenogórsk, and up the Irtýsh River almost to Zaysán Lake, then to Novosibírsk, Shcheglóvsk (now Kémerovo), and Novokuznétsk, in the area where we reserved a resettlement plot on the river Tom, about twenty kilometers upstream from Stáry Kuznétsk. How many places we inspected, how many people we met, how many experiences we had! We traveled by train, on horseback, and on foot.

At first we scouts settled on a plot of land on the left bank of the Irtýsh, about a hundred kilometers from it, in a big triangle between the Cossack villages of Bukón, Batý, and Cheshlék. Only afterwards did I realize that this would be a big mistake. What would we do with that steppe land without forests? To be sure, we could have engaged in cattle breeding and Central Asian dry farming; but as vegetarians, most of us leaned toward vegetable farming and even horticulture. Ioánn, who was familiar with sheep breeding, said there were excellent conditions here for raising sheep. A settlement could stretch out along the Cheshlék River. We could divert water from the Cheshlék to the bottom lands along the river and develop good gardens through irrigation. Maybe all that would happen, but for hundreds of kilometers all around there were no industries, no lines of communication. Where could we dispose of our products, and where could we get the funds we needed for our various expenses? But just the same, we decided then to settle on this plot. Ioánn sharpened a stick, drove it into the ground, and said: "This is where we will lay the foundation for a town."

The local authorities gave us their approval. There remained only to complete the last formalities on the next day. But evidently somebody who was "more politically developed" prompted them—and they turned us down. They said: "We need settlers here, but the frontier is not far away, and we need good fighters here—not you." And to our good fortune, in my opinion, we left that area. Once more down the Irtýsh by steamer to dusty Semipalátinsk, then northward by train into Siberia. That night and the next morning, we caught sight not of sand and thorns but of birch groves and green grass—all so near and dear to the Russian heart.

"Now, that is what suits us," we three land scouts unanimously agreed.

Afterwards we were asked, "In all that big expanse, could you really find only two places—at Kuznétsk and on the Cheshlék? Couldn't you have found a place suitable for horticulture?"

No, at that time we could not.

We visited fertile Kirgízia, but it was closed to settlers that year. In Almá-

Atá we were cordially greeted by the head of the agricultural agency for the republic: "I have heard that the Tolstoyans are good farmers, and I'd like you to work here among us." He offered us a whole village on the very outskirts of Almá-Atá, with houses ready for use, good, productive gardens, a good market for our products nearby in the city, almost no difficulties at all—in a word, come on in, settle down, and start eating apples. This offer was tempting for us, but we refused it. The inhabitants of that village had recently been driven out because they were well-to-do and would not join a collective farm.

We refused another plot of land in Kazakhstán because we were scared of the workings of irrigation farming, which was unfamiliar to us, and mainly because the land of the new settlers and the land of the local inhabitants, Cossacks, were all to be irrigated from the same water source. Water was not plentiful, and we did not want any quarrels.

We land scouts returned home in June. The commune started preparing for the liquidation of the farm. But the court sentence still hung over our heads, and we could lose our freedom, so I went back to Smidóvich. In my presence Smidóvich took the telephone and called up some public prosecutor.

"You have a case there concerning so-and-so . . . They are leaving on their own, far away into Siberia . . . I think this case can be dropped."

And with that the court case came to an end.

We made an agreement to turn our farm over to the Káshchenko Psychiatric Hospital. This hospital carried on a so-called home-care system among the neighboring villages—that is, it sent out the less seriously ill mental patients to work for the peasants in return for an appropriate wage. They decided to set up a small branch of the hospital on the site of our commune to oversee the affairs of these patients. They paid us seventeen thousand rubles in all. Our thirty-year-old horse Raven, who had turned from raven-colored to gray but was still quite strong, was sold for one hundred rubles to a peasant, who still used him in his work.

As settlers according to plan, we were given reduced fares by the Commissariat of Agriculture for the train journey and the railway cars for our livestock and baggage. In March 1931 we began to take our cargo—farming equipment, seeds, food, potatoes, personal possessions, fodder, and so on—to the Kanátchikovo station of the circle railway line. We also took the best cows, calves, and horses with us. We carried hay and food for the long journey in a separate car attached to the one with the animals. The work of loading went briskly; there was a palpable kind of enthusiasm. The commune went cheerfully on its way to a new stage in its working life.

On 22 March 1931 the commune members themselves boarded the train, and it pulled out of the Yaroslávl station on its way to Vyátka, Perm, Sverdlóvsk, Omsk, Novosibírsk, Bolótnoye, and Novokuznétsk.

From the Novokuznétsk station, the cars with our freight were sent on a branch line to the very bank of the Tom and unloaded there in the open air. It was the beginning of April, and the snow was thawing. About twenty kilometers farther on, everything had to be reloaded on horses. At first the ice on the river was swollen in the middle, and water stood on the ice along the shores; but later, water overflowed across the crumbling ice all along the river.

On 7 April we loaded the rest of our baggage onto sledges and moved across the river. It was terrifying to ride across the broad river through a layer of water, while under the water there were treacherous ice, gullies, and fissures; but we managed to pull our string of sledges onto the right bank of the Tom at Tópolniki, and only the last cart fell through the ice. But that was already close to the bank, where it was not deep, and we pulled it out.

And so, without losing anything either material or spiritual, the Life and Labor Commune safely completed its resettlement from the outskirts of Moscow to Siberia.

Never to return.

Part Two: Siberia

It was April 1931. The radiant, fleeting Siberian spring was advancing victoriously. New settlers began to arrive singly and in groups on the empty, still-unpopulated bank of the Tom. A new page was turning in the history of the Russian people, a modest page but one that was bright and filled with encouraging promise and power.

A working team of several men from our commune had already arrived here in August 1930. They had prepared the way as best they could for the arrival of the others. Several members of the World Brotherhood Community in the Stalingrad area had spent the winter of 1930–31 with them. Our work team built one house and bought three others, mowed a lot of hay, and got through the winter with the young animals they had brought from near Moscow. With the arrival of our commune and the beginning of a massive stream of settlers, these houses were quickly filled to overflowing. The entryways, the attics, the sheds—all were occupied, and people kept coming from various parts of the country. There came Ural mountaineers (according to their last place of residence), who had long been accustomed to living as an agricultural cooperative, and Ukrainians from the Subbótnik sectarian group.[13] I should add that these Subbótniks had formerly lived with the Tolstoyans and taken up many of their views. The total number of these new arrivals reached several hundred. Spring quickly drove away what was left of winter. Almost all the new arrivals were peasants, and their first thought was to get to work on the land as soon as possible.

Meanwhile an urgent new task arose: to establish mutual relations between all the newcomers and set up their economic organization. I remember

---

13. Subbótniks, "Sabbatarians"—a small millenarian religious sect found mainly in Ukraine that shares certain beliefs and practices with the Jews, including the observance of the Sabbath, and can be traced back to the end of the seventeenth century.

it as if it were today: The settlers got together in the open air and sat down on logs or on the grass in order to consider one question: How shall we live? The proposal was made that everybody should join together in one unit, with farming and property in common; but after thinking it over a little, we came to a different decision: that we should not hamper one another. The experience of our labor teams, their conversations and opinions, all spoke in favor of forming not just one but several organizations, joining together according to individual inclinations—some in a commune, others in a cooperative work team ("artel"), depending on whatever might be the guiding principles of each group.

It was decided that the Uralians would form an agricultural cooperative named "Peaceful Plowman" and settle along the Aspen Ravine, with their lands to the west of the Aspen Creek. The Stalingraders would form the World Brotherhood Community and settle along the Diving Duck Ravine, with their lands to the east of the Diving Duck Creek. And finally, the Life and Labor Commune from the Moscow area would remain as a commune, with their housing along the Tom River and their lands in the center of the whole resettlement plot. These were the three basic units, which had become close-knit through their earlier life together, before the resettlement; and all the rest of the settlers would get acquainted upon their arrival with these organizations and freely join whichever one they wished, according to their own inclinations.

Gradually still other groups were organized: the people from Barábinsk, who joined the World Brotherhood Community; the people from Omsk; and within the Life and Labor Commune, the Malyóvannians and the hand-farmers.[14]

In that first summer of 1931 there were five hundred members in our Life and Labor Commune, up to two hundred in the Peaceful Plowman, and up to three hundred in the World Brotherhood Community.

Our parcel of land consisted largely of rolling hills. One of its borders to the south was the river Tom, with its pure, blue, cold water plunging down from the mountains on its rocky bed; and stretching toward the Tom from north to south were ravines, with creeks—the Zyryánovka, the Osínovka (Aspen), the Almaatínka, the First Kamenúshka (Diving Duck), the Second Kamenúshka. Further on, beyond the border of our land, was the Górnaya Shóriya; and at the point where the Sukháya Abásheva stream flows into the Tom stood the Shórian village of Abáshevo.[15] Between the ravines were wooded ridges with steep slopes overgrown with luxuriant grass, which we mowed. Only the tops of the ridges and gently sloping sides went under the plow. Along the ravines and the slopes grew patches of woods—aspens, birches, and here and there a few mighty, gnarled pines, survivors from ear-

---

14. Hand-farmer *(ruchník)*—a person who does not believe in exploiting animals and therefore does all farm work without the use of horses or cattle.

15. Shorian (Russian: *shórsky*)—a small nationality of Turkic origin in Western Siberia (population in 1959: 15,000).

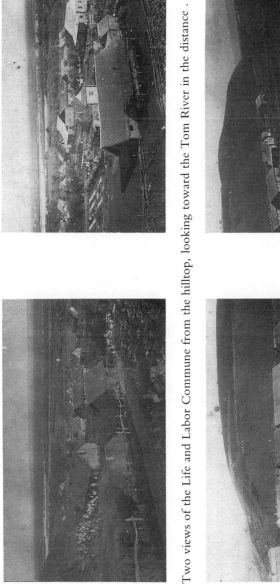

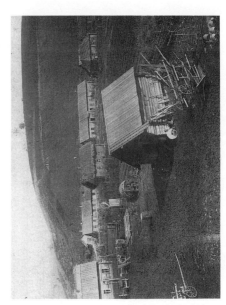

Two views of the Life and Labor Commune from the hilltop, looking toward the Tom River in the distance . .

. . . and two views of the commune looking in the other direction, toward the hills.

lier centuries. In the ravines, where it was lower and damper, the grasses would grow as high as a man and higher, with all kinds of beautiful flowers.

We were enchanted by the splendor of nature, its virginal purity, its primordial quiet. When you climbed to the top and came out on a ridge, the view that opened up before you took your breath away. Down below, whimsically winding back and forth, glittered the sparkling waters of the Tom River. Beyond it there extended for many kilometers the flat floodplains of the river, covered with bushy willows, bird cherry, and snowball trees; still further away there rose one range of mountains after another, covered with the taiga, the dark-blue, almost impenetrable evergreen forests of Siberia; while to the east on clear days we could sometimes make out against the horizon the snow-covered ridges and peaks of the Alatáu Mountains.

These were the depths of the ancient peasant Siberia, trackless and remote from machinery and cars, where even an ordinary wagon became useless for further travel up into the mountains, and you had to ride along paths on horseback. Further to the east on the Tom River, toward its tributaries the Usá and Mras-sú, toward the settlements and gold fields, humans and cargoes were carried in dug-out boats that were pushed forward by poles, since it was impossible to propel them with oars against the rapid current of the mountain rivers. To the west, from the site of our settlement to Starokuznétsk, if you traveled through the mountains, you would not see a single house; and if you went through the lowlands, along the river, there was only one large settlement, Feskí (now Boydáyevka). The summer of 1931 turned out to be unusually hot and dry for that area, but there was no real drought just the same. In the mornings there was such abundant dew that you might think a light rain had fallen. At first there were a lot of snakes on the road and in the meadows.

We lived as if we were at the ends of the earth. If you went up on a hilltop in the evening, off to the west you could see the glow of lights in the new buildings of the Kuznétsk Construction Agency, and off to the east and south, the darkness of the forest. Out there the unpopulated, uninhabitable, impenetrable taiga stretched over the mountains for hundreds of kilometers. Jumping ahead a bit, I will say that when the first friction arose with the local officials, there were some among the new settlers who were drawn to the forest. They wanted to go still further off, break away from the world with its bustle, and found a new settlement where no one would bother them. Three of the Stalingraders—Brother Yoánn and two others—left to seek a convenient spot in the taiga. They walked for several days and then came back. Everybody listened to their story with interest. At first they stumbled upon some beehives, and further on, nothing; but it was very hard to make their way through the taiga, along the steep slopes. Down below, in the ravines, there were stubborn weeds, and it was stifling and marshy; and in the mountains there was the taiga and also water—springs and streams. They found no places suitable for village life, and this idea faded away.

The only people who wandered through the taiga were hunters and gold prospectors.

Over all these places, all of nature, all the inhabitants and their way of life, there hovered the old-fashioned air of backwoods Siberia; but it was populated by a strong, resourceful, hale and hearty people. This kind of life did not last long among us—seven or eight years. Several big coal mines were opened in our area. A railway line was laid from the city to the mines, and bridges appeared over the Tom River. Horse transport was gradually replaced by automobiles, and highways were built across the roadless territory. Tractors appeared in the fields. City life now included electric lights and radio broadcasts. On the other side of the Tom from Starokuznétsk (Old Kuznétsk) there arose the big modern city of Novokuznétsk (New Kuznétsk).[16] But more about all that later.

Meanwhile, under the open skies of distant, bleak Siberia, without any help from anyone, but instead surrounded on all sides by curiosity and mistrust, a group of people gathered who for the most part were not previously acquainted—some of them with modest supplies of provisions, but others with no supplies at all and with almost no funds, some of them alone and others with families and small children.

Who were these people? What attracted them here to a life full of hardship, labor, and danger? The word "Tolstoyan" came from the family name of Tolstóy, not in the sense of singling out Tolstóy as an individual or in the sense of recognizing him as a great literary artist, but rather in recognition of Leo Tolstóy's ideas and teachings.

> A sower went out to the fields with seeds to sow;
> And then the wind everywhere these seeds did blow.
> Some by the wayside fell . . .[17]

The sower sowed, the wind blew, and the seeds fell in all sorts of places, on all sorts of ground; but these seeds were alive, and they took root and sprouted and bore fruit.

That is how the Tolstoyans made their appearance.

It is a young movement and has no ancient traditions. Into it came a former "lord and master" who began to understand the shame and immorality of his position and turned his back on his former life; and a downtrodden muzhik, oppressed by the church, enslaved by the government, then suddenly becoming aware of his own human dignity and thankfully turning his eyes and his heart toward Tolstóy, who had opened them to the truth; and a student approaching graduation, which would have assured him of respected employment, but who abruptly abandoned it all and took up the most important and essential work, agriculture; and a soldier, louse-ridden and perishing in the trenches of the First World War for the sake of powerful rulers and emperors, who suddenly recognized in himself a man who was

---

16. Novokuznétsk was called Stálinsk from 1932 to 1961.
17. The opening lines of a poem by Alekséy Mikháylovich Zhemchúzhnikov (1821–1908), paraphrasing the New Testament parable of the sower and the seed.

born not for unquestioning military slavery but for his own and the general welfare, and who thrust his bayonet once and for all into the ground and returned to a peaceful, laboring, human existence; and a worker in an armaments factory; and a Socialist Revolutionary; and an anarchist who had made bombs; and the commander of an armored train; and a Red partisan; and an investigator in the Cheká (the secret police); all of whom gave up their political activity under the influence of Tolstóy's ideas and took up the plow; and religious sectarians of various sorts who had come to understand the free and reasonable spirit of Tolstoyan teachings and given up their enslavement to primitive Biblical literalism; and a teacher in a state-run school who recoiled from the ruinous mass remolding and warping of children's souls by the state and joyfully accepted Tolstóy's ideas about a free and moral childhood education.

While Leo Tolstóy was alive, people seeking the truth reached out to him. After Tolstóy's death, there remained his followers, pupils, and friends. Their common aspirations brought them together and preserved their unity.

This is how it was: The earlier settlers had already been drawn into the ongoing farm operations, building construction, field work, and haymaking; but new settlers kept on coming. People made an effort to be attentive and helpful to them all, taking horses away from plowing and sending them to fetch the families and their property, if they had any, and giving the newcomers advice about where to find temporary living quarters in the vicinity, so they would have somewhere to lay their heads.

One big obstacle was the river Tom. At that time at Tópolniki, where there is now a bridge, there was a horse-powered ferry. In the middle of the ferry there was a vertical shaft with four poles in it, as with a horse-drawn threshing machine. Four horses would walk around in a circle, turning the shaft, the gears, and the paddle wheels that pulled their way through the water. The swift current of the river would carry the unwieldy ferry downstream; and in order to bring it in to the ferry-boat landing, the teamster would mercilessly beat the poor horses by turns, cutting welts in their backs till they bled. Work often piled up for the ferry, and sometimes you would have to wait all day long, and even spend the night.

Some of the settlers brought along some of their farming possessions: we got a wagon, a plow, a cow, beehives, even a few horses; but most of them came without anything. Ordinarily a new arrival would come to see me as the chairman of the commune council. We would get acquainted: Who are you? Where are you from? Where's your family? We'll give you a horse; have you got any property? Any food? Any money?

Then the conversation would continue in this spirit:

"Go and see Kólya Ulyánov (he was our accountant) and list everything. Give your money to him and take your food to the storeroom. And how about accommodations? Look around and try to find something for yourselves right here, or else stay for the time being in the apartment building."

"How about food?"

The first council of the Life and Labor Commune, 1931–32. *Front row:* Vasíly Bormotóv, N. A. Lyubímov, I. Ya. Kuznetsóv. *Second row:* Alekséy Chekmenyóv, A. I. Kolésnik, Sávva Blinóv, Borís Mazúrin, Anna Maloród. *Back row:* Prokóp Kuvshínov, Ye. Ye. Ivanóv, Kleménty Kraskóvsky, Dimítry Morgachëv.

Young people in the Life and Labor Commune, 1932–33.

"We take turns cooking and eat together."

Everything was simple among us. We did not yet have any established traditions. For people accustomed to other ways of living, this might shock them a bit. I remember how Níkon Shchelkunóv came from the Caucasus with his wife, a mountain type of woman, and their daughter and son. He went straight to dinner and sat down at the table without having come to see me. Shchelkunóv was an older man who came from some religious sect, a steady, serious man. He looked around with some astonishment at the commune members full of noise and laughter who were taking seats at the table. Perhaps he expected a prayer before eating, or at least a little more "decorum"—but it wasn't there. He was sitting two seats away from me, and I overheard him ask a neighbor: "How can I get to see Borís Mazúrin?"

"Why, there he is," the neighbor answered, pointing me out; and you should have seen the astonishment on his face when he caught sight of a young man in no way different from all the rest of them. Evidently, he expected to see another sort. Yes, there were such people, and Shchelkunóv did not live long in the commune; he went back to the south, got there in the midst of the famine of 1932, and they all died. Only one of his children survived.

Food enough for the time being we brought with us, and clothing too for the time being, but housing was our main worry. Nobody was misled by the beautiful, dry, hot weather. The summer months would flash by in no time, and the long, harsh Siberian winter lay ahead. We had to think, we had to act. This was what everybody talked about, in all the groups. There were many different suggestions about ways to build housing as quickly and easily as possible.

The settlers who came from forested areas thought about wood, but there was little wood suitable for construction on our parcel of land. Hauling it in from a distance was not feasible: that would take too much labor, and we did not have enough transport. Those who had come from the south thought about clay, but that too was rejected. The powerfully damp climate in this area was against it. The Uralians shared their experience with moving from Ukraine to the unforested steppe area in the Southern Urals. Over there they would hitch up several horses to a plow, fasten a pole-axe blade to it, and cutting through the ancient virgin soil, they would turn up a long, smooth ribbon of firm material. They would take their spades and cut it into bricks and build a house out of them, building them up into an arch and thus using as little wood as possible. Right up against this house they would build another (thus saving one wall), and so on. This quickly produced out of local material a long, warm building with many apartments. This method attracted general attention. The Stalingrad Community put it into practice, and they lived in such buildings. Our commune, however, rejected this method. Even though the soil in our area was the kind of black earth called "chernozem," it turned out to be loose and crumbly. A sheet of it was weak and would not hold together. We used this method to build only one house, and even then without an arch.

Something else helped us out. In spite of everything, our settlement grew up as one basically made of log houses. It was 1931, and village life in Siberia was disrupted by collectivization. Many peasants left the villages to work in factories, or moved away to other places, scattering in all directions, some of them to prospect for gold; and many buildings were for sale cheap all around the countryside. So we sent four men with money and axes up the river Tom to Burávkovo, Bezrúkovo, and Atamánovo. They would buy a house or a barn. They would mark it, take it apart, haul it to the Tom, make a raft of it, get on it, and float down the river to our commune.

There we would be waiting to meet them. We would fish out the logs, and within three or four days a house would be standing on our new street. Then another house would appear in line with it, but with five or six meters between them. Remembering the long buildings in the Urals, we would fill in the space between two houses with two walls, put all of it under one roof, and then we had a barrack with three apartments.

We also cut timber on our own land and used it for building material. We used a third method of construction too, which was especially successful for building cattle barns: we would build the framework out of thick logs and put up walls of slender poles. We would pack the space between the poles with clay mixed with long straw. We would lay the next pole on top of this clay, tamping it down firmly with mallets, and so on. The clay and straw mixture would ooze way out on both sides. When it had begun to harden, the women would coat it with another layer of clay, smoothing out the walls in the Ukrainian way, and this produced a good, strong wall. This made good, warm cattle barns. The whole place hummed with work. But the form of this work was not developed all at once. At first there was a meeting at which we discussed how we should build—all together? Or, like the Uralians, each family to itself?

There was a lot of talk; but in the end we decided that since we were a commune, we should do everything jointly. We had a lot of carpenters, so we organized work brigades; and by winter everybody had a roof over their heads. But what kind? In each house there were several families. There were bunks everywhere; and a few single persons, such as Mísha Blagovéshchensky, saved space by hanging their beds from wires attached to the ceiling. We were packed like sardines but good-humored about it. We were helped in our construction by the fact that the so-called floating delivery of logs down the river Tom had been done carelessly that year. Many logs remained along the bank, in the bushes, frozen into the ice. In the spring this timber was doomed to destruction, and in any case it would have floated with the ice into the Arctic Ocean.

Our sawyers knew what to do, and a few pairs of them turned the logs into boards and blocks. There was not much living space, and the younger men conceived the idea of building a house where they could get together, spend their leisure time, and study. They discovered a tiny cove on the Tom which the current had piled full of logs. In winter they were all frozen together in the ice, but in the spring, when the ice on the river was gone, a

The Life and Labor Commune: a view of the village in 1932.

A raft made of logs from deserted houses that the commune members had gone up the river Tom and bought, dismantled, and floated down the river to rebuild in the Life and Labor Commune.

One more house under construction, 1932.

Dwelling houses built together so as to save one wall between them. This kind of structure provided the setting for Iván Dragunóvsky's dramatic account in the last chapter of this book.

whole supply of logs remained in the cove. They got some horses and chains, and in one day they dragged out nearly eighty fine logs onto the bank. They split them in half with the saw and built a big building out of them in the center of the settlement. At once it was filled to the brim with beds; after all, people had to live somewhere!

A big group of Malyóvannians from Kiev Province arrived and wanted to live together in a separate building. They took a liking to a spot in a little pine grove at the very end of our parcel. They were all master workers, industrious people, and they quickly erected a big, long building with many rooms, and daubed it and whitewashed it in the Ukrainian style. But just the same, they later moved into our commune settlement—living by themselves was too boring.

Another need, clothing, had not yet come to our attention so much; we made do with what we had. Faddéy Zablótsky once remarked: "I have come to the conclusion that it's possible to get by with only one jacket all your life: if you get a hole in it, put a patch on it; and if you get a hole in the patch, put another patch on that." But our third need, food, became more and more urgent for us. Sometimes in the evening, when all work had ceased, Kólya Slabínsky, the storeroom keeper, would come to me.

"Well, how are you getting along about food?"

"Oh, poorly. Only enough for about three days. It's melting away."

"That's good," I would say.

"How is it good?"

"That means the people are healthy—they've got a good appetite."

You can joke like that, but then at night you lie awake and wonder where we can get food. After all, it's not a small family; there are five hundred people. It's a commune: everybody does his job, and after finishing work they come to the table confident that someone will take care of how and what to feed them. But what can we think of? We had little grain of our own to sow, and we had a drought. We harvested barely five tons of wheat, and we put that in the granary as an untouchable fund to be used as seed for the next year. True, we harvested enough potatoes and vegetables, but we also needed bread. We asked for no help, and we received none of any kind from anybody.

In the other groups it was even more difficult. The Barábinsk[18] people gathered edible herbs, dried them, ground them into flour, and baked flat cakes of them. I tried one—it was bitter.

Just as we had done before when we had to decide what to do about housing, we called a general meeting again this time. Everybody came to decide what we should do about food. And if voices had been heard at the first meeting saying, "Let every family take care of itself," this time there were no such voices. There was no doubt that this problem had to be solved by everybody together. After all, we were a commune!

We found a solution. We decided that all the able-bodied adult males

18. Barábinsk—a small town in the Novosibírsk Province in Western Siberia.

would go out and get seasonal work. It so happened that conditions were favorable for this. The building of Kuznetskstróy, the gigantic Kuznétsk industrial complex, was then under way; and alongside it there was rising the city of Novokuznétsk. Life was hard there, and in order to attract and hold the labor force, food cards were given out not only to the worker himself but also to his whole family.

And so a labor team of thirty to forty men went out to work at the gravel pit at Abagúr, loading gravel into railway cars—at that time, of course, still by hand and with shovels. A second such labor team, made up of carpenters, went into the taiga along the Sukháya Abásheva River to Siénka, Uzuntsý, and other points, to build barracks for special settlers who were awaited by the Timber Production Industry to stockpile timber. Smaller groups and individuals scattered in all directions, some to Kuznetskstróy, some to the horticultural and park administration, and so on. No pressure was put on anybody, but it was generally decided that each person would spend on himself only what was necessary for food, and would hand over the rest of his wages and especially all the food received on his family's cards to the commune storeroom. Carts were sent out every Saturday for this purpose, one to the taiga, another to Abagúr, and a third to the city. They would return loaded down mainly with baked bread.

That is how we lived through the winter of 1931–32, the summer of 1932, and part of the winter of 1932–33. On holidays the muzhiks—that is, the workers—would come home, and then everything was full, merry, and crowded; but on work days there remained only the women and three or four grown men.

In the summer of 1932 we planted more wheat and harvested more, and everybody was able to return home to his favorite work. We were fed up with being separated from our families and our own society.

Besides, the commune members had begun attracting attention even at work. Certain peculiarities of our convictions began to be noticed.

In the taiga our brigade was ordered to tear down two houses in the Shorian Tatar village of Abáshevo. We got there and found out that one was the home of a dispossessed kulák. His whole family was living in the house and would not come out.

"How can we tear it down?" we asked.

"Just tear it down, that's all."

"But people are living there!"

"Tear it down!"

Our people looked at it, stood there a while, turned around, and left. They were not about to tear it down. It goes without saying that the officials were displeased with the behavior of our commune members, and they took note of it.

At Abagúr our brigade was valued for its work: we worked fast, reliably, at any time, and without drunkenness or absenteeism; but a subscription drive was held for some kind of loan—to strengthen national defense, it seemed. Our people refused to sign. They motivated their refusal in this way:

"In the first place, how can we give a loan when we have to struggle even to feed ourselves and our families? And in the second place, we cannot give funds for war matters."

However, the loan money was withheld from their pay. Our people refused to accept the war bonds.

Then the bonds were brought in a package to the barracks and left there. Our people sealed them up and sent them back through the mail. One more mark against us—this time a big one.

It is high time I finished this description of the life of our commune during our seasonal work. I will only add that none of the commune members who went out for work was ever tempted to stay there. They all came back; and except for one young fellow, Fésik Junior, who bought himself a pair of boots, nobody broke our general agreement to hand over all our earnings to the general treasury.

I must touch on one other important question: Was the whole commune membership completely unanimous in its conscious ideological attraction to the commune? No. There were a good many people who came to the commune not through ideological aspirations, but simply through the force of circumstances—for example, some wives and older children who were not caught up by the idea. But this serious circumstance was smoothed over to some extent by the fact that the majority were peasants in their way of life, and this fitted in with the peasant tendency of Tolstoyan convictions.

All of us loved peasant work. All of our inquisitiveness, all our thirst for knowledge and creativity was focused on how best to work the land, when to sow our seeds and what kind of seeds, how to care for our plants, and how to handle the harvest so that our labor would be fruitful.

I remember how the Túla peasant Dimítry Kiselyóv once came up to me—practically running, extremely disturbed.

"Borís, Borís! What's going on here? Why, it's just as if harm were being done on purpose! Is *that* the way to get the hay in?! Among us, you know, you take a swath, step back one scythe length, and shake the shaft to dry it faster; during the day you turn it over, if it's a fine day; toward evening you make it into little shocks, and the next day you spread it out nice and thin, and you turn it over two or three times during the day, and toward evening you make it into shocks a little larger, and after that you'll look at the weather and the grass—either it will ripen in shocks, or you'll turn it over again and dry it. After all, you know, hay—that's your tea! It's like tea! But what are they doing here?" he stormed.

I knew what Dimítry was saying; that is the way we did our haymaking in the Moscow area. But the Siberian climate and the Siberian grasses disrupted the customary way and made it unnecessary.

"Come on," I called to him.

We went out a little beyond the settlement, where rows of hay mown two days earlier lay on the steep south slope (almost a forty-five-degree angle) from top to bottom. For lack of time it had not been turned over or shaken even once, and the grass had dried out under the hot rays of the sun beating directly down on it. It had dried out so much that turning it further would have only been harmful and knocked off the leaves. True, the hay here was not as fragrant as what we had at home, but this was only because the grasses here were different, taiga-region grasses.

Dimítry turned over the piles of grass, felt it, crumpled it, and said nothing. No, he did not yet agree, he did not yet give up his own way of haymaking, worked out through the centuries by his ancestors, but—but he said nothing. There was nothing to say.

Such squabbles were frequent at first. You ought to see how somebody from Central Russia from Smolénsk, for example—would look down on a man from Central Asia for the way he fastened his scythe blade to the handle with a long strap.

"Surely you don't fasten it that way! This is how we do it: with a ring and a wedge—quick and strong."

Then it was tested at work. It turned out that both methods were all right.

Almost everybody brought their best seeds with them in little bags or bundles. During that very first summer, we tried a lot of things. For example, a watermelon patch planted on the southern slope produced excellent watermelons, which we had never been able to grow in the Moscow area. We were overjoyed, but it turned out that we were helped by the exceptional summer weather, and later we had to give up planting watermelons.

The southerners suggested sowing poppy seed, which had a yield of 50 percent oil. And what oil it was! But we did not sow poppy seed; we were afraid it was too labor-intensive. The Volga people brought mustard seed. It required very little labor, brought a good yield, and made a good oil. Sunflowers also matured well—but we had to choose the varieties carefully. From the Moscow area we brought winter-wheat seed with us. We were told that it would not grow in Siberia, but we stubbornly planted it for about three years, harvesting practically nothing, until we finally learned by experience that it would not grow here.

We kept thinking about all of that even while we were still short on living space. Every field laborer thought about it and took it to heart—not the way it is now, when there is ordinarily one hired agronomist responsible for all that work, and those who work directly in the soil have only to carry out his orders more or less conscientiously. And even if the agronomist happens to know and love his work, he too is often not free to do what he considers necessary, but must carry out the directives and compulsory recommendations he receives from above.

No, we did not go from the top down, pyramid-fashion, with one man at the top, then broadening out till you get to the very bottom, the foundation—the working people of the soil. We started from below, with everybody who worked on the land themselves. But that does not mean that we steered clear of agronomy, the science of the soil, or that we did not value the labor of those who worked in that direction; on the contrary, we would seek them out and get their advice. For example, we sent Gítya Tyurk and somebody else to Omsk to the experimental grain station, and they brought

Using greenhouses and hotbeds, the Life and Labor Commune pioneered the growing of strawberries in Western Siberia.

back a lot of different kinds of wheat, oats, and barley; and by our second summer of life in Siberia, we had our own experimental field, laid out in neat little plots. We assigned the care of the field to Iván Prokópyevich Kolésnikov, a peasant experimenter and horticulturist from Vorónezh. Sávva Blinóv and I went to Barnaúl, to the Altái experimental station, for oil-yielding cereals and brought back seeds of white and black mustard, safflower, flax, and sunflowers of the early-ripening "Pioneer of Siberia" variety.

Sergéy Alekséyev, who loved gardening to the point that he said, "The garden is my religion," and who knew Esperanto, wrote to his foreign friends, and they sent us garden seeds from Bulgaria and other countries.

The northerners stuck to their favorite rutabagas, unknown to the southerners, which incidentally yielded a rich harvest and, along with potatoes, greatly helped us with our food at first, when we had a hard time getting enough provisions.

Something else that greatly helped us in the first years was buckwheat, which was not grown very much in Siberia but thrived there beautifully. We sowed it to use for the state grain procurement, especially since, pound for pound, buckwheat was given a higher value than wheat.

Beginning in our first or second year, we built a greenhouse and made hotbeds. We were pioneers in the cultivation of strawberries, which were unknown before then in that area and are now widespread all around Novokuznétsk.

We not only sent away for seeds but also from the very first years started our own seed plot. This work was assigned to the very well organized Ványa Zúyev, and he carried it out with great success. One time—much later, it is true—he produced on our seed plot eighty kilograms of first-class "nutmeg onions," which were then in very short supply. The agronomists did not believe it was possible to grow them in Siberia. Previously the Siberians had done very little market gardening. We used to take a cartload of cucumbers to the bazaar, medium-sized and green, and some Siberian would come up and ask: "Pick me out a bigger one that's yellower, riper, and crunchier."

There was an endless demand for our garden products in Novokuznétsk—both in the bazaar and in the workers' dining halls at Kuznetskstróy. We also delivered vegetables to the dining halls for foreign specialists, builders who were afraid of Siberia and always ate raw cabbage before every meal to ward off scurvy. For our gardens we rooted out the occasional bushes and plowed up a level space in the floodlands of the river, at the foot of the mountains. It was virgin soil, black and loose, and vegetables grew there wonderfully. The seeds also turned out to be good—Bulgarian seeds—and we got huge crops.

In Novokuznétsk there was a district agricultural fair—I don't remember exactly which year, about 1933. Our commune took part in it. Our cows took first place in milk yield, and another first place went to our stallion Ovsadáy,[19] who was proudly led around the circle by Artyóm Kolésnik, our stable man. Our vegetables and strawberries also took first place, and they were written up in the newspaper; but we were passed over when the prizes were awarded. The reason was clear to us—we were Tolstoyans. We were offended and decided not to take part in the fairs anymore.

The free spirit of enterprise—not capitalistic but collective, peasant enterprise—is stifled when you work for wages and on orders from above. In the commune there were no directors, no work superintendents, no approved lists, projects, bank accounts, allocations, estimates, transfers, cadre problems, production norms, categories, economists, no platoons of bookkeepers, no sick lists. We had none of all that creaking, cumbersome bureaucratic apparatus, with its deadly effect on work and on any active initiative from the workers.

Ordinarily, this is how things went. When the need arose for a mill, we got together in a production meeting. In addition to the commune council, anybody else who was interested would attend. The question was clear: we needed a mill. Various suggestions were made, some of them downright fantastic.

"Why not harness the Tom River? There's power for you!"

"But how would you harness it?"

"Let's just anchor a raft and let the current turn the water wheels."

It was tempting, and this suggestion was discussed for a while, but then it was rejected.

---

19. The name in Russian means "Gimme some oats!"

"What about a little engine?"

"Where would you get it?"

Then Mikhaíl Pólbin stood up.

"Just help me find a little steel ball, and you'll have a mill within a week."

"Let's go!"

Sure enough, he quickly built a little mill with a vertical shaft that was turned by the water power of the Aspen Creek. The water from the creek was sent through another channel dug out at a higher level and with a less steep fall, gradually getting higher and higher above the old channel, then falling back into it but from a height of two meters; the power of its fall turned the shaft.

Our oil-yielding crops—sunflower, mustard, safflower—grew very well.

"If we only had an oil-press!"

"Can you get one?"

And at once people were found who knew all about this.

"Back home in Kiev Province they were lying all over the place. They went to waste after the drive against the kuláks."

"But a heifer far away can't feed on our hay."

"Just send me and I'll bring back an oil-press," said Márko Burlák.

"But who will give you a freight car?"

In other words—a dead halt. But the idea was tempting, and we all racked our brains over it. We found a solution: to put the oil-press on the resettlement ticket of some latecomer who had not yet left Kiev with his luggage for our settlement.

So we acquired both an oil-press and a hulling machine, which were not to be found anywhere else in the whole district.

We hauled our water by horse, in barrels, from the Tom River. It took a lot of water, and hauling it could at times be both dirty and difficult.

Once when old Yevgény Ivánovich Popóv was out for a walk, cane in hand, he stumbled upon a good spring in a crevice above our settlement. That gave him an idea: it was not far away, and it would be easy to put in a water pipe and bring running water to the settlement by gravity. We cleaned out the spring, built a frame around it, got some pipe from a scrap heap in town, and soon we had water pipes and faucets in the kitchen, in the bakery, and at the seed beds. The water was pure and good-tasting.

Our farming tended more and more toward market gardening. Our production was large and our sales were good, but one obstacle was transport. We did not have enough horses even for our work on the farm itself, and the trip to the city was twenty-five kilometers, and across the Tom, where the ferry boat often caused long lines of waiting traffic.

We had to find a solution, and we did. The Stalingraders came up with the idea of traveling by water on the Tom. There was nothing new about that, of course. Every day we saw boats loaded with cargo being poled upstream and floating down the river with the current. But a boat, even a large one, could carry less than half a ton. The Stalingraders suggested making what is called a "kárbuz," a kind of boat but far bigger in both size and carrying capacity. The commune produced two of them, each with a capacity of up to six tons. The carts with vegetables would be driven right up to the kárbuz at the water's edge, and it would usually be loaded in the evening. Two sailors would take it across in about four hours to the left bank of the Tom, at Tópolniki. There we built a little house with a stable for two horses. A watchman, who was also the cook, lived in the house all the time, along with two drivers who also served as delivery men, and they would haul the vegetables around to dining halls, stores, and the bazaar. They would also haul grain, potatoes, and vegetables to be handed over to the state. That was a great relief for the commune, and saved a lot of effort and funds.

Outwardly, to the eyes of a stranger, our settlement looked like a hamlet with little houses built of logs or a combination of logs and clay. Off to one side, nearer the Tom, were the cattle barns. Along the ravine from which our water supply came (now called Cabbage Gully) were the mill, the bakery, the drying house, the blacksmith shop, the bathhouse, the granary, and the vegetable storehouse. A little farther above the settlement, where there is now the road to the cemetery, stood a few more houses on a hilly street.

We built the cemetery on a bare hilltop above the settlement. The first settler to be buried there was Andréy Pávlovich Yereménko. On the first graves there we planted birch trees, which have now grown up into a little grove. The commune has left many dear graves up there, but I dare say that just as many commune members lie in unknown graves scattered all over the boundless expanse of the North.

If our settlement did not differ outwardly from thousands of similar Russian villages, and if there lived in it the same kind of people as in all Russian villages, with the same virtues and weaknesses, still there was one thing in our lives that was special, our own. That—I do not hesitate to say it—was the spirit of Tolstóy.

That spirit was by no means expressed outwardly, the way ill-disposed people often described Tolstóy's followers—long beards, deliberate simplification in dress, wearing bast shoes,[20] and imitating peasant dialect with "ourn" and "yourn." No, there was none of that—or rather, to speak more truthfully, there was all of that: some did have beards, some did wear simple clothing, on rare occasions some did turn up wearing bast shoes, and a few of them not only said "ourn" and "yourn" but used many other dialect forms as well; but in all this there was nothing intentional.

People were sincerely just what they were.

It was the same in the matter of religion. You would have looked in vain for any signs of religiosity in our life in the sense that it is understood by church people and atheists: no rituals, no cult, no prayer meetings—we had nothing of that sort. And even if you went deeper, there were no dogmas of any kind, no catechisms, no programs, authorities, or unquestionable scrip-

---

20. Bast shoes (Russian: *lápti*) were traditional peasant footwear woven out of the fibers of such plants as hemp, flax, and the inner bark of lime trees.

tures. There was free acceptance of the understanding and manner of life that Tolstóy expressed so clearly and powerfully; and this was not merely because Tolstóy said it, but because everybody felt this to some extent within themselves, in their consciousness, in their soul. And from this there followed a tolerance for the views of everyone else.

In our meetings songs could sometimes be heard that did not express the Tolstoyan world outlook but were sectarian in content. There were hymns of the Evangelicals (Baptists), psalms of the Molokáns (Spiritual Christians), spiritual verses of the so-called Khlystý[21] or the Mormons (uncommonly musical!), and songs of the Malyóvannians and Dobrolyúbovians,[22] and many others. To my mind, all this was a distinctive tribute to the past out of which these people had come. Along with this we might hear a theosophical song, a Hindu hymn of Vivekananda, a favorite song of the People's Will revolutionaries, "Slowly passes the time . . . ," and the equally well-known poem "Convicts."

Purely Tolstoyan songs were comparatively few: "Listen to the word, day is breaking" and "The day of freedom is approaching" by Anna Chertkóva;[23] "Life is given to us that we may love," "Happy is he who loves all things alive," and "A teacher was he in a small French village," by Iván Ivánovich Gorbunóv-Posádov. We also sang A. M. Khiryakóv's "Peaceful Marseillaise"[24] and several poems written by the settlers themselves. We had several songs of Yevgény Ivánovich Popóv, a lover and collector of folk melodies ("My grain fields, my grain fields . . ."). What kind of songs did we not sing at all? Such songs as "The sharp-breasted boats sailed out . . . ," "If I had a mountain of gold . . . ," and so on.

We loved to sing and we sang a lot, sometimes with great enthusiasm, but—I must confess—not always very well. The Uralians sang the best, but the Barábinsk people too sang especially well.

Sunday was a day of rest, but even our workdays were not filled only with work. On Mondays there was a production conference. Everyone was free to participate, and often these meetings turned into lively, interesting, and useful discussions. On Tuesdays we sang and learned songs. On Wednesdays there was a philosophical study group, and on Thursdays a teachers' meeting, which the parents also attended. On Saturdays there was a chorus rehearsal. On Sundays there was a big general meeting, at which there were readings and discussions on all kinds of topics in addition to sing-

21. Khlystý, or "People of God"—a Russian religious sect of obscure origin and equally obscure practices, which dates back to the seventeenth century and was reported still to exist in some areas of Russia as late as the 1950s.

22. Dobrolyúbovians (Russian: *Dobrolyúbovtsy*)—followers of Aleksándr Mikháylovich Dobrolyúbov (1876–1944[?]), one of the first Russian symbolist poets, who later preached a message of extreme simplicity based on nonviolence, physical labor, and reverence for nature.

23. Anna Konstantínovna Chertkóva (née Díterikhs) was the wife of Vladímir Chertkóv, Tolstóy's principal associate.

24. Aleksándr Modéstovich Khiryakóv (1863–1946), an independent-minded journalist associated with Tolstóy, was imprisoned for a month by the tsarist government for the publication of his poem "A Peaceful Marseillaise."

Yevgény Ivánovich Popóv (1864–1938), an old associate of Tolstóy who spent his last years in the Life and Labor Commune, was a favorite with the commune children, some of whom are shown here with him.

Yevgény Popóv took the initiative in setting up a system that provided running water for the commune.

The dining hall and commune meeting house.

ing. Letters would be read from like-minded friends in our own country, and sometimes even from abroad—from the Dukhobors in Canada and from the commune of Tolstoyans in Bulgaria. Once in a bulletin of the pacifist organization War Resisters International (in England), we learned about an Italian who had refused to take part in the war that the Italians were then fighting against Abyssinia and had been sentenced to death. The general meeting of our commune sent him greetings and our sympathy. We did not know whether our message ever reached him or what fate befell that courageous man.

During that period, in a letter to our friend Ványa Báutin, who was imprisoned at Solovkí and was very much interested in the progress of our resettlement, I wrote: "There is nothing farfetched and artificial about our life now; it is one great stream of problems that we have to face and find clear solutions for every day, and the consequences of our solutions are also tough and harsh, so we have to resolve them seriously. What we especially value is the unity that is to be found in all important matters, despite our numerous disagreements over trivial things."

Some people said: "It was necessity that drove you closer together. If there hadn't been any collectivization, you wouldn't have been resettled and wouldn't have had your commune." But the flimsiness of such an attitude is clear to any impartial person.

The first communes in Samára Province arose as early as 1918, and our Life and Labor Commune sprang up in 1921. A great many of the people who resettled here in Siberia with us had joined together earlier for work and life in common. And how many communes arose after the February Revolution of 1917 not on religious but on political grounds! There were also communes of American re-emigrants to Russia, who incidentally brought with them farm machinery and equipment from America. Numerous facts show that the powerful stimulus to the formation of independent agricultural communes (not only on political but also, and equally, on religious grounds) was not collectivization at all, but the February Revolution. In my view, the effect of collectivization was just the reverse: to bring to naught all those genuinely independent communist organizations by replacing their initiative with the narrow framework of collective-farm regulations.

I will give here a by no means complete list of similar associations that are known to me: the Táynino agricultural cooperative at Perlóvka, in Moscow Province; the Tolstóy agricultural commune at Voskresénsk, in Moscow Province; Bódraya Zhizn ("Cheerful Life"), in Kalúga Province; Selíshchina and Brátskaya Zhizn ("Brotherly Life"), in Poltáva Province; Béreg ("The Shore"), in the Crimea; Almá-Atínskaya, in Almá-Atá; Vsemírnoye Brátstvo ("World Brotherhood"), in Tsarítsyn; Tsárstvo Svéta ("Kingdom of Light"), in Ukraine; the Vsemírnoye Brátstvo settlement, in Samára Province; Yedinéniye ("Unity"), in Túla Province; the community in the village of Rayóvka, in Bashkíria; the commune of Dimítry Morgachëv, in Oryól Province; Krínitsa, at Gelendzhík, on the Black Sea shore; Beryózki ("The Birches"), in Moscow Province; the Klínskaya commune, at Klin.

There were also many communes and communities in the Smolénsk region, in Vladímir and Ivánov provinces, in Bryansk, Sarátov, and Khárkov provinces. Here should be included the association of Malyóvannians in Kiev Province, the independent cooperatives Brátsky Trud ("Brotherly Labor") and Známya Brátskogo Trudá ("Banner of Brotherly Labor") in Samára Province, and many, many others.

From our very first days, and even earlier, from the day on which our working team arrived, our relations did not go smoothly with the outside world—the local government authorities and their individual representatives. Up to the end of 1930, this was the procedure: during the period in which they were granted special exemptions (for us, three years), settlers were in the charge of the Resettlement Administration, and not the village and district soviets. Our parcel of land had been allocated to us by the Resettlement Administration; but when we arrived in 1931, it no longer existed, and we immediately fell under the authority of the district department and the village soviet. They, of course, knew that as organized resettlers we had been granted special exemptions in connection with grain and other deliveries and taxes and labor duty. But then they sent the figure for required deliveries to the district, and the district assigned allocations to the village soviets. The requirement was high, and collection was hard, at times impossible, for young collective farms. But in the Yesaúl village soviet, we settlers constituted a large part of the population, so the temptation was great to load some of the burden on the Tolstoyans. And that is what they did. We protested and went higher up, and from there they gave orders, but just the same, we had to deal every day with those who were close by, the local representatives of the government. They got their orders from above, but of course they had the confidence of those above. And they had to choose between two evils— either fail to fulfill their delivery plan, or fail to observe the special exemptions that had been given to the resettlers, who after all were some kind of Tolstoyans. Understandably, they chose the easier course.

In the winter of our very first year, 1931–32, they demanded hay from us. We replied that we had come as resettlers according to plan and had received a three-year exemption, and we did not deliver the hay.

Once we were in the midst of our Sunday meeting. The dining hall was filled with people, all adults. Suddenly Andréy Samóylenko ran in, greatly disturbed. "A whole string of wagons has come out from the city, and they are loading our hay!"

Everybody was very much agitated: "Don't let them have it!" But just the same, despite the indignation, the rational decision was accepted that no one should go out, and that we should continue with our meeting. "That is their business; ours is not to fan the flames of evil." And when the wagons loaded with our fresh, hard-earned hay passed by the windows of our dining hall one by one, the hall resounded with the especially fervent singing of the words:

> The menacing storm begins,
> A harbinger of dawn,

Before all tsars and rulers
Let your heads remain unbowed.

The voices resounded powerfully, and tingles of emotion ran up and down our spines—not of terror or regret for what had been taken away from us, and not of animosity, but rather of quiet, firm resolve to stand on our own principles, and not to embark on the path of mutual spite.

They took the hay away. The hay was a touchstone. Nobody stopped them, nobody pointed out the unlawfulness. And so it went on and on—an uninterrupted chain of misunderstandings, friction, demands that we as organized resettlers did not have to fulfill, crop quotas that exceeded the amount of arable land we had. Once the quota was assigned and turned in to the office, everything else followed automatically: the crop quota determined the quota for the delivery of produce and the amount of tax levied by the district finance department, and all this had the effect of law. It was impossible to avoid fulfilling it; fulfill it first, and then prove your case in a legal way through the proper channels. And we went and proved it. But in the district these legal channels were the same ones that had set the illegal quotas in the first place. We would write to the regional authorities, and in reply we would get either silence or "Fulfill it!"

We went higher up and complained to the People's Commissariat of Agriculture, and we got the answer: "Go to the All-Russian Central Executive Committee; your case is being handled there. It is awkward for us. It will be better for you if you take it up there yourselves." We went to the Central Executive Committee; they looked into the matter; they understood it and sent directives to the provinces, but the same thing happened there.

There were a lot of conflicts over logging. Every autumn we would receive instructions (as did all the collective farms) to send so many men and so many horses to cut so many cubic meters of timber. We had a serious shortage of horses even in the summer, but in winter they were worked all the time: hauling hay and straw through deep snow and in the mountains, hauling firewood, hauling out manure to the hotbeds, and so on, with no let-up. In the spring the horses would come back from the logging completely exhausted, with no chance to recover their strength in time for the impending springtime work. And we would refuse to go to the logging or to send horses. They would take our horses themselves, without our agreement.

Once several members of our commune council were arrested and sentenced for nonfulfillment of the logging. Our general meeting sent me to Moscow to seek justice. I got up to Solts, who occupied a high office and was reputed to be an old Bolshevik who was a man of justice and kindness. He read our statement about the innocence of our condemned comrades, which declared that the question of logging had not been decided by the commune council but by the general meeting, and that our arguments were such and such. He read it through, wrote out some sort of resolution, and said: "Go to room number so-and-so." I left and went up to the door of the room, but something held me back. I went over to the window and read it. I do not remember it exactly, but the general sense was: "They got off too easily; review the case and increase the sentence." I put the paper into my pocket and went back to Siberia.

I will not enumerate all these skirmishes, there were too many of them, and I couldn't anyhow—I have forgotten much of it. But all this led up to a resolution by the Kuznétsk District Executive Committee to liquidate our commune.

They sent us a paper, but it made no impression on us—it was too non-sensical. We went on living and working just as we had before. But then a representative of the district executive committee came with an order to take away our seal and charter.

The commune council and many members of the commune gathered in a little room. The mood was very agitated. The representative was also very angry. He pounded the table with his fist and demanded that we submit and turn over the seal and charter. Finally he said: "For the last time I ask you— will you turn over the seal?"

"No!"

Then something unexpected happened: in a completely different tone, quietly and even amicably, he firmly shook my hand as chairman of the commune and said:

"Well, if that's the way it is, then stick to it—that's the only way you'll achieve anything."

Obviously, this simple and sincere working man saw that we were the same kind of people, and he sympathized with us. Our thanks to him.

Our commune had its chroniclers who recorded all events, minutes, documents, and facts. During the "devils' orgy" of 1937–38, all of that was lost. Only a few individual papers miraculously escaped. Here is one of them:

> To Comrade P. G. Smidóvich, Western Siberian Regional Executive Committee, Kuznétsk District Executive Committee, People's Commissariat of Agriculture of the R.S.F.S.R.
>
> Extract from Protocol No. 38.
>
> Meeting of 2 March 1932 of the Presidium of the All-Russian Central Executive Committee of Soviets.
>
> HAVING CONSIDERED the decree of the Kuznétsk District Executive Committee of the Western Siberian Region dated 23 November 1931 on the disbandment of the Tolstoyan commune "Life and Labor."
>
> HAS RESOLVED 1. to call the attention of the Western Siberian Regional Executive Committee to the violation by the Kuznétsk District Executive Committee of the resolution of the Presidium of the All-Union Central Executive Committee dated 20 June 1931 on the resettlement of Tolstoyan communes and agricultural cooperatives in the Kuznétsk District of the Western Siberian Region.
>
> 2. proposes to the Western Siberian Regional Committee (a) to immediately cancel the decision of the Kuznétsk District Executive Committee dated 23 November 1931 on the disbandment of the Life and Labor Commune, (b) to examine the economic questions connected with the establishment and strengthening of the Life and Labor Commune and take the necessary measures.

3. to grant to the Life and Labor Commune the exemptions for resettlers that are established on a general basis by law.

The document is clear, but its effect was limited to the repeal of the district executive committee's resolution breaking up the commune; its order granting us the exemptions established for resettlers was not carried out.

But in connection with military registration and military service, they held us accountable.

In the summer of 1932, call-up papers came for Lyóva Alekséyev, Fédya Katrúkha, and Yegór Gúrin to report for military service. Yegór did not go at all, and Lyóva and Fédya reported but declared that they refused to serve. In October 1932 there was a show trial. Lyóva was given five years of imprisonment, and Fédya four.

The commune submitted a declaration to the Presidium of the All-Russian Central Executive Committee, which said that we had never concealed our opposition to military service, that many of us even in tsarist times had worn convict's chains because of it, and we requested that the seriousness of our convictions be taken into consideration and the prisoners be released. And they were released about half a year later.

Recalling the early days of life in our new location, I want to dwell upon two representatives of the local government with whom we had to deal. The first was Sadakóv, the head of the district land department. We had the model charter for agricultural communes that existed at that time, but we had added to it a few words specifying that followers of L. N. Tolstóy who rejected man's use of violence against his fellow man could be members of our commune. Sadakóv did not want to register such a charter at all, but I somehow managed to persuade him, and he signed it and affixed the seal of the district executive committee. But soon he thought better of it and realized that this could be considered a great political mistake on his part, and he tried in all kinds of ways to get this charter back, but without success. So this charter lived on among us, and we used it as a trump card in court when we were accused of having an illegal commune.

Sadakóv (either he took it upon himself or else he was instructed to do it) tried to talk us out of our convictions and re-educate us. A little below average height, with shaggy fair hair, a little gray cap on the back of his head, plainly dressed, in tarpaulin boots, and above all in his convinced and insistent character and his simplicity of manner, he recalled the good Bolshevik of the early years of the Revolution who had not yet taken on the domineering, bureaucratic manner. After his ardent speeches, he would listen to our no less ardent responses, and it seemed that he was beginning to understand us a little.

The second one I remember was Popóv, the head of the Kuznétsk NKVD. He behaved simply, but you could feel that this was not Sadakóv's kind of simplicity, but a sham. In general he assumed a friendly, palsy-walsy tone with me as the commune chairman. He would catch sight of me somewhere on the street in town and shout from a distance: "Hello, Mazúrin!" Once he was at our settlement, and we sat on logs and talked. I said to him: "You shouldn't think we look on you as some kind of superior."

"As what, then?"

"Just as a man like any other."

"Of course," he agreed, "that's it."

"Whenever you need anything," he told me, "don't stand on ceremony—just stop in to see me." And such an occasion did come up. One of our people, Faddéy Zablótsky, a commune member from the Moscow area, was serving a sentence in exile somewhere in the North, and a Dukhobor from Canada by the name of Pável was in exile there with him. We knew nothing more than that about him. After finishing his exile, and having no relatives in Russia, this Pável learned about our commune from Faddéy and set out to come here. But he did not arrive—he was arrested.

When I learned that he was in Kuznétsk at the militia, I made my way up to the window and asked someone to call Pável. He came up, and I told him I was from the commune. We talked a little, and I promised him I would try to help him out. I went to Freedom Street and asked for a pass to see Popóv. I received it at once. I went to his office, and he received me cordially:

"What is it?"

I told him about Pável and added that even though he was a little strange and sharp in his speech, this man was very peaceable and not a bad fellow, and I asked that he be set free to live with us.

"Oh, what a pity!" exclaimed Popóv. "Just yesterday we gave him five more years!"

After that we never again heard anything about Pável.

With this case I may say that my friendly relations with Popóv came to an end. Afterwards, there came others . . .

Now that I have come this far, I simply don't feel like writing any further.

What awaited us in the future?

Arrests, trials, detention, prisons, convict transport—all so repellent, savage, and useless.

Anyone could plainly see that we had come together for a life of peaceful labor. We did not hide the fact that we had our own beliefs and were trying to live by them. We made no attempt to force these beliefs on anyone else; but when we were asked about them, we gave straightforward answers, concealing nothing.

What happiness it was to "live life to the fullest"—oppressing no one, groveling before no one, openly telling the truth and doing just what we wished, with the only condition being that we should harm no one else; living joyfully, without bitterness and without the slightest fear!

I remember how pained I was much later, in the camps, when I heard a petty thief say I had a "crafty look."

On his tongue that expression meant that I had already lost the ability to "live life to the fullest," to be a free man even in unfreedom. I had never felt so offended by any kind of curses, any kind of slander, as I felt from that "crafty look." But did I perhaps feel so hurt because I sensed some measure of truth in it?

And so this was the principal content of our life in the commune—life with our eyes and hearts wide open to all of God's world, living life to the fullest, without any "crafty look."

I have already said that we decided to put in a water system, and those water pipes led to the events that I will tell about now. Dimítry Morgachëv, the commune's authorized representative for purchases and the sale of our output, found the pipes we needed in the salvage dump at Kuznetskstróy. He paid for them and filled out the documents, took two horses and a young boy as a helper, and went to get them. But toward evening the boy came back alone with two empty carts.

"Where is Dimítry? Where are the pipes?"

It turned out that on their way back, Popóv and a militiaman had overtaken them, unloaded the pipes at the Feskí collective farm, and taken Dimítry into custody.

The next day, I went to look for Dimítry. For about three days I kept going first to the militia in Stáry Kuznétsk, then to the First Building to see Popóv, but they kept telling me: "Morgachëv is not here."

"Then where is he?"

"We don't know."

I was dismayed: how could that be? In the waiting room of the First Building I saw people with little bundles. That meant they had come to the First Building with parcels for prisoners in the pre-trial holding cell.

I prepared a little parcel and handed it in the next day in the usual way, addressed "To Morgachëv." I got a little note in reply: "Received everything, thanks. Morgachëv."

This made me feel indignant toward Popóv. He had lied to my face. Why?

The next day, I went back to the First Building. In my soul I heard the message: "Don't go!" But I had to go—I could not abandon a comrade in trouble!

Once again I got a pass to see Popóv. Once again he received me just as pleasantly in his office.

"What brings you back again, Mazúrin?"

Without a word, I took out my piece of paper with the signature "Morgachëv" on it and laid it on his desk.

Popóv blushed all over.

"Wait, I'll be right back." And he went out.

Afterward another military man, unknown to me, came in and said: "Come with me."

We went down to the first floor and through a long corridor. On each side were blank doors, each with a one-way peephole. Afterwards I came to know those pre-trial cells all too well.

At the end of the corridor, one room was open. A military man was sitting in it, and he said to me: "Sit here."

"What are you under arrest for?" he asked me.

I suddenly understood everything, but I disagreed with it, and I answered that I was not under arrest, I was a free man.

"You are?" he said doubtfully.

Soon there was a change in duty officers. The old one handed over the prisoners and the new one received them, opening the doors of the cells and counting the prisoners, who stood in a row facing the door. When the door of the cell opposite the duty room was opened, the prisoners stood up in a row, and both duty officers and two more men from security began to count them, standing with their backs to me. Without taking long to think about it, I went behind their backs and started down the corridor. They did not notice it. At the end of the corridor, on a stool at the door to the street, sat a guard with a rifle and bayonet on which were stuck the passes of those who had already left the building. He raised up and said: "Your pass."

I answered: "Without a pass," and kept walking. He sat back down, and I took hold of the doorknob. Out there was the street and freedom, but behind me along the corridor I heard the heavy tread of running feet and shouts: "Stop him! Stop him!"

They grabbed me, not very delicately, of course, so that my shirt started to rip, and they locked me up in the toilet. I took out my notebook and tore out what addresses there were in it, so as not to involve anybody else, and flushed it all down the toilet. The commandant arrived shortly.

"Who doesn't recognize the authorities here?" He took me back upstairs to the office of the head of the NKVD (at that time Popóv was already serving as his assistant).

The commandant sat at the table, with Popóv beside him.

"How did you get the idea of running away?"

"I did not run away. I left as a free man."

"What sort of free man are you!" Popóv yelled savagely, rolling up his sleeves with a curse and running up to beat me.

I stood there calmly, repeating: "I am a free man." Popóv did not bring himself to strike me after all, and the arm he had raised overhead dropped to his side.

"Throw him in with the criminals!"

It was very crowded in the cell, and there were innumerable bedbugs. I found a place for myself under the bunks. There was more room down there, and I wanted to be alone and calm down. Prisoner counts were made in the morning and evening. Everybody went out into the corridor and lined up in two rows.

The devil take all that comedy! I did not go out for the prisoner count. They dragged me out from under the bunks by my feet and took me out to the corridor, and then to the lockup.

The next day, I was taken to the office of the commandant of the jail house. At the desk sat a big, powerful man with a serious, stern, and some-what sad face. He raised his head, stared at me intently, and asked quietly:

"Why don't you line up for the prisoner count?"

"Why do I have to stand in line before you? What are we? Were we born differently into this world? Are we not alike?"

"That's right," he said, still speaking quietly. "But you see, we work here; we have to count everybody, and it is crowded in the cell—it is impos-sible to make a count. I advise you to get in line for the prisoner count."

"All right," I answered, to my own surprise. I do not know why it turned out that way. Probably because he talked seriously, quietly, and simply, like a human being.

Meanwhile, this is what took place at the commune. Toward evening two men drove up in a cart and asked to stay overnight. They were admit-ted. The next day they got up early, hitched up the cart, and drove up to the steps of the house. At that moment Kleménty Kraskóvsky came out on the porch. One of the two visitors suddenly threw Kleménty into the cart, jumped on top of him, and pointed a revolver at him. The other one jumped into the driver's seat and drove the horses down the street at a gallop. It was early and the street was empty, but Nína Lapáyeva happened to be out there, and she grabbed hold of Kleménty's leg and ran alongside the cart, shouting at the top of her voice:

"They've stolen Kleménty! They've stolen Kleménty!"

So they carried him off, and he turned up in the jail house. I found out about it when I heard a voice in the corridor calling out the name "Kraskóv-sky."

At that time in the Stalingraders' commune, Ioánn Dobrotolyúbov, Em-manuíl Dobrotolyúbov, and Vasíly Matvéyevich Yefrémov were at the river tarring a boat, and some people drove up and arrested them. They lay down, just as Seryózha Popóv had done in his time in similar circumstances. When he was arrested and told to follow them, he refused to knuckle under. He lay down and said: "Dear brothers, I refuse to corrupt you by obeying." The Stalingraders were put into the cart just as they were, barefooted, without their hats, and lightly dressed. In the First Building they declared a hunger strike and went without food for about ten days as a protest. And so about two weeks passed. Morgachëv was allowed to return home. Our pipes were hauled to the commune, and running water was installed.

The five of us were subjected to an investigation. The investigator, whose name, it seems, was Veselóvsky, was a pleasant young man. Once I was sitting with him in his office and he was jotting something down, and I said to him: "You really ought to give up this useless business. You are wasting your own time, and you are tearing people away from their work."

"But what could I do then?" asked Veselóvsky.

"You're a healthy peasant boy, you could go out and mow hay—that would be a lot more useful."

Veselóvsky laughed loud and sincerely. At that moment Popóv came in.

"Popóv, Popóv!" Veselóvsky called out, still laughing merrily. "Listen to what he's suggesting to us. To give up our harmful work and go out and mow hay!"

Popóv made a wry face and went out.

"No, Bórya," said Veselóvsky, no longer laughing. "I'm a corrupted man, I'm no good for mowing hay."

Once, about four o'clock in the afternoon, Kleménty and I were summoned from the cell into the corridor. There stood Ioánn, Emmanuíl, and Vasíly Matvéyevich, pale and thin from their ten-day hunger strike, and all still barefooted, bareheaded, and wearing long shirts with no belts. We greeted one another.

Where were they sending us? As it turned out, to court. From the late hour and the fact that nobody from the commune was there, we understood that they wanted to try us in secret, so as to avoid any undue clamor, since they had arrested us without any grounds. That aroused our indignation, and we decided on the spot that we would take no part in the trial.

At that time court was held in one of the long, low, wooden barracks out of which Stálinsk was temporarily built at that time (1932). We stopped before the doors of the court and did not go in. In response to all questions why, we kept silent. Two men took me by the arms and pulled me in, and did the same with Kleménty. The Stalingraders lay down on the ground. Two men picked them up by the arms and a third by the legs and dragged them through the narrow passageway to the doors of the barrack. Chance passersby looked on perplexedly at this unusual scene, which took place seriously and in total silence. They finally sat us down on the defendants' bench. Gathered in the empty courtroom were a few individuals whose interest was aroused by what was taking place, and the guards.

"On your feet! Court is in session!" resounded the cry. The judges came in. We kept our seats.

"On your feet!" shouted the judge. "What's the matter with you—are you deaf?"

We kept silent. The judges stood and talked about something among themselves, then sat down.

"Do you know what you are accused of?"

Silence.

"What is your name?" they asked the first of us.

Silence.

"And yours?"

Silence.

The third and fourth also kept silent. I was the fifth.

"Your name?"

I kept silent.

"Take off your cap!" I kept silent and did not move. Someone came up from behind, took off my cap, and put it down beside me.

Speaking requires an effort, but it is just as hard to keep silent, and that language is just as powerful and eloquent!

"So do you want to know what you are accused of?"

Silence.

The bill of indictment was read—some sort of farfetched, insignificant accusations.

Again each of us was asked in turn whether we wanted to say anything about the indictment. We all kept silent. The defendants were silent, and there was complete quiet in the courtroom. Only the judges kept talking—at times quietly and at times losing their composure and becoming irritable.

"Call the witnesses!"

In came Fatúyev, the chairman of the Yesaúl village soviet. He started by saying that we Tolstoyans agitated the inhabitants, and that Kraskóvsky had given him books by Tolstóy on war and the state.

At that point Kraskóvsky could not contain himself.

"What lies are you telling?" he shouted, jumping up from his seat. "You yourself asked me to give you something to read by Tolstóy!"

"Wait, wait, defendant; you will have the floor in a moment," joyfully shouted the judge.

The silent tension that had reigned in the courtroom was broken, and a sigh of relief, along with a nervous giggle, could be heard in the audience. Kleménty realized his blunder, and he sat down and again kept silent.

Thus ended the trial. None of us said another word. Kleménty and I, as members of a commune with a registered charter, got half a year of imprisonment under Article 109, the one for officials; and the Stalingraders, who had no official charter, got two years apiece under Article 61 for nonfulfillment of state tasks.

The arrest was illegal, the charge inflated. The sentence was light—just enough, they thought, to get the "big shots" away from the misled masses.

The trial was over. The judges left. We sat there in silence. Veselóvsky came up to me.

"Let's go, Bórya," he said gently.

I got up and left. So did Kleménty. The other three were carried out in the same way they had been carried in.

The commune of course appealed to the Central Executive Committee in Moscow. The sentence was revoked, and after six or seven months of imprisonment we were set free. But Kleménty and I were forbidden to live in the commune.

Incidentally, I will say that before, during, and after that time, whenever any members of the commune were imprisoned, we always helped them. We would send special people with parcels, money, clothing, and a whole pile of letters from the commune, which were of course passed on somehow in secret. Later they would be read with delight somewhere around a campfire in the taiga.

Life in the commune took its usual course. Kleménty and I went back, but the prohibition against living there hung over our heads.

In the fall of 1933, a long string of empty carts went past our commune settlement in the direction of the Stalingraders' World Brotherhood community. They drove up to the Stalingraders' settlement and ordered them to get together and load up their belongings.

Where to? What for? It turned out that there was an order (whose, I do not know) for them to be evicted. They would not go. But they were loaded on just the same, and their little clay cottages were left empty. In autumn, without funds, all of them—young and old—were torn away from their pitiful little huts and taken off into the unknown, to new, empty places in bleak Siberia.

The victims of this eviction were sent across to the other bank of the Tom. The long procession reached the settlement of Abagúr. They walked slowly and everybody sang, and along the sides the crowd of villagers grew larger and larger. They were brought to the Abagúr harbor. There a train of empty freight cars was brought up, and everybody was loaded onto it, with still more singing. The train was supposed to have started long before, but as soon as they finished one song, the engineer standing beside the car would beg them: "Please sing just one more!"

In Novosibírsk they were all loaded onto barges, and to the accompaniment of their songs, the barges floated off down the river Ob. They were unloaded at the harbor in Kozhévnikovo and settled in a place named after a little stream flowing nearby, the Téka.

Even there they did not disappear. They lived through the winter scattered among the huts of the local peasants, and in the spring they started putting up their own little houses on a new empty plot of ground, tilling the soil by hand, since they no longer had any livestock.

What were the reasons for this eviction from our land—an eviction that, we must assume, was sanctioned by somebody higher up? The point was that our commune and the Peaceful Plowman cooperative had charters registered with the agricultural agencies, but the World Brotherhood community and the groups affiliated with it had refused to have a charter and get it registered. They did not want to be on the books of the village soviet, give their names to the representatives of the government, or accept and fulfill any kind of obligations, or pay taxes.

Many of our settlers thought this was more consistent with the purity of Tolstóy's ideas and with free life outside the government. The firmness with which the members of that community accepted punitive measures against their way of life attracted sympathy, and later some members of our own commune and the Peaceful Plowman cooperative left us voluntarily and moved to the new settlement.

We understood their motives and sympathized with them, but just the same we held to our position that even though we ideally did not share the state forms of life, we had to take into consideration that people all around us were living that way, and we had to find some kind of common language and establish human relations with them, especially since we were often in touch with them ourselves. We saw that we too were still far from free of the same shortcomings that were present in our neighbors, and we could not be too proud and standoffish. We needed to forgo some of our interests but firmly hold to what was most important and firmly established among us, which we could not give up.

This point of view was less attractive, but it corresponded more to our real moral level.

The World Brotherhood community was taken away from us, but another agricultural cooperative with a charter, the Sower, was organized on our parcel of land. It was formed by members of our own commune. They wanted to stay on our land. We turned over to them a proportional share of the livestock, grain, buildings, and property. The land they got was basically what had formerly been used by the liquidated World Brotherhood community. Their separation took place peaceably and quietly. It did not contradict our basic purpose, which was that all settlers would unite freely, according to their own desires and inclinations, in agricultural associations. Our relations remained good, and no rupture occurred; but still it was painful for me when I learned about it after returning from Moscow, where I had gone to get permission once again to live in the commune. There were no ideological differences between us; the reasons were purely material. Two years had gone by in our new place. Our farm was growing stronger, but the personal well-being of the commune members was still very modest, even in regard to food. People would point out:

"Just look, the Peaceful Plowman came along with us, but over there each one already has his own cow, which means they have milk, sour cream, butter; and they have chickens and eggs. Over here, milk still goes first of all to the children, and we grown-up working people don't always get any. As for sour cream and butter, there's no use even thinking about it—for us it's borshch and potatoes, potatoes and borshch."

That was true, but they forgot that those in the cooperative focused their main attention on the welfare of their own family, and shut themselves off from the rest. But the commune did not shut itself off; it reached out to those who needed help and had nothing but big families with small children, often without the head of the family. For example, we took in several families of former Subbótniks. They had been acquainted earlier with the Uralians and had lived among them, but they asked to join our commune. Why? Because the cooperative members exhausted themselves catering to their own families and had neither the strength nor the means to take in destitute families with a lot of children; but the commune did take them in—gave them a place at the table and a corner to live in, and let them join in the commune life on an equal basis with everybody else. The same reception was given to several single persons—old people who had nowhere to lay their heads. Alyósha Vorónov and Agáfya Serébrennikova seemed to be closer in their views to the Peaceful Plowman, but they did not go there. They were somehow attracted to us.

The commune kept getting more and more mouths to feed, especially "small fry," but our herd of cattle grew more slowly, and this again meant we had to share, and our people psychologically had already begun to get tired of that, which was understandable. On these grounds, admission was refused to several good people who wanted to join us but were turned down when a lot of people grumbled. And of course, by refusing we offended people who had been beaten down by life and deprivation and expected brotherly help from us as people who were close to them—people whom they trusted.

The commune took on many other social concerns, which it considered no less important than personal and family well-being. On the whole, the commune members agreed that we would arrive in our own way at a standard of living at least equal to that of the cooperators, but without sidestepping or turning away from the social needs that we encountered in our path at present.

Besides losing some manpower to the Sower cooperative, we also lost some "hand-farmers." There were not very many of them. They remained members of the commune, but they took an individual plot of land, built little huts on it, and worked independently. We understood the hand-farmers and their motives: to work without the help of livestock. We sympathized with their idea and took an interest in their work. Among us there lived such a well-known supporter of intensive hand-farming as Yevgény Ivánovich Popóv, whose extremely interesting book *The Profitable Garden* had been published by Intermediary, the Tolstoyan publishing house. We knew about the experience in hand-farming of Pável Petróvich Goryáchev, who had achieved bumper crops and high labor productivity with his own aging strength, and without stupefying drudgery but with creative, fascinating, and enjoyable labor. All that was true, but we lost to hand-farming some healthy single men who could have done a great deal for society within the commune, and now their share of the work fell on the shoulders of the rest of the commune members.

There were also the southerners. They were drawn to the South. They begged for the South. They said: "We are vegetarians, our whole occupation is gardening. What sort of gardening is there in Siberia? We ought to move to the South." Ideally, almost all of us agreed with them, but practically we could not accept that. How could they move away and abandon the whole commune? And for what kind of land? Who would provide it? Where would they get the means? What we had achieved, not only economically but also by establishing the nucleus of a society based on new principles, was something we could not break up. A few individual hotheads did leave. And it turned out that they weakened our general strength here and failed to accomplish anything there, in their new place.

I happen to have preserved the following statistics. In the spring of 1933, the commune had 300 inhabitants, of whom 110 were of working age and 190 were children. We had a school and, in summer, a kindergarten and day nursery. Number of horses: 27. In 1932 (the second year of our resettlement) we delivered over 140 tons of vegetables to Kuznetskstróy. In the winter of 1932 our hothouse was in operation, and we delivered over 3,000 fresh cucumbers.

We signed an agreement with the Fruit and Vegetable Stores contracting to supply them with vegetables from fifteen hectares of garden space.

Despite the decree of the Central Executive Committee and the District Executive Committee on allocation of land to the commune no later than the spring of 1932, the commune had not yet been confirmed in its land allocation, and some of the land that at first belonged to our parcel was cut away for neighboring organizations. In the spring of 1932, our commune did not have enough land to fulfill its sowing plan.

The director of the regional land agency, Comrade Mináyev, sent a telegram to the Kuznétsk District Executive Committee asking either that more land be allocated to us immediately or else that our sowing plan be lowered to fit the actual amount of land we had. But nothing came of it, and the commune was saddled with the obligation to deliver forty-four tons of grain to the state in 1933, in connection with the increase in the sowing plan, whereas we were still supposed to be exempt as resettlers from deliveries of any kind.

Elections. I do not remember in just which year, but during that time, elections were called for the government agencies. A representative from town came out to us to hold a meeting. A lot of people came for it. They also came from the Sower and the Peaceful Plowman—the dining hall was filled. The representative made his speech.

The general meeting refused to take part in the elections and noted in the minutes: "We, being followers of Leo Tolstóy, reject violence and the organization of human social life by means of governmental violence; and for this reason we can still submit and fulfill whatever is demanded of us that does not contradict our conscience, but we cannot take part in the organization of this violence."

The representative asked for a vote on both proposals. Not a single hand was raised in favor of participating in the elections. It was half-dark in the large hall. There was only a kerosene lantern on the chairman's table, and the back rows could not be seen. The chairman stood up on a bench and raised the lantern higher so as to light up the back rows, and then repeated: "Not a single hand."

That ended the matter.

In the life of the commune, our school—a nongovernmental school—stood somewhat apart because of its particular importance.

The question of a school had arisen in the commune from the very first days of our resettlement. The children must be taught—about that there were no differences of opinion. But we all understood that in addition to the teaching of reading and writing, the school's task was to teach moral principles and build character. This was at least as important as reading and writing and a formal education. We knew that literacy and all the sciences could work to the harm of people if there were no attention to building character in our children, instilling in them the human qualities of reason and goodness through which a person really becomes a human being. Then knowledge becomes a tool in one's hands for serving the welfare of all humankind. For

Anna Andréyevna Goryáin-ova, one of the teachers in the Life and Labor School, with twenty-two of her pupils.

Gútya Tyurk, his wife Sónya, and his brother Gítya, photographed on the outskirts of Moscow in 1930, before leaving for the Life and Labor Commune in Siberia, where they spent their winters teaching in the school and their summers working as "hand-farmers."

Mikhaíl Gorbunóv-Posádov and the Tyurk brothers were close friends. In 1934 he visited them at the commune in Siberia, where this photograph was taken of him and Gútya Tyurk.

After the Second World War he visited them again at the home of Gítya in the Siberian town of Biysk, where this photograph was taken.

that reason we decided that all our children's teachers should be members of our commune, sharing the views of Leo Tolstóy that were common to our whole society.

Now I will quote some excerpts from a document that by chance was somehow, somewhere, preserved throughout those turbulent years. It is called "A Short History of the School in the Tolstoyan Life and Labor Commune in 1931–1934." The author of these notes was probably Mítya Páshchenko.

The first year of teaching, 1931–32

In the spring of 1931, when the resettled commune members had just begun to gather in Altái, when the commune had only a few huts and people were unbelievably crowded together, sleeping on the floor or lying side by side in attics, when people were bent under the weight of their heavy work, hastening on the one hand to plant the gardens and grain fields, and on the other to build at least the minimum of dwellings for the daily arrival of more and more settlers—at this very time, the groundwork was laid for the future school of the commune.

Slowly, log by log, the school building went up. By the autumn of 1931 it was ready.

Autumn, with its cold rains and early frosts, came all too soon for people unaccustomed to Siberian winters. Hurrying to finish their urgent work in the market gardens, they were not able to complete their housing. Meanwhile, it got very cold in the attics, and by the start of the school year the school building was fully occupied: forty-four people were living jam-packed in it.

The children found themselves in a sad plight. There were fifty of them in need of schooling. We had teachers, several of them experienced, with years of service; and we had a few textbooks and a little paper—but no schoolrooms. Right then, around the first of October, is when we began our "wandering schools," which moved from hut to hut—one day here, the next day there. They were welcomed everywhere. Despite the crowding and the inconvenience of the noise and dirt produced by the children, they were still welcomed. From early morning the children would crowd around their teachers' doors and ask: "Will we start soon? Which hut will we study in today?" The whole crowd, carrying their benches, tables, books, and other school supplies with them, would follow their teacher through the commune in search of a refuge where—for lack of tables—they could write on windows and trunks.

At that time we had a visit from the inspector of the Department of People's Education, Comrade Némtsev. At a called meeting of the whole commune, he protested against such an independent school as ours, called it illegal, declared it closed, and proposed that the commune open another school with exactly the same program as that required for all other schools, and with teachers invited from the city Department of People's Education.

In response to this, the general meeting answered that the commune could not accept exactly the same program, but only those parts of it which did not contradict the views that were in the spirit of Leo Tolstóy (in other words, without militarization, without arousing in the children a spirit of hatred toward anyone at all, and without suggesting to the children the legality of violence).

Then Comrade Némtsev declared the school closed for good and warned the teachers that they would be held legally responsible.

The commune submitted a petition to the People's Commissar of Education requesting that they be allowed to continue their school with the peculiarities described above, which were inherent in it as a school embodying Leo Tolstóy's ideas.

Whether or not it was a result of this petition, our school continued its existence right up to the end of the school year without any special pressures from outside. At the end of November (1932) the pupils were already using the new school building, which by then had been emptied of lodgers. But their study conditions could scarcely be called tolerable even then: in the single big room of the school building, three groups studied in the morning and two in the afternoon; and because of the continued lack of space, the building also housed the shoe shop, the harness shop, the joiner's bench, the grindstone, a food larder, and a medicine chest.

Second school year: 1932–33.

In the autumn, just before the opening of school, Comrade Nortóvich (the school director in the neighboring village of Feskí) came with a proposal to "coordinate" our school with the Department of People's Education in Stálinsk and suggested that somebody from our group of teachers go to see the director of the city Department of People's Education.

In the meeting about this matter with Comrade Blagovéshchensky, the director of the city Department of People's Education, he revealed a completely negative attitude toward our school: we were to have no school of our own; the government program must be carried out in its entirety, without any kind of changes, and with the inclusion of militarization and the Pioneer movement.[25] No teachers from among our commune members would be admissible.

Then in November here came a director for the school assigned by the Stálinsk Department of People's Education. Upon her arrival a general meeting was called, which refused to accept her as the new director.

At that time classes in our school were in full swing, with five groups totaling more than eighty pupils. In general outline, the classes were conducted according to the regular school program. The school building had been cleared of everything extraneous, and it was divided into three classrooms by wooden partitions, which were taken down when general meetings were held.

On 21 March 1933, the school was visited by a commission of three persons: the representative of the regional education department; Comrade Blagovéshchensky, the director of the Stálinsk city education department; and Comrade Nortóvich, the director of the Feskí school. Comrade Blagovéshchensky announced first of all that as a result of his trip to Moscow, relations with our school had changed; specifically, (1) we were now permitted to have a school with teachers from among our own members and (2) without militarization; and (3) in our social-studies program, we were permitted to exclude anything that contradicted our convictions—about which, however, there must be an agreement with the city department of education.

In other respects our school must have the appearance of a regular school, on the pattern of the other schools in the Soviet Union.

---

25. Pioneer movement—the Communist-sponsored national organization for children between the ages of ten and fifteen.

In May our teachers went over the four-year program of the People's Commissariat of Education.

"Extract from the minutes of the teachers' meeting in May 1933.

"Social-studies material. The proposed teaching material in all subjects (for example, the material for problems, the examples in grammar, etc.) is closely coordinated with the socialist construction of the USSR, which includes the Five Year Plan, the class struggle, and military affairs. This material will be used in the school of the Life and Labor Commune only to the extent that it does not contradict the principles of Leo Tolstóy's teaching.

"Material in the natural sciences. The material for the study of animal husbandry, hunting, and the fishing industry, studied according to the program with a view to slaughtering animals for food and for technical and scientific purposes, can be studied in the Leo Tolstóy School not for its practical application but only for informational purposes, with a view to developing altruistic feelings toward animals.

"About religion. We avoid thrusting upon children any kind of sectarian religious ideas, but we consider it necessary to give them correct ideas about life and the moral guidance that derives from them (rules for moral conduct), and we also consider it our duty to conduct peaceful work of clarification in the direction of liberation from religious and other superstitions.

"The material proposed for reading outside of class, and also for the learning of songs, can be used to the extent that it does not inculcate feelings of hatred toward anyone.

"General tendency of the school. In our school, we hope to instill in the children a spirit of active communism, that is, a spirit of equality, justice, industriousness, mutual aid, love of peace, and sober, modest behavior."

Third school year: 1933–34.

At the beginning of this school year, the school underwent thorough repair. Walls were built between the three classrooms, a vestibule and cloakroom were added, and benches were acquired. The classes were conducted in two shifts, with five groups totaling 105 pupils.

In addition to the subjects in their general education, the pupils in the fourth and fifth groups also had a rudimentary course in handicrafts—carpentry, lathe work, cooperage, shoemaking, blacksmithing, and dressmaking.

School policies and controls were worked out through meetings (1) of the pupils—by individual classes and all together, (2) of the teachers—for business and pedagogical matters, (3) of the parents, and (4) general—all members of the commune.

The school also carried on club activities outside of class time. They were as follows:

1. Stenographic club, led by Ye. I. Popóv.
2. Art club, led by I. V. Gulyáyev.
3. Singing club, led by A. S. Maloród.
4. Ukrainian club, led by A. A. Goryáinova.

In the evenings there was reading for the schoolchildren (at least twice a week). Once a week they were shown colored pictures in a course on geography and natural science.

Once a week the schoolchildren had an "evening of free games." In addition, at least once a month there were evening gatherings at which the pupils would

sing, recite poetry, give readings, give speeches (topics: Púshkin, Nekrásov, Tur-
génev—their biography and works), and put on plays, such as Tolstóy's "What
Men Live By," Fonvízin's "Young Ignoramus," Semyónov's "Spoiled One,"[26]
and "The Adventures of a Prehistoric Boy."

Excursions. The teachers took the older pupils on several excursions to Stálinsk, where they visited a model school and its workshop, and went to the museum, the theater, and the movies.

The school also had a club for the eradication of illiteracy. Classes were held
in the evenings.

On 27 April 1934, as the school year was drawing to an end, the city education department sent Comrade Blagovéshchensky to visit the commune with the
following notification from the Stálinsk City Soviet:

"Resolved: 1. that the further existence of a private school, outside the government network, is completely inadmissible.

"2. Proposed to Comrade Shlyakhánov, director of the city education department:

"a) that the school of the Life and Labor Commune be immediately included
in the government network of schools within the jurisdiction of the city education
department, and that the necessary funds from the local budget be allocated for
its upkeep;

"b) that the school be staffed with Soviet pedagogues of proven worth who
possess adequate pedagogical experience, who will teach the children in complete
accord with the program of the People's Commissariat of Education.

"3. Confirm by dual appointment the director of Factory School No. 12,
Comrade Blagovéshchensky, as director of the school of the Life and Labor Commune.

"4. Warn the Tolstoyan parents that if they attempt to keep their children
from attending the school, and if they attempt to organize group classes at home
for their children, they will be subjected to the measures of administrative influence provided by the law on universal education.

"5. The Life and Labor Commune is to allocate living quarters to the pedagogical personnel of the school.

"Chairman of the Stálinsk City Soviet Alféyev."

A general meeting of the commune members, first on 1 May and again on 20
May, rejected the decision of the Stálinsk City Soviet and resolved to appeal the
matter to the All-Russian Central Executive Committee and submit a petition that
our school be left as it was.

Mítya Páshchenko's notes about the school end with the school year 1933–
34, but our school continued to exist in 1934–35 and 1935–36. During that
period it once again "wandered," just as at the beginning when we did not
yet have a school building. Now we had a building, benches, and equipment,
but we could not use them. They were kept under lock and key by representatives of the local government.

When that happened, it aroused great indignation among the commune
members. Voices were heard saying:

26. Sergéy Teréntyevich Semyónov (1868–1922)—a self-taught peasant writer who was a
follower of Tolstóy.

"Let's break the lock and be done with it."

"We can't," others answered.

"Why not?"

"That's violence."

"Why, what kind of violence is that? After all, it's a lock, not a man."

Just the same, we decided not to break it, but to continue our own work. And so we did, even though there were more threats that they would seal the building again and arrest the teachers.

I remember one conversation I had with Ycvgény Ivánovich Popóv about the tense situation with the school.

"But the struggle for the school," he said, "seems to be taking on a political character. Is it worth that?"

I disagreed with him.

"What is political about this? We are not going beyond the interests and affairs of the commune."

I walked down the village street and saw coming toward me Anna Stepánovna Malaród, the director of the school, and her husband, Pável Leóntyevich. We stopped, and I told them about the warning and asked them:

"What shall we do?"

Anna Stepánovna looked down, deep in thought, and for a time said nothing.

"Well, what?" I asked her again.

Anna Stepánovna raised her head, looked me straight in the eye, and quietly said with a smile: "So what? We'll keep on."

That shy, gentle, physically frail woman found within herself the strength to make that decision. It was the same with all the other teachers. No one backed out, no one gave up that necessary work.

Meanwhile, events in the commune continued to develop. Another school building was padlocked, and we moved to a third, in the apiary. Teachers from outside began appearing in class—and our teachers and their pupils walked out.

Then on 11 April 1935 there was a trial.

Those put on trial were the teachers Anna Malaród and Kleménty Kraskóvsky, the three members of the commune council, and four members of the Sower cooperative and the Peaceful Plowman cooperative. The teachers from our commune were accused of teaching religious subjects in our school, and all the members of the commune council and the leaders of the cooperatives were charged with refusing to take part in logging.

Half the commune went to the city for the trial. It took place in the same long, low wooden barrack where we had been tried in 1932; but then it had been in secret, while this time the court room was jam-packed with our commune members and cooperators, who had brought with them their suntans from the fields, the white kerchiefs of the women, and the free spirit of the commune—the spirit of cheerful, harmonious people who believed in the rightness of their cause. It even had its moments of comedy. The teacher from the city education department, Zhuk, trying to prove that

Anna Maloród was guilty of teaching religious subjects in our school, declared:

"At school Maloród taught the children to sing Tolstóy's religious song "The Kreutzer Sonata." [27]

In response the whole room burst out in laughter, and even the judges smiled.

But just the same, Anna Stepánovna was sentenced to one year of imprisonment. The other teacher, Kleménty Kraskóvsky, was found innocent. I, as a witness, said:

"My eight-year-old son is a pupil in the first grade, taught by Kraskóvsky. I see that they are learning to draw straight lines, circles, and all sorts of curlicues—they are learning their letters. What sort of religious studies can you give those little tykes?"

The judges said: "That's right," and they acquitted Kraskóvsky.

Sávva Blinóv and Kólya Slabínsky each got two years. Afanásy Nali-váyko got one.

Those who were convicted were taken off to jail, and all the rest of us went with them. When the gates of the prison were opened and our friends began to go through, someone shouted:

"Let's go with them!"

"Yes, let's do!" many voices answered in a chorus, and they would have if the calmer ones had not stopped them.

As is well known, from the very first days of the Revolution there were many agricultural communes all over the Soviet Union. From 1934–35 on, they began to be switched over to agricultural cooperatives. The effort was often made to talk us into that too, but we always refused.

Once the chairman of the city soviet, Comrade Lébedev, a big, ruddy, powerful man, came to visit our commune. He asked us to call a general meeting. When we assembled, Lébedev said that communes all over the country were going over to the agricultural-cooperative system, and he suggested that we become a collective farm. We answered that we had come to the commune system through our own conscious choice and our attraction to such a way of life. We were used to living that way, it satisfied us and gave us good results economically, and we saw no reason to give up the commune.

Then Lébedev played his trump card.

"Comrade Stálin has said that at the present time only fools or religious ascetics can live in communes."

In answer to this, we said to Lébedev:

"So be it—we'll be fools, we'll be religious ascetics, but we want to go on living as a commune, and in Comrade Stálin's words there is no direct indication that communes are forbidden."

---

27. "The Kreutzer Sonata" is the title of a story by Tolstóy about sexual passion, marital infidelity, and murder that caused a sensation all over the Western world in the 1890s.

And the general meeting unanimously voted not to become a collective farm.

The alleged reason for giving up the commune system was that economic conditions at that time were not yet ripe for the existence of communes. But we realized that this was not the main thing. The main thing was that the collective farm was a purely economic organization, with governing bodies to run it; but the commune took in a much wider circle of matters connected with its activity. The commune did not have a governing body over it; it had its own council, which decided not only farming questions but questions concerning the whole life of our commune.

In essence, as long as such communes and commune councils existed, there would be no need of soviets as instruments of state power, since state-less communism would already have arrived, just as it said in the Party program. But obviously, at present that was considered untimely.

At this meeting Lébedev insisted; we answered him heatedly, and there were sharp remarks aimed at Lébedev personally. He took offense and started legal action to put a large number of commune members on trial.

The twenty-sixth of April was a Sunday—a fine spring day. We had our usual meeting, with discussions, singing, and the reading of letters from friends. I went up to my home for something and then came back. Kólya Lyubímov met me and said:

"There's a search going on at Mítya Páshchenko's; he is being arrested."

I went over there, even though I had a feeling that I too would not escape. In front of the dining hall I saw several men in the white sheepskin coats and caps of the NKVD. One of them came up to me.

"Are you Mazúrin?"

"Yes."

"Let's go to your house, I need to talk with you."

"All right."

From there on, everything went as might be expected. The search lasted until midnight, so that the children had already gone to sleep and did not see them take me away.

We spent the night on the floor in the schoolhouse: I, Mítya Páshchenko, Dimítry Morgachëv, Kleménty Kraskóvsky, and Yegór Yepifánov, who was then the chairman of the commune council. I do not remember who else was arrested on the first day, but over the next two days there were Gítya and Gútya Tyurk, Anna Grigórevna Bárysheva, Ólya Tolkách, Iván Vasílyevich Gulyáyev, and then sometime later Yákov Deméntyevich Dragunóvsky, who was a hand-farmer but was added to our case.

The next morning, we were taken to the prison in Stáry Kuznétsk. The whole commune saw us off, singing songs as they walked. On the bank of the Tom, beyond our settlement, they sang their last one:

> Onward, comrades, onward march;
> For you a glorious day has dawned.
> Break your weapons into pieces;
> Among us, killers shan't be found.

There they remained behind, and we went on, jumping across the spring rivulets flowing in the Tom, which was still covered with ice.

The commune was of course greatly disturbed by the arrest of such a large number of its members, and appealed to Kalínin. The procurator, Comrade Volobúyev, was sent out from Moscow. He had talks with several members of the commune, and talked an especially long time with Ványa Zúyev in the presence of the local procurators and the chairman of the city soviet. Evidently he gave the order to treat us courteously, not to limit our communications, and not to call us for questioning at night.

The investigation was conducted by Stepán Ilyích Yástrebchikov. His hooked nose fitted his hawkish name [which came from the Russian word for "hawk"]. I cannot say anything bad about the way he conducted the investigation; but of course he was bound by the biased directive to accuse us of counterrevolution.

Once I asked him:

"You took all my correspondence and notes. Where do you see any counterrevolution in them?"

He picked up a piece of paper on which I had started to write a poem—still unfinished—sometime in 1932 when I was in solitary confinement in the prison at Tomsk, and he read:

> From the muffled walls of the prison,
> Buried under stones,
> We silently cry out to you
> And call on you to rise . . .

"And that—isn't it counterrevolution?" he asked harshly, raising his voice.

"Stepán Ilyích," I said, "why are you doing it like that? Read on."

And he read further:

> To rise without bayonets,
> To rise without blood,
> To cast down all the fetters
> That have ensnared our reason . . .

"So there!" I said. "Where is the counterrevolution?"

Yástrebchikov did not answer, but I am not sure matters remained as they had been when he first read it, giving a false interpretation to my thought.

That is the way things went for seven long months.

It would take a big book to describe all of this, but my purpose is to tell about the commune and make it very short, and here there is an obstacle in my way. I really must lay this aside, but just the same I will tell at least a little, a few incidents.

Yákov Deméntyevich Dragunóvsky held the opinion that he should not be in prison and that he should not enter it willingly. When he was summoned and called out of the prison, he would go; but when he was taken back to the prison gates (for example, after interrogations), he would not go. He would lie down and say:

"I don't need to go in there."

I see it all as if it were today: a bright summer day, with the open cell windows looking out at the prison yard (at that time there were not yet any shutters on them); and everybody's attention was attracted to the entrance checkpoint, where some sort of noise and movement could be heard. Then the procession would appear in the prison yard. Two guards—Burundúk and somebody else—would carry in Dragunóvsky sitting on their crossed arms. Greetings and guffaws could be heard from all the windows above. Sitting in state like a tsar on the throne, with his arms around the shoulders of the guards and his beard fluttering in the wind, Yákov Deméntyevich would smile and answer their greetings with a wave. The guards too were smiling. All this somehow took place good-naturedly; Dragunóvsky was relaxed and not bitter, and the same mood infected those around him.

Yákov Deméntyevich continually wrote very long letters from prison, whole articles addressed to Kalínin and other prominent figures in the party and the government. What did he write about, that not too literate peasant from Smolénsk? No, not about himself personally, and not about his hard fate—he did not think about himself. He wrote about the contradictions between the state system and the ideals of communism; about the uselessness and harm of violence as a means of progressing toward communism; about the hard lot of the peasantry, about the meaning of morality and the life of the spirit. He did not argue, did not accuse, but appealed to the human conscience of the rulers. Where those letters finally ended up, I do not know.

It was entirely different with Anna Grigóryevna Bárysheva. She also spoke and acted frankly and boldly, but she seethed with indignation, almost with bitterness, and this mood was communicated to those around her.

Somehow, on some occasion or other, Anna Grigóryevna suggested that we begin a hunger strike. She passed a note to me. I said I was against it. I could never understand hunger strikes declared by political prisoners, and in recent times by everybody else. Even as it was, we were harmed by this deprivation of our freedom and health. So why should we ourselves contribute to it? Our aim should be just the opposite: to preserve our health, strength, cheerfulness, and calm; and to protest, should this be necessary, with reasonable words and actions. And here began a whole discussion—through notes. We had to inform everyone and find out everyone's opinion. I added my own note to Anna Grigóryevna's, and they went further and further until they had made the whole round. And then, of course, our notes had to make the rounds again in the opposite direction so that we could know everybody's opinion. The bundle of notes became quite thick; and once, when Gítya was passing them on to me, they "tripped us up" and took the notes away from us, and then the whole correspondence went to the investigator, for the dossier.

The hunger strike was rejected. Only Yegór Yepifánov supported Anna Grigóryevna.

Our trial took place from 20 to 24 November 1936 in a session of the special collegium of the West Siberian Regional Court.

There is nothing interesting to tell about the whole procedure of the trial. None of us acknowledged that we were guilty of any counterrevolutionary activity. The following sentences were handed down: four of us were acquitted; Iván Gulyáyev and Dimítry Morgachëv got three years; Yákov Dragunóvsky, Gústav Tyurk, and I got five years; and Anna Bárysheva got ten years—all under the provisions of Article 58.[28]

We were truly glad that four of us went home. We knew the commune would not abandon us—they would plead for us. And indeed, they sent Ványa Zúyev to Moscow, and he managed to catch Mikhaíl Ivánovich Kalínin on the run when he was hurrying off somewhere and told him about us. Ványa has since died, and I do not remember exactly what Mikhaíl Ivánovich replied to him; but with the beginning of the year 1937, events took a different turn.

Day and night, singly and in "bunches," without trial or investigation, and sometimes even without an arrest warrant, they began arresting people who were guilty of nothing whatever—picking them up and sending them off without a trace in a direction from which none of them ever came back. The relatives who kept inquiring about them would receive only a piece of paper informing them that no guilt had been discovered and that the person they inquired about was completely rehabilitated.

The piece of paper remained, but not the person.

We too had our Judases, probably just like every other organization and movement. They would help to destroy innocent people in order to protect themselves, to save their own skins—weak, wretched, frightened people. But still they were only a few individuals.

A dark cloud of terror swept over the commune from those arrests. Some were calm, others trembled and slept away from home every night—after all, who wants captivity? So they kept away from it.

At that time when dozens of men, heads of families, were being arrested, many, fearing everything, began burning their letters, notes, and books.

At that same time, our school became a government school; even the teachers had disappeared.

After our trial, the district authorities stopped considering our commune a commune, and treated it like some sort of collective farm.

Notification would be sent to the members of our commune about taxes and all kinds of deliveries—eggs, milk, meat, hides, and so on, even though no one in the commune had his own farmstead, livestock, or gardens. Naturally, no one paid anything, and the lengthy proceedings dragged on.

28. Article 58—the notorious article in the Soviet Criminal Code that was most commonly used by the Soviet authorities to punish anyone they considered to be a potential or actual threat to the Soviet state.

1937

I have a list of those among us who were arrested in 1937. The list is a grim one, but of course the names alone say little. Each one of them stood for a living man, with his own life, thoughts, dreams, and convictions—a man with close relatives, a wife, children, parents. Something brief should be written about each of them, but that is beyond my ability now.

Twenty-four of them never came back alive.

In 1937 Yákov Deméntyevich Dragunóvsky and Anna Grigóryevna Bárysheva died in the camps.

Of those who came back broken in health after spending ten years in labor camp, three have since died.

Besides those who lost their lives, many other members were taken from the commune either after a trial or without a trial—some not for long, some for ten years, and some for eighteen (ten years of imprisonment and eight years of forced residence).

Even though the people who were forcibly taken away from us to Kozhévnikovo in 1933 were not members of our commune, still they belonged to our Tolstoyan resettlement; so my list includes twenty-five of them who I know were arrested in 1937, almost all of whom lost their lives.

Often in frank discussions we would hear such statements as this from Communists—highly placed figures, ordinary members, and investigators, as well as simple working people:

"It's all well and good, what you Tolstoyans say. That will all come about—a stateless society without violence and without frontiers, sober and industrious, and without private property. But this is not the right time for it—right now it is even harmful."

But we did not understand that. The "Kingdom of God" that lived within us kept nudging us toward carrying out our ideals immediately, without delay. Putting off the fulfillment of our ideals until some indefinite time in the future seemed to us amazingly similar to the teachings of the church people, who urged us to be patient and endure our poverty and deprivation so that we would acquire the blessings we longed for in some future life beyond the grave.

Now more than half a century has passed since the Revolution, and the future that everyone longs for is not only getting no closer, it is even getting further and further away. Right here, close at hand, new forms of enslavement and violence keep arising. And again they try to console the doubters just as before:

"This is not the right time for it. The time will come . . ."

My thoughts keep turning back to my list of the friends who lost their lives in 1937, and I want to say something about at least a few of them now.

Semyón Chekmenyóv was a strong, fair-haired, quiet, hard-working man. He came from the Molokáns in Samára who had resettled sometime in the past in the Orenbúrg steppes, at the village of Rayóvka. Influenced by the

Children in the Life and Labor Commune.

Dinner for the commune children.

sermons of Aleksándr Dobrolyúbov, Chekmenyóv and his friends gave up their literal sectarian interpretation of life. There was no arrest warrant for Semyón. They seized his older brother Alekséy, who had been sentenced in 1916, during the tsarist period, to twelve years at hard labor for refusing to be a soldier and was freed from a Kazán prison by the Revolution. But when they put Alekséy into the car, they noticed that one arm dangled paralyzed at his side and he could not move his neck (he had suffered from encephalitis). At that moment Semyón came out on the porch. So they took Alekséy out of the car (what could they do with somebody like that?) and took Semyón instead.

Vásya Bormotóv was also one of the Dobrolyúbovians in Rayóvka. Like Alekséy Chekmenyóv, he too was sentenced in 1916 to twelve years at hard labor. During the Civil War, the Orenbúrg region was under the control of a ruler (Dútov, as I remember), who like all rulers had his own laws to sanction his lawlessness. Under these laws the peasants too had the "obligation" to fulfill all kinds of obligations. So their community in the village of Rayóvka was ordered to furnish horses for the army. They refused and said: "We cannot give them for war."

Soon the rumor went around that a punitive detachment was headed for Rayóvka. What should they do? Everybody dressed up in clean clothes, the women in white kerchiefs, and they gathered in the village square and began singing their Dobrolyúbov hymns.

Cossack horsemen appeared in the distance. Paying no attention to them, the community members continued singing. The Cossacks listened and then, one after another, took off their hats. They stood in silence, then left without saying a word.

Kóstya Bormotóv got caught by accident when he was just a young boy. He was the driver of a wagon that took a load of prisoners to the city. They left him there too.

Vasíl Golóvko was a peasant from Poltáva Province, a man of powerful build and deliberate speech. He had a gift for mechanics. In Ukraine he built a windmill all by himself, which brought him a lot of trouble even though he worked alone and hired no labor. They tried to wear him down with all kinds of taxes, but he wouldn't pay them.

"Why should I pay you?" he would say to the tax agent. "Are you trying to swindle me?"

Nikoláy Alekséyevich Goryáinov was a tall, skinny man with a white beard. He was one of the oldest people in the commune. Long before the Revolution, he and a few friends wanted to help the peasants market their products on cooperative principles, and in the Vólogda backwoods they organized a collection point for milk, where it could be churned into butter. They would float their product down the river on rafts to the industrial centers, where it was sold. At one time he worked in the cooperative colony at Krínitsa, on the Black Sea. He was one of the pioneers of fruit growing in the Caucasus, where he also organized producers' cooperatives for the marketing of fruit. I remember when he came to our commune and he and I climbed the hill to our fields. A breathtaking view opened up of the mountains covered with those thick, dark forests, and the shining, winding ribbon of the Tom River with its broad floodlands covered with undergrowth; and he exclaimed:

"This is where we ought to build a settlement—what beauty!"

"Yes, it's beautiful," I said, "but what about water?"

"Oh, water!" he answered, smiling. "We can put the water under pressure and bring it up this far."

You could feel that this man not only loved beauty but also was brimming with enterprise and inventiveness. On the day when they were arresting others, he went to the well for water. They caught sight of him—an impressive-looking white-haired man.

"Bring him along too!"

Prokóp Kuvshínov was a short, gnarled man from the Nízhny Nóvgorod peasantry, stern-looking, with bushy eyebrows, who pronounced his *o*'s with the provincial northern accent—an experienced gardener. He knew all about farm machinery. He was a good, fair-minded man. He had taken part in the workers' disturbances in 1905, and as a permanent souvenir he carried a deep scar on his head—a mark of Cossack punishment.

Ványa Svinobúrko took his wife's family name, Rutkóvsky. He had been one of the orphaned waifs of the war of 1914–18. He grew up in a children's labor colony near Moscow in which many of our fellow Tolstoyans worked as leaders. But when these colonies were taken over by the bureaucrats of the People's Commissariat of Education, our people had to leave. They organized the Leo Tolstóy Commune not far from the city of Voskresénsk. Ványa went with them and became a member of the commune. He loved horses and peasant work in general, and somehow he was a great success in everything he undertook. He was large, powerful, quiet, and not very talkative, but always cheerful.

Pyotr Ivánovich Karétnikov was from the Volga region. His parents were from the merchant class, but he did not take after them. There was nothing in him of the commercial world, in either his character or his convictions. He sought only the truth. He read a lot and loved books. He also loved farming, especially market gardening.

Ványa Lukyántsev wore a permanent smile, sometimes looking too cheerful. He was subject to fainting spells, and then he would talk to himself, saying things such as:

"Master Rulers, don't bother me, I'm not lying on your ground, I'm lying on the road; anybody can lie on the road, you know . . ."

He had come to us from the cooperative colony of Tolstoyans in Almá-Atá. His illness probably began at the time he told me about. When Kolchák was in Siberia, Ványa worked on the railroad at the Omsk station.[28] The

---

28. Aleksándr Vasílyevich Kolchák (1870–1920) was a Russian naval commander during the First World War, and during the civil war following the October Revolution, he was for a while the leader of the anti-Bolshevik forces in Siberia.

Kolchakians already anticipated their defeat and were ferocious. They arrested two hundred railroad workers and took them outside the city to shoot them. Ványa was in the group. It was at night, in freezing weather, and a heavy snow was falling. They were brought to a halt and for some reason waited a long time. Everyone was freezing, and they huddled together motionless. The convoy of soldiers stood all around. Ványa noticed that one soldier seemed to be dozing as he leaned on his weapon, and he very quietly crept past him. Then he rolled down the high railway embankment and fell through the thin ice into the water of the railway ditch. Covered all over with ice and utterly exhausted, he made his way to the home of a worker acquaintance, knocked on the door, and collapsed unconscious. He was carried in and hidden. Afterwards he and this worker hid under a pile of railway crossties, and from there they watched the departure of the last echelons of Kolchák men, and saw how the bridge across the Irtýsh rose slightly and then collapsed in a heap, blown up by the retreating soldiers.

Mísha and Fédya Katrúkha were still little boys when they came to the commune with their mother and their older brother Grísha. They grew up in the commune, began to understand life, became enthusiastic about hand-farming, and started living apart from the commune in a little clay hut in Happy Valley. Mísha was arrested when he came to his sister's in the commune on 20 October 1937, at four o'clock in the morning. He had spent the night with other people and had come only in the morning, but they were still waiting for him. They caught Fédya in Happy Valley. He refused to go. They stuffed him into a mattress, tied it up, tied it to the tail of a horse, and dragged him that way out of the valley through the snow, then tied him to the sleigh and drove him to the commune. Afterwards one of the guards at the First Building told me that Fédya would not go to the interrogations. They would carry him in their arms to the third story, and would drag him back downstairs by his feet. His head would bump on each stairstep, and he kept silent.

Tíma Morgachëv was the eldest son of Dimítry Morgachëv, a good lad, not yet married. He died in the North of exhaustion in the camps.

Anatóly Ivánovich Fomín was not one of our settlers. He somehow learned about our commune and came to us later. He said he was one of the Freedom group of Canadian Dukhobors, but not a born Dukhobor—he had joined them because of their ideas. He led discussions with the commune members, explaining his world outlook, but I could not understand it; his words seemed foggy to me, not comparable to the clear, profound ideas of Tolstóy. But some people liked his discussions. Once during Anatóly's lecture-discussion, Klcménty asked him about something and then expressed his disagreement. Anatóly then said:

"I declare a hunger strike until Kleménty apologizes."

Kleménty was upset and came to me for advice about what to do.

"But you didn't offend him, did you?"

"No, I just said I didn't agree with him."

"So why should you apologize?"

"Well, he's on a hunger strike."

"So let him have his hunger strike—that's his business," I said.

Anatóly didn't fast long. That kind of behavior was alien and incomprehensible to me—threatening a hunger strike, taking offense because of a difference of opinions. All that had nothing in common with the spirit of our commune—simple, friendly, and free.

Grísha Gúrin was from Túla Province, from a big peasant family—seven brothers. During the First World War he was a prisoner of the Germans. Over there they gave him a lot of literature in the Evangelical (Baptist) spirit, which impressed him. Afterwards, back in Russia, he drew closer to Tolstoyan views. Passionate by nature, he was also passionate in his work. Grísha told how he was sent to work for a farmer while he was a prisoner of war. The farmer told him to plow up a plot of land. Grísha had had no chance to do any peasant work for a long time. His team of horses was good, the plow was light and in good repair, and Grísha plunged into the work heart and soul. When the farmer came back to see how the prisoner was working, and whether he was asleep, the whole field was already plowed. The farmer clutched his head:

"What are you doing? That's not the way we work here—it's impossible!"

When the Sower cooperative separated from our commune, Grísha became its chairman.

I have already mentioned Yákov Deméntyevich Dragunóvsky. He was one of the peasants from Smolénsk Province. Once at a meeting he told us his life story, how he had come to Tolstóy. It stuck in my mind that he had been drafted as a soldier in the First World War. He had sweated out his military drudgery like all the rest, but once during a night attack, he was knocked out by something. When he came to, everything was quiet all around him, and he could not understand where he was or where he should go. For a long time he wandered over the deserted field in darkness, stumbling over fragments of weapons and bodies. Then he began to think: "Why am I here? What do I need here? What use do I have for this rifle? And why should I be killing these Germans?"

He began to think. It was Friedrich II, the famous German martinet, who once said: "If my soldiers ever began to think, not one of them would remain in the army." From that time on, Yákov Deméntyevich stopped being a soldier and became a thinking man.

During the Civil War, he and several like-minded people had gone through a lot of torture because of their refusal to bear arms. He had been saved from death only because Vladímir Chertkóv found out about them and personally appealed to Lénin, and Lénin set them free.

Anna Grigóryevna Bárysheva was the daughter of a peasant. During the 1914 war she was a nurse. Afterwards she taught school. As a human being in our community life, she was calm and even-tempered; but whenever the conversation turned to the unjust government system in our life, to war, or to the hard lot of the peasants, she would tense up and speak sharply, even maliciously. She had often been put on trial, sent to prison, deported.

Pável Leóntyevich Maloród came from the Cossacks of the Kubán region; but once he acquired his Tolstoyan convictions, he broke with their traditions and way of life. He left our commune to live apart as a hand-farmer.

Here I will also mention a few other former members of our commune who left at one time or another for Ukraine and lost their lives there under entirely different conditions and by different hands. That was during the German occupation.

Yevdokíya Timoféyevna Beloúsova, our former teacher, also taught school there and was burned alive in her school by the Germans.

Ilyúsha Pavlénko was tortured to death by the Germans as a partisan.

Borís Nepómnyashchy wanted very much to resettle with us, and even came to us in Siberia; but his wife would on no account join the commune, and the whole family lost their lives in Odessa as Jews.

The epidemic of exterminating innocent people is not the property or invention of any one country. It has spread all over the world, and consequently its causes are not confined to one place: they are far more widespread. It is caused by the fact that people's understanding of the meaning of life, their religion, is faulty, untrue, and does not correspond to the fundamental law of human life—goodness.

During the years 1937 and 1938, the commune could not live a full life: it had lost too many of its members. The people remained the same and still stood firm, but the commune was living out its last days. Finally, on 1 January 1939, it was transformed into an agricultural cooperative, a collective farm. People came back grief-stricken from that meeting, as if they had lost something great and precious.

Seryózha Yúdin then said:

"The commune no longer exists; now everybody can do as they please."

The houses and part of the livestock were divided up—a calf to one person, a cow to another for two households, and a fixed amount of money to another. After long years of life in the commune, people had gotten unaccustomed to such terms as "my house," "my cow," and so on; everything had been "ours." But now under the new system they were forced to turn back to the old one, with which they had freely and consciously broken in the past.

Why?

Pétya Litvínov, Alekséy Shipílov, and Lyóva Alekséyev were convicted as the last members of the commune council. One of the charges against them was aiding "enemies of the people," that is, the commune members who were imprisoned. Faddéy Zablótsky was sent by the court to the prison psychiatric hospital for compulsory treatment. Pétya Litvínov and Lyóva Alekséyev had to serve ten years of imprisonment and eight years of forced residence in the Krasnoyársk Region.

The social and work life of the Life and Labor collective farm started running on a different track. People from the outside, with entirely different convictions, began to merge with the membership of the collective farm. "Labor days," "production norms," and many other terms that we had not known in the commune came into common usage.

One woman had lived in the commune more than fifteen years and was used to thinking of the collective farm as her own and to working on it as conscientiously as possible. She told me:

> We women in the collective farm went out to tie up the rye. Well, I tied it the way I had always tied it before, in big sheaves, tight and clean; and the next day I looked and saw my name on the black list and the other women's names on the red one. Then I began to watch how those who were on the red list worked, and I myself started working like that—any old way, just so it is as fast and as much as possible, with a bit of lying to the brigade leader about the output when it comes time to count the sheaves. Then I looked, and there was my name on the red list!

Another woman told how they started living on the collective farm.

> We women became thieves; all our lives depended on theft. There were no men, and we had to raise our children and feed them. There was no common dining room, as there had been in the commune, and they paid us two hundred grams of bad grain for a labor-day of work—just try to live on that! So you swipe whatever you can. When you come home from work, you walk off with a potato, a beet, a cabbage—depending on where you work, and then at night you sneak off to the piles in the vegetable garden. And you have to feed the cow, too—she's the main provider for the family. All day from dawn to dusk on collective-farm work, and then in your "free" time you're cooking and washing and getting feed for the cow. You wake up your boy at night and go through the deep snow with his sled to the threshing floor, and look all around like a thief to see if you can bring back a little chaff or straw. That's how we lived. And that's just why I didn't want the children to stay in the collective farm and learn thieving. For me it doesn't matter—how could I get away from it?

The commune was gone. What shall I tell about in the rest of this story? Is it over? Shall I stop?

No! There were dozens of faithful members devoted to it—commune members without a commune, scattered about in the labor camps and prisons of Siberia, who had brought its bleak, uninhabited expanses under cultivation, only to fertilize it with their bones.

I cheerfully endured imprisonment and all the adversity and hard labor in the taiga. My sentence was already in its second half and was getting shorter and shorter. Hope had begun to stir within my heart that I might again see my family, relatives, and friends; but from distant Kómi I was taken under convoy back to Stálinsk. Why?

When they saw me off, my camp friends congratulated me:

"Off to a retrial!"

"Liberation!"

But they were mistaken. I was again in strict solitary confinement. And here I was in the office of the investigator—a new one, unfamiliar. When I asked him why they had brought me back there, he said:

"The sentence has been canceled by Rogínsky, the procurator of the republic."

"Why?"

"It was too mild," he barked.

Now I understood everything. Goodbye, hopes! The article was the same—No. 58—but now it was the second part, which reads: "Execution," "Under certain extenuating circumstances, not less than . . . ," and so on. Points 14 and 11 appeared. Point 14 was sabotage of state directives; almost everybody under this point went through the death chamber. Point 11 was a group point, and this added greater severity to points that were already severe enough.

"Now the death sentence," I decided. I did not know about the others, but I was sure to be first on the list.

If such a sentence had been carried out at once in 1936, it would have been easier for me; but as it was, freedom had begun to dawn in the distance, and then suddenly this.

Our sentence had already been protested in 1937 for its "mildness," with the instruction to impose a harsh punishment. But by now those of us who were convicted had been scattered to the four winds and were lost out there in the enormous mass of convicts, and we knew nothing about this until they sought us out (more than two years later) for retrial and collected all of us in the First Building in the city of Stálinsk. Our acquitted comrades—Ólya Tolkách, Yegór Yepifánov, Mítya Páshchenko, and Gítya Tyurk—were soon arrested again. They waited more than two years for the rest of us to be collected, and those poor fellows had to endure more hardship waiting for us than we did in the camps. After all, we worked in the taiga; at least a free wind cooled us, while they languished in prison in '37, '38, and '39, when the prisons were so unbelievably overcrowded that people often lost consciousness because of the closeness and lack of air in hot weather.

Soon after their liberation, Yepifánov and Gítya Tyurk died of illnesses, and Páshchenko emerged a broken man.

Our second trial took place in the spring of 1940, when there no longer existed either our commune, or Lébedev, the chairman of the city soviet, who had started the case against us, or Khitárov, the chairman of the city committee. They had all become victims of the same incomprehensible typhoon, beyond the grasp of human thought, that they had shoved us into.

The times had softened. If we had been retried in 1937, when our sentence was canceled, that would have been the end for many, if not all, of us. At the trial we got various sentences, from five to ten years, but in actual fact all were equalized; we all did ten years, since at that time, after serving a sentence under Article 58, no one was set free "until further notice."

When they took us back to the cells after the trial, Yegór Yepifánov tapped out to me at once:

"How good!"

"It's a holiday for me!" I tapped back.

Some holiday—ten years of captivity!

And once more we were swept off to the camps like leaves in the wind.

But shortly afterwards there came a new disaster—war, and in connection with it a harsh test of our convictions that we must not kill.

In 1936 an incident occurred in our commune that deeply disturbed everybody. Two drunken Shórians who were riding through our fields took it into their heads to pick our watermelons and roll them down the hill.

Sávva Blinóv went up to them and asked them:

"What are you doing? Why?"

Instead of answering, one Shórian whipped out a knife and plunged it deep into Sávva's back. People came running up. Healthy young lads grabbed the raging Shórians, tied them up, and locked them in the barn. They took Sávva to the hospital without removing the knife from his wound.

The whole population of the settlement gathered at the barn in great agitation.

Various voices were heard: "Put them on trial!" "Take them to the militia!" "What good would that do?"

Just the same, the Shórians were turned over to no one. In the morning, when they had sobered up, they began begging forgiveness and asking to go home. They were allowed to leave. They went off to their families. I do not know what traces this left in their souls; but I do not doubt that if they had been condemned according to the law and imprisoned, this would not have called forth any good feelings in them. In addition, such a punishment would have struck not so much the guilty one as his family, the little children, the elders.

Fortunately, Sávva's wound turned out not to be dangerous, and he recovered.

Called up for military service during the war, he did not refuse. We had no binding obligation about this matter, and indeed we could not have had any; everyone acted freely, as best he could according to the state of his own soul, his own conscience. Sávva went, but in view of his advanced age, and perhaps also of his convictions, he was assigned to a support unit and delivered hot food to the soldiers in the trenches and in the front lines. He was killed in 1944 by a direct hit from a shell. Sávva was there, and then suddenly he was gone. No trace remained of that big, powerful, extraordinarily gentle and good-hearted man. He was killed, and no hot arguments arose about what to do with the killers. After all, this was not the primitive knife of drunken men, but a shell, the clever invention of highly qualified specialists in the science of killing, the result of years of long experiments and mathematically exact calculations. Juridical laws condemn no one for killing in wartime. Nor do any decrees of church councils. Those killings in wartime, like all other killings, are condemned by the unwritten law that lives within the human soul and manifests itself as conscience and love for people.

I cannot say exactly, but most probably in 1938 or 1939, several young men in our commune were convicted for refusing military service. The sentences were not as harsh—from three to five years. But among those who refused in wartime, evidently there was only one who got five years—the rest were shot.

They confirmed their sincerity by going to their deaths with open eyes.

When Vásya Kírin, a man with a large family, went to announce his refusal, his wife said to him:

"You know they will kill you."

"Let them kill me, just so I don't kill anybody," he answered quietly and left.

Another who died was Seryózha Yúdin, the one who had said:

"The commune no longer exists; now everybody can do as they please."

And he did what he was convinced that he should do and what he believed in.

Ványa Morgachëv, quiet and attentive, gave up his young life. Eleven other young men from our commune were executed.

The same fate befell two former members of the commune who lived in Ukraine and Uzbekistan, sixteen who had been sent away to Kozhévnikovo, and one from the Peaceful Plowman.

This was the last blow to the followers of Leo Tolstóy. Few remained, and even those no longer had their former strength and energy. And who can condemn them for that?

Only our own conscience can condemn us for our own weaknesses.

About the fate of our commune, I have briefly told what has not faded from my memory during the decades I spent in conditions that were far from easy and sometimes almost unbearable. To be sure, there are many more details of all kinds in my memory, many of them personal, about myself and others; but I no longer have the strength to collect them and put them together in an orderly account. I will limit myself to this.

In conclusion I would like to say a little more about what led me to write these memoirs. How good it is that Leo Tolstóy founded no church, no party, no sect, and set forth no dogmas. He pointed out to people the path of life that he considered the true one. He shared his experience on this path, set a course, and left to each individual what rightfully belongs to all individuals: to think independently, to make decisions independently, and to live guided by their reason and their conscience, according to the powers and requirements of their souls. Only that kind of life stands on a firm foundation and gives strength and satisfaction to the individual and stability to society.

We had no program in advance for creating a way of life. Everything took shape by itself, since it followed from the convictions that filled our souls. Everything was genuine, not just something we thought up. We believed that what is fundamental in human beings is their spiritual essence, but we knew that this is manifested in deeds and in outward forms.

It is the same in the life of society: its spiritual essence is instilled in certain outward forms, but this does not mean that these outward forms are the goal, the basic thing. We have never worshiped programs or forms and have never sacrificed human life, the ultimate value, to them. We experienced happiness through living in a society founded on free, reasonable consent, without compulsion; a society without bureaucracy—that tomb of all life—but with freedom and initiative; a society in which there was no "mine," where everything was ours, in common. We were fortunate in recognizing the joy of labor that was not for hire and for profit, but was voluntary and satisfying.

Now, when that is all in the past and has become history, another important question inevitably arises. Did those who gathered together in the commune do justice to the name of Leo Tolstóy, with whose noble ideas we united our lives? Did we achieve in our lives the heights and fullness of the teaching we had accepted? No! Of course not. The evils of past centuries still weighed too heavy in our consciousness; we had too many human weaknesses.

And a second question: Did we strive to achieve it? Yes we did! Our aspirations were ardent, powerful, sincere, honest, and bold to the point of risking our lives.

Out of the stormy, boundless ocean of human life, with all its infinitely varied aspirations and fates, suddenly one part of it was caught up in a powerful maelstrom, whirled together into one unit, and torn away from the rest of the mass. It was carried off on the foamy crest of the wave. Then with a mighty surge it was lifted up into the air, toward the sun, and was thrown with powerful force against a cliff. It broke into thousands of droplets, sparkling with all the colors of the rainbow, then fell back into the ocean and merged with it. And it was no more. And it seemed that there had never been anything.

But there was! And the memory of it lives on in the souls of those who experienced it as something bright, great, necessary, and joyous.

9 November 1967, Tálzhino

3.

My Life

DIMÍTRY MORGACHËV

At the age of eighty, Dimítry Morgachëv (1892–1978) sat down and wrote the story of his life. It is an absorbing account of the development of a peasant boy, who got only three years of schooling and was orphaned at the age of ten, into a man who can justly be called a peasant intellectual. In addition to his experiences in two Tolstoyan communes, he tells about his life in a typical peasant village in tsarist times, his combat experience and the loss of an eye during the First World War, the famine of the early 1920s and forced collectivization in the 1930s, his repeated arrests, torture, and imprisonment, his years in the labor camps, and finally his successful struggle with the Soviet government in the 1970s for rehabilitation after his years of unjust persecution.

I WANT TO WRITE DOWN the story of my life. But will I be able to do it? So many years have gone by. I will try to recollect what I was fated to live through—the joys and the sorrows, the good and the bad.

I was born in October 1892 into a peasant family in the village of Búrdino, Terbunóv District, Yeléts Region, Oryól Province (now Lípetsk Province).

Our family was small. Grandfather Sergéy Aleksándrovich fought in the Turkish War, got some kind of decoration, and afterwards was elected district elder. I do not remember what my grandmother's name was. They had two children: a daughter and a son. They married off the daughter, and the three of them lived together: Grandfather, Grandmother, and their son—my father, Yegór.

On my father's side of the family, Grandfather's relatives were poor. I can remember how they would go off and get seasonal work in the Don coal mines, and to Rostóv Province to work on riverboats. My mother's family were rich peasants from the neighboring village of Terbuný—they had bought land of their own, and they were well off. Grandfather, being an elder, had bought about fifty acres of land. He was a man of authority and got a wife

Dimítry Morgachëv and his family, probably about 1929.

Dimítry Morgachëv at age eighty in 1972, the year he began writing his memoirs.

for his son Yegór from a rich peasant family. She was an orphan and was called Lyubóv Andréyevna. She was given sixteen acres of land as a dowry. My father married her around 1885.

My grandfather had given thirty-two acres of his land to his daughter as a dowry. He left thirty-two acres to us two grandsons when our father died—and he died young, at the age of twenty-two or twenty-three. I was two years old, and my brother, Mikhaíl, was two months old. A year and a half later our grandmother died, and within another year our grandfather, too. For that reason I do not remember anybody except for a dim memory of Grandfather—a little old gray-haired man. At that time I was three and a half years old. Our mother was left with us two children. We had a good house, made of brick. A regular peasant *izbá,* a wooden structure with a Russian stove, was connected by a passageway to the brick living quarters, called *górnitsa,* the "clean part"—all of it standing on a floor, which was rare in our region. The *górnitsa* contained three rooms: an entrance room, a living room, and a bedroom; there were two couches, a cupboard for pots and pans, and a bed in the bedroom—all of it simple carpentry work. We had a good shed for the livestock and a brick storehouse with a cellar underneath it for vegetables. In the garden there was a metal-roofed wooden barn to store grain, a threshing barn, and a shed for hay and straw. As I remember, my mother had two horses, a foal, a cow and calf, and about ten sheep. Mother managed the farm after the death of my grandfather, the last man in our family.

The village assembly elected our mother as the guardian of the property of us two young brothers. All the property and livestock were inventoried by the village elder, according to the instructions of the district elder, and turned over to my mother on her signature. An outsider also could have been our guardian. Every year Mother would give an accounting to the village assembly in the presence of the district elder.

Mother lived as a widow for four or five years and then took a husband into our home, Fedót Yákovlevich Bólgov, who had come back from military service without any property. Up to that time she had hired a workman each year. So she lived with him for five years, and they had a daughter, Anna. When Mother married Bólgov, her relatives took back the sixteen acres of land they had previously given her as a dowry. Mother took them to court. The lawsuit dragged on for a year or two. She had to go several times to Yeléts, forty or forty-five miles away. She caught a cold and came down with consumption. She was ill only a short while and then died. Mother died in 1901 or 1902, and soon afterwards our stepfather was chosen to be the guardian in charge of the property of us orphans.

We lived that way about a year. We heated the stove ourselves. I started going to school. I would get there all muddy, and they would make me wash myself off. Bólgov got married, and then we had both a stepfather and a stepmother, and they started having children.

I got to be eleven or twelve years old and began tilling the soil with a wooden plow along with my stepfather's brother Zakhár. A wooden plow is harder to use, of course, than a steel plow. Every time you turn around, you have to take a wooden plow out of the ground, clean off the dirt, move the scraping board to the other plowshare, raise the plow, turning the horse around at the same time, while you hold a little trowel in your hands to clean the plow with. The wooden plow has two handles, and you hold on to these two handles all the time while you guide the plow and lift it up at the turns. All that was not easy.

I went to school for about three years. Mathematics and religion were easy for me. The priest liked me and would always give me Biblical pictures. The priest was an old man. He wanted to arrange for me to go to school in the city as an orphan and because I was a good student, but my relatives on my mother's side would not agree with the priest—they had land: "Let him work on that."

At that time our stepfather began drinking more heavily. Once when he was drunk, somebody took two hundred rubles away from him. I do not know whose care I was under then. The neighbors told me that my stepfather was evidently drinking up our property, and I went to the district elder in the village and said to him: "Uncle, our father drinks and doesn't work; he needs to get thrown out of our house."

"And what will become of you?"

"Send me wherever you want."

The elder called in our relatives on my mother's side—her uncles. They put their heads together and agreed to take us into their homes.

A village assembly was called to discuss the question of the Morgachëv orphans. The old men confirmed that our stepfather drank, and the assembly decided to put our stepfather and all his family out of our house at once, to sell all our livestock and put the money into an orphans' savings bank until we came of age, and to inventory all the equipment and lock it up in the brick storehouse. At that same meeting they chose a new guardian—our neighbor, a deeply religious Orthodox believer. Our house was rented to the deacon. My brother and I went to our relatives to work as farm laborers—I to Iván Fedoséyevich, and my younger brother to Mikhaíl Fedoséyevich. That was about twelve miles from our native village. We worked without pay, and we had a lot of work—sowing wheat on eighty to a hundred acres. They had a lot of horses, which I had to take care of day and night. I lived like that for more than a year.

I got tired of living that way, and I asked to go to our village and see our guardian, I. P. Dorókhin. I said to him:

"Uncle, I'm not going back there, it's powerfully hard over there."

"Then where should I send you?"

"Wherever you want. Put me up with somebody else in your own village."

He took me to his sister Anísya, and she took me to her sons, Semyón and Nikoláy Myáchin. Nikoláy had once been a hired hand for our mother. Our guardian offered me to them as a hired hand, but they had already offered the job to another boy the evening before and settled the bargain with drinks. But the wives of the brothers announced in one voice that they didn't need that Pétka: he was pockmarked, and he had a father and mother, and this orphan was the one to take. So I stayed with them. My guardian settled with them for my pay—twelve rubles a year.

In a few days our relatives came to take me back, but I wouldn't go. Then they took a little fur coat and a few other things away from me and left. I stayed with the Myáchins. Even though they were not my people, they were kind and good. I lived with them and didn't feel like an outsider, and they did not look on me as an outsider either. They taught me a lot in both work and behavior.

It must have been 1906 or 1907. Spring arrived at our new masters' house. We went out to plow with wooden plows. It was hard for me. I was still weak, and the plowland was damp: I could hardly pull the plow out of the furrow. But we did finish the work: we sowed the grain and set out the potatoes. Saint Peter's Day came—that is in June. We set to work plowing fallow land for winter crops; in July we began harvesting the grain. Our village of Búrdino was big, and for that reason the fields were far away. We would work there and stay overnight. We would go out to cut the rye with long-toothed scythes. The teeth would catch what the scythe cut, and you could neatly carry it to one side and stack it up in rows, and the women would come along behind and tie up the sheaves and clean up everything with rakes. It was the custom for the wife always to tie up behind her husband. Behind me came the wife of one brother who had gone away to work as a seasonal laborer. She was a hotheaded, capricious woman, and I stacked the rows badly and got mixed up, which made it harder to tie up the sheaves.

So she started saying mass over me and praying that my awkward arms would wither and drop off. My master's wife was a kind woman, and she said to her: "Kuzmínikha, you go and tie up behind my husband, and I'll tie up after the boy."

She never scolded me, and for three whole years she washed and sewed for me. My master Semyón Andréyevich would help me in this way: When we cut wheat, he would go ahead of me, and I would lag behind him about a third of a swath. He would either help me fill a row or else go on to a new one and cut for both himself and me. So during the first year the master's wife always tied up behind me, but after that I no longer lagged behind the master and stacked the rows well.

I lived with them more than three years, up to the time of my marriage, and after that they were like a family to me. Both brothers died before they reached old age. Both of them would go away for seasonal labor, and both of them lost their health there.

My brother Mikhaíl did not live long with our relatives either. He got work as a laborer on the Beryózovka farm, at Golopúzovka village.

I made an agreement with the master to sow a few acres of grain for me: in the autumn of 1908, winter rye; and in the spring of 1909, oats, millet, lentils, and potatoes. We gathered all that harvest and carried it off to our farmstead, our home. We threshed the grain, stored it in our granary, put the straw in the hay barn, and in the autumn of 1909 my brother Mikhaíl and I moved into our home. We had worked as farm laborers for four years. In the final year I had earned thirty rubles.

We moved into one half of the house, the *izbá;* and the deacon occupied the other half. He had a large family, six children.

My brother and I heated the stove ourselves, but he did most of it. I, as the older of us, would give him directions about what to prepare for our breakfast, and for the whole day.

The deacon's oldest daughter, Shúra, was already a teacher in the school run by the village zémstvo.[1] The small parish school of about thirty pupils that I had gone to was reorganized as a large one in 1906, since the village was sizable, with about five hundred households. Shúra took an interest in me. At first I was a little afraid, but then I got accustomed to her. She wanted to become my wife, even though she was five years older than I, and I was only seventeen years and three months.

I consulted my relatives. They advised me not to marry an educated woman—"you'll be waiting on her your whole life long; on hot summer days you will draw curtains over the windows and shoo the flies away from her, and you yourself will have no time to work in the fields. Take a peasant girl; you have land, and you and she will work on the land together."

So I did not link up with an educated woman. In December 1909 my master Nikoláy took me off to arrange a match for me. The village was large and prosperous. There we found a bride from a very rich peasant family. They lived on four farms, each with nearly three hundred acres of land; but they were not divided—two brothers, the old people, and two nephews of a brother who had died. I had no good clothes, and we had not yet even bought any horses. And these wealthy people were the ones Nikoláy Myáchin had brought me to see. I will describe what the custom was: we had come to arrange a match. There is, of course, the obligatory matchmaker. He or she talks first with the parents of the bride, who will ask the parents and the groom to come to their home so that the groom may look the bride over and the bride may look the bridegroom over. And so they arrive. The relatives sit a little apart, around the table but not at the table; and when the groom comes into the bride's home, he sits near the door on a bench called a *kónik* (it looked like a chest, with a top that opened). The bride, wearing a fine dress, would walk through the whole house to the judgment bench (near the stove) and take her place facing the door, in front of the groom. Here they would glance at each other from time to time and then look down at the floor. They would sit like this about an hour, without saying a word to each other, while their parents talked about various matters—about horses and livestock in general, and about land, and how much each one expected to sow. The conversation about the real matter at hand had not yet begun.

---

1. Zémstvos—a network of local governmental institutions established in 1864, which had limited but gradually increasing authority in such matters as education, public health, etc., particularly after the February Revolution of 1917. The Bolsheviks abolished them after their seizure of power later that year.

Then the groom and his relatives and the matchmaker would step out of the house for a consultation with the groom about whether he liked the bride. They would discuss the matter in the street or in the vestibule, and meanwhile the bride's parents would inquire whether she liked the groom. If he liked the bride, the matchmakers would go back into the house and take their seats. But if the groom did not like the bride, his parents would announce that we weren't yet ready for a wedding this year, or that the bride was still too young—let her wait just one more year. Then the groom's relatives would leave without anything.

And how did matters stand with me? We went into the house of Zakhár Afanásyevich Rusín. My master was a joker, and he said:

"Zakhár Afanásyevich, we've heard you have a calf for sale."

He answered:

"That's right, but I can sell my calf only to a good master—a kind, quiet man, not a drunkard or a carouser but a hard-working man."

Then the laughter began, while I sat there without saying a word, like a licked-down ram. Later they brought a steaming samovar to the table. The bride came in and began pouring tea. She poured a glass for me too and handed it to me. I thanked her and at the same time took a quick look at her. She blushed and hid behind the samovar, and my master and her father talked seriously about the matter. During all that time, she and I did not say a word. We only glanced at each other several times. It was agreed that we should come back in three days. When we went home, I said to Nikoláy Andréyevich:

"She's powerfully small and skinny."

But he answered:

"Don't look at the warts they've got, look at what's in the pot" (that is, look at the dowry). Then he added:

"A gold coin is small but swell, Fedóra's big as they come, but dumb."

Three days later we went back and agreed on the following conditions: they would buy five acres of land for the bride, and since we had no livestock at all, they would give us a horse, a cow, and a piglet. But my master said:

"Zakhár Afanásyevich, it's the nature of everything to live in pairs, but you're giving them only one little pig."

"All right," he answered, "I'll give them a pair."

This time, after a long conversation, they brought us together and sat us down side by side. We kissed each other and smiled at each other several times at the table, but we talked very little, and I don't remember about what. It was agreed that our wedding would take place after Christmas, in other words, during meat-eating season.

While we sat at the table, we drank a little vodka. My father-in-law was an old, gray-haired man, and his wife was younger. She was his second wife, and my bride was her daughter. After taking a drink, my future father-in-law stamped his feet on the floor and said:

"We're not drinking, you know—we're getting the business done. We know they are orphans. Dmítry here has lived with you more than three years. He's a good worker, and he's got a good head on his shoulders. His brother Mikhaíl has lived with our relatives—he too is a hard-working boy, and we think they will make good farmers. They know how to take hold of things. If they are sober, honest workers, they will live well, and that is what we wish for them."

He poured out a glass apiece for everybody but us, the bride and groom, and went on: "But if they are lazy and take to drink, then no matter what you give them, they'll run through it all."

We had fifty acres of purchased land and two allotments in the association (nearly fourteen acres); this meant we could count on living as well-to-do peasants, considering the lack of land in our region.

After the agreement, I went with my guardian to the orphans' savings bank and drew out two hundred rubles. We bought the fastest horse in our village, which ran the ten miles to the railway station in twelve minutes. We bought it, as I recall, for eighty rubles. I got myself a new sheepskin coat covered with thin cloth and a knee-length beaver jacket with a collar, and we bought a fine sleigh. At Christmas time, all dressed up, I drove off with my own horse and sleigh to the home of my bride. A lot of guests were there, and I was seated at the table in a place of honor, beside her. The next day they saw me off, and we drove through the village several times in the sleigh behind our trotter. Sometimes she drove, and sometimes I did.

This is written sixty years later. Oh, where are you, my golden years?

As we rode along, we would talk with each other, joking and laughing. But our wedding could not take place between Christmas and Lent after all, since I was seventeen years and three months old, and the priest could marry us only when I was seventeen and a half, and only then with the permission of the archbishop. Indeed, there was a general law that men could be married at eighteen and girls at seventeen, so our wedding was put off until the week following Easter week. I also went to see her between Christmas and Lent, at Shrovetide; but she complained to me that she was unwell, and had some kind of illness. She said she had gone to a wedding somewhere just before Shrovetide, and in all the merriment she had drunk cold kvass, and she believed that was what had made her ill.

During Lent, as I remember, I did not visit them, since spring sowing had begun and we were busy; and besides, people said Lent was not the time for visiting. I could go to see her only at Annunciation or on Palm Sunday—but on Palm Sunday she died, she departed from this world. And so fifteen days before our wedding, I became a widower. What a joy it had been to visit them; her parents and especially she herself always greeted me so warmly. She would always meet me with a smile and a hearty kiss, if not at the gates, then in the yard. I grieved for her very much; but at my age and in my position as a peasant, I had to think about marriage. I became friendly with a girl named Nástya; but it turned out that her uncle, the brother of her father, had stolen a shock of rye (fifty-two sheaves), and this shame lay over her whole family. My masters advised me not to take Nástya as a wife: first because she had no dowry, but mainly because she was of thieving stock.

But I will finish about her. I saw her fifty years later, in 1960, when I visited my native region. She had gotten married soon after my own marriage. In 1913 her husband was called up for military service and was killed in the war. She was left with a son and a daughter, who also died—the son after he was grown. When I went to see her, she said:

"On the day you married my friend Maryána, we were setting out potatoes on our farm. Our people had gone to dinner, and I stayed behind near the cart of potatoes, in order to hang myself. I raised the shafts, tied the rope, and was about to put the noose around my neck when someone came up, and then our people came back from dinner, and so I have remained alive up to now, but I have cursed my life."

So when my bride Nyúra died, I went to my masters to grieve and think about what to do. They suggested making a match with Lóra Komaróv's daughter. My masters explained to me that her mother was dead, and she had only her father and a sister who was a nun and went around reading psalms over the dead. Even though they were poor, they were honest, hardworking people. We went and talked with her father and looked over Maryána as a bride. Her father gave us no answer immediately. At home with my masters, I said to Nikoláy Andréyevich:

"She has an awfully big nose."

He answered me the way he had done the first time:

"Don't look at the warts they've got, look at what's in the pot."

Her father went to Golopúzovka, where his brother and brother-in-law lived, to get information about me, since, as he said, "I don't know him." They told him: "Don't let this bridegroom get away; Zakhár Afanásyevich is a rich man, and even he gave his daughter in marriage to him." The next day, when we went to see them, they received us as guests and agreed to let me marry his daughter and at once turned to the agreement. Maryána's father said he would give all his property as a dowry, and since we were orphans and had no older person, he would come and live with us.

"Only, I want to settle just one thing with you: my other daughter, Irína [she was about forty years old], wants to take nothing for herself. Just get her a little house near the church, and she will need nothing else."

We found a house, which we immediately bought for 500 rubles, and five acres of land worth 450 rubles. This land was confirmed as our property under the Stolýpin law,[2] along with a horse and wagon and wooden plow, a cow, a few sheep, chickens, and all sorts of tools. At the signing of the contract, Maryána and I kissed each other and agreed on a wedding three weeks after Easter. But we still had to settle the matter of my age. We went to the priest, and he wrote a petition for me to the archbishop saying that we were orphans and I needed a woman for the housework. I took it to Oryól myself, which was faster than sending it by mail.

The archbishop lived in a monastery. The journey made a great impres-

2. Pyotr Arkádyevich Stolýpin (1862–1911), Minister of the Interior and Chairman of the Council of Ministers from 1906 till his death, attempted to reform Russian agriculture by making it possible for peasants to take their share of the land owned communally by their village and settle on individual farms.

sion on me: it was my first trip on a train and to a large city, Oryól. I stayed at the monastery hotel and slept on a spring mattress, which I had never seen in my life. The next day, I went to the cathedral where the archbishop served. I had been taught how to submit a petition: after the service, when he started to leave the cathedral, I was to get on my knees and lay the petition on my outstretched hand, palm up, covering it with my other hand. The archbishop was accompanied by a whole retinue of monks, at least ten. There were young boys, too, all of them in gilt robes. One carried the special hat of the archbishop, and another his special staff—a crozier. When this procession came up alongside me, one of the monks took the petition from my hands and said:

"Get up; tomorrow you will receive an answer—right here in the cathedral!"

The next day, the same monk called me, handed me the permission for marriage and a wedding in the church, and said:

"You may wed the girl whom you love."

"I said: "Thank you."

At the beginning of May 1910, my marriage took place with Maryána, with whom I still live to this day. We married without knowing or thinking about any kind of love, and even without knowing each other before our wedding. That is the way it was with everybody. A woman was needed in the house, to work, to do the washing and cooking. Of course, I knew, and so did she, that we would sleep together and have children, whom we would need to bring up and educate. We had ten children in all, six of whom grew up.

So that is how I settled down to married life after long years of orphanhood, wandering among farm laborers, with a stepfather and stepmother, among people unrelated to me. Her old father and sister moved into our house, and the house was filled with life. My brother Mikhaíl also lived with us, spending most of his time in the fields, with the horses. We bought a steel plow and no longer plowed with the wooden plow. Maryána told me afterwards that she had also been courted in the village where my first bride lived, but her bridegroom got an infected leg and it was cut off, so their wedding never took place.

I will tell later how my wife and I have lived out our lives, but misunderstandings between us soon began to arise over her dowry. The problem was that there were two of us brothers, and the farm belonged to us together, but I was spending her money too, which she had brought as a dowry. "Why are you spending my money on a house you jointly own?"

In our village of Búrdino there were fistfights three times a year—in December and January, on Shrove Tuesday in February, and at Easter, in April. The village was divided in half, and on Shrove Tuesday village fought village—Búrdino and Terbuný. I also took part in those fights. Our priest said that fistfights were not bad; men got training from them and would be bolder and more active in war. The fights began with boys, then with teenagers, then grown men, and after that even bearded old men. Once the old men gathered close together like a wall and pushed me up against one of the strongest old men from the other side. I knocked him down, and from that time on they considered me a strong man. They said: "How he knocked over that big granddad!" It was the rule that you should never beat a man who was lying down, whether he was knocked down or whether he fell by himself, but sometimes they would agree to hold the very strongest men up by the armpits, and other strong men would not let them fall down and would keep beating them. Sometimes the outcome was fatal. Once a wealthy shopkeeper offered two buckets of vodka to the side that won. No fewer than three thousand men got together for the brawl. Our village won that time.

While I was still a laborer, my master and I went to general meetings and assemblies of the whole village; and even though it was the old men who went there, no one raised any objection to me, since everybody knew that I was a home owner and had been interested since I was sixteen years old in social questions, and not in wenching. In the fall of 1910 the elder called a meeting of the village assembly; the village policemen notified the people to come to the meeting, saying that some kind of agronomist would be there. Nobody knew what an agronomist was, but they wanted to find out, and so there was a big crowd. I went too. The agronomist, an imposing man about thirty years old, reported to the audience: "The Yeléts Zémstvo has brought up the question of raising the level of agriculture. It is giving you free of charge a Simmental bull, a Yorkshire hog, and a woolly sheep that will produce twelve pounds of wool in one shearing." In addition, they offered to open a rental center here for agricultural machinery and tools—plows with double plowshares, four-bladed seed-planters, a grading outfit to pick out the best seeds, so that the best seeds would produce better crops, and so on. To begin with, they would give us free chemical fertilizer—bone meal, superphosphate, and slag—so that we could be convinced in our own fields about the advantage of chemical fertilizer; and for our personal plot they would give us free a few pounds of lucerne seed, which could be mowed up to four times a summer for green fodder, and some seeds of the mangelwurzel, a root plant that milk cows need. The agronomist announced further that the Yeléts Regional Zémstvo was starting agricultural courses at Yeléts lasting fifty to sixty days, with free food and housing. Lectures and papers would be read there giving scientific information about raising the level of agriculture.

"Please sign up for the courses; it's in your own interest, so that you will have good livestock and your fields will give you bigger harvests of grain and grass."

But nobody signed up. The agronomist repeated his request several times. I was sitting at the table; the agronomist looked at me, and I smiled. I wanted to go, and I was wondering whether it would be worthwhile to spend money for the trip. He pulled out his billfold, took out three rubles, and handed them to me, saying: "This is for your travel."

He wrote down my full name and told me where and when I was to go.

At that time the Terbuný District had about eighteen thousand people and eight villages and settlements. In the Yeléts Region there were twenty-one districts. In our district, A. A. Gulévsky, from a prosperous farm, also signed up along with me at Terbuný. At the appointed time we arrived in Yeléts. We were put up in the Community Center, and our courses were held at the House of Industriousness, on the Hay Square. The two buildings stood almost side by side. We took our meals free at a little dining hall. In our courses we learned about farming, horticulture, market gardening, animal husbandry, and the organizing of credit associations and consumers' societies.

All that was late in the fall of 1910. At that same time Leo Tolstóy died, and there I heard for the first time about Tolstóy in private conversations. Some said that he was an atheist and would recognize neither God, nor the church, nor the Tsar, and that he was cursed in the churches, like the robber Sténka Rázin. Others said he was a good man and a writer who was known all over the world. But all those conversations had no effect on me and left me with no impression of Tolstóy. After taking the courses, I got hold of the constitution of the consumers' societies while I was there; and when I returned home, I got six or seven people together, and we signed the constitution and sent it to the governor in Oryól for approval. Without the approval of the governor, it was impossible to organize any kind of new associations. But before approving the constitution of the consumers' society (cooperative), and other cooperative federations, the governor secretly ordered an immediate report on the reliability of the persons who had signed the constitution. I was informed about that by the village constable. But those of us who signed the constitution were peasants—all but one, the district clerk—and our constitution was approved. That was in the summer of 1911; and from the Yeléts Zémstvo I received agricultural machinery for the rental center, several hundred pounds of mineral fertilizer, and a certain amount of lucerne and mangel-wurzel seeds. The seeds were distributed free, and the machines were loaned out, also free.

The Yeléts Zémstvo commissioned me to find persons among the peasantry to receive sires of pedigreed livestock—a bull, a boar, and a ram—on the following conditions: a pedigreed Simmental bull a year and a half old would be given to someone who expressed a desire to receive it and take care of it for three years. At the end of the three years, the bull would become the property of that person. For each mating he would charge no more than one ruble, which would be for his own use. As for the boar and the ram, the conditions would be the same, except for only two years instead of three.

During the second courses, in 1911, I joined an organization called the Imperial Society of Poultry Breeders, from which I received eggs for the hatching of chicks from pedigreed hens of the following breeds: Black Minorca laying hens; Plymouth Rocks, for meat and big eggs; big Black Leghorns for meat; and wattled yellow Faverolles for meat and eggs. The aim of this society was also to spread pedigreed chickens among the peasants.

In July 1911 a son, Timoféy, was born to us. I was eighteen and a half years old.

In autumn of 1911 I joined the producers' cooperative society, whose goal was to supply its members with goods. At the same time, this unintentionally injured the trade of the private shopkeepers. Several dozen persons were drawn into the cooperative, including the local intelligentsia—teachers and workers in the district government. At the first organizational meeting, I was elected president of the governing board. For a storehouse we found a brick structure in our home, which had been built by my grandfather. Very little money was collected, and we had to buy our goods at the Terbuný station from the company of the Abrámov brothers, that is, from a private firm.

There was not yet any consumers' cooperative alliance in Yeléts. In our storehouse we had only the most necessary goods—salt, kerosene, matches, tobacco, tea, cigarettes, pretzels, candy, cakes, and all kinds of small items. We barely made expenses. The local merchants began to get angry with me.

In the winter of 1911, the Yeléts Regional Zémstvo organized a second course of study, and I was invited to go for two months. This time they promised to give us ten fruit-tree saplings to hand out to the peasants on condition that they would take care of the trees according to instructions. All this work fell on my shoulders, of course, and without pay. I had to go around to a number of orchards making up lists of those who wanted the saplings, since I was the only one in the Terbuný District.

In the spring of 1912, after sowing the early spring crops, I had to go to the nursery to get the fruit saplings. We went in several carts. There was a horticultural school in the village of Stegálovka, thirty or forty kilometers away. When the landowner Bédrov died, he willed his small estate and lands to the Yeléts Zémstvo for the building of a horticultural school for peasant children. There they told me how to lay out an orchard like a chessboard, with the trees set twenty-eight feet apart. I had occasion to visit the Stegálovka school several times after that for further instructions. Ten years later, in 1922, I myself started a fruit-tree nursery for a thousand saplings at our little Renaissance Commune.

More than fifty years have gone by since that time, and I still remember with gratitude what great efforts were made by Russian public organizations to develop agriculture and improve the well-being of the peasantry.

I kept getting involved in more and more work: the consumers' cooperative, the rental center, and the mating center for livestock—since nobody else would take the pedigreed sires, I took on all that myself. It got to be hard on my brother Mikhaíl; and since he had become dissatisfied, we got him married in the winter of 1912–13. He married a girl of peasant origin, the daughter of a boat captain. The dowry was insignificant.

Military Service and War

In autumn of 1913 I was called to the army recruiting office to draw a recruiting lottery number. The recruiting office was in the village of Kolódez in Sérgiev District, which took in recruits from five districts. This came to about 1,000 men, since there were more than 250 from our village alone. We were called up to draw lots according to lists arranged by districts, but some of the lots were blanks, or rather, big, remote numbers. In this way, if 600 men were needed and 1,000 showed up, then 400 numbers remained undrawn and were held as a reserve. I went up to the lottery box and felt all around inside, hoping to draw a remote number, for the reserves—and I pulled out number one! The next day, I was summoned to the military-medical commission. We stripped stark naked; even though it was embarrassing, there was nothing to do about it—we were not our own masters there. Then to the scales: they called out 165 pounds. I went up to the doctors; they looked into my mouth and my behind. Then: "Turn around!" Then they called out: "Fit for the fortress artillery at Vladivostók!"

After the recruitment, we were let off for a whole month of preparations and carousing. But I didn't do any carousing—I had no time. Recruits with their accordion came to see me only a few times, and I would treat them to refreshments.

There were tears in our house. My wife was pregnant with our second child, and my father and brother were with her. We put up a little house for my wife's sister down the hill near the church, just as she had wanted. Everything fell on my brother's shoulders except the cooperative. A month later the recruits from the whole district gathered at Yeléts. A verification commission for the various branches of the armed service was also there. Again they called me first, and again they pronounced me fit for the fortress artillery at Vladivostók. I asked the commission whether I could not be assigned somewhere closer to my home, since we had grown up as orphans with guardians, among people unrelated to us, and now we were settled in our own home and were farming, and I was the elder of us two brothers, and the farm needed supervision, which was my responsibility.

The officers in their gold epaulettes put their heads together and immediately said: "You will go to the infantry in Túla." I thanked them for fulfilling my request, but I really didn't want to go into the infantry. The soldiers said the infantry was hard.

I handed over my responsibilities for the cooperative to others. My wife was with me in Yeléts. I had already begun to understand what love really is. You have to smile in front of a woman and kiss her more often. After that, love becomes something joyous, and she tries to please you, and now when we separate, she weeps and I feel sorry for her.

They took several railway carloads of us to Túla. When we pitched camp, one of the soldiers in charge of the recruits kept making fun of us—"Tomorrow you'll get a taste of our cabbage soup and kasha, but I'll make it hot for you." I was afraid I would fall into his hands, and I kept praying to God to save me from him. But evidently I didn't pray hard enough—I landed in Company Four, right under him. You'd start off to the toilet and he would make you go back ten times because you didn't salute him properly.

With me in Company Four was a little soldier by the name of Chelnokóv, as I remember. He was from Yásnaya Polyána. His bed was next to mine, and once again I heard about Leo Tolstóy. Chelnokóv would say: "He was a good master, a count, a writer. He helped poor people a lot, and taught our village children in his own home. He wrote and talked to the people about God, the Tsar, the priests, and war. He said people ought to live in peace, not go to war, and help one another, not go to the army. He said the common people were deceived by the educated people, the priests, and the generals. He had a lot of children; they would come to us in the village, play with our village children, and invite them to their own home; but his wife was bad, and always wanted to punish us for timber and our livestock, that is, for cutting it down and letting them harm the crops. She even hired a Chechén as a guard to keep watch on everybody from our village."

But all those stories about Tolstóy did not have the slightest effect on me; they went right past my ears without even grazing my conscience. I replied to him: "Why shouldn't we beat the enemies when they want to take us over?" Chelnokóv also said Tolstóy taught that nobody would take us over if we refused to go to war and serve the generals, but we might be put in jail.

I quickly picked up the military ways and in January 1914 was assigned to the training unit. Our training unit was under the command of Colonel Averyánov. Once he asked me what I had been before military service. I answered: "An unskilled laborer."

"So what did you do then—clean out shit?"

"No, sir, I plowed land, sowed grain, and set out plants."

"So that means you were a grain-grower—that's the most honorable kind of work, to be a breadwinner for the nation," he said.

So I began another kind of activity and work, not agricultural and not cooperative, but military.

In June war broke out with Austria and Germany. We were in camps fifteen or twenty kilometers from Túla, in a forest. A solder picked up an artillery shell and beat it on the ground—it's war! He tore up the tents—it's war! The training unit was disbanded as a completed job. A new regiment was formed out of the Twelfth Velíkie Lúki Regiment, and I was appointed sergeant-major. Newly mobilized men began to arrive, some from our village of Búrdino. Within a few days a regiment was formed, and we were taken by special trains to the front, in the zone from Gómel to Brest-Litóvsk. But before we left, I was able just the same to spend three days at home and see my wife. My father-in-law, Larión Filípovich, had died shortly after I was taken into the army. My wife had given birth and the baby had died. During those few months, there had been changes in my family.

We engaged in our first combat on 15 August, Old Style, on the Feast of the Assumption. It was especially awful when our artillery began firing salvo after salvo, and from our trenches in the forest we could see the Austrians fall. Then with a shout of "hurrah!" we stormed them, and they threw away their weapons and raised their hands. We took two thousand prisoners. Our company was assigned to accompany them to Kíev. After turning over the prisoners, I visited the Kíevo-Pechérsk Monastery for the second time. I had been there for the first time in 1910 with my wife Maryána. I had seen a lot there that was new and incomprehensible to me.

After turning over the prisoners, our commanders decided to go to the front on foot, and so we marched for about three months. Everywhere there were quartermaster depots. We would go ten or twelve miles and then stop. Provisions were always there. But when we got to our regiment, we were treated like deserters and were disbanded and sent off by threes and fours to different companies. One officer, from a Túla company, commanded a reconnaissance unit, and he took me with him as his sergeant-major.

At the beginning of 1915 I was slightly wounded and sent to Kíev to a military hospital. There, in one of the separate buildings, I saw a frightful scene: soldiers with syphilis. Some had no noses, and some did not even have any lips. They were terrible and gruesome to look at, like skulls of the dead attached to the bodies of living people.

At the front I was not afraid of getting killed—as the saying goes, "Either medals all around or my body underground." On our way back from the hospital to our unit, a group of comrades and I walked over a level field that was covered with the bodies of dead Austrians. This field stretched for two or three miles (our dead had already been taken away). I took a gold ring off one of the dead Austrians.

Well, in the hospital it had been worse and more frightful than at the front. I had seen that many were dying from infection. Their bodies were swollen and blue. They were crying both in delirium and in full consciousness. They would call out to their wives and children and say farewell to them in their absence and would die without being of any use to anybody. The enemy was in retreat. Our men took a big railway station. Gasoline-soaked storehouses were in flames, filled with flour, sugar, rice, oats, groats, and all kinds of pastries, while soldiers were starving. Further on, soldiers were packed into some kind of underground building; it turned out that this was an egg warehouse two or three hundred meters in length, along a passageway with concrete bins along the sides, full of eggs on which a lime solution had been poured up to the top. The soldiers kept pushing and shoving, and those who were pushed into the lime solution were choking and shouting: "Help!" The officers sent guards to pull out those who had drowned and drive out the others. Still further on there was a liquor plant. Tanks full of liquor had been pierced by bullets, and the liquor was pouring out. A couple of dozen soldiers, dead drunk, were lying all around. A guard was placed here too. That went on for several hours, and then we pushed farther on. We took the city of Lvov. There two big food warehouses were on fire. We began to penetrate the forested Carpathian Mountains. The population there lived very poorly; their stoves were heated with almost no outlet for the smoke, with only a level flue placed along the walls on the floor for heating. Very rarely, two tiny windows could be found in those smoke-blackened peasant huts. Once an officer began making advances to a young woman right before my eyes. Her husband or brother started defending her, and the officer shot him to death. We soldiers—several of us there—were all torn up by that, and we barraged him with threats. He grew frightened and started pleading with us that it had happened only by accident.

The Carpathian Mountains were heavily covered with ancient forests. It was easier to go up than to come down, and we had to go on reconnaissance every day. We all came down the Carpathians and went into Hungary, and there the offensive halted. That was in the summer of 1915. We would climb a high mountain and peep out from behind a tree, and the Austrians would also peep out at us; but neither we nor they would fire.

We did not retreat from the Carpathians, but ran on without firing. We stopped for a few days around Lvov. The wheat was already ripe, but there was no one to harvest it: the population had fled into the forest. No enemies were discovered nearby. The commandant of our reconnaissance unit took three of us and went off to reconnoiter during the day through the wheat-fields. We came out onto a stretch of lowland covered with high grass. We lay down in the grass on a little knoll and took turns looking around through the binoculars. No enemy was to be seen. Then the commandant said: "Advance," and started looking through the binoculars himself. Suddenly there was a single shot. We gave a start, and the commandant stretched out without a word, without even a sigh. The bullet had gone through the binoculars and his head. He was killed outright. We ran to headquarters and reported. The regimental commander ordered us to bring back his body. Six of us started off with a stretcher. It was an open spot where the going would be frightful, perhaps under fire. One of us crawled out of the unharvested wheat to the dead man and tied a long rope to him. We dragged him into the wheat and then carried him to the regiment, where we buried him. Not a single shot more was fired on us. We did not know where that shot had come from, and it was not clear that it had come from nearby.

I will tell about one more expedition, to capture a "tongue," as we called them—a prisoner who would "talk." A nonsoldier finds it hard to understand how an armed enemy soldier can be taken alive, especially a sentry with a weapon, but an order would be given to bring one back. Only the boldest and most resourceful men would be sent out, of course. Three of us started off, with me right behind the man in charge. It is best at night, and when it is as dark as possible. You have to creep up on him just like a cat. But after a while I got used to it. This time I don't remember whether we were advancing or retreating, whether it was in Poland or Western Ukraine. The wheat had not yet been harvested. There was a highway, and beside it was a graveyard. We noticed that a sentry was standing at one corner of the graveyard, with enemy trenches close by. We started off quietly, without talking, then we crawled, and at last we reached the graveyard. The grass was high in places, and the gravestones were as tall as a man. Suddenly we heard a barely audible hiss from the enemy trenches, and the same hiss from the graveyard. We lay still. Three men were coming. Each of us stuck close to a gravestone. My cap rose on my head: my hair stood on end like the quills of a porcupine. Death was near. We thought they had heard us and were coming after us. But it was only a change of sentries. They made the change and left. The new sentries stood up: one was near the stone slab and the gravestone, and the other at the foot. All became quiet, and thus passed several minutes—although minutes there could be both long and short. Then, like cats, we threw ourselves on them—two of us on the sentry and the third on the back-up sentry. Without a sound we grabbed them by the throat, bound their mouths tight with rags, and just as quietly left the graveyard, first through the unharvested wheat and then along the road to regimental headquarters. What was done with them there, we did not know. I got a St. George, Third Class, for it, and the other two got St. George medals.

There was another incident with a "tongue." That time the situation was different. There were some enormous marshy lowlands, covered with undergrowth. A stream about twenty-five meters wide, but deep, flowed through the middle of it. Trenches, ours and theirs, were set out some distance from each other, on the opposite dry banks of this lowland. We had made a raft in advance out of four barrels and some square beams and planks. After figuring out where the enemy reconnaissance would not notice us, we quietly carried this raft up and launched it in the stream at night, and six men got on it and floated to the other side. What awaited us? Six other men waited on our bank to cover us in case we should be discovered. We got out on the other bank, which was grown up in bushes. We soon noticed something gleaming. We ran in that direction and found two enemy soldiers. We threw ourselves upon them, gagged them, and took them to the stream; but there the enemy discovered us and opened fire on us. The raft could carry only six men; two waited behind on that bank. The firing was furious but a little to one side of us. We went back for the other two men. Nobody wanted to go, but at last we brought them back. We brought two "tongues." None of our reconnaissance men were hit, but in the village near the trenches several men were wounded.

There was one case when two of our scouts were caught and shouted in terror: "Help!"—but soon fell silent. Yes, there were cases when our scouts did not come back.

Now here is the last incident, with which my military service ended forever, in July or August 1915. During an advance, our reconnaissance unit would go in front up to the beginning of combat, and then go to the rear; and during a retreat, the reconnaissance party would go last. Our armies were ordered to retreat. Some of them left the trenches at nightfall, and the reconnaissance unit occupied the whole regiment's trenches, firing off and on all night, as if all of us were in place. In the morning when it was light, we were ordered to pull out and head for our regiment. We quickly set off almost at a run down the road, not in a crowd but single file. We ran up to a big village. Two roads led into it. We caught sight of a mounted patrol on one of them, overtaking us but still a long way off, two or three kilometers. Then we looked and saw a big patrol coming into sight on the other road. We fired a volley, and they turned back. The sun was already high in the sky, and none of the village inhabitants were to be seen. We ran through the village and then turned aside, into an unharvested field of wheat. We crossed a large ravine and went further off to one side. The standing wheat kept us hidden. Suddenly a patrol of at least fifty cavalrymen rode out of the village in hot pursuit of us. They galloped ahead of us, and we remained behind but to one side. Then they turned back and scattered through the wheat, looking for us, but they did not find us and hastened back to rest near the village. We lay there in the wheat at the edge of the village for five or six hours. We could hear the army entering the village. We crept down into the ravine and went through it up to the village, kept going till we got to the river Bug, waded across it, and got back to our regiment. We were given dinner, and before we could finish eating it, we were sent off again to reconnoiter.

We had not slept all night and had run all day, but what can you do about it? We started off. This time we had a reconnaissance party of twenty-six men. Five of them crossed the Bug. Once again they came up to the same village. Three or four of them climbed up on a roof, but noticed nothing. We separated into three parties and went off in different directions, or rather in one direction, toward the enemy, but separately from each other. The wheat stood unharvested. The enemy did not know where our army was, and we did not know where they were, so both of us kept looking around, trying to sniff each other out. It had grown dark, but the summer twilight had not yet faded. We crept through the uncut wheat along the edge of the field, walking on tiptoe without a word. I was in front. We kept going that way for about 350 yards. We bent low and advanced to within about a hundred feet of the edge of the wheatfield, and stopped and sat down. Suddenly something flashed. I waved my hand—"Don't move!" Even in the darkness we could see a group of about twelve men advancing—the enemy reconnaissance. They stopped at the edge of our field and began looking in our direction, but still did not see us. Each of them had a grenade in his hand, and they entered the field and advanced in our direction. When they were right opposite us, we jumped up. I shouted, "Halt!" and with a yell of "Hurrah!" we rushed upon them. The ground was uneven. A bomb exploded; I fell; the thought flashed through my mind that I was killed, but I got up and went on. Our men had already captured two scouts. With the shout "Hurrah!" and the bomb explosion, our remaining two units and the mounted scouts of the other regiment rushed up, and they set off in pursuit of the others. I had no weapon. I was stark naked except for one boot and part of my trousers. I was covered with blood, but still conscious, and three of us took these prisoners and waded back across the Bug. We took them to headquarters. I lost consciousness at headquarters and came to three days later in a hospital train. I do not know how and on what I was carried to the hospital train and where it was standing, but I was taken to Minsk and put up in the home of the governor. Seriously wounded men were lying there. I began walking again, and those of us who were on our feet were sent to Kursk, again in a hospital train. There twelve of us were taken straight from the train to a private hospital. It was far from home. I got stronger after an operation to clean my chest and skull of hand-grenade fragments—six in my head and one in my left eye. My rib cage was smashed, my head too, and I quickly began to recover.

It was right there that I remembered about Leo Nikoláyevich Tolstóy. I asked for some reading material by Tolstóy, and they gave me a little book. I read it and meditated on it. I read a second one, a third; I read nothing but Tolstóy for about two months. I don't remember the name of a single one of the books, but I read about war, religion, the state, property, and not a single contradiction arose in my mind about what I had read. I took a liking to Tolstóy, and I believed him and his plain-spoken truth and justice. Tolstóy's books opened up a great deal to me. I had never heard any lectures or talks on Tolstóy; all of that came to my little mind after long years of experience, beginning with my childhood and ending with the war.

While I was in the hospital at Kursk, I wrote a letter home. For a long time there was no answer. I appeared before the commission and was discharged for good. Suddenly a hospital attendant called me: "Your wife has come to see you." Sure enough, there were Maryána and Timoféy. It was an indescribable joy for me after such a hellish life, threatening death every day. And all of a sudden—my wife, my son, and I was free!

In a few days we went home together, filled with joy, even though I had only one eye—the other one had been ruined forever by the war.

One thing more has stuck in my mind about war. It turns out that in every railway bridge, and even in every little crossing bridge, there is a hole in each pillar for the insertion of explosives. As reconnaissance men, we always went last during a retreat, and explosives were put in place with fuses attached—just light the fuse, there would be an explosion, and the bridge would fall into the river. Storehouses with food supplies would be blown up in the same way. In that wild, senseless way we destroyed the work of human hands, so necessary for human life.

And something else about war. When you shoot in a war, it is hard to say whether you are shooting at a man or at your own death. When a man is executed by a firing squad, it is clear that they are shooting a man. But in wartime it is another matter: it's either you or him. During the whole time you were terrible enemies, but once the fighting stopped, you would go and pick up the wounded and feel pity for your fellow man. Your so-called enemy would lie there wounded, writhing in agony, losing blood, and would struggle to raise his hand to his mouth, meaning "Water!" Even though you didn't understand each other in words, you understood through feelings, and in a moment of human kindness you would give him your last drop of water from your own flask, and as he gulped it down, the enemy would thank you with a sob. But there were also moments of cruelty when they had killed your closest friend. In times like that, many men would not see a human being in that enemy writhing in pain, and there were some—to be sure, not many—who would go up and bayonet the wounded man.

Home Again: Tolstoyism, Revolution

And so my military life came to an end. By the time I got home, I had an idea of Leo Tolstóy as a good and even godly man, fair-minded and truthful. I loved him with all my being, even though I had still read very little of him. I had freed myself from that savage, inhuman deception and had awakened from my slavery.

During my absence, our house had been burned down as a consumers' co-op—somebody didn't like cooperatives. My brother Mikhaíl was at home, but his turn was coming up to be mobilized. When I got back home, my brother had already gone to Rostóv-on-the-Don, to his father-in-law, the captain. His father-in-law gave him a job, and he was given an exemption. My brother had a farm laborer, and he stayed on with me, helping to rebuild the house after the fire, and also with the crop sowing. At the village assembly I was asked to take charge of the cooperative societies. And so I took over my baby—the consumers' co-op. I collected shares, although some people criticized me for the first payment on the shares. Our charter was old; it had been approved by the governor. I went to Yeléts, where I had not been for two years. Now there was a branch of the Central Cooperative Union. It was called the Yeléts Union of Cooperative Societies, even though there were very few of them. I found there two men I had studied with at the agriculture courses in 1910–11, and they let me have—or rather, let our co-op have—several thousand rubles' worth of goods on credit. We found a big warehouse. Our Búrdino consumers' co-op started to flourish. Private traders began to have a hard time: new members started joining us even from other villages.

And so I worked all through 1916. Revolution came in February 1917, and suddenly everything began to move in a new direction, and I got into new activity. Conferences began to be held—district conferences, regional, provincial, and even church conferences, with village assemblies meeting every day. I was sent as a representative to all the conferences—to the district, to Yeléts, to Oryól, and even to a conference of the priesthood. At one of the conferences in Yeléts, I sharply criticized both the new bosses and the old. Once during intermission, the head of the Dolgorúkovo station came up to me and said:

"I have a friend in the village—a Tolstoyan—who talks just as boldly; he even knew Leo Tolstóy personally, and he has a lot of friends in Moscow, Petrograd, and Samára."

At once I wanted to meet him. After the conference I went to the Dolgorúkovo station, and then five miles more to the village of Griboyédovo, and there I found Iván Vasílyevich Gulyáyev, who was about fifty years old. I also met his wife, Klávdiya Ivánovna. I stayed there three nights. There was a lot to read at his house, and above all, a lot to listen to. He poured a lot that was bright and pure into my soul.

It was about twenty-five miles from our house to Griboyédovo. He and

I frequently visited each other. Iván Vasílyevich painted well and wrote good poetry about life. Later, in 1931, he moved to Siberia, to the Life and Labor Commune. We were put on trial together in 1936, and we each served ten years in prisons and camps. During one of my visits, in 1922, when there was a terrible famine in the Volga region, he read me a letter from his friend Vasíly Matvéyevich Yefrémov telling about the discovery in Samára of still another group of people (nine in all, including one woman) who had been caught with a hundred pounds or so of human flesh that they were selling at the bazaars. Iván Vasílyevich Gulyáyev kept me informed about what was going on in Moscow. He corresponded with Vladímir Grigóryevich Chertkóv and other friends there. He would lend me the Tolstoyan magazines *Yedinénie* (Unity), *Gólos Tolstógo* (The Voice of Tolstóy), and *Ístinnaya svobóda* (True Freedom). I wanted to visit Moscow myself and meet Chertkóv.

Before I met Gulyáyev, even before I was called to the army, there had been a group in our village (about ten people in all) who were called "strikers." What did they do, and what were their aims? They opened a metalworking and blacksmith shop. I knew them. They invited me to come, and I would go there to have farm machinery repaired. I was younger than all of them. I did not ask them what their aims were—in those days I had no grasp of that. But I knew that the nickname "strikers" was bad. Later they opened a little poultry farm, which everybody made fun of. Evidently they had wanted to organize themselves, but it was impossible to create a more formal organization without the permission of the governor. Now, however, since the Revolution, with assemblies and meetings almost every day, I began to draw closer to them. Sometimes they had read Tolstóy in their workshop, and now they read him even at meetings. So we organized a group of friends. In the autumn of 1917, when the district government and the district zémstvo were reorganized, elections were held, and three of our group were elected: I as chairman of the food-supply board, Vasíly Andréyevich Stoyántsev as director of public education, and Aleksándr Vasílyevich Logunóv as director of the land department.

I had to give up my work with the cooperatives. At a meeting of the district zémstvo, we raised the question of building a big four-class school and put it through. My work consisted in keeping an account of the food supplies. There were three of us. I thought we would conduct a simple survey, asking the head of each household how big a supply of grain and various crops he had and how much he could turn over to the storage place for the state, but it turned out otherwise. Workers and soldiers came out from Yeléts with a printed table showing how much wheat, rye, millet, oats, buckwheat, and other grains would fit into a cubic foot. We had to go around to the barns and measure their cubic feet and give orders for the compulsory delivery of grain to the collection points, leaving the householder an insignificant amount of grain to feed his family and none at all to feed his livestock. This was called the provincial broom, or the "red broom." This work quickly became loathsome to me, since every householder would curse you like all hell, and at the first meeting of the district zémstvo I resigned that duty—as chairman of the food-supply board.

I took on the task of organizing an agricultural credit union to provide financing for the population and raise the level of less well-to-do households by lending money for the purchase of livestock and equipment. At the beginning of 1918 I took our charter to Yeléts and had it registered—this time not with the governor but at the district office. Soon afterwards the treasurer and I went to Yeléts and received several thousand rubles from the State Bank. The director of the bank warned us that we should lend money only for the restoration of farms, and only to those who could pay back the money by the end of the term, and should by no means lend it "to those you can't depend on to pay it back: you know the people out there, the thrifty ones and the thriftless." As it turned out, those who came were mainly those who had no idea about economy but were looking only for a way to get a loan without paying it back. The credit-union management began refusing a few people. The district zémstvo and the State Bank were showered with complaints. They were told that the money was only for poor peasants. Our board found itself in the line of fire. There were endless threats and complaints. I called a general meeting of the association, reported what was going on, and resigned as chairman, even though I had been the organizer of the credit union. At that time representatives of various political parties began coming out from the city: Social Democrats and Socialist Revolutionaries, calling on us to join. Most people joined the party of the Democrats, who said: "Down with the war!" The war had been going on for four years, and nobody wanted it. In general, few people joined a party, and they were mostly seasonal laborers; the peasants, who worked at home, scarcely ever joined a party. They had their doubts.

Having resigned from my work in food supply and in the credit union, I went back to my old work in consumers' cooperatives, which I had never completely given up. We old workers often got together and discussed things, and began talking about the creation of an agricultural commune. Many of us wanted that, and I spoke strongly in favor of it, even though I was the youngest. Many people started coming to our meetings. We read Tolstóy. While I was still chairman of the food-supply board of the Terbuný District Zémstvo, we had collected a railway carload of rye as a gift for Lénin and sent it with Aleksándr Vasílyevich Logunóv to Moscow as our representative. He got in to see Lénin, who said: "Not every district is sending us a gift of grain, and here your district has given us a whole carload of it," and thanks for that were sent from Moscow to the Terbuný food-supply board.

Subsequently, that may have helped us. At the end of 1918, the better-off part of the population was assessed not just ordinary taxes but higher taxes, such as had never been imposed on the population before. Some people refused to pay, saying that they did not have the money. In our village of Búrdino, such people were undressed and put overnight into cold barns in December, when the temperature was minus twenty centigrade. At the village assembly I got up and condemned such actions by the village soviet and the representatives from the district and Yeléts. One day later there was a district conference; similar cases had taken place in other villages, and at that conference several of us spoke against such inhumane treatment of people. We said: "No sooner had we gotten rid of the tsarist despots than others turn up here who are no better." On 24 December, five of us were arrested and sent to the Cheká[3] in Yeléts.

The Cheká occupied a fine, big building. A vertical sign was fastened to the wall at the entrance with the word "Chrezvycháyka" on it, and from the right and left of each letter there sprouted a snake with its mouth wide open. This sign alone was enough to terrify people. We were thrust into the cellar, where it was completely dark. In the middle was a huge steam kettle. Evidently this had once been a boiler room. Other people were already there. We remained there several days. We were taken at night for interrogation. We were accused of being Tolstoyan anarchists who were interfering with the collection of taxes for the state. After that we were sent to prison. The escort was given the order: "Take them to the rag warehouse." We knew nothing about that; it was outside the town. We walked along and laughed at the thought of spending our time sorting rags, but it turned out that people there were sent off into the dim distance for good, never to return. But they took us to the prison. When we came up to it, a little old man said: "Evidently a fine owner lives here: the gates are iron and are even double."

Stoyántsev was accused of being the ringleader, and Morgachëv and Loginóv of working as leaders under the direction and influence of Stoyántsev. Our goal had been to obstruct the growth of the new Soviet state; we had led the agitation among the people against the collection of taxes necessary for the Soviet government. For our interrogation we were taken under escort to where there was the sign with the yawning jaws of serpents, and after our interrogations, back into prison. In prison I had one meeting with Maryána. The set-up of the meeting was exactly like what Tolstóy described in *Resurrection* when Nekhlyúdov went to see Katyúsha Máslova. The room was divided from floor to ceiling by two wire nets. Between them was a passageway about two meters wide. The prisoners sat on one side of the netting, and those who came to see us on the other, and an armed guard walked back and forth in the corridor between the netting. We had to shout in order to hear each other. Noise, shouts, tears, spiritual anguish.

In the investigation it was explained, however, that we had been active workers on the governing board of the district zémstvo and had spoken out at our meetings against the illegal and inhumane activities of persons who had rudely mistreated people during the tax collection. We were set free in March 1919 and went back home. At that time elections to the soviets were

3. Cheká—an acronym made up from the Russian initials *ch* and *k* of Chrezvychájnaja komíssija po bor'bé s kontrrevoljútsiej i sabotázhem (Extraordinary Commission for Struggle against Counterrevolution and Sabotage), the first name given to the Soviet secret police. Chrezvycháyka is a familiar form of this name.

taking place. The district zémstvos had been abolished. I was well known as a socially active man, not only in my own village but also in the district, and would no doubt have been elected; but I categorically refused either to elect or to be elected.

Our group of close friends came to the conclusion that we needed to create a commune under group leadership, with a communal farm managed according to the principles of justice, brotherhood, and rejection of private property, from which humankind suffered, and so did we. All the evil in the world came from private property, and our chief goal was to educate our children by living in a communist spirit, so that the children should not know "it's mine," but would know that it was ours in common, necessary and indispensable for all the members of the commune, and also personally for each worker in the commune.

At last we came to an agreement. We must get to work, and for that we needed land in one place. We made a request to our Búrdino association to assign us in one place the land that was due us as our individual allotments, and since we planned to build on it and live there, we asked that it have water. So that no one could envy us, we requested that this be worse-than-average land. The land association strung us along for a long while and discussed our request at numerous meetings. At last they refused us: "Don't go thinking up all kinds of newfangled ideas—you'd still fight among yourselves when you got together. Live together with us; we won't give you any land." We didn't want to go against the land association.

We were made up of nineteen households, plus two more from other villages. We agreed to accept them on our land allotments. There were fifty of us in all, including children. After the Revolution we had received a land allotment—two acres and a half for each person of either sex. I continued working at the consumers' co-op in our village, and at the congress in Yeléts I was elected a member of the governing board of the Yeléts Consumers' Union. But I refused to accept an office in the district, because we still had another goal: to create an agricultural commune, no matter what. But I remained a part-time board member of the Yeléts Consumers' Union, and I was invited to the more important meetings.

Even though I worked at the consumers' co-op, the district executive committee began nagging me—why wouldn't I join the Party and let myself be elected to the soviet? There were members of the district executive committee who were already in the Social Democratic Party. In the winter at the beginning of 1920, when I was at a congress of the Consumers' Union, for some reason I had to drop in at the headquarters of the Yeléts District Executive Committee. Acquaintances of mine were members of the soviet. I had been to the Yeléts District Zémstvo many times formerly; I had seen how orderly everything was. Everybody spoke politely—"Please sit down and tell me . . . ," and they would immediately give you advice or give an order about what you needed. But what disorder, what an uproar, in all the government offices since the Revolution! Even at the table they would swear at one another in the most repulsive language and then laugh at their own vulgarity and stupidity. Or they would shout: "Up against the wall—execute him!" And how much time it would take for people to settle down again.

In the summer of 1920, we friends finally decided to get together in a commune anyway; but since the association refused to allot land to us, we decided to get land near the boundary line of the village of Yazýkovo through voluntary exchanges with the citizens of our own village. The land was our private property, turned over to our village after the Revolution. It was good land: a peat meadow for fuel and fertilizer. Through exchanges, we collected a little over thirty acres of tillable land without a meadow. In July after the rye harvest, we got ready to move. My wife Maryána Illariónovna did not want to join the commune—we already had three children. I gave her some time—three days—to think it over, and if she decided she would not go into the commune, I would leave her the whole farm and still join it myself. I am writing these lines forty years later, and if my wife had not joined the commune, I really would have left her at that time. But she said: "Do whatever you want, and I will be with you."

The first building in the new place was my hay barn. We took it apart in the village and carried it to the new place, and we did all this at night, not far from the village of Yazýkovo. We carried the harvested grain from the fields to our new place, and after the threshing we covered that big barn with straw. Then we set to work moving my two granaries and one more that belonged to Pyotr Vasílyevich Úlshin. We built houses out of them—not very big ones, but still we spent the winter in them.

However, most of the members of our commune, our friends, thought better of moving there, explaining that their wives did not want to; but they helped us move. The houses in the village were made of brick; we had to either sell them or tear them down and carry the bricks.

In the spring of 1921, we plowed up the meadow and set out cabbage. The cabbage did well, and in spite of the cold year, we sold cabbage in exchange for wheat. The winter wheat was bad. The spring crop was tolerable. We had sown black vetch for fodder, and it turned out to be not bad at all. As is well known, 1921 was a year of great famine, especially in the Volga region, where all the grain had been hauled away in 1920. In 1921 the crop failure and famine were terrible. Autumn came. The village soviet demanded that we turn over grain for the starving in the Volga region. We said the population was starving there through the fault of the government, which had taken grain away from the people; and besides, there were harvest failures in the Volga region periodically. We were willing to take in ten or twelve children from the Volga region as innocent victims and feed them till the next harvest, but we would not give any grain. At the beginning of 1922, we were arrested and sent to the Yeléts prison—the third time for me. An investigation got under way. We simply told the investigator that the government was to blame for the famine, because it had taken grain away from the peasants. The investigator was a young man. Sometimes he would call us for questioning and talk with us about Tolstóy, since he knew nothing about Tolstóy. He would ask: "Was Tolstóy really the kind of man you say?" He would ask one of us and then read the first one's testimony to the second one, and he would ask the others: "Do you agree with that? What else do you want to add?"

At last we appeared in court. There were a lot of people at our trial. We said the same thing in court that we had said at the investigation, and asked them to give us a few of the starving children to feed, since the children were innocent creatures. People whispered: "They've lost their minds—talking like that about the government." The court asked a lot of questions. The judges held a meeting that lasted more than two hours. It was evening when the judges came back and read out the sentence: in view of the sincerity of the defendants and of their beliefs, the court had decided to free the accused but to take without payment, as confiscation, all of their grain that could be found.

Late in the evening we were taken from the court to the prison. There was a heavy snowstorm, but we were ordered to get together at once and leave. We asked them to let us stay there till morning, but they turned us out at once. When we left the prison, the storm was whistling, howling, swirling, and blowing. We walked to the railway station, about four kilometers away, and spent the night there. We had not stayed long in prison that time, about a month and a half.

During the winter of 1922, starving people from the Volga region, women and children, kept wandering in the direction of Moscow. Extremely weak and exhausted, they got as far as where we lived. Many of them froze to death on the way. Sometimes a mother and one or two children would be found lying at the side of the road, frozen to death. It was pitiful and painful to look at those hungry children. Many people shared what they could with them. I met one woman who told about her sister. They lived in a village near Samára. Where there is starvation, there is also sickness. Her husband died. The neighbors dragged the dead man into the cellar while his wife lay delirious and kept begging for food, and the neighbors cut off some meat from the dead man and cooked it and fed it to his wife. She began to recover and walk around a bit, and then stumbled onto the remains of her husband, realized what they had fed to her, and went out of her mind. If she had not found out what they had given her to eat, she probably would have lived and stayed sane.

About two weeks after we returned home from the trial, an order came down to the village soviet to take the rest of our grain away from us. No member of the village soviet was willing to do it. Finally, one did agree— Abrám Volýnkin. We lived seven kilometers from the village. They brought several carts, but nobody would go up to our granaries. At last they got up the nerve. We did not even go near and did not look at what was going on. They cleaned us out completely, and even took the women's sackcloth to pour grain into it. We had no grain left, yet we had to eat. We decided to sell our cows. We set out in the direction of Lívny, where there had been a harvest, and in one settlement we sold two cows for about four hundred pounds of millet. The cows were very good. Then we decided that if ever we had to buy anything that people were selling out of need, we must pay the real price for it, and not just the price they were asking in desperation.

How painful that was—to sell a cow for almost nothing because we were starving.

In the commune we had to establish the scantiest kind of rations—100 grams of bread per person. But still, our bread was made of grain, while others baked bread almost entirely of chaff and oak bark; and whoever had goosefoot plants for flour would say: "It isn't really bad if there's goosefoot to be had; but what is really bad is when you can't get either bread or goosefoot." Many people said that the children could not understand why there was no bread, and would keep begging and crying: "Give us some bread!" But that was a mistake. The children did understand. During our starvation, a ration would be handed out to everybody, and the children would look at their piece, lick it, and then put it away. Some would even save it till the next day, and show it to the others the next morning and say: "I still have mine, and you don't." None of us ever said anything to the children, and the children never asked for extra bread.

In the spring when the grass started growing, we would cook and eat it; and when the sorrel came up, we boiled it in big pots and fed on it.

We sowed spring wheat. One of my acquaintances gave us a little seed— forty or fifty pounds—since everyone knew that all our grain had been taken away from us. In 1923 the harvest was good—both winter wheat and spring wheat. We harvested everything—grain for the wheat bins and straw, chaff, and hay for the hay barn and the livestock.

In autumn of 1923 we built a little house for a school, since the children needed to be educated, and we had with us a schoolteacher, Raísa Ivánovna Ivanóva, a single woman, the daughter of a blacksmith from the neighboring village of Soldátskoye. She was very kind. We put up all the children of school age in the school, where they lived with their teacher, and cooked their meals there. We kept the children separate so that they would be brought up without family squabbles but in mutual helpfulness, and so that they would not know personal property but would recognize property as public and make use of it jointly. We also admitted children to our school from the village of Yazýkovo, which was less than a kilometer away. The adults in that village were almost all illiterate. Their children came to us only for their classes. We took no pay at all from them.

We had broken entirely with the church. No one ever went there. We did not have our children baptized, and did not even register them at the village soviet. Not only in our village but also in the surrounding villages, people began saying that we had some kind of new religion. I already had three children, unbaptized and unregistered, and the rumor went around among the people that horns would start to grow on unbaptized children. When my wife had occasion to take the baby to the village, women would stop her to see how the horns grew on unbaptized children. When they saw that there were no horns, they were astonished that people said such untrue things. My wife and I had one baby who died, and we buried it on our communal farm in a young orchard. Later the mother of one of our commune members died, and we buried her in our orchard too. Then the rumor went around among the villagers that this old lady who died without sacraments and was buried without a priest walked through the fields at night and wept. Many people said they had seen her, more than once and in many places. Less than a kilometer from our village were ditches with water in them for soaking hemp. One peasant got up early one morning and went to get his soaking hemp. He began piling it onto his cart, and it seemed to him that something was groaning in the sheaves of hemp, and a human voice seemed to say: "Don't disturb the sheaves, I am comfortable here." He jumped on his cart and in a frenzy drove his horses some six kilometers, but the old woman pursued him right up to the village. He became ill from fright and died soon after. Then still more started saying that all this was because she had been buried without a priest and the sacraments. Some people said we should go to the priest and have a requiem performed; otherwise she might frighten a lot of people to death.

"But just what sort of religion do you have?" many people kept thinking and guessing. Finally someone got the idea that we must be Catholics, and started calling us "Kettle-iks," as they pronounced it. They also said we would pray to a kettle full of water and try to jump over it, and whoever jumped over it showed that he was a saint, but whoever caught his foot on it was sinful and had to look at the kettle all night until a voice told him either to walk around it or to have a rest.

The most absurd tales circulated about us. I often went to the village, and people would ask questions of me and others about this. Sometimes we would joke about it and say sure, it was all true, and sometimes we would laugh and deny it; but they still didn't believe us. That shows how hard it is for people to accept new and unusual views on life.

In the village of Yazýkovo, with only twenty households, a passerby once stayed overnight and stole something, so they stopped taking anyone in for the night. Instead, they would send them to us: "Over there is where the Kettle-iks live—they never refuse to let anybody stay overnight." And we really did refuse nobody; we did not even latch or bar our doors. There were times when some stranger would arrive at night and wake us up and ask for lodging. We never locked our granaries either.

In 1924 the women in the commune began to squabble more and more. When the grain was threshed, it had to be hauled off in carts to the granary, but there were almost no bags. My Maryána had a big piece of sackcloth. She would spread it out in the cart and pour up to half a ton of grain on it, but the others had no such cloth. One man came to me and said:

"Your wife won't lend her cloth to anybody."

I went and said:

"Maryánka, lend them the cloth."

"I won't. Let them lend their wagon, and then I will."

"But they haven't got one."

"What's that to me?"

I tried for a long time to persuade her but failed. In anger I struck her on the head with my jacket, and the belt button hit her under her eye. Her eye swelled up and turned black. Afterwards I was ashamed of myself, and I never again raised my hand to her in all our life together.

We came to the conclusion that we should form a collective farm, especially since many of our friends had already agreed to join one. In autumn of 1924 we accepted the charter of a cooperative agricultural work team *(artel)* and registered it with the district executive committee. Now the land organizers allocated land to us. We distributed our property among all the members without taking into account who had contributed what. The orchard, too, we divided up among the members.

Thus ended our commune. The women had played a big role in its failure. The questions that agitated us about property, communes, communal labor, the education of children, and other important and fundamental matters were alien and incomprehensible to them. They remained at the previous level of traditional individual peasant life. I do not know whether they should be blamed or pitied for that, but we could not make them understand and sympathize with the ideas and aspirations and everything that we lived by. Our life in common could not withstand such a divergence, and so we went down to a lower level.

I don't know whether I am right, but all that has left within me a feeling of bitterness and lack of respect toward women, even though I know they are not all like that: there were some who could be considered equal comrades in our work.

Although I lived in the commune, the leadership of the co-op rested on me, even though I was not always there. For example, with my agreement, the managing board got forty head of cattle ready for delivery, and I reported this to Yeléts. In reply they told me to bring them to Yeléts, where they already had two hundred head of cattle. According to their contract, they had to send them all to the Moscow slaughterhouses, and they empowered me to take the cattle up there and deliver them. I agreed, since I had long wanted to go to Moscow and get acquainted with Vladímir Chertkóv. We loaded the cattle into railway cars, and we men who were taking them got into a freight car along with the feed and our own provisions. Even though I was in charge, a specialist on cattle deliveries and meat grading went along with us, since the price for the meat would depend on its quality. We arrived in Moscow, and a branch line of the railway led us straight to the slaughterhouse. The next day, we set to work slaughtering our cattle. The norm for two butchers was forty to forty-five head in eight hours. They worked so fast that they would cut the carcass in two parts—fore and hind—and drop them into the refrigerator while the muscles were still twitching.

After finishing with the cattle at the slaughterhouse and settling our account at the bank, I was free; and I went to look up Vladímir Grigóryevich Chertkóv. I found him, I don't remember where—either on Lefórtovsky Lane or Newspaper Lane. He gave me a friendly reception, and we talked for at least two hours. Then he said: "Come back this evening; we are going to have a meeting."

When I went back, there were about thirty young people there. Then Vladímir Grigóryevich arrived, and we all took seats. His first words were: "We have a visitor here from the Yeléts District in Oryól Province. I talked with him today, and I will ask him to tell us about his life."

Everyone present said with one voice: "Please do!" I went up to the table, stood beside Vladímir Grigóryevich, and briefly told as best I could how I had heard about Tolstóy for the first time in 1910, and for the second time in Túla from the Yásnaya Polyána recruit, and then in 1915, when I was lying wounded in the hospital, how I had remembered the words of that recruit about Tolstóy and how he was opposed to war, and how I had asked for some books by Tolstóy and read them with enthusiasm and taken to heart everything Tolstóy said. I told about the court trials, the first one and the second, and how we had still been found innocent. I told about our organization of the commune.

Chertkóv got up after me and said: "Friends, you have heard what this man told us about his life. Such people are native talent from the heartland. He grew up as an orphan, among working people. He knew nothing about Leo Tolstóy. The great truth discovered by Tolstóy casts its light into the darkness of the common people and awakens them to reason and awareness. Here before us stands this man, almost illiterate, and yet he has been at work all the time. This is not what you have been doing: you go to meetings, you listen to speeches and lectures and you yourselves give them, and many of you have been shown the true path by your parents, but these people are illiterate, they have found their own way to the path of truth and goodness. . . ."

Vladímir Grigóryevich said a lot more about us and the city youth. Voices resounded: "We too want to start a commune."

The next day, an old lady invited me to come for some books. I went to Newspaper Lane, the headquarters of the Moscow Vegetarian Society. A lot of books were for sale there. The elderly woman who had been at Vladímir Grigóryevich's the previous evening asked me what kind of books I had. I named a few, but they were my friend I. S. Gulyáyev's. She picked out some books and booklets for me and recommended that I read *Papálagi,* about a young Indian who went to London or Paris and on his return home told about seeing high mountains in which many people lived, but without knowing one another. Here on our island we know everybody, but there they did not even know who lived next door on the same mountain. This was about the tall skyscrapers where people live that way even to this day.[4]

Vladímir Grigóryevich treated me kindly, like a son. I also met him later, probably when I went to see him in 1931 about our resettlement in Siberia. I remember that he gave me a package to take with me. I put it into an outer

4. *Papálagi*—the Russian translation of a fictional work published in German in 1920 by Erich Scheurmann, giving a satirical description of Western European civilization as seen through the eyes of a tribal chief from one of the South Sea islands. Modest though it is as a work of art, it has been translated into at least eight languages and continues to be published around the world.

pocket. He took it out and said: "That's not where you carry things in Moscow. You're not in the village here. Here you have to keep a sharp lookout; they'll cut your shoe soles off while you're walking." And he put the package into one of my inner pockets.

I have already said that in the place of our commune we organized the Renaissance Agricultural Cooperative (that was the same name our commune had). At the beginning of 1925, we decided to get an American Fordson tractor. One of us was sent off to take a course for tractor drivers. We received the tractor, and it was a marvel: we could both haul and plow with it. Our tractor was the first one in the district. Even though we had no great ties with the district, the authorities warmed up to us, knowing that our collective farm, in their district, had a tractor. When there were district meetings, they would ask us to come with our tractor. We would report on how it worked—plowing, mowing, hauling—and the district authorities were proud: "Here is what the Soviet authorities give to the peasants."

Everybody knew that we had broken with the church. I happened to go to a district meeting on the tractor. There were a lot of people. The chairman of the district executive committee came up and asked me to tell the people something about the church. I agreed to, but I made it short:

"Comrades! The priests in the churches preach from their pulpits and deceive the people, fogging over the truth. The time is not far off when the people will hear reports from the pulpit by scholars and academicians about raising the standard of living among the people, and especially the peasantry." Here they loaded me down with so much applause that you couldn't even have hauled it away on the tractor.

A big highway passed not far from us—the Yekateríninsky High Road, from Oryól to Vorónezh, seventy meters in width. The district executive committee gave us permission to plow up two-thirds of this road for our collective farm. We broke a strip of virgin soil two kilometers long. We sowed it in wheat that we had received from the Khmelínets sugar factory. In our locality, people did not sow wheat but rye. Our wheat produced a good harvest. We gave grain in equal portions to every living soul in the cooperative, and not just to the workers. We decided to buy a pair of millstones to use with our tractor. Our tractor driver, Pyotr Vasílyevich Úlshin, went to Oryól, bought them, and brought them back, and we built a flour mill in the village of Búrdino. A miller's measure had to be set aside for the state from every job we did.

In 1922 there was the famine. For a kilogram of grain we would pay in money and goods whatever was asked, but in 1924 our rye cost twenty kopeks. In 1927 our rye harvest failed, and some members of the collective farm had almost no grain. As chairman of the cooperative, I gave out a part of the miller's measure to members who needed it for food, and we were severely questioned about the miller's measure. A representative of the district executive committee made a check. The miller's measure showed on the records but was not to be found. A report was drawn up and sent to the court. In the district executive committee, they looked askance at me because

I would not join the Party. The court sentenced me to three years of imprisonment, with confiscation of my property. I appealed to the regional court and carried my appeal to Yeléts in person. The regional court overturned my sentence, but ordered us to pay the miller's measure out of the next year's harvest.

Forced Collectivization, and Resettlement in Western Siberia

With the coming of the year 1929, collectivization began in the district where our collective farm was the only one in existence. All the district leaders began agitating for collectivization, but everybody reproached them and even laughed at them: "You want to get us into a collective farm, but you're not going into one yourselves." Then they started applying for admission to our farm so that it would be easier for them to agitate for collectivization. We did not like that bit of trickery, and at a general meeting of the cooperative we refused to admit the leaders of the district executive committee. That greatly offended them, of course, and set them against me. Some of the Party members were on my side and advised me to leave, or even move away completely:

"Now they'll persecute you at every step—they'll eat you alive. You're a capable man; go off and take the course for collective-farm directors."

But I would not leave: I was going to stick it out to the end, no matter what.

At last the district leaders got even with me: they expelled me from the collective farm as a "Tolstoyan sectarian" and dispossessed me as a kulák, taking my cow and my goods and chattels. My horse, though, was in the collective farm. I went to Yeléts, where many people knew me. They were all astonished at the incomprehensible action of the district authorities, and the decision of the district executive committee was overturned. My goods had disappeared, and my cow was not returned for two or three months. It had been taken by relatives of the chairman of the village soviet. They offered me any cow that had been confiscated, but I refused to take anybody else's cow. I demanded my own, and I finally got it back. The district bosses still wanted to deport me as a kulák, but the village Party activists would not agree to that, first because we were orphans and I had lived for more than four years as a seasonal worker, and second, because I had worked more than fifteen years in consumers' cooperatives, and all the poor peasants and all the Party activists in our village of Búrdino were on my side. I continued working as the chairman of the collective farm, which was composed entirely of our friends, and they refused to elect anybody else in my place. I went ahead, regardless of obstacles. There were such incidents as this: during my absence, an effort was made to get the most active poor peasants to take some sort of decision against me, but not a single one would raise a hand against me in my presence. One Party leader practically went out of his mind at the sight of the poor peasants taking my side. That is the way things went all through

1929. During the threshing, the district procurator came to arrest me, but I was on top of a stack of straw that was being hauled by my horse. So they just stood there and talked with me but did not seize me.

Collectivization began at the end of 1929 without the agreement of the peasants. Horses, cows, heifers, and sheep were gathered together in collective farmsteads. Plows, harrows, wagons, and fodder were taken away from the peasants' barns. Then suddenly in January or February 1930, there appeared Stálin's article "Giddiness from Success."[5] The next day, the peasants joyously trooped off to the collective farms to get back their own livestock and equipment. But the Party activists were very dissatisfied. They said: "You won't be crowing long. Come autumn, we'll rub a few butts with acid and you'll dance another tune—you'll come running into the collective farm without looking back." That was what we heard from the chairman of the district executive committee, Aleksándr Alekséyevich Úlshin.

In 1930 everyone worked individually. In August some were saddled with forced grain deliveries of nine to fifteen tons—a clearly impossible demand. In September and October, these people were tried in court and given sentences from three to eight years in the camps, with confiscation of their property. My brother Mikhaíl Yegórovich got three years, and Timoféy Semyónovich Vólkov got six years. At one time he had started to join our commune, but his wife would not agree. He was sent to Karagánda, where he lost his life. My brother Mikhaíl survived but never went back to farming. He remained in factory work.

In the winter of 1930, collectivization began again, and this time there was no giddiness; everything rolled along smoothly, without squeaking. Fifteen or twenty men were convicted, and the rest—the more well-to-do middle peasants—were the first to join the collective farm. Some of the poor peasants still had their doubts and hesitated, and some of them went to work in the factories for good, taking their families with them.

I found out from I. V. Gulyáyev that Chertkóv had submitted a petition to the All-Russian Central Executive Committee requesting an allotment of land for the establishment of communes and agricultural cooperatives by the followers of Leo Tolstóy. Later Gulyáyev told me that peasant representatives had gone to pick out a plot of ground for the settlement, and still later, that land had been reserved in Western Siberia.

In January I went to Moscow. I had not been there since 1924. I went to see Chertkóv. He welcomed me cordially, like an old friend. He told me about the preparations for the resettlement. I told him that I too would like to resettle with like-minded friends of Tolstóy. Chertkóv sent me to the Life and Labor Commune, on the outskirts of Moscow. I went there with Dmí-

---

5. The collectivization of 54 percent of all the farms in the Soviet Union during the five months from October 1929 to March 1930 was so disastrous for Soviet agriculture and so brutal and costly in human lives that the government was forced to order a retreat. Stalin's article "Giddiness from Success," published on 2 March 1930, allowed the peasants to take back their own livestock and equipment from the collective farms.

try Kiselyóv, who had come from Túla also to see about resettling. Dmítry was a merry fellow, and on the way he laughingly told me how they kept hens and did not kill the roosters, and how many there were, and how they crowed, each one in his own way!

We arrived at the commune. The chairman was Borís Mazúrin. He had a thorough talk with each of us. When it was time for dinner, we were invited to the common table. After dinner we helped cut a little wood for the kitchen. In the evening we talked some more with Mazúrin. He asked us about our families and our property. I told him that even though I had some property, I could not take it with me because there were eight in our family, three of them grown. Mazúrin jokingly asked me another question: "Aren't you too lazy to work for such a family?" I also answered jokingly: "I may be lying to you now, of course, but I didn't use to be lazy." I told him what kind of property I had, including about a hectare of orchard I had set out in 1923. Then I told him I was not going back home, but said that if he did not accept me, I would get some kind of job here or else take some courses. I said I had a recommendation. At supper that evening a lot of commune members talked with me and questioned me, and they decided to accept me.

In autumn of 1930, the commune sent a working team to the site of the new settlement in Siberia to prepare housing and living arrangements. A few days before I joined the commune, the working and producing livestock had been loaded into railway cars and sent off with Pyotr Yákovlevich Tolkách. Now another group of commune members were getting ready to leave, and I went with them. We got into a car of a passenger train and started on our way to Siberia. For all our little group, Siberia was a new and unknown country.

Everything was still covered with snow. On the fourth day we arrived at Novokuznétsk. Horses and light carriages were sent to meet us. We got in and started off. We reached the Tom River. Water was already flowing over the ice. Crossing was risky, but still we made it across safely. There was a settlement on the other side of the river. It turned out to be Kuznétsk—the old town. There were little wooden houses, and on the mountain above the town was an old fort. Dostoyévsky had once served out his exile in the town. But I was most surprised by the village of Feskí, through which we passed. Its little houses were also of wood. I went into one house to get a drink. Its cleanliness and neatness, the flowers in the windows and even on the floor in tubs, the painted floors—we thought of Siberia as a land of convicts, and yet people live far better here than in Central Russia. Among us, floors in peasant huts were a rarity, and flowers were found only in homes of the priesthood, never in peasant homes.

So here we were in our new settlement. Not far from the bank of the Tom, a few little houses clung to the hillside. We spent the night in our new place. The next morning, we were off to work. A cooking stove had to be built under an awning. Nobody knew how to build stoves, or make a cauldron or an oven. They asked me, but I not only did not know how, I had never even seen one built. Nádya Gúrina said to me: "Come on, I've seen cooking stoves built." So she and I set to work, and by evening we had built a complete stove with a cauldron and an oven. It had a good draft and would boil and roast quickly. During the winter, a big new building was built. Even though it did not yet have a roof, we needed to build a stove in it. I had now become the stove-builder, and I set to work building stoves with three to five heating chambers in them. As soon as we put up stoves and let them dry, the residents would move in, and a new family in the commune would start to grow. We began buying houses in the surrounding villages, hauling them back, and putting them up. I kept on building stoves.

In the evenings we would talk about how to organize the family life of the commune in the best and freest way. We all came to the conclusion that a separate room or house should be made available to each family. We knew that our new settlement would get several hundred families from various parts of the country, representing different nationalities and different varieties of the Christian religion. The new settlers received no material help from the state or anyone else. They received only free resettlers' railroad tickets issued by the People's Commissariat of Agriculture. Again according to the rules, whoever had grain or fodder would turn it over to the local authorities in exchange for a resettlement receipt, and here they would receive the same amount back from the local grain-procurement office. This was very convenient. In April 1931 the last members of the Life and Labor Commune arrived after liquidating their property near Moscow. Settlers began pouring in from various republics and provinces of the Soviet Union.

We did some sowing in the spring. There had been no winter sowing. It was hard to find living quarters for the newcomers, and we had to put several families into one house or one apartment. New arrivals who came with money were authorized to buy houses for themselves in the surrounding villages and then take them apart, haul them in, and put them up again with the help of the commune. For those like me who came without any means, the building was done at the expense of the commune, without making any distinction.

All the property brought along by the newcomers, including their livestock and grain as well as their money, was appraised and received as joint property of the commune and noted down in the personal account of the donor.

More and more settlers kept arriving, and they even started coming on their own, without resettlers' railroad tickets, not only Tolstoyans but members of various religious movements—Subbótniks, Malyóvannians, Baptists, Dobrolyúbovians. I must say that in their way of life, these groups were close to Tolstoyan teachings. There were Subbótniks who even in tsarist times had been sentenced to twelve years at hard labor for refusing military service. The Malyóvannians and Dobrolyúbovians also refused to take up arms. Almost all of them were vegetarians. All of them rejected the church religion, with its rituals, icons, sacraments, and so on. So it goes without saying that they led a more or less moral way of life: they did not drink, smoke, or use foul language. They decided not to inhibit each other in choosing their own way of life; and the newcomers could unite according to their own wishes in communes, cooperatives, or communities. Thus, in addition to the Life and Labor Commune, there were formed the Peaceful Plowman Cooperative (Subbótniks and Ukrainians) and the World Brotherhood Community, whose members had come from near Stalingrad and considered themselves followers of Tolstóy. A group from Barábinsk organized a settlement three or four kilometers from our commune. A group from the town of Biysk set up a farm near the Abáshevo coal mines. The group from Omsk was not very large. And so a number of independent groups settled on the land allotted to the Tolstoyan settlement in the Kuznétsk District of Western Siberia.

I was already in the commune, but my family was still at home, where our first commune had been organized. In June 1931 I went back after my family. I had to travel by way of Moscow, and our commune council gave me several commissions. Some of our commune members who had come from Kirgízia had been deprived of their civil rights. The commune interceded for them, pointing out that the deprivation of their rights was illegal, since they had not been exploiters. I arrived in Moscow and went to see Vladímir Chertkóv. I had been given an oral commission to find out whether we could settle beyond the borders of the country—I do not remember just where, but it seems that it was on some island.

Vladímir Grigóryevich arranged an appointment for us with the deputy of M. I. Kalínin, Pyotr Germogénovich Smidóvich. On the appointed day, Chertkóv's son Díma, Vásya Shershenyóv, and I went to Kalínin's reception room. Kalínin and Smidóvich had one secretary between their two offices. Kalínin's reception room had eighteen offices in all where peasants were received with requests and petitions about all matters, and the secretaries themselves decided in Kalínin's name where to send the petitioners. Kalínin's office was on the second floor, and people were admitted there only by pass. We were admitted, and we sat down in the secretary's office to wait for Smidóvich. M. I. Kalínin came in. I did not know him. Everybody stood up and said: "Good morning, Mikhaíl Ivánovich." I stood up too, recognizing who it was. Kalínin was a short little old man, who looked very much like his portraits. Going past the secretary, he went into the office on the left. In a few minutes a man came in and asked: "Has Mikhaíl Ivánovich arrived? I need to see him."

The secretary answered: "Just a moment."

The man said: "He gave me a commission yesterday, and I need to talk with him."

"Just a minute—I will ask." The secretary went into Kalínin's office, then came out at once and said: "No, Mikhaíl Ivánovich cannot see you."

The man shrugged his shoulders. "Then give him this file." I thought to myself, How are peasants able to come and see Kalínin when he evidently would not receive a member of the government?

At last Smidóvich arrived and invited us into his office. He closed and bolted the door himself and drew the heavy curtain. Our conversation began.

I handed him the commune's petition to restore voting rights to those who had been deprived of them. He read it and said: "This is very bad; they are not our people." We talked about it for a long time. Finally Smidóvich said: "I will talk this over with my comrades. You come back in a few days." Then he ordered glasses of tea for us and some cakes.

Then we mentioned resettling abroad, on an island. He looked at us in astonishment and said: "No, friends, we will not allow that, and I cannot raise that question with my comrades. They have unemployment over there, and we need workers, so live here in your own place and be examples of communist social life in our country." That is what Pyotr Germogénovich Smidóvich said.

Before my trip back home to get my family, I received a letter from my wife telling me that a big package had come for me, but the village soviet would not let her have it, and even railed and swore about me. The package contained the resettlement documents from the People's Commissariat of Agriculture, allowing my family to make the railway trip to Novokuznétsk station in the Western Siberian Territory at the low rate for resettlers. I told Vladímir Grigóryevich about this. He advised me not to go myself to get my family; in those uncertain times I might be imprisoned. "Write to her," he said, "and tell her to bring the children and come to Moscow." But I did not take his advice, and told him I would not let anyone see me there. Vladímir Grigóryevich was really displeased that I went. It was four hundred kilometers from Moscow. I arrived at the Terbuný station just before evening. It was seven or eight kilometers to my home. I went on foot by a road through the fields. There was a Communist living in my house. I went through my orchard. It was already dark, but the Communist's wife saw me. We greeted each other. The next day, I quickly gathered up our few possessions, took them to the station, and sent them as baggage to Moscow. That was at the beginning of July, and I went with my family to sleep in the barn. My wife and I talked for a long time about Siberia and the commune. Toward morning, several men and the chairman of the village soviet came and arrested me. They wanted to seize what was left of our belongings, but I had sent them off in time as baggage. They took me to the village of Búrdino and put me in the watchman's room at the church. Chertkóv's suspicion had proved correct.

The village soviet was right beside the deacon's house. A general meeting of the village of Búrdino had been set for that day. The news of my arrest spread quickly through the whole village. Friends and acquaintances began gathering at the watchman's room to see me. I jokingly said to them: "I've come here to get part of the church property. After all, I gave here for many years." Then we talked about Siberia and the commune. The watchman's room was overflowing with people. Then the chairman of the village soviet came and told them to go to the meeting, and assigned an odd young fellow who was not very bright to stand guard over me. Toward eleven o'clock, my son Ványa came and brought me some boiled eggs for lunch. I ate a little of the lunch and then offered some to my guard, and then I myself went out. I walked around the church. Inside the church wall there was a grave-yard where my people were buried—my father, mother, grandfather, and grandmother. I walked around their graves and stood for a while before the grave of my mother. Then I walked up to the brick wall. I looked around. There was nobody on the road, and instantly the thought came to me to leave. I jumped over the wall, crossed the road, and climbed down in a gulley toward the blacksmith shop. There I quickened my pace and turned toward the vegetable gardens sown in wheat and hemp. Bending down, I ran up to and into the woods. I had gone about two kilometers when I heard shouts and laughter from the whole meeting: "Find him! Find him!" But now it was too late to find me. Where would they look? After all, no one had seen where I went. My guard had waited for me and then, seeing that I was not there, had gone and told the meeting that I had run away. Then came the shouting and the laughter.

I walked about five kilometers to a place opposite our settlement, but it was still about five more kilometers to the settlement itself. It began to grow dark, and I walked straight ahead through the wheat. It was dark when I came to our house. When I was convinced that everything was quiet, I let my wife see me and then went to sleep in the unharvested rye. I spent the whole night there and got sick at my stomach. My wife came and saw me writhing in pain, and she started crying. I spent the whole day there with a fever, and in the evening I somehow managed to get to Pyotr Vasílyevich Úlshin, our tractor driver. I drank some tea with preserves and began to feel better. Then I went to sleep and recovered completely.

I was in a difficult situation: our house was occupied, and whatever things we had were on their way to Moscow. Where could my wife and six chil-dren go, with only one of them grown—Tíma? Everybody would have to leave. Even though the horses belonged to the collective farm, the people who lived there were ours. They gave us horses, and my sister drove my family to the station at Terbuný. We bought tickets, but not for the train that went nonstop to Moscow, in the middle of the day. The district bosses knew and hated me and often went to meet that train, and for that reason we got tickets for the early morning train, with a change at Yeléts. My wife and children sat down on the platform, and I stood near the church on the other side of the train, about forty meters from the track. When the second bell rang, I ran to the train, grabbed hold on the other side, and climbed into the car after it had started moving. At Yeléts we changed to another train by way of the Leo Tolstóy station and arrived safely.

The next day, I went to see Smidóvich alone. I waited a long time for admission to the second floor. The guard told me to get a pass from any of the secretaries. I started going from secretary to secretary; no one would give me a pass, and no one would call up Smidóvich's secretary, who knew I was supposed to see him. At last one of them did call. Smidóvich's secretary told her to give me a pass, and so I got in to Smidóvich. I went in and greeted him. Pyotr Germogénovich began asking questions about the location of the commune. I explained that it was a mountainous spot, a spur of the Altái mountains, and there were woods and hayfields. We were building houses and a cattle-yard with our own forces. We were buying draft animals. In a word, we were getting ourselves well prepared.

"That's good," said Smidóvich, and asked further: "How far away from you are they building the factory? Aren't the local people asking to join your commune?"

I answered that the factory was being built twenty-five kilometers away, and that so far none of the local inhabitants had asked to join us.

Finally he said to me:

"I spoke to my comrades about your request for the restoration of civil rights to your commune members. They agreed to satisfy your request, and you will get an announcement of it in writing."

Smidóvich was in a good humor and was very much interested in the commune. But when I told about myself and said that during my absence I had been deprived of my civil rights as a Tolstoyan sectarian, Smidóvich's mood changed at once, and he frowned.

"That matter is worse," he said.

I explained my situation to him, and told him that I had gone to the commune earlier with a construction team, and now I had come back to get my family. My family was already in Moscow. I had shared Tolstóy's views since 1915. I had organized a cooperative in my village and had organized a commune in 1922–24, which had later become a cooperative farm, the first in the Yeléts District.

Smidóvich asked me a lot of questions. Finally he said:

"I will give you an official order to the Moscow Soviet for resettlement documents and tickets."

I thanked him. When we parted, Smidóvich said:

"I wish you success in building a new social form of life—a communist form."

I was in a joyful state of mind when I left him; I was glad both for myself and for others.

The next day, the Alekséyev brothers—Pétya and Ilyúsha—went to get my baggage. They went with me to the Moscow Soviet to get the documents and railway ticket—a booklet in which were written the names of my family and me and a few other persons who were going to the commune.

We arrived at the commune in July 1931. We were assigned a little house, a former bathhouse, where I lived till 1936 and my family till 1947. I went back to building living quarters and farm buildings, and my son Timoféy joined a field team.

Experiences in the Life and Labor Commune

I feel the need to describe my experiences and impressions in the Life and Labor Commune; but I have lived through so many vivid, impressive, and varied experiences that I cannot include them all, especially since my memory has grown weaker. So I will tell what has not yet faded entirely from my mind.

In autumn of 1931 there were more than five hundred people living in our commune. The harvest was small, and we lacked grain. It was expensive on the market, and one loaf of bread cost forty to fifty rubles. Very little cash remained in the commune, since we had bought houses and draft animals. The commune council called a general meeting to settle the burning issue of food. It was decided to empower the council to seek work for all able-bodied men. Soon work was found. We made an agreement with the timber-supply office to build houses and supplementary lodging for timber workers on three plots of land at Kamenúshka, Slentsý, and Uzuntsý, along the Abáshevo River, which flows into the Tom. According to our agreement, rations of grain and food supplies were distributed not only to the workers but also to the members of their families. So all the able-bodied men in the commune went to work at Górnaya Shóriya. The money we earned and, above all, the supplies we received as rations greatly lowered the tension over food in the commune. I worked at the middle plot, Kamenúshka, where the work was led by Grísha Gúrin. We finished an enormous clubhouse toward spring, and then our work team started building a railway branch line to the timber harbor Abagúr, where rations were also handed out to family members.

In 1932 the commune sowed more wheat and vegetables. From then on, vegetable growing supplied the commune with its basic income. The market for vegetables was unlimited, since the gigantic Kuznetskstróy (Kuznétsk Metallurgical Combine) was under construction about twenty-five kilometers away. There was a great need for vegetables, and the local population had never gone in for vegetable growing.

Toward July all the members of the commune came back from their outside work and got busy improving its facilities and building houses, cattleyards, barns, vegetable storehouses, and so on. In 1932 the population was a little smaller than in 1931. The same natural process took place as in all new settlements: some were afraid of the difficulties; the climate did not suit others; still others did not find what they had expected in their dreams. By that time the commune had people of various specialties in all the branches of work necessary in agriculture. The farm grew by leaps and bounds. There were people who had a middle and even a higher education, and this helped us organize our own school. So our children received a great deal of serious attention.

We built two greenhouses to grow seedlings for the early transplanting of cucumbers and tomatoes. We laid the foundation for hothouse farming with three hundred glass frames. During the winter we grew cucumbers and tomatoes in our greenhouses. Our vegetable gardeners were experienced: Seryózha Alekséyev and Prokóp Kuvshínov. At first Vasíly Shipílov was put in charge of marketing the commune's vegetables, but he became ill and then I was chosen.

Our commune was located on the Tom River, twenty kilometers up-

Grinding grain into flour at the Life and Labor Commune, 1932–33.

Loading produce on a big boat called a *kárbuz* to float it to market down the river Tom to Novokuznétsk.

stream from Stálinsk. On the bank of the Tom we built a little house to serve as a transfer point. There we would moor our flat-bottomed boats, which we had acquired to facilitate the transport of our vegetables, potatoes, and grain. We would unload them and deliver them on carts to the dining halls of Kuznetskstróy. We would pull our boats back up the river by cables attached to horses. I would spend the whole working day going around to the factory dining halls, negotiating over who needed what and how much.

In the evening we would gather in our little house on the river bank, and I would give instructions to each one about how much should go to which dining hall.

We cleared a section of floodlands by the river for a vegetable garden, and vegetables did well there. We set out no less than three hectares of them. On warm days the growth would reach a ton and a half per hectare in twenty-four hours, while on cooler days it would fall to less than four hundred pounds per hectare. I remember this because I myself did the marketing. If anything was left over after we had supplied the dining halls, we would send the vegetables to the market. I would tell who to take it to and how much to sell it for. The dining halls settled their accounts with us through bank transfers; and the cash from sales to the market was turned over to me, and I would pass it on to the commune or deposit it in our account at the State Bank. Everything was based on honesty, on conscience. I already knew, for example, how much was supposed to be received for a wagonload of cucumbers, and when the person who had sold them handed the money over to me, I saw that it was right; but there were some cases where you would have the feeling that not all the money had been turned in. Still, I said nothing to anybody about that, and did not even give a personal reprimand to that man, and I am writing about it only now, thirty-five years later. Yes, conscience is a great matter, especially when people trust you, and that man himself feels the sin of misappropriation upon him. He was always ashamed, and not only in front of me but in front of other people too. He felt that everybody knew about it, that he had violated the confidence we had placed in him.

In Stálinsk there were special dining halls for foreigners, engineers who were building the factory—Germans, Belgians, Frenchmen. Some were building the blast furnaces; others, the rolling mills; still others, the hydroelectric station; and others, the waterworks. They did not ask there about the price—"Just give us fresh vegetables." When they sat down at the table, they would chew raw cabbage—they were afraid of scurvy. Representatives even came to our commune from the city soviet, begging us to supply the foreigners with fresh vegetables.

For the building of our commune we needed iron, nails, glass, and other materials, even cotton textiles. At that time those things were hard to find for sale, and I would have to get them through the factory management or the shop dining halls. That meant walking all over the factory, because there were an enormous number of departments, with something or other in each one. If you went empty-handed, that is, only with money, you would get nowhere; but I found out how to do it. In the winter I would put a few kilos of fresh cucumbers and tomatoes in a basket, go to the necessary department, and quietly show them to the bookkeeper or manager. They would start trembling all over and beg me to sell them. I would say, We have a lot like that in our commune, and you have a lot of what we don't have but need. I would hand over the basket, and they would empty it and send for what we needed—always for money, of course. We needed glass for our big greenhouse. I found some greenish glass reinforced with wire. I took a sample home to the gardeners, and they said: "Get it quick!" We also needed a small motor for wheat threshing, and we went all the way to Mundybásh to get it, but with an authorization from the Kuznétsk factory.

Some people would come into the commune with some hesitation for one reason or another, and then would go back home after getting repaid for the property they had brought into the commune with them. But those who joined the commune in earnest would turn over their property for good and never ask for it or get it back.

Without any special arrangement among individuals, there was formed in the commune a kind of backbone made up of sincere, honest, upright people who loved our communal life—not backbone but granite; no, not granite but diamond. And once there was diamond, there was also sandstone—but more about that later. There were some who hesitated, and they would leave. But after leaving, sometimes they would come back and ask to join again—and how they would beg!

From October 1931 till July 1932, all our able-bodied men worked in factories, receiving rations for their dependents. Thanks to that work, the commune painlessly got through that very difficult situation with regard to feeding our big family at a time when food was very expensive or was not to be found at all.

Our food in the commune was vegetarian, without any meat. The commune members were unwilling to sustain their life at the expense of other creatures. Even though we had milk cows and chickens, the milk and eggs went chiefly to our children. In addition to our school, we also organized a kindergarten. The children were under the supervision of a specific person, a teacher, with whom they took walks, went to bathe in the river, and visited the gardens, where almost all the women worked. Later we laid out an orchard in the commune and a strawberry patch for marketing and for the children.

The commune decided to put in running water. I was given the task of getting the pipes. In the upper colony there was a salvage dump where there were a lot of pipes—new ones, rejects, bent ones, but quite adequate for us. After reaching an agreement with the foreman of the salvage dump, I brought some workmen; and we picked out the pipes, loaded them onto three- and four-horse wagons, and wrote out the invoice. I paid the money, and we crossed the river and started down the road to the commune. At the village of Feskí we were stopped by a representative of the OGPU (the secret police), a man named Popóv, who ordered us to unload the pipes and arrested me and took me to the First Building.

Of the ten brick buildings constructed in Novokuznétsk in 1931, the first one was occupied by the OGPU. The chairman of the commune council at that time was Borís Mazúrin. He went to look for me. Everywhere—at the GPU,[6] at the militia, and at the prison—he was told that I was not there. But I *was* at the GPU. Popóv went after me and tried to get what he wanted out of me. He offered me material aid: "We know you're one of the poor peasants, you have a lot of children, we'll help you; but you must talk with us, and none of the commune members must know about it." I told him that I needed nothing, that my family and I were well provided for, that I was ready to talk with him, but openly, so that all the commune members would know about the conversation, and that wherever there was secrecy, for me there was lying and meanness. Popóv got angry and shouted at me: "You will rot here within these walls!"

I answered: "It's all the same where I rot, and your time too will come to rot."

Once they put a young woman into the cell with me. She sat there with me for two or three days and nights, complaining to me that they were tormenting her for nothing at all (I cannot remember what reason she gave for her arrest). But I understood that she had been put in there in order to tempt me and to find out something from me.

Once Popóv called me in at night for an interrogation, even though it was an ordinary case, and asked me this question: "Do you recognize the Soviet authorities?" That was a ticklish question. I pondered how I should answer the investigator. Thoughts ran through my head one after another, and I kept silent. The investigator several times demanded an answer. "What's wrong—haven't you got a tongue, or does it not work?" I thought hard and finally came to the conclusion that since I had set out on this path, what could I fear? I would answer sincerely.

"I don't acknowledge any violent authorities."

Popóv, louder: "And the Soviet authorities?"

I answered: "Not any at all."

Finally Popóv shouted at the top of his lungs: "And the Soviet authorities?" and jumped up and hit the table so hard with his fist that the table bounced, and folders, ink, and everything on it fell to the floor. I sat there without moving and looked at the investigator, and then I decided that I would not talk with him any more. He sat a little while, then stood up and began picking up off the floor everything that had fallen from the table. Finally he started asking me about something else. I kept silent. He said to me several times: "Why don't you answer?" I said I did not want to talk with him.

"Why not?"

6. GPU—the same as the OGPU: (United) State Political Administration. This name replaced Cheká in 1922 and was in turn replaced by NKVD from 1934 to 1943, NKGB in 1943–46, MGB in 1946–53, and KGB since 1953—all of them representing essentially the same branch of the Soviet government: the security agencies.

"Because you are crazy: you hit the table so hard that nothing stayed on it."

He burst out laughing and said he was normal now. But just the same, I kept silent. He called a guard and said:

"Take this scum and give him enough to make him crawl down the stairs from the third story to the bottom."

I was held there for several days. Once I caught sight of one of the commune members and shouted that I was there. Mazúrin kept coming to Popóv about me. He went on denying: "We don't have Morgachëv." Finally Mazúrin caught him in the lie, but was arrested himself and later convicted.

Once they let me out to go to the toilet. When I came back, I saw some arrested commune members sitting at the end of the corridor: Kleménty Kraskóvsky, and Vasíly Matvéyevich, Ioánn, and Emmanuíl from the Community. I walked past my cell and went up to my friends, shook hands with them, and sat down beside them. The guard on duty shouted: "Come here!"

I answered: "I won't leave my friends."

The guard was a hefty man. He came up to me, grabbed me by the neck, and squeezed so hard that I became helpless. He took me to the cell and shoved me in so violently that I landed face-down on the floor against the opposite wall. At first I could not raise up; I hurt all over, especially my neck.

About two months after my arrest, the investigator called me in and said: "We are letting all of you go. It turns out that the pipes were properly bought, but you must give us a signed statement that you will not tell anybody what was said here." I gave no signed statement. "Well, look here now—remember and keep quiet." I understood that the pipes were only a pretext: they just needed to find a man who would secretly give them information about our commune.

I arrived at the commune in the evening, and that same evening there was a general meeting, at which I reported what they had asked me about, what they had promised me if I would talk with them, and what they had said about not telling anybody about all that. I said we must always remember that many of us might go there, but we must always behave honorably toward our friends.

I got busy again with my duties. During the wheat harvest, I came back from town to the commune. We used a simple reaping machine called a "brow-heater." The knife would cut the straw and drop it onto a platform, and the man sitting on the seat would throw it onto the ground with a pitchfork. It was very hard work. I took my seat and started throwing it off and could hardly make one round. "Brow-heater" was really the right name for it. I went to the city and looked up the agricultural supply center and found two reapers there that would drop the straw automatically. I bought them and sent them to the commune without getting the approval of the commune council, even though I was a member of the council, but of course I was alone. Two or three days later, the commune sent me thanks for the automatic reapers. They said they had sent the brow-heater off to retirement, and—most important—the men got some relief from that hard labor.

I have already said that we took our meals in common. We built a large dining hall with an attached kitchen. Many families would take their meals home; others would eat in the dining hall. It was also possible in the commune to get dry rations and take them home to prepare for yourself, but there were almost no requests for that, because everybody was loaded down with work—the men, the women, and the teenagers—so nobody felt like spending time cooking at home. There was a lot of work to be done, because we were building the commune in a new place, without any loans from the state. We did everything with our own means and our own forces. For that reason people would take dry rations only on their holiday, Sunday, if some housewife wanted to cook something in her own way.

On Sundays, especially in summer, people from all the groups with their various tendencies would gather in the commune, dressed in simple but clean clothing—especially the young people, blooming like those Altaic mountain flowers. Each group would get together and sing their favorite songs or recite poetry. We also had some songs that were common to all the groups, which we would sing together. Everybody was in a joyful, holiday mood. The old people would talk about their affairs. The young people would take walks to the bank of the Tom and hikes into the mountains. In the years 1931–33, even the Subbótniks from the Peaceful Plowman cooperative would come on Sundays. There were Russians, Ukrainians, Belorussians, Poles, Jews, and Germans in the commune. As for religious beliefs, in addition to the followers of Tolstóy there were Subbótniks, Molokáns,[7] Dobrolyúbovians, Malyóvannians, and Baptists—not the narrowly sectarian ones but those who had caught the free spirit of Tolstóy. Some families of Subbótniks did not work on Saturdays, and others would substitute for them; but they in their turn would replace their substitutes on Sundays, so that even here, with our reasonable and tolerant attitudes, we found a common language.

In the course of our work and life together, new questions began to arise about our convictions. A group of "hand-farmers" sprang up—people who refused to exploit the labor of animals as a work force, or to exploit milk cows, believing that the milk belonged to the offspring of the cow and that the horse should be able to live in freedom. This group asked to be allowed to farm by hand, with a shovel and hoe. After discussion and criticism of this question, the commune decided to let them be hand-farmers during the summer, but with the understanding that they should take part in the general work of the commune during winter, and should provide for their own food supply. The hand-farmers included the Tyurk brothers, Gútya and Gítya; Sónya Tyurk; the Katrúkha brothers, Fédya and Mísha; Valentín Aleksán-

7. Molokáns (also known as "Spiritual Christians")—a pacifist Christian sect that arose in the second half of the eighteenth century.

drovich Kudryávtsev; Yefím Bezúgly; Ványa Lukyántsev; and several other persons. Ványa Zúyev and Iván Stepánovich Rogózhin worked without horses in the commune as seed-growers.

On the one hand, in our machine-age century, hand-farming seems irrational and even absurd; but in reality, if you go into the matter a little more deeply, it is both rational and moral, honest and noble. Our hand-farmers demonstrated that it was entirely feasible when they worked from five- to seven-tenths of a hectare under cultivation in grain and vegetables. They got from 290 to 360 pounds of wheat per tenth of a hectare, and after feeding themselves they still had a surplus. But under our present state system it is impossible to admit this (hand-farming): for every farm worker there are now several hundred dependents, holding out their hands for bread, vegetables, fruit, meat, milk, and eggs. Hand-farming is possible only when each person carries his share of the burden of peasant labor.

I have already said that we had our own school with our own teachers. I am not a teacher, and I cannot properly tell about the work of our school. When our school building was taken away from us, I said at a meeting of the commune with representatives of the city department of people's education that if they took away our school, we would study in somebody's house. The city education representatives said they would take the house away from us, and I said: "We will give up every last house for our school, but we will not send our children to your state school." My statement served as an indictment against me in both court trials, in 1936 and 1940.

In 1933 some of the members (including my son Timoféy) left our commune and formed an agricultural cooperative *(artel),* which they named the Sower. These members quit because they wanted to live materially better than we were living in the commune, since we had a lot of disabled and elderly people, widows with children, and large families. But the same fate awaited all of us: in 1937–38 many men and women were arrested, both members of the commune and members of the cooperative, and almost all of them lost their lives.

In the commune we kept an account of each person's labor days, but not of how much each person produced. We considered that what was important was for each person to have the desire to work honestly, but it was not important who had how much strength and who could work how much. No reprimands were made for absenteeism, although the chairman was obliged to explain why a person did not appear. Usually it was for sickness, laundry, or whitewashing the house. Money was not charged for absence from work. No deductions were made for food for commune members and their families. Money was given to both adults and children for clothing, shoes, underwear, and bed linen according to the following system: an advance was given for the year, and at the end of the fiscal year, when we knew the total income of the commune and the total number of appearances for work, we would combine the appearances of the husband and wife as a family and add 25 percent of the father and mother's combined pay for each child—50 percent for two children, 75 percent for three, and so on. The same arrangement

Hand-farmers from the World Brotherhood Community, plowing without the use of livestock.

The commune apiary, 1933.

A young people's gathering in the Life and Labor Commune, 1932. In the foreground on the floor is Iván Dragunóvsky. On the wall the sign at the left says "Loving kindness conquers all and is itself invincible," and the one in the center says "Overcome evil with good."

A Sunday religious meeting of commune members next to the schoolhouse, 1933.

existed for disabled persons and old people in families; single disabled persons were given the average pay for adults. The commune had a bookkeeping system, with a record of income and expenses, provisions, fodder, and labor days. A personal account was kept for each family and single person, which included a list of all personal property and real estate as well as livestock.

We ate no meat in the commune, but we did have productive livestock, and so the question arose about what to do with the young and old animals. At first this question was discussed in private conversations, but later it was taken up in a general meeting. The decision was made to keep old cows until their natural death and to give unneeded steers and heifers free to the surrounding population for breeding purposes, on condition that they would commit themselves to raising them for breeding. We gave some of our young livestock to a beekeeping collective farm of former Cossack officers in exchange for bees. There were cases where a man would accept a free steer or heifer for breeding purposes and then take it off in the bushes, slaughter it, and sell the meat to the market in town.

Something else about the feeling for property: yes, dear reader, it is hard, very hard, and takes a lot of thought for a natural-born peasant to deliberately give up all personal property. When he is hunted down and his livestock and other property are taken away from him, he will groan and say nothing. But when he has come into a commune voluntarily and handed over his property not free but by appraisal, that is hard on him, and for some it seems better to go back home. And he puts in an application to leave. The commune settles with him in money (the commune never returned anything in kind), and he goes home to his native region and sees what is happening there: it is impossible to live individually, and he turns around and comes back to the commune. He has used up all his money on the trip. He makes another application to join the commune. He begs, almost weeping: "Take me back—that was my big mistake, leaving the commune." People like that did not have the strength of diamonds, they were weak sandstone; but the commune would take them back into the family. Personal property was in many cases a cause of dissension, even among the followers of Tolstóy. The husband would gladly join a commune, but his wife would not even hear of a commune, and then began the shouting and weeping. But with us it was not the same as collectivization; it was a free matter. In view of such family quarrels, though, many men who were convinced still hesitated to join against the wishes of their wives. To be sure, many wives have agreed to go to a foreign country, to distant territory, to join their husband's fellow believers; but they went not through conviction but through necessity. People like that are the kind who turn into whisperers and tale-bearers; they are dissatisfied not with themselves but with others.

Many people, especially women, lived in the commune not as proprietors but as workers: they worked honorably, and that was all.

I worked for a little over three years in marketing and buying. I got tired and fed up, and I asked for a change. The commune council agreed on condition that I would acquaint new comrades with this work—Vásya Bormotóv and Yegór Ivanóv. I introduced them to all the establishments and individuals they would have contact with. I myself took over the beehives and started a new kind of work—interesting and in the open air. I moved the beehives to a broad gulley opposite the settlement of the people from Barábinsk and worked in seclusion.

The Destruction of the Life and Labor Commune

In the summer of 1935, as I remember, I came back to the commune one evening, and my wife said that all the members of the council had been arrested and they had asked about me. I said: "I won't go there right now, not before morning." Suddenly the door opened, and in came the chairman, Blinóv, and said: "The investigator wants you to come, and then he will let us all go before morning." Well, I agreed, and we went to the investigator. It was eleven or twelve o'clock at night. When I got there, the investigator said:

"Well, now you are all here; I will get all your signatures that you will report tomorrow morning by nine o'clock, and then you can go home."

They began to sign; but when my turn came, I refused. "I might die before morning; for that reason I won't give any promises in advance, but I will not go anywhere and I will not hide." Vásya Bormotóv and Vásya Kírin also refused to sign. The investigator got upset and said: "I can send all of you to jail right now." Then Bormotóv and Kírin signed, and I was sent at night with a militiaman to the OGPU in Stálinsk. But they would not accept me there: no reason was given in writing for my arrest. Then I was taken to the prison. There, of course, I was accepted.

About three days later I was taken to the OGPU for interrogation. The same investigator said to me:

"You are to be among the accused as a member of the council, but we have decided that you will be a witness. Do you know the chairman well?"

"Very well," I answered.

"Then tell me how he works and who goes to see him."

"Ask him yourself. He did not authorize me to speak for him, and I will not talk about any other council members either."

The conversation was long.

"I can tell everything about my own work."

"We already know everything about your work."

He tried to scare me with the court and prison, and then he got out a little book, the code of laws, and started reading to me:

"For refusal to testify to court and investigative authorities—a prison sentence of three to six months. Do you understand?"

"I understand," I said, but I was simply glad it was not a long sentence; I would serve it out and would not talk about anybody.

The investigator wrote down the protocol, but I refused to sign anything.

I was sent back to the cell, in the prison. In about two days I was taken to the investigator again, and again I would not sign the protocol. Then two men certified to my refusal and signed for me themselves.

This time that was the way the matter ended for me. As for the council members, who was sentenced and for how long I do not remember. Two or three times I was summoned to court in connection with this case, but I did not go.

In April 1936, ten persons were picked up: Mazúrin, Páshchenko, Yepifánov, Gulyáyev, Dragunóvsky, Gítya Tyurk, Gútya Tyurk, Kraskóvsky, Bárysheva, and Ólya Tolkách. In May they took me too, and I remained imprisoned until June 1946.

The interrogations began. We were all put in separate cells.

In reply to all the investigator's questions, I answered only: "I have done nothing bad to anybody, but you want to accuse me." The same answer to all questions.

The investigator cursed:

"Why do you keep saying the same thing like a parrot? Your answers are beside the point."

I would not sign a single protocol about the questions. I do not remember how long the investigation lasted, but they kept taking us first to the Kuznétsk prison, then to the cell for preliminary investigations in the First Building. The Kuznétsk prison was down the hill, and the road was higher, on the level of the second floor. In 1936 there were not yet any blinds on the windows, and whenever I saw anybody from the commune walking along the road, I would sing a verse through the hole in the window which Mazúrin had written in prison:

A stormy wind makes merry outside;
At times it starts howling around the jail;
Suddenly it blows through the bars of my window,
And my thoughts fly out behind it.
Oh! they probably fly over our field
Through the wheat like waves.
And also down along the Tom
Waves splash and beat against the bank.
I'd like to go to the commune, where freedom breathes,
And lie under grain-filled spikes of rye,
But malice is the ruler here in prison—
A clot of blood, violence, and lies!
But there shines still within my soul
Unclouded joy, and faith in goodness.
My mind flies higher than prisons;
It must not be in confinement.
And I here, behind the bars, will know
How to feel life as a blessing in my soul.
May I only be able to rule myself,
May I only be able to be patient and forgive . . .

So we remained in prison all summer, up to November 1936. The investigation ended. I refused to get acquainted with the facts of the investigation, because I did not want to awaken within myself, in my consciousness, bad feelings against those who had given bad, false testimony about me.

The trial took place in November. We were tried by a special board of judges from the Western Siberia Territorial Court in Novosibírsk. We all rejected the official defender: we would defend ourselves against injustice and lies. I was given three years, and other comrades got from three to ten years. Dimítry Páshchenko, Gítya Tyurk, Yegór Yepifánov, and Ólya Tolkách were acquitted and set free. Kleménty Kraskóvsky was released from the investigation. The six of us who were convicted—Borís Mazúrin, Gútya Tyurk, Iván Vasílyevich Gulyáyev, Yákov Dragunóvsky, Anna Bárysheva, and I, Dimítry Morgachëv—were taken off to prisons and labor camps.

The prisons arise in my memory without any sort of order: the dark, ancient, enormous Mariínsk; the Novosibírsk, also enormous. It was said to have been built by the Agricultural Institute but was turned into a prison because of the insufficiency of such cultural establishments in our time. Then back to the Starokuznétsk prison, but now remodeled, with dark blinds on the windows, with careful searches, stripping the prisoners naked, and so on. At one time we were held in a small cell. Opposite us, door facing door, was the death cell, with a tiny, heavily barred window high up, just under the ceiling, a concrete floor with the bed legs cemented into it, a latrine bucket chained to the wall, and hovering over all of this the tangible stench of death. Once during the night, the locks clanked in the death cell. Somebody was taken out and led along the corridor, and he said in a soft voice: "Farewell, farewell, farewell. . . ."

When they got him to the door, he became silent, evidently because they put a gag in his mouth. We did not sleep that night. We sat and talked the whole night through.

We were taken to the prison in Tomsk, built at one time for humanitarian purposes by the merchant Kukhtérin, whose son or grandson was in charge as late as 1932. We were also in Górnaya Shóriya, where the camp was situated between the mountains and the impenetrable Siberian forest, called the taiga; but the camp had no firewood, since it was very hard to bring it down from the steep mountains covered with a two-meter layer of snow. We were taken there to the bath, where icicles hung from the faucets, and the barracks were so overcrowded that no one had space of his own: you would stand up to shift around a little, and the space where you had just been would instantly close up. On the prison gate was a sign in big letters: "WELCOME!" That sort of thing sticks in your memory to the grave.

The court of appeals confirmed our sentence, and then we were taken to the camps, I no longer remember just where—let's just say to Prokópyevsk, the center of the Kuzbáss mines, to load coal into railway cars. We had to work day and night. It was hard work, by hand and dirty, at forty degrees below freezing, centigrade; but many men would throw off their padded jackets in order to load the cars faster. Then into the duty room; and if you loaded it faster than required—a sixteen-ton car in an hour and a half, or a fifty-five-ton car in two hours and forty minutes—the coal mine would give you out of its own supply a supplement to the camp rations: five hundred grams of bread or tobacco and sugar. Later we were sent to a logging camp at Moryakóvka, a settlement on the bank of the Tom River, where we loaded logs onto barges. In the winter we stockpiled the wood. We would haul it up to the bank of a cove where enormous barges were moored, and toward spring we would load this wood by hand, putting down the enormous, heavy logs in a layer lengthwise on the barge, then putting down a second layer crosswise, and so on until they were eighteen or twenty layers high. As it was loaded, the barge would settle deeper and deeper in the water. Most of the prisoners would roll the logs up to the barge; and on the barge itself, five men who were the strongest and most agile with logs would lay them in place—"tuck them into bed," as we called it. For relief from that drudgery, we would sing the old song "Dubínushka." There was a coal miner with us from Prokópyevsk, Alyósha Kiréyev. He led the singing very well, and would make up new verses of his own. When we were served a meal of watery gruel made out of some kind of trash, he would start singing:

"Ekh . . . heave-ho!"

Or:

"Once more—bim, boom, bam, now we'll get three hundred grams. Heave-ho!"

And on and on in that spirit. He could lead us in a lot of songs, and that helped us at work. Later Kiréyev was arrested in the camps by the Third Section.[8] They kept after him: what do the Tolstoyans talk about? What do they think? Don't they try to lead you astray with their religion? Kiréyev worked in the same labor unit with us—Kiréyev, Mazúrin, Morgachëv, Gútya Tyurk. After that, we divided into two units—Mazúrin and Kiréyev, Morgachëv and Tyurk. They fulfilled their norm by 120 percent, and we by 105 to 107 percent, yet we received the same supplementary ration: three hundred grams of bread in the evening, in addition to the camp ration of six hundred grams. But Kiréyev never let us down, never did anything mean, never slandered us in any way. I don't know what ever became of him— most likely he lost his life. Later we were driven like cattle to Tomsk, to the Cheremóshniki staging post. Here the timber that came from the lower reaches of the river Ob was unloaded, stacked up in piles, and then loaded onto railway cars. The work was very hard—handwork, or rather shoulder-work. Here Borís and I worked as partners. We would take a load of boards from the barge, put them on our shoulders, and carry them fifty to a hundred meters on a swaying gangplank to the shore. There we would go up a gangplank to the top of the pile, and at the word from the man behind, "Let's drop it!" we would throw down the boards, lay them out in order, and go

8. Here Morgachëv refers to the Soviet secret police by a term used in tsarist times. The notorious Third Section was established by Nicholas I after he became tsar in 1825 and was abolished at the beginning of the 1880s.

back. In spite of the little cushions on our shoulders, which we called "dumplings," our shoulders ached, and so did our leg muscles.

At Cheremóshniki my son Timoféy and daughter Tósya came to see us. At the guardhouse my son was asked, "Aren't you afraid that if you come and visit your father they'll arrest you too?"

After all, that was in 1937. My daughter wept bitterly; and after our meeting, when I was back in the forest, I wrote this poem:

> My daughter wept, she bitterly wept,
> My breast was wet with her tears.
> Don't cry, my daughter! I too was in tears,
> I was pained by her childhood grief.
> Years of captivity and ordeals
> Will not bend me, I know;
> But the tears of a child, innocent tears,
> Weigh on my soul like lead.
> When I awoke from the darkness of superstition,
> When I ceased to serve violence,
> Then I decided to devote my life,
> Without any doubts, to peace and the welfare of people.
> I know, my child, when you are older,
> You will understand your father.
> In your own soul you will justify my path,
> And you will wipe away your childish tears.
> Dear little daughter, take back to your native commune
> Brotherly greetings from the prisoners.
> Tell them to live free and fearless:
> Suffering for the truth is not pain but light.

In early spring, eight hundred of us carpenters were loaded on barges at Cheremóshniki, hitched onto a steamer, and taken north to Narým. At first we sailed along the Tom. Then the Tom emptied into the Ob, the river became very wide, and it was evident how the waters of two rivers flowed in one river: one was pure Tom water, and the other was muddy Ob water. We sailed past Kolpáshevo, and sixty kilometers beyond it, and disembarked on the uninhabited left bank of the Ob. Big frames for tents had been made here out of reeds, but no tarpaulins had been brought along, and everything was covered with straw mats, through which light could penetrate, and—even worse—so could the rain, which began in the night. A cold wind blew in from the river. Double bunks had been made in the tents, also of reeds. The men were soaked, and we huddled together from dampness and cold. Borís and I stripped down to our underwear, put our clothes under us, lay close together, and covered ourselves with what we had; and on top of it all we put my big coat, which was waterproof. That way we slept remarkably well. That coat, which saved us, had been given to me by Lyóva Alek- séyev—thanks again and again to him! In 1936, when I was arrested and was sitting in a cart, Lyóva came home from work, saw me, took off his coat, and threw it in the cart, saying:

"Take it, maybe it'll come in handy."

And indeed it did come in handy.

We built large, clean barracks at Narým, not far from the river bank. When we asked what these barracks were for in such a deserted place, we were told that this would be a fish-canning combine. But when they started to enclose the completed settlement with a high prison fence, they began saying that this would be a political isolation camp for the families of important Communists who had been executed: the sisters of Tukhachévsky, the wives of Yakír and others.[9]

My wife Maryána and Kólya Ulyánov came to visit us there. We caught sight of them from a distance, but they were not allowed to approach us. They were even threatened with arrest and locked up in a barn. They destroyed all the letters they had brought to us from friends in the commune. Kólya hid in the forest, and the authorities kept asking Maryána: "Where is he? Who did you come with?"

"Leave," they told her threateningly. She bought tickets for both of them, and she and Kólya got away safely.

Borís and I had worked well, and we asked the head of the camp to let us meet with them, but he gave us a look of astonishment and said:

"Nobody has come to me."

Borís and I still maintained our vegetarianism, and we persuaded the authorities to prepare our food separately. One day they brought mess pots with dinner for the brigades and called out: "Such-and-such brigade, such-and-such brigade," and then: "The Italians!" Nobody answered. Again: "The Italians!" We understood that it was for us. We took the three-liter pot, carried it to the barrack, dug into it with a spoon, and found it was full of meat. At the kitchen when they were told to cook separate meals for the "vegetarians," they thought they heard "Italians,"[10] and understood that they were to cook better for the Italians; and so they tried. We had to go and explain.

At the end of autumn, barges came with provisions for the future inhabitants of the settlement. The provisions were all very good.

Sometimes we had to go with the brigade to the forest, a wild, desolate place with wind-fallen trees and clearings. There we came across some dens dug out of the earth and covered with rough planking. These turned out to be the first refuges of "kulák" peasant families, who had been deported to these desolate places.

Late in the autumn, when the last steamers sailed by before winter, blowing their whistles as a sign that they were on their way to winter quarters, all of us "counterrevolutionaries" under Article 58, about seven hundred persons in all, were hastily loaded onto a ship and carried off to Cheremóshniki. About a hundred service personnel remained from among the nonpolitical

9. Mikhaíl Nikoláyevich Tukhachévsky (1893–1937) and Ióna Emmanuílovich Yakír (1896–1937) were among the top Soviet military leaders executed by Stalin on trumped-up treason charges during the terror.
10. The Russian words are *vegetariántsy* and *italiántsy*.

prisoners, and later they told us that women had spent the winter in only one barrack, and no one was allowed to get near them. It was unknown who they were.

In the winter we were driven on foot from Cheremóshniki to a logging camp in the Forty-First Quadrant of the forest, about forty kilometers from the Tom, on the other bank. We were given no carts for the baggage, and people grew tired and began discarding their suitcases along the road. I did so too, but I did not cast aside a bag of ground-up straw that served me as a mattress, and they all laughed at me—"Look at the farmer who won't let go of his bag of dung." Late at night we got to our new living quarters. It was a barrack made out of newly cut green wood, with bunks made out of green, frozen planks. We had about thirty degrees of frost, and we were all sweaty. There were two iron stoves. We built a fire in them, and the smoke went into the barrack instead of the chimney. It was fiercely cold, but fatigue knocked us off our feet for a while, so I put my sack on the ice-covered bunk and lay down on it, and Borís laid his big dogskin mittens nearby, and we fell asleep.

There was terrible despotism in that camp, the kind you might think would be inadmissible in a land of workers and peasants. In winter, in freezing weather, we were driven out in the darkness to work before daybreak, and we were kept waiting outdoors at the pits for two hours or more while the officials made the rounds of the barracks, hunting up everybody who was sick or would not go out, and driving them out to work. At last we would start on our way. The sick men lagged behind and were beaten and driven forward. In the forest we came to an enormous plot of ground that the guards had surrounded with a fresh ski trail: one step beyond the ski trail was considered an attempt to escape. Everybody separated by brigades and then by units of two to four men, and the felling of the trees began. Sometimes the snow was up to two meters deep. It was impossible to walk through it. Each unit would have to get down on all fours and crawl through the forest to their place. Some would work, and some would freeze around the bonfire—on their last legs. The workday ended at dusk. Five or six kilometers back home to the barracks, swirling snow on the road, the guards demanding order in the ranks, the sick men falling, unable to walk, and still getting beaten and driven. Borís and I asked permission to carry a sick man on our shoulders. The guard agreed, and we asked our comrades to pick up our tools—our saw and axe. We carried the sick man to the camp, turned him over to the hospital, went back the next morning to see how he was, and found out he was already dead. Everybody would arrive wet and frozen at the camp and hurry to the barracks, and suddenly there would be a shout: "Prisoner count!" And everybody would come back out into the frost and stand in line, sometimes for an hour and a half or two hours, while the guards counted them all—rarely only once, more often twice or three times. At last the shout: "Dismissed!" Then to supper—a bowl of sloppy gruel and six hundred grams of bread if you had fulfilled your norm, three hundred if you had not.

In summer we four hundred "counterrevolutionaries" were driven out of the barracks into underground vegetable cellars. Dampness, darkness, mold, smoke from the iron stoves and oil lamps, and all the while grains of sand falling from overhead, so that you could not eat a spoonful without sand in it. People quickly weakened and died here. Sometimes during one night in the camp, there would be from eight to nineteen deaths.

Finally we were herded into the camp at the Taigá Station. There the barracks were old, but at least they were barracks, and everybody began to recover. The food was better, the regime was not so harsh, and you could buy food in the camp store. My wife Maryána and Boris's wife Alyóna came to see us there.

That's the way it is in life. You think, I am in the most terrible situation; things cannot possibly get worse, but that is not right. There is always something worse. So it was with us. At Prokópyevsk, loading coal into the cars night and day, dirty all over, gulping down dust, suffocating, spitting up soot, you think: Oh, if only they would move us somewhere else. They move you to Cheremóshniki, and you carry heavy boards and crossties on your back for ten or twelve hours—could there be any place worse? From there to the Forty-First Quadrant it was even worse. And again you think: where could it be even worse? And we land in Narým in autumn during the rainy season, living under the translucent roof of one floor mat. But at the Forty-First Quadrant it was the worst of all.

As early as 1937, rumors began to reach us that many friends in our commune had been rounded up and taken off into the unknown. My son Timoféy was taken, and he died there. In 1938 still more were taken, and the rest lived in the expectation that their turn would come too. Some lost heart, and there were even some who took the path of Judas to save their hides. More and more rarely were letters sent to us from the commune. It became dangerous to visit us. Finally all contacts with the commune were broken. At that time this poem was born:

> Where are you, answer, you courageous tribe
> Of faithful, fearless strugglers for the truth?
> Or have you perished in those brutal prisons,
> Crushed by the weight of all that heavy labor?
> Or are you stifled by those worldly cares?
> Have trifles dragged you down to the very bottom?
> No answer comes, the darkness grows still thicker,
> All the world has turned into a prison.

More than thirty years have gone by, and it still makes my flesh crawl when I remember how we lived, not for hours or days but for whole years, in that savage, inhuman life where people died like flies in autumn from the hard labor, from starvation, from the smarting consciousness of our innocence and our undeserved infamy and punishment.

At first there were three of us. Then Gútya was taken under convoy to the Far East, and in the summer of 1938 Borís too was picked for prisoner

transport. Previously we had more than once asked the officials not to separate us, but either to leave us both or send us together, and they had done it.
But this time the chief would not agree: they were picking only healthy,
powerful men, and they recognized Borís as one, but they did not take me.

Within the general zone of the Taigá camp, there was another zone enclosed by a wall of tightly linked posts sharpened at the top and about six
meters high. Inside this zone there was a barrack. It held those from our
brigades who had been imprisoned under Article 58,[11] Points 2, 8, 9, 11, and
so on—about seventy men. It also held the Germans from Slávgorod who
worked with us—the Gegelganses, father and son, Lay, and others. The prisoner Dóbrusov (from Gúryevsk) worked at cutting bread; he was ordered to
bring forty rations for the transport from our colony. He cut it and then
waited for them to come and get it. Nobody came. He waited and waited,
and still nobody came, so about midnight he took the rations to the guards
on duty. Beyond the gates, everything was flooded with light; carts were
waiting, and the guards were not from the prison but were soldiers. On the
carts lay men tied hand and foot, with gags in their mouths. When the guards
saw Dóbrusov, they threw themselves on him with a shout: "Who ordered
you to bring bread here? Get away from here, don't look around, and keep
your trap shut, or we'll tear your tongue out." I think they were being sent
with a prisoner transport "into the hazy distance," never to return.

In 1939 I was summoned for transport, the only one from Taigá Station.
I was taken to the Kémerovo prison. Iván Vasílyevich Gulyáyev was already
there. We were glad to see each other, and embraced and exchanged kisses.
About ten days later we were put on a train again and taken to our Kuznétsk
prison.

Iván Vasílyevich and I were put into one large cell, with women's cells
on each side of us. In one cell there was a hole in the wall. I asked through
it: "Is Ólga Tolkách among you?" They answered that she was next to us
but on the other side, and told us to tap to her and she would answer.

Then I began to think and try to figure out how to tap to Ólga. I tapped
on the wall to her and got an answer. Iván and I thought that must be Ólga,
and I remembered that Borís had said there was a special alphabet for tapping
through a wall. It came back to me: you wrote down the alphabet, row on
row, with five letters to a row—six rows. But I myself had never tapped
messages. I remembered only that you first tap the row and then which letter
in the row. For example, to ask the question "Who?" you first call by tapping. When you get an answer, you tap the letter "w"—fifth row, five taps,
a brief pause, and then the third letter in the row, three taps. Then "h"—
second row, two taps, and third letter, three taps; "o"—third row, fifth letter. All this taps out the word "who."

You tap out family names and so on in the same way; but for all this you

11. Article 58—the notorious article in the Soviet Criminal Code that was most commonly
used by the Soviet authorities to punish anyone they considered to be a potential or actual threat
to the Soviet state.

have to know the alphabet, learn it by heart, and then practice, and soon you can go rather fast. In prison we had plenty of time. I had a little black bag, and I ripped it open on the seam, spread it out on the bunk, and drew thirty squares on it with a piece of soap. Gulyáyev and I filled in the letters, and then after checking them I tapped out: "Who?" The answer came back: "Ólga."

Iván Vasílyevich just couldn't memorize this alphabet, but he helped me: I would walk around the cell, and he would give me the letters—which row and in which place. I even tapped out whole poems.

At that time the Kuznétsk prison was filled with prisoners under Article 58. There were a lot of very literate Party members, and some of them learned to tap very fast. Kurgánov, the secretary of the Stálinsk District Committee, could tap especially fast and well, as if he were telegraphing.

We were taken from the Kuznétsk prison to the First Building OGPU. I sat there and did not know what it was all about. I wrote an application, then a second and a third, to the investigator: "Why have you held me for six, seven months without saying anything?"

At last the investigator summoned me and told me I was not yet convicted, but only under investigation, and he read out to me that owing to the protest of the procurator of the RSFSR Rogínsky, the sentence I had received from the Western Siberian Territorial Court had been revoked because of its "mildness" (even in 1937). For that reason, those who had been acquitted—Páschchenko, Yepifánov, Gítya Tyurk, and Ólga Tolkách—had shortly afterwards been re-arrested and had been in prison more than two years while those of us who had been convicted earlier were being collected from various camps all over the Soviet Union.

The last one to be brought in was Borís, in September 1939. In the inner prison of the OGPU there were fifteen cells and one isolator, which held a coffin instead of bunks. I was held in the fifteenth cell. Somebody was alone in the fourteenth cell, and he and I tapped back and forth to each other out of boredom. Every day he would tell me what the investigator had asked him. At last he tapped: "Sentence: ten years." Two days later he tapped: "I am leaving," and the fourteenth cell was left empty. Later I heard somebody walking around in it, evidently in boots. I called by tapping for a conversation but got no answer. I called again and got no answer, but two days later he answered. I asked: "Who?"

He answered: "Borís."

"Where from?"

"From the commune." And he asked me: "Who?"

I answered: "Dimítry." And so we became neighbors, even though through a wall, but that was a great joy.

On the other side of the fifteenth cell, beyond a wall, was the dining hall of the OGPU. We could hear whenever they had a party, and after their parties the prisoners got better food—the scraps from the parties. Between the fourteenth and fifteenth cells there was a tiny hole along the steam-heating pipe, and I decided to write Borís a note and pass it through that hole. But here a whole series of problems arose. What would we write on? What

would we write with? How would we push it through the hole? At last I
thought of something: to write on rags. I tore up a little white bag. And
what to write with? Ink? I dug a lot of dirt out of my boot, dissolved it in
spit mixed with sugar—and there was my ink. In the toilet I collected half-
burned matches and split them—there was my pen. I printed my letters. I
don't remember what I wrote; most likely, since I had memorized from Gulyáyev a few thoughts from Tolstóy's *Circle of Reading,* I passed them on as
the most necessary thing. There remained the task of pushing the note through
the wall. I pulled out a few slender twigs from the broom in the toilet and
carried them back to my cell under my shirt. I took the rag with my message
on it and wound it around the twig, then pushed it through the hole to
Borís. Then I tapped out to him: "Take it!" Sometimes we would arrange
to hide notes for each other in some prearranged place in the toilet. I would
occasionally get notes from Páshchenko, even though his cell was very far
away. Once during evening inspection, I noted that the guard on duty looked
carefully at the pipe along which we had been passing our notes. After passing our next note, I smeared sugar mixed with spit on the pipe and sprinkled
it with whitewash I scratched from the wall. It quickly dried and left no
trace.

And here is how I met the Tyurk brothers. Gítya had been languishing
for about two years in the stuffy, overcrowded cells through which new
"residents" passed in an unending stream—coming and going, some to the
camps and some to the grave with a bullet in their head. They came and they
went, but he kept pining away in there, overtaxing his already too frail health.
Then his brother Gútya was brought from the Far East and put into the cell
next to him, but at first they did not know that. Here is a poem by Gítya:

> Tap, tap, tap!
> Where is that tap?
> Someone is tapping behind the wall,
> Someone insists on finding out
> Who I am.
> Tap, tap, tap,
> I answer the tap.
> "I have come from afar, friend,
> I'm tired and I want to rest.
> I have come for a new trial."
> Tap, tap, tap—
> Again comes the tap,
> Blow by blow,
> He taps my name out of me.
> In excitement I tap back:
> "How can you know me?"
> The tapping comes slowly,
> Footsteps are muffled behind the door,
> The sounds split up and flow together:
> "I am your brother, I am here just like you."
> The locks hang heavy,

The doors are bound in iron,
The bricks in the wall are strong,
But just the same they were not able
To shut us off in their stone circle.
Tap, tap, tap.

Why do I include poems in my life? Because even if I did not write them, they reflect what we lived by during those years of captivity. Not without reason did Tolstóy and other wise men of the East say: "There is one soul in all," and what one of us has lived through is intimately felt by another.

Here is another prison poem, written by Mítya Páshchenko:

A gray light splashes over the town,
O sleepless night, go away, go away!
My heart is ripped apart again by captivity.
The days are paralyzed within my breast.
What is leisure when it has frozen stiff,
Throttled by the boldness of the prison executioners.
How much youth and life is rotting away
Behind the barrier of ghastly nights.
I am in a prison reeking of tobacco smoke,
O, my mother, worn out by grief!
Like a madman, I am tormented by thirst—
Thirst to live, to breathe in freedom.
And for what? For what was I thrown into prison,
I, a son of the fields and labor, a peasant son?
Am I perhaps an uninvited guest on this earth?
Grow cold, kind heart, grow cold!

During the time I spent in prisons and the camps, I saw and experienced so much savagery and cruelty that I found myself at a loss to understand where I was and who was doing all this. Could this be done by the representatives of Communist power, whose ideal—the withering away of the state, and a society without violence—was dear to them and to me alike? Could all this be perpetrated by the same people who had grown so indignant about the savagery and arbitrary rule of the tsarist authorities over the common people? But I know that in those days the politicals and even the revolutionaries—forthright enemies of the existing order—were nonetheless able, even while living in exile, to write their works, study the sciences, and have books and paper. At that time there were people who could criticize harsh treatment in the prisons; this criticism restrained the jailers. But now? Against whom would you direct your criticism? Against the Communists? But their idea was the essence of humanity. Now nobody can express any protest or dissatisfaction with the harsh treatment of people in the prisons and camps. You cannot even speak for yourself, much less stand up in defense of others. What is the sense of all those searches—stripping you naked and standing you in a corner while they feel and rub their hands over all the seams in your clothing? "Come here, raise your leg, turn your butt around, lean over, pull those cheeks apart, get dressed." Letters from your family, so precious to you when you are imprisoned, are taken away from you despite the fact that they had already been checked when they were received. There are no grounds at all for seizing them, but those who impose a search on you have unlimited power, and of course it is well known that tsars are not the only ones corrupted by absolute power. These people had neither shame, nor conscience, nor reason, nor even intelligence; they were steeped in gross dishonesty, foul language, and effrontery.

That is why we had to conceal every important event in our lives, every line of verse, and keep it in our brains, which the jealous arms of the law could not reach into, where they could not rummage around in your experiences even if they cut open your skull.

What a divinely marvelous storehouse that is! However securely they hold you in their prisons, in subordination and silence, good thoughts, kind feelings, and loving relations among people still slip through the stone walls with their iron doors and big, massive locks. They slip through silently, without words, so as to bolster your spiritual and at times even your physical strength when it is exhausted by these harsh, inhuman conditions, where rational human beings are kept like wild animals.

And so they gathered us all once more for a second court trial. They gathered us, but not all: two of us were no longer among the living—Yákov Dragunóvsky and Anna Bárysheva, about whom the investigator remarked to me that they had been "sent off into the hazy distance." Then I sighed and understood where they had been sent, and the investigator understood that I understood it. But he asked: "Why did you sigh like that?" To which I answered: "And where is the hazy distance?" He answered: "Somewhere in the North."

When I got acquainted with the dossier on the accusations against us, which consisted of several thick volumes, I discovered two little papers—the notification by the Stálinsk OGPU that Dragunóvsky had been taken under the authority of the "Third Section" in December 1937, and that Bárysheva had been taken under the authority of the "Third Section" in January 1938. Bárysheva was in the Mariínsk camp, and Dragunóvsky was in the "Róza Orlóva" camp. I studied the dossier for several months. The investigator began to get angry with me, because he had to sit with me all that time; but I had little interest in the dossier. I was trying to memorize I. V. Gulyáyev's poem "Living Corpses," but I still did not succeed in writing it down in my brain library.

Our trial took place in the early spring of 1940; and like the first one, it lasted five days. We all got long sentences, but nobody was sentenced to death, even though we thought we could not avoid that. We appealed our sentences, and while we were appealing, they held us all together in the Mariínsk central prison, a good strong one, dating from tsarist times. Despite the fact that the prison was surrounded by a high brick wall, its courtyard had been divided up into little courtyards, each of them enclosed within high plank walls. We would be herded out there for a walk of some five minutes, sometimes even less. With our hands behind our backs, we would walk around in a circle single file until the guard gave the order: "Turn around!" and we would walk in the opposite direction so as not to get dizzy.

Gítya Tyurk made up the following poem about these little courtyards:

> The boards reek of the damp morning air,
> And here today is just like yesterday,
> Two pitiful green teardrops,
> Two little blades of grass in the courtyard corner.
> Every morning, sad and shy,
> After all the torments we have lived through,
> How glad I am to meet in the prison box
> Our close-knit brotherly circle.
> How dear to me are those pale faces,
> Their smiles and the cheerfulness of their words.

After confirming our sentences, they began to pull us out of Mariínsk and send us in all directions. I was sent to the Orlyúk agricultural camp; Gítya and Gútya, after being shifted from camp to camp, finally met in one of them, to their great joy. Gulyáyev and Páshchenko remained somewhere in the Mariínsk system of camps. Ólga Tolkách landed in a camp near Novosibírsk. After the appeal, Yegór Yepifánov was allowed to return home, where he did not live long and died of tuberculosis. Borís was sent back to the North.

Somehow I received a letter from him in which he wrote as follows: "Dimítry, I am glad you did not get sent here with me. You would not have survived it. In one winter here in our colony of 1,200 persons, more than 500 died, and in the whole Ust-Vymsk camp, 36 percent died. May God grant you long years of health and allow you to survive all this and return to your family and those of your friends who are still among the living."

On 30 May 1943 I completed my sentence in Orlyúk, but I was not released. I was sent on to another camp, in Yurgá, where I was assigned to work "as a free hired worker." All this was based on some Directive No. 145. I worked there as a beekeeper and manager of supplementary farming.

The war ended in 1945. The year 1946 began, thus completing ten years of my imprisonment. I was informed that because of my good work, the directive had been withdrawn from me and I was free to leave, but not to go anywhere I pleased. I was asked where I wanted to go. I answered, "To Kirgízia." I had heard from my friends Vásya Bormotóv, Sergéy Semyónovich Shipílov, and Vásya Kalachëv that life was not bad there. But for a long time I could not settle down; I kept moving from place to place. Later in Frúnze I met the director of a farm on Lake Issýk-Kul. He told me he needed a man like me. He took me to a restaurant for dinner, and during dinner he wrote out a certificate and told me to go to Przheválsk, and in two or three days they would send for me. In a few days they really did come for me and took me to my new place of work. They gave me a four-room apartment with curtains on the windows and doors, with chairs, tables, and a spring mattress such as I had never slept on before in my life. With great difficulty, my family succeeded in breaking away from Stálinsk and joined me there.

Tósya and Vitály were studying in Stálinsk at an agricultural college. Tósya had to give up her studies and help her mother with the move, and Vitály was allowed to transfer to Frúnze. Even though Tósya was not given a transfer, she was accepted just the same in the second year at the college. They both finished with honors. Tósya went to work at Issýk-Kul, closer to us, and Vitály entered the agricultural institute in Frúnze.

I did not like living there, and I resigned, but I had accomplished a big task in memory of myself: I had set out an orchard of several hectares and surrounded it with ornamental trees—that will be a remembrance for eighty years or so.

I bought a little house in Przheválsk—nothing special, it is true, but with a nice little garden. We are still living on that farmstead to this day. We built a new brick house on it. In 1949 I went to work as beekeeper at the Przheválsk timber-industry enterprise and worked there five years. Work for hire could not compare to the commune, but work that I loved in the midst of nature made life much more bearable. The apiary was sixty kilometers from town, in the mountains. It was inconvenient, very far from home; and five years later, when the timber enterprise asked me to move to another place, I refused and resigned. In autumn of 1954 I gave up the apiary. I had my four beehives there, and in the spring I bought fifteen more, found a place for them on the farm of a Kirgíz in the village of Dzhetý-Ogúz, and went into beekeeping. In 1967 I bought myself a little temporary house and six-hundredths of a hectare of land in the same village, enclosed it in a *duvál* (the local word for a wall made of clay and gravel), set out an orchard there, with more than thirty trees and currant and raspberry bushes, and made a summer house covered with ivy. Now we had a real holiday cottage, except that the house itself was poor. I had never gone after personal property and wanted to organize my life without it, but did not have a chance to. I love to work, and prosperity just thrusts itself upon me.

In 1958 or 1959 I invited Gútya Tyurk to come from Tashként and join me in beekeeping (by that time Gítya had already died in Biysk). He came with his family, bought a little house with an orchard, and took up beekeeping. On 20 March 1968, Gútya died of heart trouble. I have an inflammation of the spinal nerves that I brought away from the camps. All around us there are health resorts with hot springs, but they do not help. It is twenty-two years now since I was released from camp. My children have grown up and gone out on their own.

A few more words now about the communes. Communes sprang up even before the Revolution—usually on landed estates made available by owners who had accepted the commune idea. At that time the majority of commune members were intellectuals who had been carried away by that idea. But it

Gútya Tyurk, Iván Dragu-
nóvsky, and Dimítry Morgachëv standing before a statue
of Leo Tolstóy in Dzhcty-
Ogúz, a health resort in Kir-
gizia not far from Przhe-
válsk, the town where Morgachëv spent his last years.

was hard for them to get used to peasant work, and because of that, the
communes did not last long and soon fell apart.

After the Revolution, a lot of communes were organized, and at first they
were welcomed and encouraged by the government and the Party. Many
people in these communes were not very serious: they received property,
squandered it, and then went their separate ways. But there were also many
communes that set about their work with conviction and good management
and were soon firmly established. The members of those communes were
almost all peasants. They did not need to get accustomed to working hard,
but there did remain the difficulty among older people of overcoming outdated ideas and attitudes about life.

Not a single one of those communes remains today, and all because
someone who did not work in the communes and took no part in their life,
but thought he had the right to lord it over people and make them live his
way, took it into his head to close the communes with one stroke of his pen.
The liquidation of the communes was confirmed by laws and strong iron bars.

And now a few words about the first "Renaissance" commune, near the
village of Búrdino in Yeléts District, where I lived and which my comrades
and I organized. It was built on a bare plot of ground by peasants of average
means. We took down our buildings in the village and hauled them to the
new spot ourselves. We set out a big orchard, with several rows of ornamental trees all around it. Seven or eight years later, many people found it hard
to believe such a flourishing place had so recently been a plot of bare ground.
After collectivization, our whole settlement was moved into the old village.
The orchards were used for a few years by the collective farm, but during

the war all the orchards were ruthlessly cut down. Thirty-one years later, in 1962, I went back home and walked over that same place where my friends and I had built the commune. There were only rows of green shoots where there once had been fruit trees. It is probably like that still.

Here is a list of the Tolstoyan members of the Renaissance Commune from 1915 to 1930:

1. Vasíly Andréyevich Stoyánov. Arrested in 1922 at Rostóv-on-the-Don. There his life came to an end.

2. Aleksándr Vasílyevich Logunóv. The same one who hauled grain to Lénin. Left his native village in 1930.

3. Iván Vasílyevich Astáfyev. His wife would not join the commune, and he ended his life as a suicide.

4. Timoféy Semyónovich Vólgov. Deported in 1930 to Karagánda, where he died of starvation.

5. Timoféy Yevdokímovich Vólgov.

6. Pyotr Vasílyevich Úlshin.

7. Leónty Ivánovich Dorókhin.

8. Vasíly Vasílyevich Úlshin.

9. Iván Deméntyevich Úlshin.—All these people died at home in the village of Búrdino.

10. Daníla Ivánovich Vólgov. Died at Rostóv-on-the-Don.

11. Raísa Ivánovna Ivanóva, our schoolteacher. Died in the village of Soldátskoye.

12. Mikhaíl Grigóryevich Úlshin. Died in the Donéts Basin.

13. Filípp Yegóryevich Bélskikh. Died.

14. Dimítry Yegórovich Morgachëv. Resettled in Siberia in a commune of Tolstoyans. I invited my friends to join us there, but they were afraid of Siberia.

Once again I ask myself: why were those people not allowed to live? They were industrious people, local people; their whole life was like an open book. I never heard anything from them about aiming at or trying to get any kind of political power; they had no trace of such a thought. One could say that their only aim was to make their work flourish for the benefit of others and as an example to them. But no, with a stubbornness worthy of a better aim, they were kept from living and laboring. And who kept them from it? The government of workers and peasants, with the ideal of communism marching at their head. But it seems to me that the workers and peasants themselves had nothing to do with it; there was only the naked arbitrary power of the bureaucrats, sitting on top of the people and not serving them at all.

Our Life and Labor Commune in Siberia, which sprang up in December 1931, grew in size and strength year by year, and then was wiped out at the end of 1938.

Iván Vasílyevich Gulyáyev, a member of our commune who at one time engaged in friendly correspondence with Tolstóy, wrote a poem about the destruction of our commune. It begins with these words:

> What were the Tolstoyans guilty of
> Before the free country?
> Why were they denied their right
> To live in a commune of labor?

And it ends like this:

> Perhaps they were guilty only of this
> Before the free country:
> That they strove to follow their conscience,
> As Leo Tolstóy teaches.

Between 1936 and 1940, sixty-five persons in our commune were arrested and sentenced. Only a few of them came back, and the sick ones soon died. The rest did not return to their families at all.

Between 1941 and 1945, more than forty men from our Tolstoyan commune and other Tolstoyan groups were arrested and sentenced for refusing to bear arms and go to war. They never came back. That was more than a hundred persons in all. These people gave their lives for their sincere beliefs.

May their memory live forever!

Conclusion

I have lived my life. Now I look back at the whole path I have followed. Labor has been the entire condition of my life—labor of necessity, labor of love, labor out of conviction.

But for me labor has never been a path to profit, a way of getting rich by accumulating possessions. I have been used to an active life, in constant movement. Now my physical strength is failing me, and I have reached old age, a situation I am not accustomed to, and I must confess that it sometimes brings on a feeling of depression, a feeling of my own inferiority and uselessness. But I am overcoming this feeling. Everything in its time. When I had strength, I used it unsparingly. Now I have to live an old man's life. And with the view of an old man who has seen a lot, lived through a lot, and become somewhat wiser through experience, I examine my path and still have no doubt that the cause to which I have devoted my strength—the cause of drawing all people together in brotherly union on the basis of freedom, reason, and labor—is a truly good cause.

Even now I would leave everything without hesitating, leave my secure and peaceful corner and set off into the unknown, off to labor and hardships, if only I could take part in building the kind of commune I have striven for all my life. The approach of old age has only strengthened my opinion that this is the right path, one that is worthy of reasonable people.

But there are still questions that have weighed me down all my life, and to which I have still found no answer in either my life or my thinking.

There is the question of the family. What should it be? How should we live so as not to bend others to our will and not to subject ourselves to the will of others? It is natural for a man to seek a mate for himself so as to live as a family, and this takes place in his youthful years, when he has not yet gone very deeply into questions about the meaning of life. But it is also natural for a man not to stand still in one place, but to think, to meditate about life and come to certain conclusions, which cannot be compared to clothing—give me one shirt today, another tomorrow, and the next day I'll go without any shirt at all. No, if your convictions are sincere and firm, you can't brush them aside; your soul will not allow it—you would lose your self-respect.

And so, as a young man who lived "like everybody else," I got fed up with all the blessings of government-organized life, its patriotism, militarism, and property—all sanctified by the church. I saw through all that deception.

That kind of life became alien to me; I could no longer believe in all that, even if I faced death for it. I longed to create a personal and social life on other, more human, principles.

I felt cramped by the narrow family life that was confined to the interests and well-being of only one's own family. I understood that no family well-being could exist apart from the whole of society, and this distressed me. I thought it would not be right if I had plenty when those all around me were in need. I wished the same good for others that I wished for myself; and I believed that if things were all right in society, then they would also be all right for me and my family.

I understood all this and began to live by it, but it was alien to my wife. She could not understand why we should be concerned about problems far away when we had our own problems, our own needs, our own family. I do not blame Maryána for anything. She is a good, honorable, hard-working woman, a caring mother and wife. But I cannot blame myself, either. How can I harmonize her understanding with my own in our family life? I know this is a sore subject, and not only for me. I know that many others have agonized and do agonize over it. I know that in a lot of families—both those that are religious and those that are political—many a woman, even though she has no profound understanding of her husband, still considers that he is right, and believes him, and not only does not argue with him but supports and defends him against attacks. Life in such families goes much more smoothly and easily for both the husband and the wife. But the question still remains: Is that right? Is it good or bad, that kind of voluntary subordination by the wife? In any case it is easier for both husband and wife than eternal squabbling, dissatisfaction, and tears. It is better for them, and it is better for the children. I never tried to force Maryána to believe what I did, and besides, that would have been impossible; but in certain cases I did show firmness: for example, I never allowed her to speak badly to me about other people. If you have something good to say, then say it, but if not, keep silent. I will not condemn other people or listen to bad things about them.

Sometimes I wonder what the man I believe in so completely—Tolstóy—

would say about all this. I know he would say that order in life, not only within the family but also in society, can exist only when people are sincere, when they have one thing in common, a good and reasonable understanding of life, when they have a religion in common. Then everything that is so difficult, even impossible, to settle just settles itself. And I agree with that; but we are living now in an age when people have no philosophy in common. The old one has been outlived and no longer has any power, but no new one has yet taken shape. And from this comes all the suffering, the chaos in life, that we see all over the world.

I also think about the courts. In my long life, I have often been tried in court; and I have spent a big chunk of my conscious adult life as a slave, behind bars, under the bayonet.

For some reason the judges, the investigators, the procurators, the learned lawyers had to present me as some sort of enemy of the people, a criminal. I do not know why that was necessary—perhaps because that is how they earn their living? Let that lie on their conscience. But my conscience is clear before the people. I have never sought power over other people. Since my youth, I have worked with all my strength for the welfare of the people. I have always wanted only good for others, only what they themselves wanted for themselves: freedom and peaceful work; and in this respect my conscience is clear. Even the courts during the first years after the Revolution, when they were closer to the people and had not yet become bureaucratized and officialized, took note of my sincerity and lack of malice even when they put me on trial—and set me free out of respect for it. And by setting me free they glorified themselves, demonstrating that they were thoughtful human beings, and not soulless bureaucrats.

And now I bring this account of my life to a close. Even though my life has not yet ended on this earth, the end is near. I am not afraid of death; it does not frighten me. It is more frightful to be a living corpse.

I will struggle with all my might to feel the joy of life not only in active labor but also in the weakness of old age, in stubborn struggle within my soul in the same direction I have gone all my life.

In 1976, three years after finishing these memoirs, Morgachëv sent the following statement to the Procurator of the USSR demanding his rehabilitation:

Declaration concerning rehabilitation. I declare that I, Dimítry Morgachëv, a member of a Tolstoyan agricultural commune, am one of the few friends and followers of Tolstóy still alive. I was arrested along with a group of ten or twelve persons in April 1936. I was sentenced in November 1936 to three years of imprisonment in a labor camp. In November 1937 my sentence was revoked during Stalin's cult of personality because it was too mild. There was a second investigation. A second trial took place on this same matter in April 1940, four years after my arrest. My sentence was increased to seven years in a labor camp. After serving out this unmerited sentence, I was ordered under Directive 185 to continue working in the camp as a hired laborer, where I worked for three more years. I did ten years' time in all. Our commune of friends and followers of Leo Tolstóy had been resettled in Siberia on the basis of a decision of the Presidium of the All-Russian Central Executive Committee in 1930. We created a large agricultural communist economy, without any "mine" but with everything in common, ours, without putting if off like the Communist Party till sometime in the future. We did it right then, at that time, and we paid very dear for it with the lives of commune members. Very few friends and followers of Tolstóy are still alive. We were cruelly beaten for that peaceful, humane ideal. Such an unparalleled commune in the Soviet Union ought to have been taken under the protection of the law as a model communist farm. But only a few rare animals and birds are under the protection of the law. I am a fortunate man! I am still alive after being arrested in 1936. And after being put on trial twice. I endured everything. Those who were arrested in 1937–38 and 1941–45 never came back to their families and children. They went to an unknown death. The whole Tolstoyan case against the members of our commune, created during Stalin's cult of personality, was farfetched and false. Even though several thick volumes of lies and slander were written against the friends and followers of Tolstóy, I never admitted any guilt, since I had committed no crime, and I never signed the protocol of accusations. I accepted the teachings of Leo Tolstóy in 1915 during the First World War, and I have adhered to that ideal doctrine for sixty years. All men are brothers. I will take this teaching with me to Eternity. I sent you an application for rehabilitation in 1963— twenty-seven years after my arrest, and seventeen years after I had served ten years of imprisonment for being a follower of Leo Tolstóy's teachings. I was then seventy-one years old and a war invalid second class. In reply I received a pitiless refusal. I am still alive, and I still share Tolstóy's views on life. Now I am eighty-four years old. Forty years have passed since my arrest, and thirty since I served my sentence in the camps. I request that you rehabilitate me before I leave for Eternity. Signed: D. E. Morgachëv, 24 July 1976.

Not quite three months later, on 13 October 1976, Morgachëv received an official reply informing him that action had been taken to revoke the sentence he had received from the Novosibírsk Provincial Court in 1940, and that similar action had been taken for the other persons who had been sentenced along with him. By that time only two of the others were still alive—Mazúrin and D. I. Páshchenko. In January 1977, all three of them received certificates of rehabilitation from the Supreme Court of the USSR.

4.

From the Papers of *Yákov Dragunóvsky*

Yákov Deméntyevich Dragunóvsky (1886–1937) is the only contributor to this book who did not survive the Communist terror. The circumstances of his death in the labor camps in 1937 are still unexplained. In 1915, while lying wounded in a military hospital, he wrote an account of his experiences in the First World War, including a memorable episode on the Russian-German front in Poland during Easter week of 1915 when the German and Russian soldiers climbed out of their trenches and started fraternizing. He discovered Tolstóy's religious writings during the new freedom of the press after the first revolution in 1917; and by 1919 he had built up a personal library of over a thousand books, dealing mainly with Tolstóy and religious and philosophical matters. His generosity in lending his books soon attracted the suspicion of the new Soviet government. In 1920, during the Civil War, he was arrested for refusing military service on grounds of his Tolstoyan convictions and was tortured almost to death.

The selections from his writings included here are taken from the unpublished biography written by his son Iván on the basis of materials that had miraculously survived his father's death—diaries, autobiographical notes, poems, essays, and correspondence.

An honest, courageous, impassioned man, intolerant of compromise and hypocrisy, Dragunóvsky was not always easy to get along with. Even after their years of association in the Western Siberia Tolstoyan colony, Borís Mazúrin said upon reading the son's biography: "The impression it gives me is awesome. It fills me with joy, pity, and regret: joy for his power, his striving for the truth, his constancy in his journey toward reason; pity to the point of tears for the enormous suffering that fell to his lot; and regret that I never got the chance to draw closer to Yákov Deméntyevich and talk frankly with him as a friend."

1886–1914: My Life in Outline

BORN ON 7 OCTOBER 1886. Large peasant family. Orthodox religion. Our childhood fights. I was a crybaby. My education. Schooling in the village.

Yákov Dragunóvsky

Learning how to work. Unquestioning obedience to elders. From 1900 to 1906 I was an obedient and valued worker. Lack of land in the Smolénsk region. Purchase of land. Increasing work. Religious observance of the fast days. Prayers before holidays and on holidays. I got rheumatism from my poor footwear and clothing. I got pneumonia. No fear of death. When I was seventeen, our family, which had grown to twenty-one members, was divided into three households. My mother and her ailing husband (my father) no longer hesitated to live as a separate family, having five growing children, beginning with me, a seventeen-year-old, on whom my uncles placed their hopes for a good worker who would manage the farm well. In reality, I could still be a bad manager; I had been a good, obedient worker, never disobeying my uncles' orders, and now I was under the guidance of my mother, which was not at all bad for me—not to have any cares in my youth.

Conclusion: a valued worker, a peasant, an obedient drudge with several good moral qualities. I got acquainted with cabinetmaking; I wanted to find a teacher of cabinetmaking. I was too bashful. I became an eligible bachelor, but was afraid of girls, afraid of society. To a certain extent I was downright unsociable, satisfied to be a homebody. I was more devoted to religion. I loved to go to church. The Russo-Japanese War filled me with a vague horror. The 1905 Revolution was incomprehensible to me. The Union of the Russian People.[1] At the age of nineteen I spent a month and a half with a cabinetmaker. The cabinetmaker's stinginess and my hungry existence.

As if to spite my bashfulness, a feeling of love for girls crept into my soul. I could have fallen in love with the first one I met. This sincere, heartfelt love got mixed up with some kind of hazy, passionate attraction. A neighbor took me to the girls' folk dances at the market fair so as to pick out a bride for me. But I had no girlfriend right up to the time of my marriage.

My mother got ready to marry me off. "You need a helper for the farm." I did not know how to answer. I said I was not going to get married, but the neighbors advised my mother to marry me off. In spite of my stubbornness, my mother made a proposal for me to a girl I did not know. They brought us together in the church to look each other over. As future husband and wife, we stood about ten paces apart and admired each other. Without getting to know each other better, I found it hard to say whether I liked my prospective bride. The neighbor who had helped me look her over said: "They ought to do better than that for you." I agreed and was filled with sadness. When I got home, I could not eat. But Mother kept after me to give her a definite answer. I could not say either yes or no. A woman who came from the village where the bride lived tried to persuade me that a better bride could not be found. At last I was convinced. My mother and brother took some vodka to the bride, and the wedding took place two weeks later: on 7 May 1906, Tolstóy's Alyósha Gorshók was married off.[2]

---

1. Union of the Russian People—an organization of nationalist extremists, nicknamed the "Black Hundred," that sprang up during the Revolution of 1905 and carried out anti-Semitic pogroms.
2. Readers familiar with Tolstóy's short story "Alyósha Gorshók" (also translated as "Al-

If up to that time I had not been able to love any specific girl, I did give that first love to my wife. If I had been a homebody before my marriage, after marriage I was even more so. I greatly disliked attending big celebrations (weddings, parties, festivities). My wife was just the opposite. I would give in to my wife and attend a few rare carousals with her; and I could not stand it when some of the men would get into conversation with her, or when the same man would dance with her several times. I passionately hated dancing; what was the point of all that crowding together, all that stamping and stomping, all that senseless turning and twisting, all that stupid bobbing up and down? In a word, all those affectations were repulsive to me. I was very sorry that my wife took part in that nonsense. I became jealous and suffered from it. But I could not persuade her. I could not pass on to her my own character, my own dislike of carousals and dances. But in general, my wife and I had a good, harmonious life together.

Toward the end of our second year together, there appeared a link that bound us closer to each other—our son Ványa, born on 25 January 1908 (Old Style).

Autumn. Called up for military service. I was a recruit. Began to drink vodka. Accepted for military service. I adopted the family name Dragunóvsky.[3] My first time in a train. In the military barracks. I was a dumb sheep.

I was a soldier from the end of 1908 till November 1911. I was very homesick, and often wept. I found joy and reassurance in church. Probably my upbringing in our religious family had planted within me the desire to go to church on every holy day. All through 1909 I was taught discipline, taught to "march," to be not an independent rational man but a humble servant in the hands of the authorities, at whose command I must defend "the Faith, the Tsar, and the Fatherland from all enemies foreign and domestic." Those enemies greatly frightened me. What if I was ordered not just in words but in fact to kill? What could I do then, when I was horrified at the very thought? Still, I was curious to see the Tsar, whom I would have to defend from imaginary domestic and other enemies . . .

The year 1910. The soldiers got drunk at Easter, and protested against a bad sergeant-major. As punishment for that, I was ordered to stand under arms for ten hours. A revolver disappeared. I was given thirty days in the guardhouse. Fear of prison made me afraid I would never get out again, never return home from military service. Tolstóy's death. First acquaintance with Tolstóy's works. I read *War and Peace*.

The year 1911. In the summer we did guard duty in Petrograd. I got acquainted with the city, the museums, a few parks—the Taurian Gardens, the Zoological Gardens, the Community Center. I bought and read Tolstóy's *Resurrection*, "The Coffee-house of Surat," and others. The reserve soldiers

yósha the Pot" and simply as "Alyósha") will appreciate the wry humor of Dragunóvsky's identification of himself with Tolstóy's character.

3. Dragunóvsky—he made a family name out of the name of his native village, Draguný, having been known up to then, like most peasants, simply by his first name and patronymic, Yákov Deméntyevich, "Jacob the son of Deménty."

with their drunkenness kept me under arms for ten days. They raised my fears again that I would never get out of the service. The severity of the service increased my aversion to it. Discipline. Fear for one's life. Bitterness. Superstition has not changed. I was on guard duty twice at the railroad when the Tsar was passing through. Abstention from vodka. Church, books. I love to read Tolstóy. I haven't yet taken in the truth. I am still a dumb sheep. Demobilization. Thank God, I have been discharged. I am at home and happy, and my family is glad that I have come back. I brought a few books back with me. I am beginning to love books; I read them and acquire still more. Something draws me to Tolstóy's works.

Life at home. Peasant life, materially satiated, drunken, not very sensible. Basically, it is work, work, and work, acquiring more and more, a kind of competition with each other. Again the church gives me a certain spiritual rest and peace. I read the canonical hours, and I am very glad that I can read loud, clearly, and correctly. I am beginning to read Acts. Along with that I am still attracted to Tolstóy's works. Our seven-month-old son Alekséy died in the spring of 1913. That had a powerful effect on my soul. In autumn of the same year, my wife nearly died of a hemorrhage. My brothers Pyotr and Timoféy went off to Ríga for seasonal labor. I am busy with cabinetmaking at my uncles', who have moved to Dolgomóstye. I am earning money to buy a lathe. Auction sales at a landowner's. Wedding at my Uncle Abram's. I was dead drunk. Afterwards I was sick for three days and disgusted with myself. A dry summer. We got our wheat in quickly.

Mobilization from 20 July 1914 to August 1915.

(Written in the 1920s)

1914–1915: War

After arriving wounded at the hospital, I took it into my head to write my own diary-story from the beginning of the first mobilization up to the present.

It was July 1914. The weather was hot and dry the whole time. We laid in a supply of green, fluffy hay. The mowed meadows began turning yellow under the scorching sun. The air was stifling. Shortly afterwards we harvested and stored away the rye. Half of the field work was done by 15 July. Only the spring crop remained, which was still a little green, but the hot sun made it start to wither prematurely. In several villages they had already begun to harvest the spring crop: they would mow the meadows and pull out the flax. Everything seemed to be going along fine: we worked away in peace and joy. Then suddenly, on somebody's orders, all this was rudely disturbed. Mobilization was announced on 18 July. Everybody was suddenly filled with gloom. You could no longer hear merry songs or conversations among the muzhiks sitting on the mounds of earth packed around their huts and talking about their peasant affairs. Rumors of war started flying in all directions. The muzhiks were gloomy, and the old women wept. I too felt stunned. I walked around as if I were tipsy. The mobilization order caught me just at the time when I was reading one of Tolstóy's books. I plunged into thought, laid the book aside, and started walking back and forth. I saw my wife crying, and she threw her arms around my neck and bawled. I tried to persuade her that I was not the only one to go to war, and not everybody would get killed, and maybe I would come back alive. I kept trying to persuade her, and yet my own heart was aching. All right, then: whatever will be will be. I asked for the bathhouse to be heated. I would bathe myself for the last time and leave. I washed all over and put on the underwear I had brought back from the service. My mother said: "You've dressed up as if for your death," and burst into tears. The night passed full of anxiety. I dreamed all kinds of nonsense about war: first I thought about suddenly getting wounded, maybe seriously, and how long it might take to recover. Then I would imagine myself killed outright, with never a chance again to see the beauty of nature, my homeland, and my dear family. How clever our little son had become, now in his seventh year. The past winter I had taught him to read a little.

On 19 July all soldiers were ordered to assemble in their district, and also to bring horses. They said the soldiers would ride in wagons to military headquarters in the regional capital. I got to the district at eight o'clock in the morning. A lot of men and horses had already gathered there. I saw that we had nothing to do for the time being, so I went to the church. After the service I asked the priest to recite a farewell prayer for me. I prayed fervently and sadly, asking God to have mercy on me and let me come out of the war alive. I had no stomach for dying at such a young age and in such good physical health. After he recited the prayer, the priest offered me best wishes. I went back to the district. At that time I heard shouts among the soldiers: "Let's smash the liquor store! Why won't they let us have vodka? This may be the last time we'll be here alive! We've got to have farewell drinks with our kinfolks!" The constable ordered the shopkeeper to open the liquor store, and everybody rushed in. I harnessed my horse and rode back home. At home I started walking all around, as if to bid farewell to everything dear and familiar to me. I felt sad about all of it—my family, the house, the garden, our field, the cabinetmaking and lathe-turning trade I had just learned, and the books I had acquired. It was good that two of my brothers were still at home and the third was away on seasonal labor, but inquiries had already been made about him for mobilization.

The morning of 20 July was dull and overcast; it had rained a little during the night, and the air had cooled off. All nature looked festive, as if inviting us to a peaceful, happy life; but my heart was heavy and sad. This was the day I had to leave for the war. Perhaps I was seeing my family and this beautiful world for the last time. We lit candles before the icons. Our hut was filled with women and children, and they all helped me pray to God. I started reciting the prayer that is recited before battle, the one I had learned during active service: "O my Saviour!"—but I could not finish it. I forgot and stopped at the words "to overcome our enemies." Most of all, I prayed that I would be able to come back home.

It was a little over twenty miles to the regional capital, and we got there around noon. We went to military headquarters and found out that the soldiers had already broken into two liquor shops. The drunken men were shouting, cursing, pushing their way into the office, and thrusting their military cards toward the officer in charge. Suddenly we heard shots. We were told that the soldiers had broken into a third liquor shop.

The physicians pronounced us fit. I thought: fit for what? But my thoughts did not go beyond that question. At the railway station we were distributed among the cars, and the train started off.

On 10 November 1914 we arrived in Warsaw, and there it became clear to us that we were being taken to the German front. From Warsaw they took us to the town of Grodzisk, where we saw signs of previous battles: the devastated railway station and houses burned down or blown up. On the evening of the twelfth we got to Skierniewice. There we unloaded.

In Skierniewice we ran around and looked for the first time at German prisoners of war, who were surrounded by a convoy of our soldiers. It was interesting to see what kind of people we were going to kill. It turned out that they were the same kind of people we were. They stood around and stamped their feet from the cold. Their faces were sad and downcast, as if they had a foreboding about the suffering to come.

Our first battle took place on 14–15 November. A fine snow was falling, and it had already begun to cover the ground. The regimental commander arrived on horseback, greeted the soldiers, and we started moving. We went some two miles and met about a hundred soldiers, who were driving one German along in front of them. In reply to our question where they were coming from, they said: "We are coming from our position. There were several battles, and this is all of us left alive from the whole regiment." We could hardly believe they had fought to the point where only a handful of men were left from a whole regiment. We could hear the thunder of guns not far away. The soldiers were walking and crossing themselves as they walked, calling on the help of God and Christ, who commanded us to love our enemies. They went on like dumb sheep.

We were ordered to take the village of Belyávy, where the enemy had dug in. We walked through a level plowed field. We crossed a ditch in the middle of this plowed land. In the sky there were scattered, scudding clouds, with the moon peeping out from behind them. The night would by turns grow dark and then bright and festive. Nature called us to quiet, happiness, and joy, but where and why were we marching? But such questions rarely arose in our minds, stupefied as we were by delusions, discipline, and the mass hypnosis of the state.

We kept moving forward and had gone nearly a mile when suddenly bullets started whizzing over our heads—zing-zing! zing-zing! We threw ourselves down on the plowed ground. Bullets kept whizzing by, but we did not fire. The company commander ordered us to rush forward, and we advanced on the run, but under the rain of bullets we lay down, trying to lie between the furrows. Suddenly: z-z-z-boom! After the explosion I raised my head to see where the shell had exploded. A thick cloud of smoke was rising not far ahead of us. After that they kept exploding closer and closer to us— boom! boom! Well, here it is, I thought to myself—this is the end. A shell will land right on us and blow us to pieces.

Our moving line was clearly visible to the enemy in the glow of the fires, and our company was advancing right into the light of the burning houses; but the company commander kept ordering us forward, forward, and no one dared disobey him. It had to be hypnosis.

Two or three hundred paces ahead, there were trenches that had not yet been occupied by the Germans. We hastened to take them. Crouching down in them, we opened a heavy fire on the Germans.

Our forces began surrounding the village on the left flank. Seeing this maneuver by our troops, the Germans put them under heavy fire. Finding themselves under this fire, our soldiers thought it must be coming from us, sitting in the trenches and shooting at them by mistake; and they shouted: "Russians! Don't shoot! It's your own men!" The Germans increased their firing, and our men began to retreat from the village.

Suddenly a few Germans climbed out of their trenches and started running straight toward us. At first we could not understand what they wanted— were they running to attack or to give themselves up? On our side we shouted: "Hurrah!" and ran toward them. The Germans took fright and ran back, but we ran after them, and they stopped and surrendered.

Walking past the German trenches, I saw a terrifying scene. The trenches were filled with dead men, most of them shot through the head, and some of them with their heads blown off. I stepped into one trench and jumped out in horror: a corpse was lying in the straw, and I had stepped on it. Walking past other trenches, I saw a lot of wounded. Some of them had fallen asleep and were snoring, but many were pleading for help. But how could I help so many when I was all alone? We came up to a barn where wounded Germans were groaning and begging for help from us, their enemies. Some of them begged in the German language, and others in Polish. Some here were not wounded, and they were taken off at once to headquarters. Walking further, I heard a soldier from our company call and ask me to bandage his back. I looked at his back and was horrified: how could I bind up that enormous wound, torn open so wide by a piece of shrapnel that you could not cover it with your two hands! His coat was soaked in blood. I told him I could not bind up such a wound, and then he asked me for water. Fortunately, I had a full flask of water, and he eagerly gulped it down. He asked me to lead him back to the unit. "I don't know anything and can't figure out which way to go," he said. I agreed to, and he and I went past the trenches where dead Germans were lying. I heard someone ask for help. I went up and saw a wounded German begging for water. I let him drink from my flask. The German put his hand on his heart as a sign of gratitude. We went further, and suddenly we heard somebody not begging but shouting and waving to me. I saw a wounded German lying on the plowed ground, far from the trench. I told my wounded comrade to wait there a minute and

I would go and find out what was the matter. I saw the man lying on his stomach, motioning to me: "Drink!" I gave him a drink too. The German pointed to his trousers pocket. I reached in there and drew out an old wallet. I asked: "This?" He shook his head and said something. I reached deeper into his pocket: it was wet. I pulled my hand out; it was covered with blood. The German saw that I did not understand him and pointed to his leg, above the knee, asking me to bind it up for him. But what could I do? Here is my own comrade, badly wounded and hardly able to stand, waiting for me and begging me to tie up his wound. I couldn't do it for him, and now you beg me, and not only you but many others in the trenches are begging for my help. My heart ached with pity, but there was no way for me to help. I put my hand on my breast and said: "I can't, brother." He understood me and didn't beg anymore, and I left him, full of pity for that poor sufferer. My wounded comrade and I went further. Another wounded German asked me for water, and I gave him a drink, and I gave another drink to my wounded comrade. I do not know how I came by so much water: I gave a drink to so many men and still had some left.

We came out of the village into a field. Two dead horses were lying under the trees, and not far from them were about a dozen dead men— Russians and Germans. Evidently there had been hand-to-hand fighting, and now they all lay together, like senseless brothers.

It was now almost dark. We tried to dig trenches, but the ground had already frozen, and we could not do anything with our short spades.

Shouts could be heard from the front line: "Hurrah!" We kept hearing those shouts for a long time, but we did not go to their aid, and no general battle took place. They gradually quieted down, and at last it was perfectly quiet. We were lined up and started off somewhere. We marched for a long time and made stops along the road, during which I began to fall asleep, and others did too. A heavy frost hit us, along with wind. We halted, lay down on the frozen ground, squeezing close together so as to warm ourselves a little, and started dozing off, but we could not sleep long; our feet were freezing to the point of pain and numbness, and we would jump up and run around till we were thoroughly tired, but still we could not get warm. Utterly exhausted, we would lie down and doze off, but in a few minutes we would jump up and run and run. The thought struck me: what is the use of all this? I remembered that it was Sunday, and my thoughts carried me back home to my dear family. Were my people thinking about me? Did they know where I was? How I was freezing and suffering, and for what? Dimly, as if in sleep, the thought came to me: after all, we soldiers are a flock of dumb sheep; the shepherds drive us wherever they want, and we do not think for ourselves, but blindly obey them.

Day dawned. In a neighboring trench, an old soldier was reading the breviary and the prayers; a heartfelt groan, almost a sob, could be heard in the words and his voice. Suddenly a German shell exploded close by. The soldiers pricked up their ears. The doleful chanting of the prayers could be heard as before from the trench. Shells began exploding one after another, but they all either fell short or went beyond our trenches, and we thanked God.

Among people who have lived the most moral lives since birth, their instinctive faith often takes irrational, superstitious forms and can be shattered unless it is supported by rational arguments. The old soldier has been a good man from birth. He feels sorry for his own life, which at any moment can be cut down so stupidly and cruelly; he feels sorry for his own and the German soldiers who are inflicting suffering and death on each other. He neither sees nor feels an enemy in anybody; but he swore an oath and was made to take up arms and kill whomever his commander ordered him to. It was terrible!

In moments of reflection, I began to notice that I was becoming brutalized. When I shot at the Germans from a trench, I did not feel any pity for them. I was told that they were our enemies. When the priest, our holy father, sent us into battle with his blessing, he called us soldiers "a Christ-loving host," and said we were going into a holy war, for the Tsar and the Fatherland. Our compassion for human beings disappeared. Our mind, feelings, and will were in the power of mass hypnosis and discipline. I had been a dumb sheep, and that is what I remained.

In the morning I saw them burying soldiers who had died of their wounds during the night. We would dig ditches three and a half feet deep beside peasant houses and under apple trees, and wrap the dead men in their coats. The priest would read a prayer over them, and the dead men were dropped into the ditch and covered with dirt. How many such unknown graves there are, scattered over the Polish land.

We were taken to the Kurdvánov farm. We halted and began cooking potatoes, since there was no bread. After eating, we started off like a herd of sheep, heading for our position. When we had gone a little over half a mile, we saw German shells falling on the farm, and soon the shells started exploding off to one side not far from us. The soldiers scattered in all directions. We were placed in a line and ordered to dig trenches. I dug out a little hole for myself and remembered that it was Sunday. I washed myself in a nearby ditch, prayed to God, and began to eat the rest of the last night's meal. The morning was calm and sunny, with a little bit of frost.

How many times did I read the letter from my brother at home; and on that wonderful, clear morning I was at home in spirit, among those people who were so dear to me. My brother wrote that my wife had given birth to a daughter (Kláva), but that our brother Timoféy had been taken off to the army in a military transport.

Suddenly my thoughts were interrupted by the deafening crash of exploding shells not far away. Large-caliber missiles were exploding, and fragments of them were flying into our trenches. Soon the shells started exploding very close, right over our trenches, and several men were wounded. During this heavy bombardment, our company got the order to go and cover the battery. It was terrible to climb out of the trenches into the open field, but what could we do? We had to climb out and fulfill the orders of the commanders. The hypnosis was still as strong as ever.

The company commander picked me and a few other soldiers to go on patrol into a nearby forest and look around, find out what roads there were in the forest, and so on. We were glad to get the assignment to go into that beautiful forest. It formed a square a little over half a mile by half a mile, surrounded by a wire fence. It was some kind of park or reserve.

Once we got into the forest, we felt as if we were at liberty. The snow was melting and dripping off the fir trees, and the air had a resinous fragrance. The stillness of the forest was disturbed only by us men and the big flocks of pheasants and quail that we frightened. We scared up a wild goat, and we met a lot of rabbits, dozens of them, which to our surprise showed no fear of us and let us get quite close to them. Nature melted away the hardness that the fratricidal battles had produced in our hearts. It was incredible that nearby the most intelligent of creatures—human beings—were stealthily looking for each other and taking aim and killing each other like wild animals. What for? Why?

We spent Christmas and New Year's Day of 1915 in peace and quiet, without any battles; only we were terribly disturbed by lice, and we battled them every day. On 14 January the Germans had some kind of holiday. We heard that it was Wilhelm's name day.[4] All day long we heard merry drunken singing from their trenches, which were about eight hundred paces from us.

The first six months of the fratricidal war were celebrated on 18 January. I went to the field chapel, which had been put up in the forest. It was strange to hear the words of the priest, who called for new victories among Christians who are supposed to love their enemies.

Day by day the weather grew warmer. It got easier to carry out our duties. We were anticipating the great holy day of the Resurrection of Christ, who taught us to love our enemies. What mockery! I kept thinking: if only this great holy day can pass in peace and quiet. And indeed there was a feeling that things were leading toward peace with our opponent. What joy that would be!

On Thursday, 19 March, three days before Easter, we had done our night sentry duty as usual, and after drinking our tea we had lain down in our dugouts to get some rest. Suddenly we heard joyful shouts from the soldiers. We scrambled out of our dugouts, and all the soldiers climbed out of theirs, too, and looked out at the German trenches. A strange scene appeared before our eyes. All the German soldiers had also climbed out of their trenches, and ten men had separated from the rest and were walking toward our trenches. For us it was a joyous miracle. I too ran over to find out how this peace had taken place.

The ten Germans were coming toward the left flank of the First Com-

4. Kaiser Wilhelm II was born on 27 January (14 January, Old Style) 1859.

pany. Our battalion commander would not let us go over there, but the Germans got together with our soldiers in the middle of the flank and began conversing with them. One of the Germans came over to our trench. We gave him a loaf of bread, and he started complaining about how little bread they were allotted.

This peaceful fraternization between the Russians and Germans, fighting and shooting at each other on the orders of their officers, might have continued longer and most likely would have ended in peace. But it was broken up by the frightful oaths of the commandant, who stormed at his soldiers for fraternizing without the permission of the officers. He telephoned the artillery and ordered them to shoot at the Germans. Two shells of shrapnel burst over the German trenches, but the soldiers did not take refuge: they just kept sitting above their trenches and carried on their peaceful conversations. Fifteen more shots were fired far beyond the German trenches. The simple, rank-and-file soldiers felt compassion for each other.

After that, the firing ceased, and the Russians and Germans went back to their trenches after agreeing not to fire on each other. "Why should we kill each other?" they said on both sides. "Let's get along with each other!" The day had turned out to be so marvelous—calm, clear, and warm—that these worn-out fighting men were involuntarily drawn toward peaceful, kindly feelings.

All day long and all night long, not a single shot was heard. Everybody walked around in the open, all the soldiers had happy expressions on their faces, and songs filled the air. The Germans started waving white handkerchiefs at us from their trenches and shouting something to us. We answered them the same way. Two volunteers from us went over to see the Germans, and guests from their side came over to us. All the soldiers on both sides climbed out onto the big open space and watched this precious, peaceful scene for about an hour. That night, while we were on duty at the embrasures, we kept hearing the Germans singing songs. At daybreak, two of our soldiers went to visit the Germans. They were so well received, and so well treated to vodka and snacks, that they could not walk back to our trenches by themselves. The Germans took them by the arms and guided them back to us with the words: "Here—take your boys."

That morning the battalion commander got the idea of writing notes and fastening them to stakes, and he ordered the stakes to be carried out in front of our trenches and driven into the ground. On the stakes was the message: "If you come over to us, you will be taken prisoner; and if you run back, we will shoot."

On the morning of the twentieth, two Germans came toward us on a friendly visit. When they got to the stakes, they stopped and read them. One of them grabbed a note and ran back. Three shots were fired at him, but he disappeared, and the other came on. Only our officers talked with this second German, about what we did not know. The rumor was started that this German had said the Germans did not want a peaceful arrangement, but wanted to make only a pretense of it so as to lure as many of our soldiers over to their side as possible and take them prisoner. But we could never find out what the truth really was. We thought that but for the officers, the ordinary soldiers would have reached an agreement and made peace among themselves. But the officers only got in the way of this good work and sent us off, like wild animals, to fight each other.

And so our friendship with our "adversaries" was broken up. Although there was no more firing at each other, we were forbidden to walk around in the open.

It was a Sunday in May. The village in which we stopped to rest had suffered very little from the war, but the fences had been torn down for campfires. The soldiers strolled through the village. My comrade and I went into a blossoming orchard, lay down under a currant bush in the thick green grass, and admired the neighboring field, in which tall, green rye was rippling like waves. Further away, beyond that field, another village could be seen, surrounded by orchards. My comrade and I lay back in the grass to finish reading *Anna Karénina*.

The next day, at five o'clock in the afternoon, we were marched off again to our position. As we walked out of the village, a cuckoo accompanied us with its call. Soldiers say that is a bad omen, it leads to misfortune; but what kind of good fortune could await us when we remained an obedient flock of dumb sheep on our way to the slaughter?

And sure enough, as soon as we got to regimental headquarters, we heard that one company was already occupying trenches on the other side of the Rawka River. It fell to the lot of our company to go and seize those trenches. We crossed the river on logs and started occupying trenches that had been hastily dug in rough-and-ready fashion. We got settled in them toward morning on 5 May, and after posting sentries, we lay down to sleep.

When I woke up, the sun was already high and warm. I started examining the terrain. About six hundred paces away was a half-devastated village occupied by the Germans. Closer to us was a line of their trenches, where we could even see the holes of their embrasures. In front of their trenches was a strong barrier, but our barriers had collapsed. I went down to the river and washed, and when I got back to the trench I started reading my prayer book. A soldier lying beside me listened. At noon we ate some bread and butter mixed with dirt. At two o'clock the Germans started firing on our trenches. They fired for an hour, then stopped. Toward nightfall it grew overcast, and during the night we had a heavy downpour that soaked us to the skin and left deep puddles of water in the trenches. During the rain the Germans fired very little; but as soon as the rain slackened off, they began a heavy artillery bombardment of our trenches from three batteries. There were frightful explosions of both shrapnel and heavy shells, and some of the explosions would make the whole earth shake. We heard that there were a lot of killed and wounded in the third platoon, and that the men in that platoon had begun deserting to other trenches, where shells were not falling so often. Our artillery kept silent and did not fire a single shot, while the Germans kept firing right up to morning, stopping only at daybreak. The day was overcast. During the day the Germans fired a few shells at us and then fell silent. Four of my neighbors were killed, and ten wounded. My heart was heavy, but I remained at my post; no changes had taken place in my thinking. I still thought this situation was necessary and willed by God. We had enemies and we had to kill them.

The sun went down. The medics carried the dead and wounded off the field, which would have been dangerous to do in daylight. Once again the German guns started pounding us furiously. Not many shells fell on our trenches at first; most of them were fired at the regiment next to us. But soon deadly shells rained down on our trenches. Our artillery sent a few shells into the village and then fell silent. After that, we were bombarded still more wickedly and murderously by shells of various calibers. A lot of batteries roared, and the ground shook from the explosions. Our dugouts started collapsing, and our embrasures fell apart. A hollow place I had dug in the wall of the trench fell in, almost burying me. All hell had broken loose on us. Soldiers lay flat and silent in the trenches, their faces pale, expecting death at any minute. I crouched against the front wall of the trench, which still held together, and after each explosion I would look over the rampart to see whether the Germans were coming. The other soldiers were surprised that I looked out of the trench so boldly and openly.

Midnight came, but the shelling did not die down. It was time for us to be relieved, but no replacements came. Evidently they were waiting until the bombardment subsided. The commander of the tenth company ran up and asked: "Where is your commander?" Before he could get a reply, we were deafened by an exploding shell. He squatted against the wall where I was standing. We saw that we were still unhurt.

"Your Honor," I said, "we've gone through plenty of terror today."

"Yes," he said. "I don't know what will become of us and how we'll get through our shift." With those words he went off to look for our commander.

During that hellish din of guns and shells, the soldiers passed the word down the line that in the third platoon a bomb had fallen on a dugout full of men and collapsed it. I grabbed a spade, dashed out of the trench, and ran to the scene of the catastrophe. I ran and shouted to the soldiers: "Where is that dugout?" The soldiers stuck their heads out of the trenches, pointed it out to me, and then disappeared again in the trenches, because the shells were exploding constantly. It was a strange situation: at that moment I had no fear in the face of the death that was flying, roaring, and exploding all around me. There was just one thought in my head: to save the comrades who were buried under that dirt. Out of love for those men, I showed some courage in spite of myself. Jumping into the crater left by the bomb, I hurriedly started digging into the earth, and soon an arm appeared. Seeing the arm, I began to dig in the spot where the head must be. When I cleared the dirt away from the head, I saw that the man was still alive. I freed his chest and body and pulled him out of the ground. The man groaned weakly and then told me to free his legs, which pained him a lot and must be injured. His legs were pinned down by a lot of dirt and by ceiling beams torn apart by the shell. Somehow I freed him from the beams and dirt and started pulling him out, but he yelled in pain: "Take hold of my leg!" Another soldier ran up in response to my call, and together we pulled the man out. He said that two of them had been in the dugout. I quickly started digging and soon felt an overcoat with my spade, and a little further there appeared the strings of a kit bag thrown over a shoulder, and then I dug out a man's head. I could see from his face that he was dead. I began pulling on his waist and arm, but the arm cracked and came off, shattered by the shell. I left him there, realizing that he no longer needed help. A medic ran up and started bandaging the man we had saved, whose right leg was badly injured in several places.

The hellish din of the guns continued as before. Several shells burst above my head, and under their frightful crash I crouched in a pit. Then I ran back to my own trench and again started looking out over the top. Soon word was passed on to me that the man I had saved was calling for me again. I ran back and saw that he had again been buried under dirt by the powerful explosions and shaking of the earth. Even the medic had not managed to get away, but the medic had no spade on him, and so he had nothing to dig with. Together we pulled him out of the ground, and the twice-saved man begged us to carry him away from that tomb. But we had no stretcher, and besides, how could we carry him across that open space under the rain of shells? But then the shells started falling less frequently, and medics came up with stretchers and began carrying the wounded away.

Toward morning the bombardment died down, and only one battery kept firing. We went off duty in the morning, and we breathed a sigh of freedom and joy, now that we were in the forest and completely safe. There we learned that the Germans had fired more than a thousand shells of various calibers at our trenches, and I also heard that a piece of shrapnel had struck the head of my good comrade with whom I had almost finished reading *Anna Karénina*. That good comrade of mine died soon afterwards in the hospital, and I wrote to his relatives and told them. That terrible night is one I will never forget.

But it turned out that not all creatures were busy that night with what occupied the most intelligent creatures—people. Here beside us, above a little stream in the forest, a nightingale poured forth its silvery notes and trills all night long. In the backwaters of the stream, the frogs were croaking away, and they too appeared to be undisturbed by the senselessness of men. In the daytime, lapwings, uttering their strident calls, flew over the warring lines, higher than the flying projectiles. All these lower forms of life probably did not know what those reasonable creatures—human beings—were doing to each other.

So what can we boast of to those lesser brethren—animals and other creatures? Our intelligence, which we have perverted and turned into an instrument of evil and suffering? No! It is not for us to boast but rather to be ashamed before the animals!

A month later, Dragunóvsky was ordered to take forty men and go out on a dangerous scouting mission. He was wounded in the foot and sent on a troop train to a hospital in Petrograd—the new name given to St. Petersburg in 1914 after the outbreak of war with the Germans. While he was in the hospital, he wrote the account of his war experiences given above.

1915–1921: My Life in Outline

I was given three months' leave, from 15 August to 15 November 1915. I recovered very well at home, but I was seized with horror at the thought that I might be sent back to my unit. I could find no rational way out, and for that reason I began secretly reopening my wound; but that was not enough, so I ruined my hearing in one ear, which has remained deaf ever since. During that leave I let my relatives know about my new understanding of life.

Despite my reluctance to be a military man, the commission sent me to a reserve battalion, which was not far away.

Seeing that self-mutilation did not work, I began seeking a way out through insubordination to the authorities and nonfulfillment of my military duties, for which I was subjected to prosecution and sent to a disciplinary battalion for "reform." There I was filled with fear that I might never be set free.

The year 1917. Revolution. A joyous awakening, which moves me to tears. I am free. My deaf ear frees me from the military profession. A feeling of anger about the oppression of the old regime. I am at home. I am working with joy, and I wish with all the strength of my soul to help in the building of a new life. I am glad that land is being taken away from the priests and landowners. In the zémstvo I passionately take part in the elections to the Constituent Assembly.[5] I agree to serve in a credit union. Crop failure and starvation in Smolénsk Province. I was sent to Oryól and Vorónezh provinces to get food. I bought several railway carloads of flour. On the way back, our cars were fired on. Just as before, there is no peace in the world: first the Whites and then the Reds rob the peaceful inhabitants. Their names are different, but evidently their hearts are alike. The Revolution has not changed their outlook: both groups are materialists and egotists and are looking out only for themselves. I am glad I was able to buy and bring back food for our starving population. I am delighted that my brother Pyotr is more active than I in the provincial assemblies and was elected a delegate to Moscow, where he saw and heard Lénin.

I feel an increasing need to play an active role in building our new life, but I do not know where to play it. I have been elected to the district executive committee, as vice-chairman, and appointed to the financial section and

5. The zémstvos were a system of limited local government established in 1864, which gradually gained more authority, especially after the February Revolution in 1917; but the Bolsheviks abolished them after seizing power later that year.

the military commissariat. In all this work I feel a powerful contradiction in my soul. I am against violence, but my official position makes me use violence, demanding war taxes and contributions, requisitioning wagons and provisions from the population. I see that by serving in the government, I am taking part in violence. I am dissatisfied with myself for not living and acting the way I think.

At home I am rough and at times brutal with my family members. I lose my temper easily. I feel that my character is not improving. I will never forget my severity with my five-year-old son because he had not learned his prayers and letters well. Once I kicked him hard because he had learned some bad words from his playmates; and later, when he was in school, I often punished him with birch rods or pulled his ears till the blood came because he did not do well in reading and writing. I was rude to my wife when she did not always agree with my opinions and did not want to share my vegetarianism. I would get angry when others did not think and act as I did, and this only made the people who were closest to me feel cold and distant. I was unduly demanding toward others and always wanted my children and my wife to do whatever I said.

I do not know how I might have lived further in my Orthodoxy, whether I would have become gentler in my relations with others or whether I would have continued sternly fulfilling the rules of Orthodoxy; but all this came to an end. I began to think I ought to join some kind of peaceable, reasonable organization. I had heard that there were communist anarchists who rejected violence. I got acquainted with them and had talks with them, but for some reason they did not accept me. I heard that about twenty miles from our village there were some Tolstoyans, the Pýrikov brothers. I soon got acquainted with them and felt a spiritual kinship with them. I got some pamphlets by Tolstóy from them, and I stopped eating meat for good. Heart-to-heart talks with Yelizár Ivánovich Pýrikov opened my eyes in many ways to the meaning of life.

With great pleasure I gave up my feverish activity in the district executive committee and replaced it with activity much closer to my heart—reading books by Tolstóy and having serious talks with my friends—and I resolutely gave up my "military" profession. I started taking frequent trips to Smolénsk and brought back bushels of books, and by the autumn of 1919 I had a large library. I set up a bookbinding shop and taught my son to bind books, thanks to which he got in the habit of reading them.

The library attracted many readers. I gladly lent books to them, and in this way I acquired many friends who were sympathetic to my beliefs. Some of them stopped going to church and began refusing military service. When the village priest heard about this, he became alarmed. He took Tolstóy's books away from some of my readers and burned them. Through the Pýrikovs I became a member of the Moscow Vegetarian Society. I was a "Tolstoyan." Soon I started a local "Society of True Freedom in Memory of L. N. Tolstóy."

The year 1919. I am reading Tolstóy and corresponding with the Moscow Vegetarian Society and with several new friends. The execution of seven men who refused military service, among them my cousin Semyón, horrifies my soul but does not frighten me away from my newly discovered truth. The arrest of the Pýrikov brothers adds both horror and determination. I write my first letter to V. G. Chertkóv about the horrors and about my intention to remain firm and to rejoice in having to suffer for the truth, which is not the same as suffering and awaiting death in war.

(Written in the 1920s)

Letter of 20 February 1920 from Yákov Dragunóvsky to the Society of True Freedom in Moscow

Dear Friends,

Even though you already know about the Society of True Freedom organized in the village of Draguný in Smolénsk Province, I think it may not be amiss to write you more about it. Up to last spring I was only a sympathizer with Tolstóy's views, and I did not even know such a society existed. Then on 6 April I became a member of the Society at the Donéts post office in Smolénsk Province, about twenty miles from us, which was organized by the Pýrikov brothers. It was there that I applied for membership in the Society in Moscow.

At the Pýrikovs' I bought some of Tolstóy's pamphlets. Only then did I begin to get better acquainted with Leo Nikoláyevich's philosophy of life, and I even began to think, How could I have failed to understand all this earlier? I would have tried long ago to put these ideas into practice. But then I realized that it is never too late to strive for goodness. Later I read the letter of the Moscow Society of True Freedom "To All Friends and Like-Minded People," which gave me the idea of organizing such a society in our neighborhood. This was helped along by Fyódor Alekséyevich Strákhov when he arrived at the Pýrikovs', and also by Yelizár Ivánovich Pýrikov himself. I occasionally attend the discussions led by Fyódor Alekséyevich. His friendly talks, his kind words, and his purely childlike love have such an effect on you that afterwards you feel like rejoicing or weeping for joy! You begin to feel that you are entering a new world; even the sun, which had been shining all along, now seems different. You begin to see something beautiful and dear in the rain, the bad weather, the cold, the winter; you feel like throwing your arms around everybody. All evil disappears before my eyes, and I want to show my love toward everything alive, even wild animals; I want to tell everybody that we will live this kind of life, and not merely tell them—I want to shout out loud that this is life, that everyone needs to live so that everything will be good. And it's not enough just to shout; I feel like doing something more or less heroic—even a miracle. I feel like doing something as if by magic. I had occasion to confess these impulses to Yelizár Pýrikov, who told me there was no need to try to perform any kind of miracle over people; rather, you need to work on yourself, and then you will see how everything gets picked up and passed on without any effort on your own part. I have been going deeper into what he said, and I agree completely with the justice of such arguments. But still I somehow don't feel like keeping silent; I want to say what will make everybody understand this. But since I don't know how to speak and express my ideas, I have begun collecting books and circulating them among people. But I already have a lot of books, and now I want to do something more: start a Society. I asked F. A. Strákhov to come to the formal opening, but he could not come in such cold weather because of his health. Yelizár Pýrikov agreed to come, however, and on 14 December 1919 he and I together organized a meeting, at which about sixty persons were present. Very few of them actually became members, but our principal aim was not that, but rather to say publicly what had been whispered privately, to put in leaven, like the woman in the Gospel, so as to leaven all the dough. And now the fermentation is beginning. Agitation is arising among the powers that be, the clergy, and those who cling to outward ceremonies. They almost all cried out in one voice that these people are causing harm, and so on. But the truth does not fear slander, and the people who have begun to follow in the footsteps of truth are not afraid of any kind of terror; all fear disappears before them, and they see above all just what they are striving toward—a new heaven in which truth has its dwelling place!

With brotherly greetings and love,
Yákov Dragunóvsky, 20 February 1920

(From the periodical *Ístinnaya Svobóda* [True Freedom], No. 2, May 1920.)

Memoirs about Arrest on 31 October 1920 for Refusal of Military Service

Only one militiaman took the twelve of us to the politburo of the regional town of Demídov. Even though we were already arrested, and thus would have been looked on in former times as dangerous people, only one militiaman was with us, and not all the time at that—while we were on the way, he went about his own affairs. It is clear from this that we were not considered criminals who had to be kept under strict guard, and there was complete confidence that we would not run off anywhere. And in actual fact, what had we done that was criminal? After all, if we were arrested, the people who made the arrest could simply have made a mistake.

About noon on 3 November we were already in the politburo. The corridor in the building on the bank of Góbza River, where we were told to stand, was very small and already filled to overflowing with people. We twelve men were barely able to squeeze in. The people there were the same kind as we: fourteen people from the Svistóvichi District. In that tiny jam-packed corridor, we still had to make room for people to pass in three different directions. When the politburo workers walked through there, or rather climbed through, they would curse us for getting in their way, using such horrible unprintable words that it would turn your stomach. In general today, people have begun swearing terribly in "free" Russia, in the midst of our "freedom and brotherhood." It is not unusual to hear savage cursing in the name of "mother," "Christ," and "God" and all that is good and holy. "Oo-oo, how many holy devils got packed in! Pull back a little, apostles! Let me through, you stinkers!" And then would follow a string of nasty curses. One of those pushing their way through us while we were pressed against the wall was Yershóv, who had arrested us at home and carried out the search. As he went past me he said hello, shook my hand, and said: "Here you are, all twelve of you, Tolstoyans in the real sense of the word—not at all like those guys" (pointing to the men from Svistóvichi). With these words he left. I took a good look at these men who were so "unlike" Tolstoyans. No matter how hard I looked, I saw no signs by which you could distinguish people's spiritual life.

"Ignát Polyakóv!" I winced a little when I heard the first call for an interrogation. They took him away. My heart beat faster in my breast, and my thoughts carried me into the interrogation room. Can that young Polyakóv hold up under all those difficulties? There was little time to think about it. They had a brief talk with Polyakóv and sent him right back. One of the politburo workers came out behind him and shouted: "Yákov Dragunóvsky!" I followed him into a hall lighted by electricity. We did not stop there but went through a door on the right and into a small room about six by nine feet, with one window in a narrow wall space. In front of the window was a table at which two men were sitting; three more were standing, one of them a boy of short stature. I at once recognized the two men sitting at the table: one was Shurúyev, who had come to our village in August with a detachment of soldiers to get butter, the order for which we did not then fulfill. He had shouted long and hard at the time, threatening us with execution, but we parted on good terms just the same. The second man was Parfyónov, the former manager of the district office of public health, whom I had known ever since the district assembly. Now he was here as the investigator: he kept the record, with his lame leg lying across two chairs and his crutches leaning against the wall beside him. When I went in, they asked me to sit on a chair at the end of the table. I was perfectly calm: I calmly came in, calmly sat down on the chair they offered me, and calmly answered their questions. My racing heart had slowed down, and not a muscle moved. Parfyónov took a sheet of paper on one side of which was printed "Record of the accused," followed by a series of questions: place of birth, single or married, previous convictions, and so on—in a word, a detailed "questionnaire," which was to be filled out upon first acquaintance with the accused. They gently asked me the questions on the form and quickly filled in the answers. After the last question, "Previously on trial or under investigation?" the indictment began. Here things did not go as smoothly as while they were filling out the questionnaire: I was asked a lot of questions, showered with a lot of curses, threatened with the provincial Cheká,[6] execution, and everything else the human mind could think up.

"When did you become infected with Tolstóy?" asked the investigator.

"For a long time I have wanted to be a man who neither did nor wished any evil on anybody," I answered.

"For a long time?! But didn't you serve under Nicholas?"

"Yes, I did. But what could I do? I was serving then not out of conscience but out of fear. And even though I had to be at the front, I never saw the enemies I was ordered to kill. On the contrary, when I had occasion to see the Germans, I felt pity and a kind of awakening love for them. I not only did not want to kill them, I wanted to embrace them as brothers; I wanted to help them somehow."

"Don't sing psalms to try to pass for a saint. Tell me, how many months were you at the front? And make it short. Don't string out your answer."

"Seven months."

"When did you leave your position?"

"On 23 June 1915."

"In what way did you leave it?"

"I just left it—I landed in the field hospital."

"And after that, where were you up to the Revolution?"

"Until the February Revolution I just wandered around behind the lines— I kind of deserted. And up to the October Revolution I was at home."

"Why didn't you refuse then, instead of just hanging around?"

"I hadn't yet worked all this out in my mind—and besides, I was still overcome by fear."

"And you're not still overcome by it?"

"No, now I obey my conscience."

"What does conscience mean—where do you keep it?"

"I'm not the only one with a conscience—you have one too. And if the life we live is even a little bit good, it's only because people listen to the voice of that conscience."

"All right, that's enough of your nonsense. Now tell me, where did you learn this doctrine?"

"I began finding out about it at the front in May and June 1915. As time went on, I learned more and more about it. After the February Revolution, when Tolstóy's forbidden works began to be freely published, that is when I started to find out about a reasonable life. I had a pretty sensitive soul even before, but then I met a really great soul through books. Just imagine—I had never heard that there were people who didn't eat meat. The first time I read

6. Cheká—an acronym made from the initial Russian letters of the original name of the Soviet secret police, *Chrezvycháynaja komíssija po bor'bé s kontrrevoljútsiej i sabotázhem* (Extraordinary Commission for Struggle against Counterrevolution and Sabotage). Later called the NKVD (People's Commissariat for Internal Affairs), and more recently the KGB (Committee for State Security).

Tolstóy's little booklet *The First Step,* I stopped eating meat right then. And now I know I can't eat meat, not just because of what Tolstóy said about it, but because my innermost feelings won't let me even consider the idea that it's possible to eat meat. I never killed animals—except for one chicken, and I'll never forget that as long as I live."

"How is it that you won't eat meat but you still wear a fur coat?"

"I can't justify wearing a fur coat. It really goes against my conscience to wear it. That just makes it clear that I'm still a sinful man, and I still haven't figured out how to get along without a fur coat in winter."

"So your doctrine is something incomprehensible—first you live according to your conscience, and then you dodge your conscience a little. Is that why you talk one way in front of us but live another way?"

"Yes, there is a lot of bad in me that I ought not to do, but I do it because of my human weakness and because I can't think things out."

"Then tell us, is there any specific thing that you Tolstoyans strive for?"

"Yes, there is! It's God, and people take different paths to get to Him. Every individual has his own cross to bear. That's why one person may follow his conscience more and another less: There aren't any perfect people; but the main thing is that we must do more good and keep further away from evil, and try to increase our love for others, and 'not do unto others what you don't want done to yourself.' "

"Well, enough of that. Now tell us: has your year been called up yet to the Red Army?"

"No, it hasn't."

"Then why, you blockhead, are you refusing military service when you haven't even been called up?"

"I figured that I could be called up soon, so I made a declaration to the court well in advance."

"Well in advance! And now when you're locked up in prison, you'll find out about your 'well in advance'!"

"Well, to tell the truth," I said, "there's no way to please you. I didn't please you by refusing military service when I hadn't even been called up; and my brothers didn't please you by refusing when you tried to make them go off to war right now. Just when, in your opinion, should we refuse that terrible business?"

"War now is not what it was under Tsar Nicholas: then they were defending the capitalists, but now we must defend our right to land, to factories, to running our country. For that reason it's criminal to refuse to fight for those rights! Do you admit your guilt of that?"

"No, I don't."

"Why not?"

"Because fighting for rights means going out and killing people, and every murder is the greatest evil on earth. I have long believed in my heart that I could not do that terrible thing—killing people. No matter who may order me to do it, Tsar Nicholas, Kérensky, or Lénin, I cannot and will not do that."

"And so you think every kind of government is violence?"

"Absolutely."

"And you don't see any good purposes in the Soviet government?"

"I see a lot of good purposes, but you won't reach them by that road. In order to achieve such great ideas, the old-fashioned way of violence won't do. Surely it's not hard to understand that a good, noble deed has to be done in a good way. If it's done badly, how can anything good come out of it? Dear friends!" I went on. "Where are your fine slogans that were written on your banners in 1917: 'Down with war!' 'Down with capital punishment and every kind of violence!' 'Long live equality and brotherhood!'? There's no trace of those fine slogans anymore—they are drenched in blood. And the people who want to put those great ideals into practice are now considered some sort of enemies. They are persecuted, put into prison, and even shot."

"But don't you know, you blockhead, that the war won't last forever? As soon as we wipe the bourgeoiseys and the parasites off the face of the earth, the reign of socialism will start and we won't have any more war."

"Yes," I went on, "but I can't believe in some sort of distant future. Just as I can't believe in the future paradise of the priests, I can't believe in your future paradise either. I am living only in the present—today. I don't even know what may happen to me tomorrow. How can I do something terrible today for the sake of some benefit tomorrow? If I want something good for tomorrow, which doesn't yet exist, then I must do only good today. So that if we wish good for people—both today's and tomorrow's—the best thing we can do is do the very best right now. We live only right now, and only at this minute can we have control over our actions, which can lead either to good or to evil."

It was clear that my explanation did not please the interrogators.

"Well, enough of that nonsense. Let's get down to business. Tell us, have you agitated against the Soviet government?"

"No!"

"How can you say no, when first you and now your brothers have refused military service?"

"That happened without any agitation. They themselves came to realize that they must do no evil to anybody."

"But you organized a library in your home, you know. That too is agitation, because you lent books to other people! How many books do you have?"

"That's right, I did organize a library and did lend books to other people, and I have over a thousand books in my library. But I didn't organize it for any bad or selfish purpose, only for the sake of education. I figured that in this way I would be helping the Commissariat of People's Education, which aims to create a dense network of libraries all over Russia to enlighten the ignorant masses. We have illiteracy in the villages. I myself got only a primary education, but through my own efforts I've been adding to my education. I organized my library with that in mind—to enlighten myself and other people."

"You don't admit that you're guilty of agitation?"

"No!"

"But why didn't you take part in the food requisitioning?"

"Because that was demanded for the army," I answered, "and I cannot and will not either serve or help it through my work."

"And is it true that the village authorities came to you with soldiers to requisition grain and you would not give any?"

"That's right. They came and took two hundred pounds of rye, and we didn't protest."

"Why did you not fulfill the order for wagons, and when they sent out for people to build storage cellars for potatoes, why would you not help?"

"All for the same reason—it was connected with war," I said. "Peasant wagons were demanded mainly for the soldiers, in order to take provisions away from the peasants. I would not go and help build potato cellars for the same reason. I can't help in all that."

"And so you won't admit your guilt?"

"No!"

The two men sitting at the table asked me all those questions while the others only listened. Some questions they asked in a gentle tone, and others very rudely. When I tried to explain my thoughts in more detail, Parfyónov (the interrogator) shouted at me: "Shut up!"—which I had to do. But when I kept silent and refused to answer a question, he would shout his order to answer. When they finished the interrogation, they started rummaging through the documents they had taken away from me in their search. They came across a document given to me by the United Council of Religious Communities and Groups as their authorized representative in Smolénsk Province.

"Who the devil gave this document to a fool like you? What kind of authorized representative can you be? Just look at yourself—you're a complete fool! So he was going to defend other people! He can't even say anything for himself that makes sense. He's talked such devilish gobbledygook that it makes you want to puke. Tell me, you nasty devil: do you confess to being guilty of agitation against the Soviet government?"

"No, I don't!"

"How is it you don't, when you've admitted you have a library? That in itself is proof of agitation! Now, confess it: if you weren't a troublemaker, there wouldn't be so many objectors to war around here."

"What's the use of talking?" said another. "Just write down in the protocol: 'I confess that I am guilty of agitation against the Soviet government,' and he'll sign it afterwards."

I said nothing. They wrote out the protocol.

"All right, listen to the protocol," said Parfyónov, and he started reading it.

I listened attentively, but did not listen to the end, since what they wrote down was "I confess that I am guilty of agitation against the Soviet government." After those words I stopped listening. I could not agree with such an accusation.

When they finished reading the protocol, they put it on the table before me and said: "Sign it." I refused to sign it. My refusal upset them. Shurúyev, who had sat at the table during the interrogation, stood up.

"Why won't you sign it?" he shouted at me.

"Because I don't consider myself guilty of agitation."

"So you won't sign it?" they shouted at me from all sides.

"No, I won't."

"Sign it, you devil-head, or else it'll go hard for you!"

"No, I won't. Write out a protocol I can agree with, and I will sign it."

That maddened them still more.

"Oh-h-h! So we have to pamper him, rewrite the protocol, take a lot of time with him when we've got nine more waiting out there! Listen, you idiot! We're giving you one last chance; if you don't sign it, you've got only yourself to blame."

I categorically refused to sign it. Then they showered me with the most frightful, loathsome curses the human mind is capable of thinking up. Along with their cursing, they got still more excited and started walking around the room. Finally, they ran out of curses and evidently could not think up any more.

"Here's what!" shouted Shurúyev, as if he had discovered something new and reassuring. "Sit down and write instructions to the Provincial Cheká to shoot the hell out of him, and in the protocol we'll write that he has refused to sign."

All four of them quickly signed the protocol, and one of them wrote the order to the Provincial Cheká. Again the same questionnaire, but in a different form, and again the same questions were asked, which I calmly answered. In general I had felt calm the whole time. They shouted and cursed, and I kept sitting there calmly, as if all that did not concern me. As if the threats of execution did not frighten me. Let happen what may.

When they had finished writing the order, they turned to me again:

"Do you know, you muddle-headed devil, that because of your stupid stubbornness we can hand you over to be executed? The Provincial Cheká won't stand on ceremony with you the way we've done."

"Well, that's your business, and my business is to forgive you for not knowing what you are doing."

"That's enough, enough of your nightingale songs, devil take you! We'll see how you sing before the Provincial Cheká!"

Accompanied by those words, I left the interrogation room and went back to my friends, who had been waiting for me anxiously. Even with two doors between them, they had been able to hear the curses and shouts, and that had disturbed them. When I sat down, several heads leaned closer in the darkness and started asking me: "What happened to you during the interrogation?" I briefly told them what they had demanded and why they had sworn at me.

My friends were relieved when they learned that I had not been beaten.

Our conversation was interrupted for a few seconds by the summons of Ignát Polyakóv again. I was asked once more what kind of questions had been put to me and how they had listened to my answers. They wanted to know everything, but our conversation was interrupted for good when two men went down the corridor to the interrogation room. In less than a minute they called out: "Yákov Dragunóvsky!"

One of these two men (as I later learned) was the head of the politburo, Letáyev. As soon as he had arrived, he was evidently told that the most important one had been interrogated and refused to sign the protocol. When I went into the interrogation room and stopped at the door, he was standing in front of me. Somebody behind his back said: "There he is—their ringleader, the agitator against the Soviet government. He won't admit his guilt and won't sign the protocol."

"Why won't you sign the protocol?" shouted Letáyev, his eyes flashing savagely. It was evident from his face that he was a master of his trade. With his eyes alone he could terrify a man; and when he distorted his face and opened his mouth, with its two missing upper teeth, he became so frightful that he looked abnormal.

"I don't agree with the accusation of agitation," I answered.

"So you won't sign?"

"No, I won't."

Before I could say those last words, punches rained on my left cheek. Letáyev was of medium height but powerfully built, and his blows were so strong that I could not keep my place. I was knocked back and would have fallen if the wall had not held me up. I received about half a dozen blows. At the first one I felt a powerful pain in my jaw, and then felt dizzy. Seeing that he had knocked me to one side and had knocked off my cap, he halted, as if to get his breath and gather new force. At that moment I picked up my cap and remained standing in front of him, feeling dizzy.

"Now will you sign the protocol and admit you are guilty of agitation?"

"No, I will not admit I am guilty of agitation, and I will not sign a protocol that I don't agree with."

My firm, categorical refusal awakened the wild beast within him. He began kicking me with his booted foot, blow after blow, right between my legs. The pain was unbearable. I felt I was just at the point where one more blow would mean death. Everyone knows that is the most sensitive part of a man's body, where one well-aimed blow can kill him. Tears were flowing from my eyes. Instinctively I took my cap and tried to cover the part of my body he was kicking; but Letáyev was savage and agile, and that defense did not stop him. He hit the spot he wanted with a well-aimed kick from below. Several times his boot struck my hands, with which I tried to cover myself, and they started bleeding. I thought the sight of blood would stop him, but it only delighted the beast that had awakened within that man. Without the slightest embarrassment, he kept on kicking me with all his might. I saw that he was trying to kill me on the spot, and I began begging him:

"Brother! Come to your senses! Brother! I beg you!"

But neither my entreaties, nor my blood, nor my tears had any effect on him. He beat me till he was exhausted, and only then did he stop.

"Now will you sign the protocol?" he shouted.

"No I won't." A kind of stony firmness had arisen within me. While he beat me, I felt horrible pain, but I still could not sign that terrible protocol. Letáyev did not beat me any more. As if nothing at all had taken place, he proposed that I myself write about my beliefs. I wanted to refuse that too, but then I decided to write them down. I was taken out of that room and into another one, an empty one. They sat me down at a table and gave me some paper. But how could I write when I was so dizzy, my mouth was so dry, I was in so much pain, and my hands were bleeding? I sat there and started thinking about how and what I would write when I could not collect my thoughts. Shurúyev had come out with me. Seeing that I could not write, he leaned over the table toward me and gently showed me how to fill out the questionnaire. When I finally completed it, with great effort, he said:

"Now write about your beliefs."

With those words he went back to the torture chamber. There they beat the Polyakóvs one after the other, who begged their butchers just as I had. It was very hard for me to write in those circumstances. I had to think a long time in order to write each word. I do not know how long I wrote, but I do know that they finished interrogating both Polyakóvs and had already started in on Yefím Fedósov. Twice that sinful waif who waited on and was corrupted by the politburo came in to get my statement. When he came in the third time, he started to grab the paper out of my hands:

"Give it here, they won't wait any longer."

There was still a lot I wanted to write, but they would not let me. Well, let them have it. My friends were sitting in the dark room without moving, only sighing and shuddering as the sound of the blows and groans came out of the torture chamber. Seeing my condition, they did not try to talk to me; nobody wanted to say a word. We were all seized by the horror of the beatings. Now we could hear the blows and screams: Yefím Fedósov was in the torture chamber. They were beating him, and he kept begging them not to torment him.

It is a terrible thing to endure when you yourself are beaten, but it is even worse when they are beating and torturing someone else and you can hear the sounds of the blows and groans. The tears and suffering of others tear at your heart. But then all grows quiet, and at once you imagine something horrible: there, they've killed him, the man is dying. It's awful! awful! Somebody runs through the corridor with a big bucket of water. You imagine that they have beaten the man into unconsciousness and will now pour water on him.

But it turned out that Fedósov himself had asked for water, since his beatings had made his mouth very dry.

"Yåkov Dragunóvsky!" came the shout once more. I went in thinking that they were going to interrogate me still more.

"Which of your brothers are in that room?"

I said only my brother Vasíly.

They summoned Vasíly and sent me out. About ten minutes went by, and then they called me again. I went in for the fourth and last time. My brother was sitting on a chair, and Letáyev, the head of the politburo, stood over him demanding that he sign the protocol. My brother refused to sign, because in the protocol he was accused of desertion. He asked that the protocol be read to him. It was indeed drawn up as if against a deserter: "Protocol of defendant accused of desertion under the cover of 'Tolstoyism.'" My brother read no further; he put the protocol down on the table, saying: "I will not sign such a protocol." Then Letáyev turned to me:

"You are their teacher—make your pupil sign the protocol."

"We have only one teacher—Christ—and among ourselves we are brothers. I can't make him sign the protocol, because he has his own mind."

"But you wrote yours and signed it, you know; so why won't he sign?"

"Let him write his own, and then he'll sign it."

"Wha-a-t!" shouted Letáyev. "If we let each of you write his own, it'll take all night!" And turning to my brother:

"Will you sign the protocol?"

"No I won't."

They sent me out at once and started beating my brother. That same brother who had refused to fight under the French, and refused when he was under Deníkin to fight against his fellow Russians, now refused under the "Reds" to commit that awful deed and kill people who were just like himself—fellow Russians—except that they bore the label "Whites." And now he was being terribly beaten and called a "vicious deserter." I suffered indescribable horror. Through two doors I could hear the noise, the groans, the muffled blows, and the terribly painful sighs. I could hear feet stamping, stamping, and again the muffled blows.

I do not know how long that went on, but to those of us sitting next door in that dark room and hearing it all, it seemed an eternity. My brother kept silent for a long while under the blows; finally he could stand it no more, and he shouted:

"Brothers! Shoot me instead!" But even after that shout, they went on beating and beating. Then everything died down; several agonizing, eerie minutes of dead silence passed. Again I wondered whether they had beaten my brother to death—right there, next door, at that very moment.

They beat my brother Vasíly until the beaters themselves were exhausted and their victim was unconscious. Then they sat him down unconscious in a broken wardrobe that was standing there, and one of them ran out to get water. They knew that cold water would bring a man beaten half to death back to consciousness, but . . . Vasíly did not take it. Why he did not take the water, he himself does not know. Afterwards he said that he was practically out of his mind at the time and did not understand what was going on. A little later, when he had come to and was extremely thirsty, they did not offer him any water, and he himself would not ask for any. They pulled him out of the wardrobe and took him into another room and sat him on a chair. He came back to us much later, after he had regained consciousness.

Kozhurín was summoned to the interrogation and torture chamber. That young man was also fiercely beaten. Of the ten men called for interrogation that night, only two were not beaten: Iván Fedósov and Gusárov. But the rest of us who were subjected to beatings had a very, very hard time. Those who came last were beaten less, since it was long past midnight, and the politburo workers were impatient to finish their "work"; besides, such "work" was exhausting both physically and morally.

"Take them to the militia!" they ordered.

As we were going out, one of the politburo workers, Shurúyev, lighted our way through the corridor and peered at our faces.

"What's the matter?" he said to those who did not look in his direction. "And you call yourselves Tolstoyans! But you know Tolstoyans are not supposed to get angry."

I went last and looked in his direction.

"It's obvious you looked on purpose, but you're angry just the same."

With those parting words we were sent on our way, beaten and tormented, back to our friends, who were awaiting us full of impatience and anxiety. When we came to that dark, cold building, we felt around until we found a little free space. Groaning and storing our sacks of rusks under our heads, we lay down as best we could.

I woke up only toward morning. Iván Fedósov had not slept all night long. He kept thinking, sighing, and saying: "Why did they beat everyone but me, as if I were holier than the rest?" He had wanted very much to be beaten, and more than anybody else. He would have been able to endure it; but as if on purpose, they had passed him by.

In the afternoon they made a prisoner count. We were lined up by twos and sent off to prison under a five-man convoy.

(Written in the 1920s)

Letters from Yákov Dragunóvsky in the Demídov Prison to Vladímir and Anna Chertkóv

FIRST LETTER (DECEMBER 1920)

Dear friends,

I had just finished writing the last words of my first letter when I looked out the window into the prison courtyard and saw a detachment of armed men. Part of the detachment went up to the second story of the prison with some ropes. We assumed that they were going to take some dangerous criminals to the courtroom. But imagine our horror when we saw them bring out the fourteen men, tied together in pairs, who had been sentenced to be shot. What could be done to get away from that horror? I could not bear to look at the men being led off. I was filled with horror; my chest ached, and I felt a stabbing pain in my heart. O my God, my God! What is going on in this world, in broad daylight, and who is doing it? Men—reasonable creatures, created for life and joy. Just what kind of joy in life is created by men? Oh, horror—not joy but grief and madness! Either I myself have gone so crazy that I feel this way and feel so horrified, or else those who are bringing on these horrors have gone crazy.

There they have been taken out, all fourteen men—four for banditry and ten for refusing to go to war, condemned to death for refusing to kill people, for their purely human feelings of kindness, because they cannot cause harm and do evil to others. All those living men have walked off on their own feet to the pits that have been prepared for them. They will see with their own kindly, intelligent eyes the bed that has been prepared in the damp earth for their bodies. And with their souls and minds, they feel that they have sacrificed themselves in the cause of love.

They have been granted the privilege of leaving this life and uniting with all that is good. They are no longer among us. Here are their names: Mitrofán Filimónov, Iván Terekhóv, Vasíly Terekhóv, Yeliséy Yeliséyev, Vasíly Pávlovsky, Vasíly Petróv, Varfoloméy Fyódorov, Iván Vetítnev, Gleb Vetítnev, Dmítry Volodchénkov.

Their case was up before the People's Court, and testimony had been received from the United Council in Moscow[7] confirming the sincerity of their convictions. Yeliséyev had even been sentenced by the People's Court to some sort of prison term, but just the same they were all condemned as deserters and shot.

I cannot write any more. If I remain alive, I will write in more detail.

SECOND LETTER

In a prison convoy, 17 December 1920

Dear friend Vladímir Grigóryevich,

I am sending you additional information about our prison experiences and about the ten men who were shot for refusing military service because of their religious beliefs. The additional information is as follows. A priest from the village of Svistóvichi in the Demídov Region, Prokófy Bogdánov, was a secret agent of the Demídov regional politburo in the betrayal of the Society in Memory of Tolstóy and its members. This priest was arrested by the politburo for his careless performance of his duties and was kept for nine days in the prison where we were held. His carelessness consisted in the fact

7. The United Council of Religious Communities and Groups, known by its Russian acronym OSROG (Ob'edinénnyj sovét religióznykh óbshchin i grupp) was founded in October 1918 on the initiative of Tolstóy's close associate Vladímir Chertkóv, who served as its chairman. In addition to the Tolstoyans, the council was composed of representatives of the Baptists, Evangelical Christians, Mennonites, Seventh-Day Adventists, and other religious organizations. The first and most important result of the council's activity was the decree signed by Lénin on 4 January 1919 "About exemption from compulsory military service on grounds of religious convictions." This decree granted to the United Council the exclusive right to determine the sincerity of men claiming objection on religious grounds to military service. Further information about this matter is to be found in A. B. Roginskij's notes to the Russian original of this book, *Vospominanija krest'jan-tolstovtsev* (Moscow, 1989), pp. 465–468.

that the whole population found out about his activities in betraying the Tolstoyans. His prison mates, L. Ulyánovsky and I. I. Belyáyev, passed the following information on to us. On the very first day, this priest asked them what could happen to him and the people he had betrayed. They answered: "You'd all be lucky to escape being shot." The priest was filled with alarm and started tearfully repenting of what he had done. Belyáyev and Ulyánovsky asked him what his duties had been. He told them he would report whether Tolstoyans went to church, got married in church, and had their babies baptized, and also about their behavior in everyday life. Belyáyev tried to console him in the midst of his bitter tears, and told him: "Enough of your weeping and wailing—it's not fit for you as a priest to go to pieces like that." But the priest was so upset that he could not help weeping and unburdening himself. He was probably also alarmed by the fact that the ten Tolstoyans facing an unknown fate were being held in the jail. But when the court sentenced those ten men on 11 December to be shot for refusing military service because of their religious beliefs, the priest was no longer in prison.

No one knows how he felt when he learned that about ten or eleven o'clock on the morning of 13 December, those ten men were shot, and three of them were his neighbors from that same village of Svistóvichi.

In the course of his sincere confession, the priest said that all the priests in the Svistóvichi District had been asked to undertake that work, but all of them except him and one other unknown priest had refused.

These are the kinds of things that are beginning to take place, dear Vladímir Grigóryevich. It must be that a time of inquisition has come for free religious movements. With brotherly greetings and love,

Your brother,
Yákov Dragunóvsky

Documents from 1921

1.

Extract from protocol No. 30 of the session of the Kásplya Village Soviet in the Demídov Region of Smolénsk Province, 10 November 1921.

Heard: current business, about the arrest of "Tolstoyans" as counterrevolutionaries, introduced by Comrade Sídor Mikháylov.

Resolved: to bring to the attention of the authorities that there are no bandits in this district and that the population stands for the achievements of the October Revolution. The arrested men—Yákov, Pyotr, Timoféy, and Vasíly Dragunóvsky, Iván Yevdokímov, Nikanór Mishchénkov, Sergéy Polyakóv, Maksím Mishchénkov—are known to the Council of Soviets in the best sense; no counterrevolutionary agitation and nothing blameworthy has been observed in them.

Signatures, seal.

2.

From the United Council of Religious Communities and Groups, 23 November 1921.

No. 3694. Moscow, Petróvskiye Voróta.

To the Administrative Commission of Smolénsk Province.

We enclose herewith the declaration of the following prisoners in the Smolénsk forced-labor concentration camp: the brothers Yákov, Pyotr, Timoféy, and Vasíly Dragunóvsky, Sergéy Polyakóv, Iván Fedósov, Nikanór Mishchénkov, and Yegór Ivanóv. The United Council requests the Provincial Administrative Commission to free them from imprisonment by applying the amnesty of 4 November 1921. Points 3-a and 4-a, concerning the liberation in all cases of sectarians not connected with counterrevolutionary organizations, and Point 3-c, concerning the liberation of deserters, apply to them completely.

The United Council submits a similar petition in behalf of Citizens Nikoláy and Iván Ivánovich Pýrikov and Kleménty Yemelyánovich Kraskóvsky, who are in the same situation as the above-named eight persons who have submitted a declaration.

The United Council of Religious Communities and Groups certifies that all the above-named persons are well known to it for their sincere, steadfast, and consistent effort to live according to the free-Christian philosophy of life, the most outstanding exponent of which was Leo Tolstóy. Moreover, the United Council vouches for the fact that the above-named citizens are free of any kind of counterrevolutionary tendencies or organizations, and have acted exclusively from religious motives.

V. G. Chertkóv, Chairman; N. Rodiónov, Council Member; N. Dubénsky, Secretary

3.

Verdict.

In the name of the Russian Socialist Federative Soviet Republic, on 10 October 1921, a Special Session of the People's Court in the Demídov District Bureau of Justice, in an open court session under the chairmanship of P. P. Petróv and the People's Assessors Stepánov, Púle, Boródkin, Nóvikov, Komónov, and Lavróvsky, along with the secretary, E. A. Shulkóv, having examined the case of the petition from Citizen Yákov Dragunóvsky, of the village of Draguný in the Kásplya District, for exemption from military service because of religious convictions by substituting work for the benefit of the people and society, *finds:* that Citizen Yákov Dragunóvsky, according to the expert testimony of the Moscow United Council of Religious Communities and Groups on 2 January 1920, No. 9494, on the strength of his religious convictions in the spirit of his free-Christian philosophy of life, is indeed unable to perform either combatant or noncombatant military service; and for that reason, on the basis of Point 1 of the Decree of the Soviet of People's Commissars on 4 January 1919, the Special Session of the People's Court of the Demídov Regional Bureau of Justice has determined: the citizen of the village of Draguný in the Kásplya District, Yákov Dragunóvsky, age 35, on the strength of his religious convictions is exempted from military service, and if his age group is called up, he shall substitute work in contagious wards and infirmaries. This determination is final; it may be appealed at the Smolénsk Provincial Soviet of People's Judges within a period of two weeks.

Chairman Petróv, People's Assessors Stepánov, Púle, Boródkin, Nóvikov, Lavróvsky. Certified as an accurate copy of the original by Shulkóv, Secretary of the Special Session of the Demídov Regional Bureau of Justice.

Yákov Dragunóvsky to Vladímir Chertkóv, 28 December 1921
Dear friend Vladímir Grigóryevich,
In reply to your question about the "defection" of two of the ten men who spent a year in prison for refusing military service on religious grounds, I am writing to say that several reasons are involved here, but the principal one is the prison. Since this question interests you just as much as it does me, I am glad to write and describe this case impartially. And, even though only in a few brief words, I will touch on the reasons that led them to question the truth of the ideas they wanted to adhere to. This is how it was. When we were all put into prison, they were men steadfast in spirit. We could only rejoice in them. Just consider: they had undergone horrible torture and been threatened with execution, but they still remained firm. You would think that even if they had been obliged to stand before the tribunal and hear those terrible words: "To be shot," they would have remained firm even then. Such was the astonishing power of their spirit. On 18 November two men from the politburo came into the prison to make one last proposal to the objectors: give up their undertaking and join the Red Army, or else it would go badly for them; either rot in prison or be taken out and shot. But even this final proposal had no effect on them; they remained firm in their decision. During the first half of December, the court condemned and shot twenty-four men, among them ten of our fellow Tolstoyans. We expected the same fate ourselves, but no one considered backing down.

Finally we were sent to another prison, the Provincial one, where we saw and experienced great horrors. Here, too, people were taken out and shot, and we did not know how our own case would end. We might be condemned in absentia, then summoned and put into an automobile, taken out to the pit, and killed, just as many others had been taken out and killed. But on the seventh of March we looked out the window and saw six men working from noon till evening in a scrubby field, digging a ditch about three hundred meters from the prison. Each one of us could not help wondering, "Are they getting it ready for me?" All this—the horrors we had gone through during torture, the horror of executions in first one, then another, then a third prison, and also our unjust treatment by the officials of the concentration camp—plunged many people into serious thought. So when they were faced with all this horror, all this outrage, they began to have doubts about their own consistency. It was not that they questioned the truth of that great idea of love, but they began to doubt whether it could ever be achieved after all. You might keep on being shuttled from prison to prison, or even worse—you might be shot and just throw your young life away. "Wouldn't it be better just to live like all the rest? War is war; let's not refuse it, but help it along. After all, not everyone gets killed in a war; in most cases they come back home safe and sound. And better still, you may be a soldier and not even go off to war, but just get a good assignment somewhere, the way a lot of people do. And you not only won't go through any suffering, but just the other way around—you'll be satisfied with your work. So let's just make use of all the rights of man, let's even defend our rights in court. Otherwise, you know, there's something awkward about trying to fulfill Christ's ideas according to Tolstóy. You can't stand up even for what's yours; if they take it, you just keep quiet; if they beat you, you just present your body for the blows. Somehow it turns out to be odd—can't you give as good as you get? Surely that would be more advantageous—you wouldn't just stand there like a milksop. After all, there are people who live without arguing about anything in particular. They probably hope the Kingdom of God will come some other way, all at once, without any special efforts by individuals; or else in the Orthodox way, by some miracle; or else in the revolutionary way, through struggle. And for that reason there's no need for each one to fritter away his own little forces by himself; instead, group them together in one big mass—that way your chances will be better. But the main thing is that as an ordinary person, you'll have some rights everywhere. Otherwise they'll beat you and then blame you for the beatings; and you can't even think of making a legal complaint, because you yourself don't recognize the court system!" Indeed, that is just how they thought and talked—"Why do they put all the blame on me? First they beat me when I didn't bother anybody, and then they blame it all on me. That's a stupid situation!"

The point was that when they began to interrogate us at the Provincial Cheká in Smolénsk about the beatings we had gotten during interrogation at the district politburo, we wouldn't talk about it, because we were afraid those people might be punished and even shot for their brutality. We had forgiven them and didn't want to make a complaint, and for that reason we would not testify. But the investigator said: "Look, by keeping quiet about it you're just breeding more evil, whereas it ought to be wiped out. If you weren't so stupid, you'd understand that the Soviet government is fighting against that kind of people; right now it is dismissing worthless elements from the government agencies. By keeping quiet, you are concealing them; you want to leave them free to beat even more people. For that reason you are not getting rid of evil, you are increasing it."

When I heard that kind of argument, I thought the interrogator was joking. After all, he must have understood very well that you can get rid of evil in the world only by not resisting evil with evil. But imagine our astonishment when the Provincial Cheká put us into prison and read us the accusations against us—along with "counterrevolution," "agitation," and so on, we were also accused of "nonresistance to evil"! They forgot that we do indeed resist evil, only not with more evil but with good. That accusation seemed ridiculous to me, but some of the others were puzzled: "How can that be? We got beaten, but we get the blame for it!"

In a word, all of that, one thing after another, greatly undermined the spirits of those two young men, and toward the end of their year of imprisonment, they lost all belief in goodness. Seeing around them so much evil and falsehood, which was encouraged by all but a handful of people, they began to forget all the holiness of spirit which had been their support. Just as the Bolsheviks had forgotten their noble slogans: "Down with war!" "Down with capital punishment!" "Down with violence!" "Long live freedom, equality, and peace among men!" For some people, the first indications of this "freedom" had been foul language, drunkenness, smoking, debauchery, and other irrational things. We often heard those two young men blame all religious people who were led by their consciences to refuse military service. "They're all chicken-livered. It's not that they won't kill other people, they're just afraid of getting killed themselves—that's why they won't go to war!" They forgot that they themselves had been just that "chicken-livered." They forgot that they once had no thought of saving their own skins: they had been beaten and still held firmly to their rational convictions. They must have forgotten the time that one of their number had not suffered the beatings the others went through during their torture-interrogations, and afterwards he had not slept all night, and kept wondering: "Why was I spared? I'm no holier than the others!" He wanted to go through the same beatings as everybody else. They forgot that at that time they had been threatened with execution, but even then they were not cowardly—they were firm in their convictions. And finally, they forgot, or began to forget, that religious people were shot for refusing military service.

They began forgetting about that under the influence of their prison conditions. They began thinking of themselves as "chicken-livered." "But we won't be like that anymore," they decided. "At the first call we'll join up. We'll try to become commissars, and then we'll hunt down and prosecute those so-called 'religious' objectors to military service!" One of them had been summoned to court (at the beginning of his refusal) because he had submitted a declaration refusing military service on grounds of his religious beliefs; but he had not appeared in court. He said, "I won't go to any courts now about this matter." And so he didn't.

I visited the other one in his home after he was set free. He started bragging about his "independent life," without any kind of Christs and Tolstóys as his authorities; but he got embarrassed when he looked me in the eye. He saw that I did not share his views, and he fell silent.

Let us not condemn those young men for betraying their convictions. I would rather cast blame on those terrible prison conditions. That is what corrupted them—and not only them. It has corrupted and still corrupts many of "these little ones."[8] But these men have not completely lost their conscience.

I think this is a temporary depression that has come over them. After all, they had already reasoned their way through these vital questions, and they had been firm. This present betrayal of their reason is temporary. The time will come—soon, I hope—when they will understand their mistake, and then they will set out more earnestly than before on the path to goodness and truth. At first I tried to persuade them, but that was like throwing oil on a fire. It made them furious. Then I decided there was no use in trying to influence them from the outside. Let them think through their mistake for themselves.

I believe you too, dear Vladímir Grigóryevich, will not cast any reproaches on them, just as none of the Jews cast any on the woman in the Gospels.[9] They deserve not reproaches but sympathy and sorrow.

That is all I have been able to report in a few words about the defection of these two men. I do not write their names here, because I think that would be awkward. And now stay healthy and prosper, dear old man. With love from your younger brother Yákov Dragunóvsky.

1921–1929

My Life:
A Summary Account

After the amnesty and liberation, I was filled with optimism for some two months. Any kind of weather made me happy. I went to Moscow. A joyful meeting with friends. I visited Bonch-Bruyévich and had a talk with him.[10] An excruciating homesickness took hold of me. I arrived home and still could not calm down: I was unable to shake off my depression. I had given my son a wrong and unreasonable upbringing. I was unhappy over my wicked heart but did not know how to change it. My new world outlook had not changed me for the better; my character had not improved. I rushed about hither and yon, hoping to find some support from outside.

In June I was back in Moscow. I made several close friends, including Sergéy Mikháylovich Popóv, with his remarkable, reasonable system of hand-farming. I was glad to get better acquainted with and draw closer to the old Tolstoyans V. G. Chertkóv, I. I. Gorbunóv-Posádov, and others; I talked

8. Dragunóvsky's allusion to Jesus' statement reported in three of the four Gospels, e.g., Mark 9:42: "And whosoever shall offend one of these little ones that believe in me, it is better for him that a millstone were hanged about his neck, and he were cast into the sea."

9. Dragunóvsky's allusion to Jesus' words reported in John 8:7 about the woman taken in adultery: "He that is without sin among you, let him first cast a stone at her."

10. Vladímir Dmítrievich Bonch-Bruyévich (1873–1955)—a leading prerevolutionary Bolshevik who was the executive director of the Council of People's Commissars from 1917 to 1920 and who had an active scholarly interest in the various religious sects in Russia throughout his life.

with them as with equals, but just the same Chertkóv appeared to be a kind of authority, and I somehow could not understand Seryózha Popóv's "spiritual monism."[11] I visited the Living Church, where I heard a sermon by Antonín.[12] I visited the Evangelicals, listened to their singing and their organ, but all that did not satisfy me.

Once again my wandering around among friends impelled me rather to turn homeward. I was glad to be back home—but not for long: I was often depressed, often angry, and unhappy. I was astonished at what was going on within me. Comparing my life in Orthodoxy and now, I found differences—my character now seemed to be getting even worse. I worked, but in my soul there was dissatisfaction and great melancholy, though from what, I did not know. My wife had a great misfortune: she became seriously ill. We had to take her to the provincial hospital. My heart was filled with alarm; I was afraid I might lose my dear friend. I was overjoyed at her recovery and homecoming. But soon I again grew angry and spiteful. My character was not improving.

Moscow again. Golítsyno. Zvenígorod. I visited friends in a colony in the woods. They proposed that we organize a commune. Somehow I was afraid to squeeze my family into such an organization. I was intimidated by their alien (upper-class) buildings, just as I had been intimidated in 1920 when I visited I. M. Tregúbov at the People's Commissariat of Agriculture.[13] My acquaintance with Kornílovich gave me a push. The life and philosophy of Sergéy Mikháylovich Popóv made a profound impression on me. I visited many friends: O. A. Dáshkevich, the Strákhovs,[14] Bulgákov,[15] Pleshkóv,[16] Dobrolyúbov;[17] I visited the Quakers, the Bahaists,[18] and the Abstainers from alcohol. In the Vegetarian Society I had occasion to do some cabinetmaking: I made some benches, a showcase, and so on, for which they promised to buy me a ticket for my trip. I liked the work and wanted to earn some money.

The English Quakers, with their wealthy bourgeois circumstances and

11. Spiritual monism—the doctrine of Pyotr Petróvich Nikoláyev, according to which there exists only a spiritual substance, and there is no matter. His book *Dukhovno-monisticheskoe ponimanie mira* (The spiritual-monistic conception of the world) was published in Russia in 1914 and republished in Belgrade, Yugoslavia, in 1929.

12. Bishop Antonín Granóvsky—one of the leaders of the Soviet-sponsored "Living Church" splinter group within Russian Orthodoxy during the 1920s.

13. Iván Mikháylovich Tregúbov (1858–1931)—a former student at an Orthodox seminary who became a follower of Tolstóy and worked for some time in the Tolstoyan publishing house "Posrédnik" (Intermediary).

14. The family of Tolstóy's follower Fyódor Alekséyevich Strákhov (1861–1923).

15. Valentín Fyódorovich Bulgákov (1886–1966)—a follower of Tolstóy who served as his secretary during 1910.

16. Iván Dmítrievich Pleshkóv, like the previously mentioned Seryózha Popóv, was also fascinated by P. P. Nikoláyev's theory of spiritual monism.

17. Aleksándr Mikháylovich Dobrolyúbov (1876–1944[?]), one of the first Russian symbolist poets, who later lived a life of extreme simplicity and acquired a following through his example and teachings based on nonviolence, physical labor, and reverence for nature.

18. Dragunóvsky uses the word *begaíty*, but he evidently had in mind the Bahaists, who had aroused the interest of Tolstóy in the last years of his life.

food, did not offer anything positive for me.[19] I liked the free exchange of opinions among the Bahaists; the hysterics of the Abstainers repelled me. For some reason I did not visit the meetings of our friends [the Tolstoyans]. On 29 December I did not attend a public debate which led to the singling out of V. F. Bulgákov for deportation abroad. Alarm among many friends. We expected arrests. M. Kúchin and I watched a demonstration in Moscow against Christmas. I have come from the Quakers and decided to go home, as my family has been tearfully begging me to do.

Desire to lead a cultured peasant life; this possibility could come only through a transition from the village to individual farms (Stolýpin-type farmsteads).[20] Those farmsteads were not successful. My brother Timoféy is going to the Caucasus to look for free land. A telegram and letter from my brother have definitely made me want to resettle. Returning land scouts have brought back papers accepting us in an agricultural cooperative.

Moscow. Troubles in Moscow are both alarming and calming. Resettlement has been approved. I went to see the Chertkóvs again, and also Tregúbov, Veresáyev,[21] Smidóvich, the People's Commissariat of Agriculture, and M. I. Kalínin.

At home. I felt alarm in my heart about the sale of our property; and since I was occupied with the sale and our resettlement, I devoted too little attention and help to my wife, who had fallen ill. My four-day absence caused my wife to end up in the hospital, but fortunately she is coming home.

I went back to Smolénsk for six days to see the head of resettlement. I had a premonition of misfortune. I was alarmed the whole time, and on my last night I fell seriously ill. On 13 December I returned home and found out that my wife had died.

(Written in the 1920s)

After the death of his wife, Dragunóvsky took his children to the south of Russia and spent five difficult years organizing and managing a collective farm made up of an assortment of people from all over the Soviet Union who had little in common, not even a background in farming. In

19. English and American Quakers had been engaged in famine-relief work in Russia, particularly in the Buzulúk area, since August 1921. With the end of the relief work an effort was made, beginning in 1924, to transform the Quaker administrative headquarters in Moscow into a Quaker international center to foster greater mutual understanding among people of various political and religious points of view. According to English Quaker sources, their representatives in Moscow had some contacts with Chertkóv and other Tolstoyans in the Moscow Vegetarian Society during the years from 1924 to 1930, when the Quaker center was forced to close.

20. Pyotr Arkádyevich Stolýpin (1862–1911), Minister of the Interior and Chairman of the Council of Ministers from 1906 till his death, attempted to reform Russian agriculture by making it possible for peasants to take their share of the land owned communally by their village and settle on individual farms.

21. Vikénty Vikéntyevich Veresáyev (1867–1945) created a furor in the early 1920s with the publication of his novel *V tupiké* (In a blind alley; English translation published as *The Deadlock* in 1928), an astonishingly honest account of the moral and political conflicts involved in the civil war that followed the revolution of October 1917.

1928 Borís Mazúrin, the leader of the Tolstoyan Life and Labor Commune near Moscow and one of the major contributors to this book, began corresponding with Dragunóvsky. The following correspondence tells what happened as a result.

Boris Mazúrin to Yákov Dragunóvsky

FIRST LETTER

Life and Labor Commune
2 February 1928

Dear Yákov Deméntyevich,

Even though you and I are not acquainted, I know a little about you, since we have several acquaintances in common. I saw you once and heard you speak on Newspaper Lane,[22] when you told about what you and your brothers had suffered for the truth. I also heard from Yelizár Ivánovich[23] about your unsuccessful attempt to live in some sort of labor cooperative in the south of Russia. I was very sorry to hear about that. There are so few people willing to devote their energies to group life and labor—and they never seem to turn up where they are needed.

So this is what I have in mind, Yákov Deméntyevich. I am writing to you from the Life and Labor Commune, about six or eight miles from Moscow. It was organized during the years when a lot of communes were being organized and a lot of people joined them. We started with nothing and created a rather strong farm. In any case, we don't live badly, but the bad part is that there is hardly anybody left. Some leave for jobs, others for studies. The whole burden of work falls on us, a handful of people, and we are looking for some comrades for life and labor, the kind who would not be trying to move elsewhere, who would not be tempted by life and work in the cities, and who would be satisfied with a peaceful, honest life of labor.

Last Saturday, 28 January, I was at a meeting on Newspaper Lane and learned from Líza Shchénnikova that she had received a letter from you and wanted to write and invite you to live in Perlóvka.[24] I came home and told Kleménty Kraskóvsky (he lives with us), and we decided to write to you too, in order to find out what your intentions are for the future, and—if you are thinking of leaving the Stávropol region—to invite you to come and live here with us. Maybe you are not thinking about moving at all; in that case let us know. But if you really are thinking about it, then of course we ought to discuss it all in more detail in an exchange of letters; or better still, you could spend a little time with us: then everything would be clear.

---

22. The address of the building that served as headquarters for the Moscow Vegetarian Society and as a general meeting place for Tolstoyans.

23. Yelizár Ivánovich Pýrikov, Dragunóvsky's acquaintance from his earlier years in Smolénsk Province.

24. The Táyninskoye agricultural cooperative existed at Perlóvka until it was liquidated by the Soviet government in 1927. See Mazúrin, p. 41.

Our postal address is Life and Labor Commune, Bogoródskoye Village, Teplostánskoye Postal Agency, Moscow.

> With friendly greetings,
> Borís Mazúrin

SECOND LETTER

22 March 1928

Dear Yákov Deméntyevich,

I have received your answer. I fully understand your situation, and I think you can best see what you ought to do. If your affairs end badly, we will always be glad to have you (if we ourselves are still alive). I have not replied to you for a long time, and I am writing very little now because I haven't got a single free minute. We are now building a house—fifteen carpenters. We have to furnish the material, and we are short of people in the commune. Best regards to you for now. If you have time, write to us about your life. We will be glad to keep in friendly contact with you. Our address is Life and Labor Commune, Tyóply Stan, Moscow.

> Borís Mazúrin

THIRD LETTER (UNDATED, BUT WRITTEN BETWEEN MARCH 1928 AND APRIL 1929)

Dear Yákov Deméntyevich,

I received your second letter long ago, but I have gotten around to answering it only now, and even now only by taking advantage of being on duty tonight, because I, just like you, have been in the commune for five years and still haven't got the free time I ought to have for rest, reading, and answering letters. It's true, though, that things seem to have gotten easier in the past year. My position in the commune is much like yours. Evidently such is the fate of all people who unselfishly and ardently devote their energies to the common good. Many people when they join a commune cannot get used to working responsibly, and they work in a slipshod way, shove all responsibility onto other people, and then suspect them of mercenary motives or even a plain desire to throw their weight around and be the boss. As one of the organizers of our commune, I had occasion when I was struggling against parasitism and careless work in the commune to hear myself called "the boss" (in an offensive sense for a commune member), "the dictator," and even "the policeman," both behind my back and to my face. Well, so what? I thought to myself, there's no use getting upset about it, even though it does cause a lot of bad blood. But just the same, I believe my situation is a little better than yours: I do have somebody I can fall back on—two or three people, close friends, standing together, shoulder to shoulder, are a great help.

You write that you regret not having been able to settle down among friends. But you know, what is hard for you to put up with from people who are perhaps not very close to you, is even harder to put up with from people you wanted to consider close friends and then found out you were mistaken about them. Unfortunately, I have been severely tested by that over these five years. But still, being close to a center such as Moscow and the Vegetarian Society is a great help: you go to hear a talk by some powerful spirit, some dear old man like Iván Ivánovich Gorbunóv-Posádov, Vladímir Grigóryevich Chertkóv, or Nikoláy Nikoláyevich Gúsev, you meet and talk with young people, and you shake off some of the dust of everyday cares that had settled on your soul.

You write about the children, but what can we give them except a personal example? I think our whole task in bringing them up is to live the best we can ourselves, and what takes root in the children's soul and what becomes of them is not within our power. In our commune we also have about seven small children, ranging from one year to twelve. They see their elders constantly at work, in nature and among animals. But there are also many other aspects that can hinder the proper upbringing of children, and one of them is family disagreements: the husband is drawn toward the soil, toward freedom, and the wife toward the city and slavery. So if you are having a hard time, Yákov Deméntyevich, we too have a lot of troubles of our own. It's probably not our business to try to keep them from existing, but rather to relate to them properly. I myself sin in the same way by devoting too little attention to sincere, heart-to-heart work with people, but instead spend too much time on superficial everyday trifles, with too little time left for the principal thing—living according to God's will. After all, the time will come when you're face-to-face with death, and you'll no doubt be horrified at where your life has gone, what has become of your strength, how much of it has been wasted on trifles and how little has been devoted to what is most important—our souls. I write this, but I am afraid you may not understand me correctly. I don't mean to say that we ought to work less ardently, that it all leads to nothing—no, I stand firmly in favor of persistent, diligent, necessary work on the land, and I refuse to give up the effort to create new outward forms of life.

I know how hard it is to achieve mental equilibrium, but we do have to strive for it. Without that it would be too hard to live, and that must not be. Not without reason did Tolstóy teach that "life is a blessing." So we must strive for that blessing in life which is life itself.

A little information about our farm: we live six or eight miles from Moscow, and we have about 135 acres of land, half of it under cultivation. Ours is basically a dairy farm. Our fields are adapted to the needs of cattle raising: grasses (clover), vetch (natural meadows), root crops (beets, rutabagas, potatoes), and grain (wheat, rye). We now have nineteen cows and some horses. We have the beginnings of an apiary, with about ten hives, nearly three acres of old orchard, and we are thinking about setting out a new orchard. We have started building a new dwelling house this year (the old one is very dilapidated).

In general, from an economic point of view we can get along—thanks, of course, to our very modest requirements.

I also want to tell you (even though I haven't talked it over with the rest of the commune members, but I am sure nobody would be against it, especially since Kleménty Kraskóvsky knows you personally) that in case of failure down there, we can find a place for you here in the commune.

It is a dream of mine to be able over a period of years to gather a little group of people in our commune who are sincere, more or less close to one another in outlook, hard-working, and not cantankerous. I think we could then get a more normal life going than what we have right now.

I am sorry that the best forces are so scattered and are struggling separately, but sometimes I think maybe that is the way it has to be.

Well, I will finish now and wait for an answer. The address is: Borís Vasílyevich Mazúrin, Life and Labor Commune, Tyóply Stan, Moscow.

FOURTH LETTER

8 April 1929

Dear friend Yákov Deméntyevich,

I have received your letter and have also read your letter to Lev Semyónovich (he now lives here with us). How shall I answer your burning questions?

Right now my head is spinning. About Perlóvka, you already know that they were partly to blame for their own disintegration from within, but now yesterday's newspaper published the decree of the Moscow Soviet about the liquidation of the Leo Tolstóy Commune at New Jerusalem.[25] There the commune members were guilty of nothing except their unwillingness to accept as fellow residents people who were unknown to them and had a different world outlook. Action against us has already been started by the district executive committee, and we have no hope of escaping destruction. Many of the New Jerusalem people as well as our own have nowhere to go; we are not likely to be allowed to divide up our property. All our many years of hard work will come to nothing. So the situation is difficult, but God grant that everything may be for the best. None of us are losing heart.

Please excuse me for writing so little. I can't think straight now. Maybe after they have freed us from our cattle and the rest of our farm cares, I will have more time; then I will write more. How is it where you are? Is there any possibility of getting an allotment of land? Is there any possibility of living there? Would it cost a lot to build a little house? Would a horse and a cow cost very much? Please send me all this information. It will be good to have various possibilities in mind in case of resettlement. My best and brightest wishes to you.

Borís Mazúrin,
Life and Labor Commune,
Tyóply Stan,
Moscow

25. See Shershenyóva's account of this in chapter 1 above.

FIFTH LETTER

29 April 1930

Dear Yákov Deméntyevich,

I have received your letter and I hasten to reply. I am very glad about your readiness and interest in joining us, but I hasten to warn you: don't move too quickly, and don't take any steps without weighing them carefully and getting in touch with us.

The reason is that we have tried very hard to get some kind of guarantees and special decrees out of the highest agencies of government that we will be left alone in our new location, *but we have not obtained them.* We were told orally that "we cannot make such exceptions for you"; but they promised that when we relocate, they would give instructions to the local provincial executive committee about us, but those are merely unsupported assertions, and for that reason we are cutting down the scope of the resettlement.

In the first place, we consider resettling and accepting this task to be a touchstone for us, both our commune and the commune of our friends near Stalingrad.

The fact is that our commune just cannot hold out here any longer. You are astonished that we have held out even this long—and indeed it is a sort of miracle. The pressure was powerful: they took everything away from us—our stamp, our seal—and then they brought in new people, formed a council out of them, and put us on trial, and so on. But we didn't lose heart, didn't give in right away, and here we are, still surviving, even though we have lost all the time from 13 January to this day for our work. Just yesterday the Regional Appeals Court confirmed the sentence of the People's Court, which had condemned Kleménty and me to two years of exile, and three more people to a year apiece; but we are going to keep struggling. We were condemned as the council of a pseudo-commune even though we refuted all the court's accusations—but then the whole matter had been decided outside of the court.

The Stalingrad commune also survived only through their unshakable firmness, but they lost all their property (it was taken away from them). Just the same, they got their entire harvest in by hand and on two decrepit old nags. They have now been left where they are, but they are an energetic crowd, and they want to try their luck together with us.

So any day now we three land scouts expect to leave and pick out a place either in Semiréchye or in the Kuznétsk District (Altái). When something is decided, I will let you know. Meanwhile just keep working away. But in case it becomes impossible to remain there, write to me at the commune; maybe it will be possible for you to join our commune at once.

To start with, don't try to draw people into resettlement, especially those who are hesitating; it is better to begin with fewer but stronger. After we have gone and picked out a spot, we will send out a working team to prepare housing and do other work. I will write about everything when it all becomes clearer. You write, too, about how things are going with you. Address it to Kleménty, at the commune. I will probably be traveling one or two months.

All this is just our plans; we can make them, but we have to live the way we must. If our plans work out, good; but if they don't, so be it; we won't grieve over it. God's will be done in all.

Farewell,
Borís Mazúrin

Yákov Dragunóvsky to Vladímir Chertkóv
Donskóye, Stávropol Region

26 May 1930

Dear friend Vladímir Grigóryevich,

Before I received your letter No. 3 of April, telling me that you had asked the government to allocate land on the outskirts of the Republic to the Tolstoyans, and that the government had agreed to this and indicated the Kuznétsk District in the Altái region of Siberia, I had already learned of this situation from Borís Mazúrin in the Life and Labor Commune. In reply to Mazúrin's information, I agreed to join the friends who are resettling, but in his second letter Mazúrin cautioned me not to move too fast but to stay where I was for the time being.

Your letter fired up my desire still more not to put this off, but to get into serious correspondence right away about joining the Life and Labor Commune and then moving with it to Siberia.

After I got your letter, the following plan took shape in my mind: this autumn, after getting in the harvest, to sell everything we don't need and go to the Life and Labor Commune in Moscow. The only thing is, how should I do this so that after working here through the summer I could take enough food supplies with us to last my family for a year, so as not to be a burden on anybody? If I don't manage to lay up any food supplies at all from the harvest, will I be able to earn enough over there to buy food?

I don't know whether I ought to stock up on things for the trip. Here is the fix we are in: this is our seventh year down here, and we still have not been able to climb out of this bad material situation. It's no laughing matter: for my family of six I have thirty-five acres under cultivation in crops of all kinds, and what weighs on my heart is whether I can lay up enough food to feed my family for the year. If we don't get any rain right away, there won't be any harvest at all, just as there hasn't been for all the last six years.

In a word, I have to arrange our material situation somehow in the commune, only I must by all means fix things up so that they will accept me and my family of six, in order for me to go with the working brigade to put up buildings at the new location.

In regard to my wanting to live together with friends, I can't brag about anything in advance, except maybe my strong wish at all costs to join together with like-minded people. In order to give you a full account of what I have been working toward in social life, I enclose my report on my organization and five years of back-breaking work building up a voluntary collective farm out of nothing, with people of all kinds of views and philosophies.[26] Thanks to my persistence and long-suffering, I built up a good farm, but just the same I couldn't stand it any longer, and last year I quit the farm I had built up, leaving my creation in good shape.

There were a lot of reasons why I left my own collective farm, as you will see when you read my report, but the chief reason (which is not indicated in the report) was connected with the persecution of religious collective farms, the destruction of well-equipped farms, and the arrests of their leaders.

I saw that for all my back-breaking, self-sacrificing labor, I was threatened with prison—and only because of my religious convictions.

Another reason why I left was fear of the militarization of all the collective farms. I was horrified when I read *The Collectivist* for February 1929, published by the Center. The whole issue was filled with war stuff, not of any use to a collective farm. It advised creating military reading rooms in all of them, giving all collective farmers training in target shooting, even teaching military science to women, taking as models the military reading rooms already existing in some collectives; and finally, the journal said: "Collective farms, one and all, must take a stand for the defense of the Soviet Union in case of enemy attack."

If I do not acknowledge having any enemies at all, if I earlier refused military service and all participation in violence and militarism and was sent to prison for it, I feel still less of a military obligation now, when I am in a collective farm. And if the powers that be should say: "Here, this is an enemy—kill him, strangle him, cut his throat," then I too, as an active collective farmer, liable for military service, would be supposed to carry out all their orders. That journal opened my eyes and made me see that I did not belong in the collective. I clearly understood that with my convictions, salvation was outside the collective farm, and for that reason there was nothing surprising about it when I picked up the rest of my belongings and cleared out.

After leaving the collective farm, I lived for a year in a very difficult situation, but I was in good spirits—I had not been mobilized into the ranks of executioners.

The campaign for complete collectivization scarcely touched me, except for the shouts of a few unreasonable people: "We'll ruin you! We'll send you to Solovkí![27] We'll wipe you off the face of the earth!"

---

26. This report is not translated here but is to be found in the Russian edition on pp. 375–386.

27. Solovkí—one of the earliest Soviet labor camps for political prisoners, set up in 1920 on the site of an ancient Russian Orthodox monastery in the far north.

But several "activists" were afraid to have me in the collective farm, as if I were a collective-farm plague, a religious disease, that could undermine the foundations of collective-farm violence.

Nothing frightened me. I firmly decided not to go into a collective farm built on violence, into one that ruined the lives of the people called "kuláks," all of whose property was taken from them and put into the collective farm, without leaving the "kulák" children even a piece of bread, with the ill-clad little "kuláks" thrown out of their huts in the dead of winter. How could anybody take part in that kind of robbery, that nightmare, and then rejoice when the collective farm got rich by ruining other people? To be in such a collective farm, be a participant in that robbery, be such a butcher, commit such acts—God forbid! I have not yet gone out of my mind.

After the decree of the Party Central Committee and Stálin's article,[28] things seemed to get a little better, but they still kept making threats: "We still won't let you live on individual farms; we'll still drive you into the collective farm."

My close associates told me: "Be careful, Yákov Deméntyevich, they've had their eye on you for a long time. They are sorry they didn't arrest you when you read the Party Central Committee's decree about voluntarily joining a collective farm to that meeting of peasants."

At one meeting, the chairman of the executive committee sternly reproved individual peasant-farmers for their allegedly malicious disruption of the crop-sowing campaign. I got up and spoke in defense of justice, and said the crop-sowing campaign had failed not because individual farmers had maliciously decided not to sow; the evil of disruption had been created back in the autumn, when brigades accompanied by bands and dances made off with the seed grain of hard-working farmers and in return for the good work of certain peasants reclassified them as kuláks. And so, out of fear that they too would be labeled kuláks and be held guilty for their work, the peasants stopped working, so that they would have nothing left over that could lead to their undeservedly being called "kuláks"! That was what caused the disruption of the crop sowing.

For that well-justified speech of mine, the chairman was ready to arrest me on the spot. In his final statement, foaming at the mouth and trembling all over, he shouted at me, called me a yes-man of the kuláks and a counter-revolutionary, and in conclusion asked the meeting to "give a severe rebuff to my slander." But the meeting responded to his shouts with silence, whereas they had greeted my well-justified evidence with applause. Now they are telling me: "Be careful, Yákov Deméntyevich, now they'll throw you in prison for nothing at all—they are furious with you. After all, you were an active collectivist, and now you stubbornly refuse to join the collective farm. Your leaving it is being called agitation against collectivization."

28. A reference to Stalin's article "Giddiness from Success," published on 2 March 1930, which allowed the peasants to take back their own livestock and equipment from the collective farms they had been forced to join.

The sum of all these circumstances has made me ready to escape from here any day now. Back in 1924, when I came to this bad material situation here in the Caucasus, I dreamed of organizing a colony of friends and like-minded people, but there was no solid basis for that. I actively corresponded with one close friend, but I did not succeed in going out and finding a place and starting an organization, and my idea of such an organization remained only a dream, one I haven't forgotten to this day.

That is why I don't want to wait till those two organizations move out there to get settled and start a new life and then invite us to come when the pie is ready to eat. While my health is still pretty good, I want and am able to be a useful cabinetmaker and carpenter for housing construction in the new location, and for that reason please don't turn me down for admission to the Life and Labor Commune, and help me with advice about what I need to do now: probably just wait till the land scouts reserve a plot of land; after that, probably, get in the harvest, if only it doesn't fail completely; and then toward autumn, take my family and our belongings and move up there to you in Moscow.

I repeat: How can I arrange all this so that I will not be a burden to anybody when we arrive?

With friendly greetings and love,

Yákov Dragunóvsky,
Donskóye, Stávropol Region

Borís Mazúrin to Yákov Dragunóvsky

25 July 1930

Greetings, Yákov Deméntyevich!

We came back not long ago from our journey. We traveled about eight thousand miles, and we found and reserved a plot of land for resettlement in the Kuznétsk District of Siberia. I won't describe it all to you now (a long, detailed letter will be sent out soon); but I will say that even though the plot is located on some rather high ridges, it is well provided with tillable land, meadows, woods, and water. The soil is rather good. We can find seasonal work. The Tom River is nearby. By the time you get this letter, our friends (about eight men, including Kleménty Kraskóvsky) will very likely already have left for there. We are in a hurry with this matter in order to get in at least a little haymaking, because it will be hard to buy fodder. I know from your letters that you want to resettle, and this is what I believe is the best way to do it. If you had no luggage or equipment, the best of all would be to come to our commune without delay. We have enough work now (a few people are leaving), and in the spring we would be moving as a whole commune to our new location. Meanwhile the work team would be preparing a few dwellings and thus ease the resettlement of the rest. But you have equipment, and it would be far better to keep it (the valuable items, at least) and transport it to the new location, but that will have to be done toward spring, since it would be rather hard to go there during the winter, when nothing is prepared, and the main thing is that it takes a lot of time to get documents allowing a low price for travel and the transport of equipment. After all, we can't just go to the People's Commissariat of Agriculture and get an individual ticket for each person (there are a lot of requests); you have to write back and forth about it, draw up lists of everybody, and then go and fill out the documents. Maybe it won't be possible for you to get through the winter. In that case you can come to us here. We have enough space and work, and we would be glad to have you. I seem to be writing this all in a jumble, but right now I feel thickheaded. I hope you will understand how the situation is and what is best for you to do.

Heavy clothing will also be needed for the new location; the winters are rather cold. Summers are warm enough. The main crops there are spring wheat, winter rye, oats, barley, and millet. All kinds of vegetables grow there. They say you can even grow watermelons and cantaloupes. There are no orchards, but we believe we will be able to develop some Siberian breeds. There is plenty of rainfall, and no drought. It's a beautiful region. The valleys between low mountains are covered with evergreens and deciduous trees— birches, aspens, pines, firs, and so on.

Even though we're rather sorry to give up our old home and all the work we've put into the soil, still we look forward to seeking our fortune in the new location. It's a place where we can live, but it will be hard to put down roots at first. I will look forward to hearing from you soon.

Borís Mazúrin

Documents

1.

The Council of the Life and Labor Commune hereby certifies that Citizen Yákov Deméntyevich Dragunóvsky and his whole family are accepted as members of the Life and Labor Commune of Moscow Province, which is now resettling in the Kuznétsk District of the Siberian Territory, in accordance with the decree of the Presidium of the All-Russian Central Executive Committee on 28 February 1930, Protocol No. 41.

On this basis it is ordered that Comrade Dragunóvsky's departure not be hindered, and also that settlement of his accounts not be delayed.

B. Mazúrin, Chairman of the Commune Council,

30 January 1931

2.

To Yákov Deméntyevich Dragunóvsky,

District Executive Committee of the Northern Caucasus Land Administration

On the basis of the directive of the All-Russian Central Executive Committee, deliver without delay, through the appropriate district land departments, resettlement documents with the right of reduced railway fares for new settlers as far as the Kuznétsk Station of the Tomsk Railway to the here-indicated followers of L. Tolstóy, who are settling to reinforce the Tolstoyan communes on the parcels of land at Úgolny, Osínovsky, and Kuréyny in the Kuznétsk District of the Western Siberian Territory.

In case of necessity, furnish the district land departments with blanks for resettlement tickets, and at the same time inform them that the period for resettlement is established up to 1 January 1932, and that kulák elements and persons deprived of voting rights are not eligible for resettlement and resettlement tickets at reduced fares. Those who are departing must be loaded as far as possible by groups.

> Member of the Collegium,
> People's Commissariat of Agriculture (Murzá-Galíev),
> Secretary V. Shershenyóv, 17 March 1931

Yelizár Pýrikov to Yákov Dragunóvsky

Moscow, 13 May 1932

Dear Yákov Deméntyevich,

I have intended to write to you for a long time, but I somehow kept too busy, and on top of that I am a poor one for writing, but do excuse me for it, even though you are even with me. I wanted to see you in Moscow before you left for the Altái. I started to go to you but then changed my mind. I changed my mind because it was hard not to see you, but it would not have been easier if we had seen each other, since there was nothing encouraging I could say about your move. I knew how many troubles you had faced in the labor cooperatives, and then you had more hardships here. Above all, I didn't want to undermine your enthusiasm when you were already halfway there. I thought, and still think, that you will be very useful to the commune with all your experience of life, and they will value you. I myself came near leaving for the Altái ahead of you, but I had misgivings about my bad character. In labor cooperatives and communes, I like to be free with my own opinions. I thought that if I traveled several thousand miles just to get into squabbles, it wouldn't be worth it; and it is a fact that squabbles would be inevitable, since things were not discussed seriously on the spot.

And so I am now writing these lines out of my deep respect for all of you people who are striving in action to create a good life of labor on the land, keeping busy with the agricultural work that is natural to humankind. I myself tried to live on the land in labor colonies, but as soon as we started working together, we ran into friction, so that we not only lost our ability to work together but even lost the good human relations we had enjoyed before our life together on the land.

Before our friends left for the Altái, I expressed my opinions to some of them about how they should get settled there. For example, settle down and work with a group in which everyone has already come to feel close to one another. Or else with a group that has come to an understanding not on spiritual but on purely business grounds—to put it bluntly, on the basis of a work plan. For example, suppose a group takes as its goal the creation of a certain kind of farm and is inspired by that idea—well, there you have your group. For others you may appear to be preoccupied with trifles, but for you it is to a certain extent a cause that is dear to your hearts. And without love for the cause, it is no longer a cause.

In this way your commune would break up into numerous groups and associations, but there is no reason to grieve over that, since each group or individual person would thrust his plow only as deep into life as he is capable of pulling it out without bringing the common cause to a halt. This would lead to the free labor of separate groups and individuals. But in this kind of group life, one thing must not be forgotten: if you want to be free, you must not hamper the freedom of others; if you do not want your labor to go in a certain direction, do not halt the labor of others. And by halting that of others, I do not mean the income they earn by their labor (the rent) from the land you occupy. That ground rent must be contributed by every group or individual to the common fund, which has to exist for the support of the necessary social and cultural institutions—schools, hospitals, the elderly, and so on.

The collection and dispersal of ground rents must be managed by a council of communes elected by all the inhabitants of the district in which this activity takes place.

Further, it seems to me that after the expiration of your years of exemption as new settlers, the government will begin to collect taxes from you on a regular basis; and this may again produce friction both within the commune and in its relations with the authorities. Within the commune, because of differences in convictions, some will say (and it seems that there already are such): "I don't recognize the state, and therefore I will not pay any taxes"; and others will say: "Since we have received the use of railroads for our resettlement, along with other things, from the government, we must pay for it." The authorities (especially the local authorities) may impose an unjust burden on you in the form of a large tax, and you will have no firm grounds for resisting. You can only pound on the door of the All-Russian Central Executive Committee with your bare hands. But if you introduced ground rents among yourselves, you could take firm data to that same All-Russian Central Executive Committee and say: "Even before you (that is, during our years of tax exemption), we collected rent on everything that belonged to us and spent it on our public needs; so now take for yourselves the part of that rent that you think is fair, but leave us a part of it to support our own public services." And for everybody alive, it would be clear that if the government takes part of the rent, it still acts justly by leaving part for social needs. If it takes all the rent, that means it is unwilling to devote anything to your cultural life, and you will have to support it yourselves, but once again the government is committing no great injustice. If it goes further than the rent, however, then you have a right to declare: "This is rent (render to Caesar the things that are Caesar's); take it, it is the nation's (since you are its representatives). But allow me to dispose of my own labor." And it seems to me that you can reach an agreement with the government (here in Moscow, of course), since they will understand the justice of your arguments. Besides, they do not collect rent as a part of land taxation.

But there is nothing new about all I have been writing to you here. Leo Nikoláyevich agreed with it all, and he himself wrote favorably about Henry George.[29] I wanted here only to confirm to you my view about the organization of a good, neighborly form of living together on earth.

Yákov Dragunóvsky to Vlas Belénkin

[1933]

Dear friend Vlas Yevímovich,

Forgive me for not writing to you for such a long while. I don't know now where to begin in order to acquaint you briefly with our life here. I know you are interested in knowing my experiences, and I want to share them with you as a close friend. So I have decided to describe my life here to you from the beginning up to the present day.

I arrived in Kuznétsk on 22 September 1931. We got a bleak welcome from the dirty, cold city of Kuznétsk (now Stálinsk),[30] which was just getting under construction. On 24 September we arrived at the commune. The commune settlement had also just gotten under construction, and people kept coming and coming. There is not enough living space and not enough food, and for that reason we have to get jobs in production. A cooperative work team of carpenters and cabinetmakers from the commune was already working in the taiga, a little over fifteen miles away, and I was to join it. Since 29 September I have worked in the taiga as a cabinetmaker for eight months without any days off. Before leaving for the taiga, I worked for four days in the commune, helping to dig potatoes. During those four days, I got oriented. I saw how the settlement was laid out. It is a quarter of a kilometer from the broad river Tom, whose silvery waters rush off to the Arctic Ocean over a bottom covered with large, clean pebbles. The settlement lies at the foot of a hill, the tillable land is on the hilltops, and the meadows are on the steep hillsides. The soil is very soft and fertile but weedy. Grass grows wonderfully in the meadows, but with a lot of weeds and ferns, so that a lot of the hay goes to waste. There are groves of birches and aspens on the hillsides. When you climb to the summit of the hill, a beautiful view opens up of hillocks, groves of trees, the broad, level plateau along the Tom, the taiga, and luxuriant thickets of vines, bird cherry, and cranberry trees. So far there are no fruit trees here. The bird cherry counts here as a fruit tree, and we have cranberries and black currant bushes. Off in the taiga there are raspber-

29. The philosophy of the American economist Henry George is obviously reflected here in Pýrikov's discussion of taxation.

30. Kuznétsk was called Stálinsk from 1932 to 1961. It is now Novokuznétsk.

ries, strawberries, and rowanberries; and they say that about twenty miles into the taiga, there are Siberian pine groves with nuts, also inaccessible so far to us. Because of our urgent work, we have had no time to go raspberry hunting in the forest. So far, we have to be satisfied with bird cherry and cranberry trees. Evidently, fruit trees have not so far been able to survive the severe climate, and northern breeds have not yet been produced.

The winters are really long and severe. The temperature sometimes gets down to sixty degrees below zero (centigrade), and the average is considered thirty to thirty-five below. The summers are short and warm, sometimes hot. You have to hurry with your work in both spring and fall. In spring, while it is still cold, you have to plow and sow, and in the autumn you must hurry with the harvest, or the frost and the early winter will swallow up your work. In general, you have to be very energetic, climbing up and down steep hills and hurrying through your work. But what is remarkable here is the abundance of sunshine and the nature of the soil. The sun is not stingy with its light in both summer and winter, and this takes the edge off the severity of nature. The soil is so rich that you have only to work it at the proper time and get rain at the proper time, and you are sure of a harvest. The only burdensome thing is the steep hills where you have to work. Only four kinds of natural wealth make you reconciled to the severity of the North: the life-giving sun, the good fertile soil, good water, and good heating. You can heat with wood or coal for about sixteen rubles a ton. There is a coal mine half a kilometer from our settlement. All the hills are full of coal here; you have only to dig into a hillside a few meters and you will strike coal.

Such, in short, is the wealth in this place. And if I were asked where it is easier to live, in our village of Draguný or here, of course the Altái spurs are better than the poor soil of Smolénsk.

But I am not attracted to this place. I long for the South, I long for warmth; I long to root around in the orchard and raise fruit trees. The local fruit—bird cherries and the fruit of the cranberry trees—does not satisfy me. I don't know whether I will be able to fulfill my dream—horticulture and a heavenly diet of fruit. Now, you know, I don't need the broad expanse of a farm, cultivated by horses or even machines. Four hectares, cultivated by hand, are enough for me. And for that reason the South, the South—that is what I'm dying for. Under no circumstances would I ever agree to live here permanently.

Even for fruit growing, the climate of our Smolénsk Province is better than this. But will I ever have a chance to fulfill my desire under the present-day collectivization and militarism? I have a terrible dread of the barracks and compulsory labor, and that is inevitable right now.

But let us wait and see. And now let's take a look at the taiga and the barrack where I lived and worked during 1931–32. I will not speak about the work, since that is the same everywhere, but I will tell about my friends and our relations with one another. We work communally: we work together, we receive a ration, and all our pay and dependents' rations go to the commune. I have not become close friends with any of my acquaintances here. Either I was too individualistic and egotistic, or else there was no appropriate friend, but I have remained as much alone here as I was before I came to this society of friends. All winter my whole interest has consisted in observation, listening to conversations, and on rare occasions taking part in discussions.

In the end these discussions led to a desire to reorganize our communal economy—to have not just one commune for all the 350 assorted members, but to break up into groups drawn together by spirit, temperament, and mutual attraction.

With such a grouping it would be more expedient and productive to manage our economy and carry on our work, and there would not be some privileged people and others in more difficult situations.

But such a regrouping turned out to be impossible, because the leader of the commune, Mazúrin, and those who supported him were opposed to such an innovation. The reformers had to limit themselves to picking a group of sympathizers, who separated from the commune and formed an independent cooperative farm. They brought the list of the cooperative to me and asked whether I wanted to join the new organization. I signed the list for the cooperative.

With the beginning of the spring work, our organization began plowing and sowing independently. The poor situation of our new organization did not allow all the members to take part in the field work. We did not have enough seed or enough food, so I worked until 15 June in production in the taiga.

During the first year of its life, our cooperative worked communally, without keeping any account of our labor, and taking meals in common. Only in autumn was there distribution of food products according to the number of mouths to feed; and with this, arguments began to arise about who did the work for whom. The single people tried to prove that they worked more than those with families, but the family men tried to prove that their families did not lag behind in cooperative work. Arguments arose over whose property predominated in the economy of the cooperative, and those who were well off started demanding that their capital—part in money and part in property—be divided up so as to establish an equal share in the cooperative property for all of them. And so it was done. Concerning equal participation in voluntary work, it was decided to allocate the work by families, so that each family would work off its share of each cooperative task. Each family was to sow its own vegetables and potatoes independently.

Through this cooperative arrangement, we intended to avoid reproaches and quarrels. It was especially hard for me, a sick man, almost an invalid, to think that somebody else was doing my work for me.

Here I must mention that when the commune was divided, my son Ványa did not go with me to help me, an invalid, but stayed in the commune. For that reason it was hard for me in my condition to think that my own family was being maintained at the expense of able-bodied people. I wanted very much to see a new arrangement set up within the cooperative, where we would work not as a commune but by families. Then I could make use of what I was physically able to earn.

During the summer of 1932, our cooperative got on a firm footing, with enough grain, produce, and money to last the whole year. After that, in the winter of 1932–33, no one had any thought of going out for seasonal labor.

With the coming of spring in 1933, our cooperative doubled in membership: there had been thirty-five people, and thirty new ones came in. Some of the commune members began to envy us and decided to leave the commune and join our cooperative. At that time my son Ványa came over to the co-op.

With the expansion of our farm, our project for working by families was disturbed. Only three households remained faithful to this project, and the other three-fourths of the cooperative started farming communally. Even though my son Ványa had come over to the cooperative, he did not work with me and help me, but went to work in the big communal group. He persuaded my older daughter Kláva to go over and work with them. There were only three of us left: me, an invalid, my old mother, and my twelve-year-old daughter Lyúba.

Yákov Dragunóvsky to L. S. Lúrye

I am now in my fourth year among friends in the Altái region. From my letters up to August 1933, you know something of our life here. I must fill you in about my activities for the past year and a half, but in order to make the picture clearer, I will begin with the spring of 1933.

During most of 1933, I lived in a cooperative of almost seventy people. The chairman of the cooperative was Grísha Gúrin. The internal organization of the co-op was as follows: a majority, three-fourths of the members, under the leadership of Grísha, decided to farm on the communal pattern; and the other fourth, three households, insisted on the cooperative arrangement, so that each of us would have separate garden plots for vegetables and potatoes, but we would hold everything else in common, cooperative-fashion.

In the middle of October, three big groups of our friends in the Altái were taken away from us because they would not register any kind of charter and they refused any production plans and payment of taxes. They were hauled off to the Kozhévnikovo District, nearly 350 miles to the north and about sixty-five miles from Tomsk—a remote district where wholesale collectivization has not taken place. Here, around the Kuznétsk industrial complex, a region of full collectivization, life would be impossible for such sinners as those who refuse to recognize the compulsory instructions of the government.

My Ványa went off with the exiles to Kozhévnikovo without saying a word to me or even informing Gúrin. There he landed in the good company of Vasíly Matvéyevich (of the Stalingrad group). After staying there three months, he had second thoughts about it. He wrote to me saying: "I was wrong for not helping you, my sick father, during those two years I lived in the Altái. I repent of my error, and I want to return to my father like the prodigal son. We will live together; I want to atone for my wrong by helping you in your illness. We don't have to move anywhere else, neither to the South nor to Kozhévnikovo. We will live right there, in the Altái, and do hand-farming."

My son and I became like-minded people, close friends, hand-farmers. In January 1934, Ványa came back from Kozhévnikovo.

This winter a fifth group separated from the commune. They split up into three camps: one part is staying here in the Altái, another is going to Kozhévnikovo, and the third is going south, to Central Asia.

I have taken an active part in all three groups. But in the end I have decided to join the group of Southerners. There are twenty persons in this group. My children have agreed to go to the South. My mother, my youngest daughter Lyúba, and I have stayed here to liquidate the rest of our property. After that, in May, I too will leave.

Our Southerners left on 24 March. Three members of my family went with them: Ványa, Kláva, and Ványa's wife Frósya (Ványa got married just before they left).

When I sent the children to the South, I thought the whole family would be together there by May; but my children's disastrous situation has stopped me and cooled my ardor. It is good that I did not hasten to sell everything. Some sort of foreboding held me back.

On 11 May I received this message from the South: "Stay where you are and sow spring wheat in the Altái."

On 14 May I began digging up the ground with my mattock, and my thirteen-year-old daughter Lyúba harrowed it with the rake. Then I made little furrows six or seven inches apart with the corner of my mattock, and Lyúba dropped seeds in them and smoothed out the furrows with the flat part of her rake.

We dug and sowed, dug and sowed. We had to hurry, because we were already half a month late. I wanted to sow as much as possible so as to have enough food for the whole family, including our Southerners, who intended to come back. We worked like that for a month and ended with twenty hundredths of a hectare in wheat, twenty-four hundredths in millet, thirteen in buckwheat, thirty-three in potatoes, and six in other plants. Almost a hectare in all.

Oh, how I liked that work—hand-farming! In spite of the difficulty, my health, and my haste, I did not get tired and I had a good time. When you are happy in your work, your fatigue quickly passes. I dug up five or six hundredths a day, and where the ground was soft, even eight. If the land had been near the settlement, I could have grown enough produce to feed a family of five or six by myself, but the sowing took place nearly two miles from the settlement and on very steep slopes.

We had barely finished the sowing when shoots from the first seeds came up, and we had to keep them weeded, loosen the soil, and help the plants make a successful struggle for rapid growth.

How pleasant, how joyful it is to look after crops, study the life of plants, and learn when to help plants. You enter into that joyful work and become wholly absorbed in it both physically and spiritually. But sometimes there are cases when you are powerless to help the plant. I carried out the last sowing of millet and buckwheat in completely dry soil. I hoped it would soon rain and the crop would come up fast, but I was wrong. The spring was dry, my crop lay there for about a month without coming up, and the late-sprouting millet did not have a chance to ripen. The morning frosts in August nipped it in the bud, and I failed to get a single grain from it. The other crops yielded the following harvest: wheat, 720 pounds; buckwheat, 450; potatoes, eight tons; the millet was a failure, and the other crops produced nothing. If the frost had not struck down the millet, the result would have been fine.

How good it is to work without the help of animals! You feel that you have liberated innocent animals, and you have liberated yourself from the various burdens of looking after the stock. When you work with a horse, you often have occasion to get angry, lose your temper, and beat the gaunt ribs of the weakened animal with a stick or a whip, which is unworthy of the name of a vegetarian, and in general unworthy of the name of a kindly, rational human being.

I will never forget my bitter experience in the spring of 1933 during spring sowing, when we were trying to fulfill the plan assigned to us by the government. Our cooperators were in a frightful hurry, and with a shortage of horses they were having a hard time coping with the big quota called for in the plan, especially on our steep hillsides. They not only wore our horses down to a frazzle, but two horses could not hold up under the burden and dropped in their tracks.

What do we vegetarians, we Tolstoyans, have to say for ourselves after that? We don't eat meat because of our sympathy and love for animals; we consider them our friends. And then at work we cruelly beat our friends with sticks and torment them to death. Hand-farming sets us free from that cruelty, that sin. Still, how sad it is that so few people are aware of this and willing to do something about it. But just the same, how good it is that there are at least a few people willing to set a good example for the rise of a more humane life in the future.

Even though circumstances beyond my control have kept me from achieving fully satisfactory results in this first year of my experience with hand-farming, and my grain crop was skimpy, on the other hand I had an abundance of potatoes. It seems rather bad that we have no vegetables to sell. We even had to buy nine hundred pounds of cabbage, since we had none of our own.

And now the powers that be are threatening to ruin us and send us away to forced labor if we keep on farming this land that is of no use to anyone and don't pay taxes. This year they have already tried to shake up a few hand-farmers, but so far this cup has passed from me.[31]

It seems that the government itself has set aside this place in the Altái for so-called Tolstoyans. But it is too bad that the commune and the cooperative have been fulfilling nearly all the state requirements for the past two years.

Those who were exiled to Kozhévnikovo did the right thing. But let them exile everybody rather than torment them with the yoke of taxation. Let the exiles suffer persecution rather than strengthen the power of the state, that organ of violence which brings harm to all the people on earth.

By staying here among the taxpayers, you seem to have greater power to act as your conscience dictates. Let them even take away everything for non-payment of taxes. But by acting in this way, the people in power are taking us into account somewhat just the same, since they know that people here have no hidden political aims, and refuse to take part in building up the state out of religious convictions. But in a new place nobody knows whom they would be taken for.

Another advantage in staying here is that there are people here who are products of the commune, and they think about it and are beginning to apply it to life. In general, you can feel spiritual support when you yourself have not yet become wholly strong.

The hand-farmers sowed quite a lot. When we finished sowing the spring wheat, the powers that be started visiting us to measure and register the crops. In the middle of the summer, a whole commission of five people was here. We would not help those men either. In autumn the chairman of the village soviet came several times and demanded that we pay the tax, or else they would come and take it. "Well, so what? Come on, take it, but we won't pay it ourselves."

And of course they took it, but not from everybody.

Some hand-farmers were afraid they would be ruined, and one not only paid his tax but even went along as a witness when they broke the lock of a hand-farmer neighbor and took his tax by force.

Representatives of the government came out and thanked the commune for its complete and timely fulfillment of the requisition of grain, money, milk, and hay. But such gratitude jarred upon many commune members.

Even Mazúrin said: "We fulfill it through our own weakness, even though, of course, we ought not to be supporting any state."

For refusing to do timber cutting, their horses were taken away—eight from the commune and two from the cooperative. For refusing to fulfill the meat requisition, two of their best cows were taken. For refusing a government school, the commune's school building was taken away for use by the government school. The case of the school will be examined by the All-Russian Central Executive Committee, but meanwhile the commune teachers are teaching the children wherever they can find a place, and according

31. An allusion to Jesus' prayer in the Garden of Gethsemane (Matthew 26:39).

to last year's program—in other words, without interference from the authorities and without filling the children full of class consciousness and militarism.

Our friends here observe Moses' Law: six days of work, and on the seventh, Sunday, a day of rest and talk. At three o'clock in the afternoon: singing, sometimes readings, but rarely discussions. We have not advanced very far. The singing takes on a ritual form, as in the Orthodox Church. On some days they will sing for four hours at a time, without any readings or talks. That sort of ritual is boring. Just the same, there are some lively, thinking people in the commune, but in the cooperative I dare say not a single one. The cooperators will sometimes come to the commune meetings, sit there for a while, and then leave. They have no time for any kind of intellectual work; otherwise there would be nothing to eat, and no shoes and clothes. So what's the use of looking at some kind of idea? We'll have time to talk about an idea when we're well fed and clothed and warm and can see how to keep the cooperative farm from falling apart.

Materially, at the present time the cooperators are wealthy. And doesn't there seem to be some kind of law that when persons or organizations get rich, they get greedier? Last year the cooperators were not wealthy and were gentler, and now they've grown rich and rude.

I am an invalid, but I do not envy such wealth and such wretchedness of spirit. Even though we have a scanty diet, with little bread, potatoes can fill your stomach and build your muscles and blood. You can live on potatoes. The Irish live almost entirely on potatoes. With potatoes as your diet, it is possible to live and even to think. And what is more, without envying anybody. The health I have from potatoes cannot be called normal, but still I'm not about to despair. Sometimes my leg aches so hard that it even keeps me from working. But no matter—I carry on a stubborn battle against illness. Through fasting and undereating, I ease my pain, and I intend in this way to drive out illness completely. In the first half of 1933, I went through seventy-five fast days; in February 1934 I fasted twenty days, and in July, eight days, and I often fast one day a week. I have eaten once a day for the past two months, and at the present time I am fasting again.

My leg ailment has led me to try all kinds of experiments on myself, and I think I may get some results: this all too deeply rooted illness may give way before a good quality of blood.

Some people are surprised that I have produced foodstuffs when I am so sick. I am now in close, friendly contact with the spiritual monist Pável Leóntyevich Maloród. We are getting acquainted with P. P. Nikoláyev's philosophical conception of spiritual monism. We are exploring our consciousness and clarifying the meaning of our life. How good and joyous it is to work in that direction.

After three years of life in the Altái, I have come to see that I was mistaken here too. Wherever I ran, I could not run away from myself. Without spiritual effort, a reasonable life cannot be created by itself.

(1935)

Autobiographical Note

The year 1934 was materially disastrous for me. My mother left me for her home region, considering me bankrupt and having no more hope of better food for her ailing body. Ványa, Kláva, and Frósya came back from Central Asia.

When the authorities seized everything I owned, all my belongings and food, that did not frighten me. But the children were afraid of hunger and went back into the commune. Only Lyúba stayed with me. In the spring I was presented with a plan for sowing 3.5 hectares and delivering 2,500 pounds of grain and 1,200 pounds of potatoes. I refused, and they took my whole harvest and all my things. Lyúba also became afraid there would be nothing to eat, and she too joined the commune.

I was not terrified by this ruin. In the spring I wrote an essay against the military tax, and on 10 November a poem. I expected that I would be arrested for the tax, but that did not happen. On 29 December two government agents came: one from the Territory and one from the Stálinsk City Soviet. I told them I would not give a single kopek for war. I already have full confidence in the principle of rational life, and I cannot support an irrational organization that serves to disunite people. People are rational creatures, and they must manifest within themselves a consciousness of true life.

(1935)

Yákov Dragunóvsky's Statement Addressed to the Government (Written in Connection with Arrests at the Commune)

25 May 1936

Dear friends,

We are looking at a picture!

In front of the so-called court on the so-called defendants' bench sit the so-called Tolstoyans.

I describe the scene in that way because nothing in it possesses absolute ideal truth, and for that reason it has no constant, positive character, but is only temporary and relative.

The court? Can the court claim that it possesses absolute truth, that it is infallible in the decisions and punishments it metes out to others? Of course not! The judges' decisions are only approximate and sometimes contain serious mistakes, in a word, whatever comes into their heads.

The Tolstoyans? Can the Tolstoyans say they possess absolute truth and inerrantly display it in life? Of course not! To a certain extent, the true meaning of life becomes apparent only in part, and only after a fumbling search.

The defendants' bench? Is the line that divides people into the condemned and the condemners an indispensable and constant thing, even if the life of people should be other than it is now? Of course not! That bench will exist until people have found a point of support that will unite people into one whole.

In many respects, even though unconsciously, the society of the proletarian state is already guided by reason, that altruistic international means of uniting people for the building of a new way of life, a new, classless society, an ideal communist commonwealth.

Tolstoyan society is founded on the same reason, the same higher consciousness, as the society of the proletarian state, and in part is consciously beginning to manifest that reason in its life. But often, of course, reason is not always manifested consciously among Tolstoyans either, just as it is not among the people of a state society.

If reason, this common source of human unity, were the basis of its highest achievement at the present time and were manifested in the life of of both societies, then misunderstandings between these societies would be eliminated. That would result in the disappearance of the defendants' bench, that border dividing people into the punishers and the punished. Only then would people more readily understand one another, and understand the common ideal toward which they strive.

In the present case, what we have cannot be called a legal process, where truth and justice condemn falsehood and injustice, but rather must be understood as a kind of dialogue, an exchange of opinions, a clarification of the basic questions of life for clearer mutual understanding and respect, for the introduction and examination of vital concepts under the general rubric of reason.

If, however, despite our reason and all that is fine within us, the court still judges and condemns people as criminals, then such a situation contradicts our highest consciousness. In that case reason will be held up not as a guiding and unifying principle, but as a soothing word to conceal our mistakes. Reason will be considered not the basic source of life but an appendage. And then judgment will be passed not on the imaginary Tolstoyan criminals who have committed no crimes, but on an idea. Judgment will be passed on a philosophy of life. Judgment will be passed on a world outlook that takes Reason as its foundation. The very limb on which we are sitting will be cut off.

But there still is hope for a positive outcome. There is hope that the proletarian state will understand the positive side of Tolstoyan society, the aspirations and ideals of these pioneers of a new and better life. And having understood this, it will forgive the shortcomings and imperfections that the members of Tolstoyan society have not yet overcome.

In their turn, the Tolstoyans will better understand the struggles and the ideal of the society of the proletarian state. And having understood it, they will forgive the shortcomings and imperfections manifested by the people in that society.

Having understood each other, both sides will value according to its merits all the best that exists in the aspirations of both societies, and will rather help each other to overcome the shortcomings and imperfections that hinder unity.

The Tolstoyans are looked on not only as opponents but as counterrevolutionaries who are hindering the building of socialism and a classless communist society, and for that reason all efforts are directed at liquidating this obstructive element and at knocking this rational understanding of life out of people's minds.

But just what are the shortcomings and mistakes of the Tolstoyans? Just what is their counterrevolutionism, and how are they hindering the building of socialism? Is it possible that these shortcomings consist only in what the commission from the Stálinsk City Land Department noticed? "The farm of this commune is not exemplary, there is nothing significant about it. The egalitarian system of pay is abnormal. The school has a crippling influence on the children and does not teach them by the state program. There is only one communal pot, in which the same white meatless potato soup is always prepared."

That is the naïve accusation by which said criminals are judged. But is there anything counterrevolutionary here? Is there any kind of criminal sabotage hidden here that is hindering the building of socialism? Of course not! These are simply people whose philosophy of life leads them to believe that superfluous riches are harmful, and so they are not trying to make a wealthy showpiece out of their farm. The Tolstoyans consider that a person ought to have just as much as a simple life requires.

In exactly the same way, equalized wages are no crime. All commune members demonstrate their capacity without any calculating self-interest and consider the needs of all to be the same.

And the school? Can the Tolstoyans possibly be blamed so much for their school that the teachers had to be arrested and tried in court? Is it really impossible for them to bring up their own children in the moral spirit that is necessary at this time? And can the Tolstoyan school possibly be considered bad merely because it does not teach class hatred and the state militarism that prepares young men for military catastrophe? And because instead of class and state antagonism, the Tolstoyans want to teach their children altruism, humanism, and internationalism?

Dear accused Tolstoyan friends! It is not you they have put on trial, because you have committed no crime; they have put on trial the idea you wanted to support! What is on trial is the philosophy of life based on reason. What is on trial is your higher consciousness. What is on trial is our reason. And so much the better for the people who are putting this idea on trial. They will understand sooner when they put it on trial and examine it than when they don't think about it at all.

Friends! The criticism is made against us that Tolstoyans do not understand, value, and take part in the building of socialism, the building of a classless, communist society. "The Tolstoyans are counterrevolutionaries!" This accusation is absolutely untrue. Tolstoyans see and value the enormous efforts and exertion of people who wish to build life on new, reasonable principles. How much heroism has been shown here, how much self-sacrifice has it taken to prove the falsity of the existing irrational class society, the irrationality of the feudal and capitalist system. To prove the irrationality and brutality of laws that acknowledge the right of one man to use a thousand hectares of land, while it was impossible for a thousand men to have a few rows of garden plants. To prove the irrationality and brutality of laws that give one factory owner the right to take the labor of a thousand workers in order to live in luxury himself, while dooming a thousand families to a pitiable existence or even to death from starvation!

All these desires and aspirations are theoretically so great and valuable that neither the Tolstoyans nor any reasonable person can fail to recognize their real and vital significance. And not only to recognize it, but to take part in building something new, great, and reasonable.

But when our revolutionary friends took the helm of our new, reasonable life, when the theoreticians of those great ideas of equality, brotherhood, and classlessness began applying the outdated, conservative, and counterrevolutionary methods of violence, here the Tolstoyans categorically parted company with them. And in their disagreement they see nothing conservative or counterrevolutionary; on the contrary, they feel themselves to be pioneers of that great and rational life which is the desire of all thoughtful, reasonable people.

Do the Communists know their own contradiction, that their beautiful theory about the ideal society is the positive side, but their method of violence for the attainment of their reasonable goal is something else entirely— the negative side?

The idea of communism in theory is in harmony with our reason; the method of violence contradicts reason. The idea, based on reason, is world internationalism; the method of violence is egotistical, divisive despotism. What is there in common between these two ideas?

Do the Communists really know their imagined "enemies," the "counterrevolutionary Tolstoyans," who reject violence as contradicting reason, and recognize only the reasonable and beautiful as the basis for the new structure of the classless society, the new structure of communism?

Do the Communists know that the Tolstoyans, in their idea and method of nonviolence, are not the enemies of communism but its friends? And not only ordinary friends, but pioneers of this new structure?

Do the Communists know that both theories—the theory of communism and the rational religiousness of Tolstoyism—are necessary, vital, and timely?

Do the Communists know that these two tendencies are not so hostile to each other as to have this dividing line between them—the defendants' bench? Evidently the Communists do not know all that, since this picture exists of the judges and the judged. But if the Communists and Tolstoyans have known little of each other up to the present, now it is shameful not to know, now both of them must understand; and instead of pronouncing an undeserved and severe condemnation, they ought to hold out a hand to each other for mutual understanding and for the achievement of a common rational life.

We can understand that man, as he strives toward truth but still commits errors through ignorance, is not as guilty as it used to seem to us. We can understand, rather, that he is guilty who knew the right path to a higher life but deliberately turned away from it or deliberately perverted it. If a person knows what true life consists in but does not follow this knowledge or even perverts this knowledge, that is an unforgivable abuse of the spirit of life; it is the burying of one's talent. And the enemy is certainly not he who openly and boldly speaks out and warns against danger; rather, the enemy is he who keeps quiet while knowing the danger, or even sticks out his foot when humankind is rushing toward the precipice of enmity and hatred. But the person who sincerely desires and strives for a rational life, even if he should make a mistake through ignorance, is not guilty.

Is a person guilty for understanding that he is not just a lump of clay that can be molded into any shape for anyone, but is a spiritual being, unique in all spiritual life?

Is a person guilty when he has understood his spiritual essence and ceased to fight against other such spiritual essences as himself for selfish personal advantage and material benefits?

Is a person guilty when he has understood his spiritual unity with all life and has begun to harmonize his actions with the requirements of that life?

Every thinking person not only will say that such a person is not guilty for understanding spiritual unity, but also will say that all of us need to understand this unity and begin struggling with our imperfection.

Having briefly set forth the world outlook of the so-called Tolstoyans and their bloodless revolutionism, I believe the people of the court, the people of socialism and communism, will understand the great significance of the moral and rational ideas of their supposed enemies, and will see them not as enemies but as close friends, who are helping to build life on reason. Once they have understood the ideas and aspirations of these defendants, they will understand their own mistakes in connection with them, and in general the mistakes they are perpetrating against reason, against life. They will stop perpetrating them and begin reforming themselves under the guidance of reason.

The Tolstoyan friends will also better understand and feel the vital significance of reason and our highest consciousness, and with this understanding they will be led in all their actions by reason and will begin making fewer mistakes.

I believe that by drawing closer to this case from all sides and—most important—by illuminating it with reason, with our highest consciousness, we can avoid the juridical quagmire that could swallow us up. And for this reason, my sincerest desire for both the judges and the judged is to try to avoid juridical tangles, try to avoid misunderstandings both in the present court case and in general in our everyday lives. Ours is not to judge and condemn but rather to forgive one another, remembering the saying, "It is better to pardon twenty guilty persons than to punish one who is innocent."

Yákov Dragunóvsky

Letters from Yákov Dragunóvsky to His Children after His Imprisonment in Labor Camp

31 May 1937

On 7 May I handed in a package to be sent to the Academy of Sciences. It contained a few of my articles, copies of all my statements to the NKVD, and a copy of the P. P. Nikoláyev article. In all, the material amounted to 360 pages. Now I don't know whether my letter was mailed or not. I gave a ruble to register it. During this time, some sort of melancholy mood has taken hold of me. All my former memories of my irrationally spent life came back to me. I started blaming myself for not being able to give you children all that my heart felt like giving you. I began regretting all the time I had spent to no purpose. It is painful that I have lived half a hundred years and hardly been of any use in life—I haven't even learned how to express my thoughts correctly. For example, I had a great desire to express my ideas on Reason before learned people—but suddenly there were a whole lot of mistakes.

On 21 May I looked out the window at the steppe. About thirty or forty paces from the window there is a plot of farm land—about twenty hundredths of a hectare. Last summer it was all in cabbage. I felt like working a little with a hoe, putting in a small crop. I decided to ask about it. I feel that my leg is a lot better than it was last year—I can work even while they are treating it. I told the hospital nurse, and she talked with the doctor, after which the following conclusion was reached: "Nobody will allow a crop to be sowed on an individual plot of ground, since all sowing is done in common, by machinery; and besides, a prisoner could not undertake such work as that for a year, or even a summer, since he might be sent off at any moment on a prisoner transport, and for that reason you need to take on only the kind of work you can leave at any minute. After all, a crop requires constant care for at least four months. If you want to work and your health permits it, then right here in the hospital we need to get the flower beds and grass plots into shape. Nobody will force you to do it; just work as much as you want to and feel able to."

I decided this wouldn't be a bad thing. I could at least brighten up a little plot of ground for the patients, where sick prisoners walk and rest on warm days in the sunshine.

On 22 May I began work with a spade, carving out grass plots and round flower beds, and digging little holes and ditches to set out trees. I did eight days of tedious work, and the result was beautiful: the vacant plot blossomed with currant bushes, five or six little birches, two bird cherries, one hawthorn, and two dwarf fir trees, hauled in from ten kilometers away. In a word, my work has pleased the patients, the doctor, and the hospital nurses. The planting of the trees was a little late. I finished them only yesterday. The currant bushes are in bloom, and the birches have put out leaves. In order for the trees to take root, I've had to carry a lot of water. I pour sixty buckets on them each day. I carry the water about fifty meters in buckets on a yoke.

Ványa, you write, and so does Pável Leóntyevich [Maloród], that he expects to be in our parts. If you have time, do copy two pages from the first volume (of Nikoláyev), about which I reminded you earlier. Enclose all the passages I have copied from the books—I think they are all in one place. Enclose my notes on Reason, and the others, too—they are all in one place. Enclose my article on taxes and the notebook "Defense of Friends in Court," the notebook of my biography (the outline). Put in four ordinary notebooks, pencils, a penholder, pen points, the book on the spiritual monistic conception of the world (Introduction), the book *A Guide to the Beginning Poet,* the book *How to Work with a Book,* and *The Brain and the Soul* by Chelpánov.[32] I would also like to ask you for *The Path of Life, A Circle of Reading,* and *What I Believe.*[33] What a pile of requests I'm loading you down with; but I don't need any food.

21 June 1937 (excerpt)

For the present don't send me anything; you have a lot of work there, and I don't want to disturb you with my requests, especially since I do it for no special reason, just incidentally. I feel spiritually well, and I need those extracts and the paper only because I wanted to write a few things. But if I have no work, then I think, and that is the best, most necessary work.

Goodbye for now.
Yours, Yákov

From the Memoirs of Iván Dragunóvsky

About My Father's Trial

Many members of the commune, including me, went to the trial of our commune-member friends. There were no outsiders, and the trial took place in a small courtroom in the First Building of the NKVD.

My father refused to walk to the court proceedings, and he was carried into the court by force, but when the judges announced that in the concluding remarks the defendant could say whatever he wished—about his beliefs and about his life—my father went to the courtroom on his own. When his turn came, he stood up and began speaking.

His voice was pure and sonorous, and he spoke clearly, eloquently, simply, and intelligibly. During his speech his face became animated, his eyes

---

32. Geórgy Ivánovich Chelpánov (1862–1913)—a philosopher and logician who was also one of the founders of experimental psychology in Russia. The book mentioned here (Russian: *Mozg i dushá*) was published in St. Petersburg in 1900.

33. Of these three books by Tolstóy, the first two (not available in English translation) are compilations of daily readings of a religious nature to which Tolstóy devoted a great deal of attention during the last decade of his life. They are taken in part from his own writings and in part from many religious and philosophical works of all times and cultures.

sparkled expressively, and a wealth of mimicry enlivened his well-reasoned speech.

My father began his story with his birth and continued in the same order that I have given it in his biography. He spoke about two hours, and during that time he brought his story up to the First World War.

My father believed the judges and really did think that in the concluding remarks he could talk as long as he wished, until he had told all about his life: about how he had searched for the meaning of life, how he had made irrational mistakes, how he himself as well as other people had suffered from them, and how he had found the true Reasonable path of life, which had brought joy to his soul and a spiritual rebirth.

But the judges stopped him and said: "We do not want to hear any more; it is time to pass sentence." My father stopped talking and would answer no more questions from the judges, since he considered them unreasonable.

After the verdict, all of us commune members were allowed to talk with our condemned friends and relatives. Pável Leóntyevich and I talked for a long time with my father, who was cheerful and calm and paid no attention to the term of imprisonment he had received from the judges.

About the Death of My Father

In 1938, after I myself had been arrested and sentenced to ten years of imprisonment by the same judge who had sentenced my father on the same strange charge of "counterrevolution," I heard the following news about my father from a fellow prisoner named Kórgov in one of the transit prisons: "I knew Yákov Dragunóvsky and was in the same camp with him. He boldly talked and wrote about the uselessness of violence, about the unreasonable lives people lead, and about much more. He was tried by the camp court for his words and writings and sentenced to be shot."

5.

From the Book One of My Lives

IVÁN DRAGUNÓVSKY

Iván Yákovlevich Dragunóvsky (1908–1991) grew up under the strong Tolstoyan influence of his father. Other important influences on his spiritual development were the execution of his uncle Semyón Dragunóvsky in 1920 and the arrest of his father for refusing military service. "My father, his brothers, Uncle Semyón, who was shot," he said, "and others who refused that evil business of military service seemed to me bolder and higher than all the other heroes on earth. I wanted to share their fate in prison. I wanted to help somehow, which I did to some extent when I visited them in the camps with food packages. I wanted to be just like them, doing good to all people." In 1924, at the age of sixteen, Iván moved with his father to the Stávropol territory, where his father organized the Peaceful Plowman Agricultural Association. Iván completed training there as a tractor driver and drove the American tractor that the association acquired. In 1931 he and his father moved to Western Siberia and joined the Life and Labor Commune. The extract from his autobiography published here begins at that point.

ON 14 SEPTEMBER 1931 we left the beautiful foothills of the Caucasus. In Moscow we went to see V. G. Chertkóv and talked things over with him. On 24 September we found ourselves in the foothills of the Altái Mountains and were welcomed by unfamiliar but kindred members of the Life and Labor Commune.

Voluntary work according to each person's strength and abilities, without any compulsory norms, was just what I liked. Not only I but all the other commune members liked that free, unconstrained way of working. As a result, the work went well; it was pleasant, merry, conscientious, and of high quality. Everybody treated our helper-horses kindly, without any shouting and goading, without a whip, without unduly heavy burdens, without exhausting our lesser brothers.

What I especially liked about the people in our new society was their

Iván Dragunóvsky in Happy Valley in 1937, the year before his arrest, holding his little son Alik and sitting with his wife Frósya on his right and his sister Lyúba on his left.

Iván Dragunóvsky on his seventy-fifth birthday, 8 February 1983.

simple, friendly, sincere relations with one another. You met with never a single coarse, abusive, or even ill-natured word, no drunken speeches, no clouds of tobacco smoke. Even the older people called each other by their first names—Pétya, Ványa, Mísha, Yegórushka, Tánya, Fénya, Mótya.

We young people quickly made friends with one another, because we all had the same sober, reasonable aspirations and amusements. We organized a choir under the direction of Anna Stepánovna Maloród, performing mainly religious and moral songs, and poetry and music from the Russian poets Púshkin, Lérmontov, Nádson, and Iván Gorbunóv. We organized a string orchestra conducted by Mísha Blagovéshchensky.

In 1936 about ten people in our commune were arrested, among whom were the teachers in our free, nongovernmental school and other members of the commune. My father wrote an "Appeal" to the government. Two other members of our commune were arrested for refusing military service: Lyóva Alekséyev and Fédya Katrúkha.

Our commune school was closed, but it was soon opened again, and government teachers were sent to it. The children of the commune members started going to that school, since they did want to learn how to read and write.

I remember one of the government teachers, Pyotr Ivánovich, who from the very first day behaved arrogantly and defiantly with his pupils. During recess he would come out in the street with his accordion and play bold, devil-may-care ditties, boastfully laughing before the commune members, as if to say: "See how bold and powerful we are. We took over your school and your children, and we're teaching them just the way we want." But after living for a while among the commune members, seeing every day how sober, kind, and friendly they were toward him, seeing that and knowing why our teachers and other commune members had been arrested, he changed his attitude toward us. Imperceptibly he became a kind and intimate friend of the commune members. The children loved and respected Pyotr Ivánovich as the best teacher in the school.

That is how a kind and loving example can influence other people.

I will not whitewash the life of our commune, since there were certain shortcomings in it, just as there are everywhere. For example, a small group of members separated from the commune and organized themselves as a cooperative agricultural work team, with a small amount of personal property, such as houses, gardens, and cows, and all the rest owned in common. Another separation involved a small group of hand-farmers, that is, people who tilled the soil only with their own hands, making no use of animals at all. That group was not officially registered anywhere. They occupied steep hillsides that were of no use to anyone and did not pay any taxes, since they had no extra property.

The commune and the cooperative work team paid taxes on their land in grain, vegetables, and money. But when the government demanded that they hand over cows for meat delivery and horses for the army, they refused. The government agents came in person and took as many horses and cows as they wanted.

The moral distinction of the commune consisted in the fact that it included many single old men, widows with children, orphans, and invalids, who felt completely at home there.

A group of hand-farmers built a little mill on a creek to grind their grain, since turning the millstones by hand was rather hard work, and the water flowed idly all the time. The village soviet found out about it. They came over, tore down the mill, and threw the millstones off a cliff into the Tom River, saying: "The water is state water, and nobody can use it free."

The village rulers took almost the whole pitiful crop of grain that the hand-farmers had harvested from those formerly useless hillsides. The hand-farmers took no offense and did not complain, but just lived on potatoes and other vegetables, looking with sorrowful compassion on those men gone astray who called themselves the "potentates of this world." The commune did not pass by these offended people in their calamity, but took them in like their own brothers.

And so these people who had consciously and willingly decided to live a nonviolent life of brotherhood, according to the law of nonresistance to evil by violence, meekly endured suffering and death from the surrounding world and the "potentates of this world below."

During our Sunday discussions in the commune, nobody tried to force his own views on anyone else. Instead there was a free exchange of opinions and ideas. Outsiders were able to attend our meetings, since the commune members did not conceal their opinions from anyone and engaged in no politics. Our meetings were often attended by teachers from the government school who had been given orders from on high to "keep tabs on what was going on."

At these meetings my father would often tell stories about his life, his sufferings, and his errors, and about his search for the meaning of life, and his refusals to do military service and the beatings he received for that.

Klávdiya Zhuk, the wife of one of the teachers, would often attend our meetings, listen to my father's accounts, and then report them to the NKVD in a completely distorted version. The investigator Yástrebchikov began coming out from town to see my father. He would carry on long conversations with my father in his home. Stepán Yástrebchikov, as an intelligent, educated, serious man, found nothing "counterrevolutionary" in Father's words, and after bidding him a friendly goodbye, he would go back to the city with a profoundly thoughtful expression on his face. (Later, during the Stálin inquisition, he was executed by his own fellow materialists, possibly for his "softness" on the Tolstoyans.)

On Sunday, 8 August 1936, we were all at home: my sisters Kláva and Lyúba, my wife Frósya, our little year-old son Álik, and I. My father was lying on the bed, wrapped up in a wet sheet. The day before, on his way back from his little field, he had fallen into a hole he had failed to notice in the tall grass and broken open an old wound on his shin, from which the blood had spurted in a stream. Accustomed to pain, Father did not groan but lay quietly with compresses to ease his physical suffering.

Toward evening, two young men with weapons drove up to our home in a wagon and came into our house. They went up to my father, lying on the bed, and told him to get up, get dressed, and go with them, since they had come to arrest him and take him away. My father lay there without speaking and fixed his sad eyes on the young men in astonishment. Then they took the cover off him and unwrapped the wet sheets. There before their eyes lay his gaunt, naked, worn-out body with his bloody leg, covered with ulcers.

Any human being would have shuddered with a feeling of compassion at the sight of that body. Evidently the young servants of the law, for all their armor (against that weak man), were not yet completely lacking in compassion. They stood in perplexity before the gaunt, naked body of our father, not knowing what to do with him now. Even though they still had the good human feelings nature had given them, their minds were perverted by the false teaching in which they had grown up and which they had studied in their government school. Now they were servants, blind enforcers of that law; and having nothing reasonable of their own in their souls, they carried out the will and orders of that law; they were hypnotized by the law.

The enforcers of the law turned to the four of us and asked us to help them dress our naked father "so as to hurt him as little as possible." All four of us refused to give such "help."

Then, overcoming their embarrassment, they started looking for his underwear and other clothes and began dressing him as if he were a corpse. After somehow getting him dressed, they took him by the arms and legs and carried him out of the house and to their wagon in the street, near which a large crowd of commune members had gathered in anticipation of something bad. The young enforcers of the law laid our father in the wagon, got in themselves, and quickly rushed out of the village, fleeing from the eyes of the people who had silently and sadly watched their unnatural, unreasonable, inhuman actions.

On 20 November 1936, the anniversary of Leo Tolstóy's death, the court passed judgment on his followers, the Tolstoyan commune members. They were condemned because they did not march in step with a society that supported violence, murder, and church and state superstition. They were condemned for their human convictions about love of their fellow human beings, for their nonresistance to evil by *violence*. The people in government, the judges, told them: "You are building communism too soon; it is too early for you to refuse to support violence and murder. First we have to become materially wealthy and feed everybody until they are full; then communism will come by itself, without any effort on our part."

The terms of imprisonment varied. Father was sentenced to five years in the camps.

I have no desire at all to tell about the terrible years 1937–38, because my heart feels heavy when I remember what Russians in their delusion did to their own fellow Russians, arresting them, beating them, condemning them, deporting them, putting them to death. When they arrested and deported one another to the North by the hundreds, thousands, and millions, those people bore no malice toward one another. Often they were even good-hearted people, but they were stupefied by government hypnosis; they blindly believed that the millions who were deported (and put to death) really were "enemies of the people," which is to say that they were their own enemies. But the principal evil was in the people themselves, in their imperfect souls, in their personal egoism, in their eagerness to save their own skins, in their blind faith in "matter," in the objective reality of their body as the only value, for the preservation of which people will resort to the most immoral means, including the betrayal of one another. What a great delusion!

It was October 1937. Toward evening I left the commune settlement and went through deep snow to the apiary, which was located in a beautiful forest about three kilometers from the settlement. Lev Alekséyev and Anatóly Ivánovich Fomín had gone there before me. Lev and Anatóly had climbed into the loft of a big thatch-roofed beehive shelter, and I settled down on the floor in the little hut where our beekeeper, Blagovéshchensky, lived with his wife Dúsya.

We slept poorly and uneasily. At midnight there was a knock at the door. A moment later the unlatched door swung open, and four men with a lighted lantern came in. Three of them had pistols in their hands, pointed into the room. The fourth was unarmed—Onúfry Zhevnováty, a member of the commune. They shone the light on my face, asked Onúfry my name, and said: "No, that one's not needed now," and went into the other room, where Mísha and Dúsya were. They ordered Mísha to get dressed and started searching the whole house. They rummaged through everything, scattering books and other things about the floor, but they found nothing except literature and books on beekeeping. Three of them went to search the beehive shelter, but in half an hour they came back without finding anyone or anything. They did not climb up in the loft.

They took my good friend Mísha Blagovéshchensky, a dear, kindly, frail man, off into the darkness of that cold winter night without letting me say goodbye to him. I never saw him again, and never will see him in this earthly life.

At dawn Anatóly and Lev came down from the loft, blue and shaking from the winter cold and from fright produced by the intelligent but misguided men. They remained in the house to get warm and calm down, and I set out for the commune settlement; but on the way I decided to stop in at Happy Valley, where Fédya Katrúkha, an independent hand-farmer and the brother of my wife Frósya, lived alone in his hut.

Climbing down through the deep snow into the little valley overgrown with brushwood, I noticed a lot of human footprints beside his hut and some household utensils and piles of ashes scattered about in the snow. I went in. Fédya was lying on the bed under a blanket with his eyes wide open and a serious, sorrowful look on his face. Strewn about the dirt floor were his pitiful belongings and pages torn out of books. I asked: "What happened, Fédya—did they come here too?" He gave no answer and continued to lie quiet. Then I noticed that his face and neck bore the marks of a beating. I sat there with Fédya for about half an hour, and during all that time we did not utter a word. Words were unnecessary; even without them everything was clear. I did not ask him to show me his beaten, disfigured body; that would have been unnecessary curiosity. All his books were destroyed; some of them had been burned right there in his hut on the dirt floor, and some outside. His possessions and utensils were broken and torn apart, and some of them had been carried away.

When I got to the commune settlement, I went to see Fédya's mother and told her about him. She left to see him, and I went home.

When I walked up to the entrance of my house, I stopped in astonishment. The good strong front door had been smashed to pieces. I went in the house. Frósya and my sister Lyúba sat pale and silent. Our two-year-old son Álik sat in his mother's lap and clung to her with a frightened look on his face. This is what they told me.

At two o'clock in the morning there was a knock on the door. Frósya went to the vestibule and asked who was there. They shouted from the yard: "Open up without any talk, we're from the NKVD!"

Frósya answered: "Ask one of our neighbors to come with you, and then I will open up; otherwise, I don't know you."

Then the men who claimed to be the NKVD picked up a birch log from the pile of wood lying in the yard and started beating down the door. When the door was beaten to pieces, they carried a log into the vestibule and started ramming the second door to the room. Frósya realized they would tear the second door to bits and then she and the baby would freeze. She opened the door.

Several armed and drunken men calling themselves the NKVD came in. They immediately started shouting and using obscene language; they climbed down into the cellar and began searching the house. Their first question was, "Where is Mikhaíl Katrúkha?" (Frósya's other brother).

Frósya answered: "I know only about myself, I know nothing about other people," and she would answer nothing more. The drunken men shouted and cursed for a long time, threatening Frósya and Lyúba with their weapons, and still insisting: "Where is Mikhaíl Katrúkha?" But this time they could not get anything out of her. For some reason they did not ask about me.

That night many commune members were taken off to prison, and almost none of them ever came back to their homes or to this earthly life.

Mísha Katrúkha and I continued to spend our nights wherever we could: sometimes in the communal bathhouse, sometimes in the drying room, sometimes in the field in a haystack, sometimes in the woods. We wanted above all not to be caught by those wild hunters and placed behind bars, without knowing what for and without feeling guilty of any kind of crime.

Possibly it was egotistic on my part to avoid suffering and death and to protect my own self. It was a kind of denial of the unity of life. If life is one and indivisible, then we ought to share both joys and sorrows in common, on the basis of mutual responsibility: one for all and all for one. But I did not see any sense in enduring this unnecessary suffering and premature death. I do not want to believe in any kind of superstitions: neither about the church nor about the state. I do not want to be hostile toward or make war upon anybody on the whole planet; I will not and cannot kill either people or our lesser brethren the animals—not for sport and not for food. Can they possibly want to punish me or take my life for that? How savage and senseless it is!

I spent one of those anxious nights at the Karétnikovs', who lived right beside us, just beyond the wall. At that time their son-in-law Mísha Ovsyúk was already in prison, and his wife Kláva and their little daughter Véra were living at home. Dúnya Aguréyeva was spending the night in our room along with Frósya, Lyúba, and Álik. Mísha spent that last night with the Chernyávskys.

I awoke suddenly during the night as if from an electric shock. I do not know why I woke up—whether it was from an inner foreboding of disaster or from the loud noise on the other side of the wall. I could hear the stamping of feet in my apartment. I heard something strike the wall behind which I lay, and after that I heard a cry of anguish from little Álik. I woke up Kláva Ovsyúk and begged her to run to our home and ask one of our neighbors to go to our home and find out what was happening. Kláva ran off, but quickly came back in great agitation and said that armed men would not allow her to go in, and that in general it was frightful out on the street: they were seizing everybody, throwing them into sleighs, and carrying them off.

I could stand it no longer, and I ran out through the backyards to my apartment, barefooted and in my night clothes. It was a moonlit night and freezing weather, but I did not feel it. At that moment no one was in the yard, and I crept along the wall right up to the vestibule of our apartment. Through the window in the moonlight I caught sight of two human figures. Looking closely, I saw that one of them had a shining pistol in his hand, with the barrel pointed at the head of the other person. Even though I was no more than three steps away, I could not make out whom he was aiming at.

"Speak up, where is your husband?" I heard a coarse masculine voice.
Silence.
Frósya! So it's you, poor darling! I trembled as if I were in fever. That pistol is aimed at your head! They are torturing you and threatening you with death because of me! No! That cannot be! I will jump up and shout: "Here I am! Turn her loose!"

But—I did not jump out of my hiding place, I did not cry out, but crept up closer, one more step, almost against the window, expecting things to come to a head.

What was it—cowardice or mute terror that locked my lips? I do not know. If the man with the pistol had turned his head a little toward the window, he probably would have seen me; but all his attention was riveted on the outwardly calm face of Frósya. I decided to wait at the window to the end of this nightmare, even though my feet were frozen and I could no longer feel anything.

"I ask you for the last time: where is your husband? Or else I'll blow your brains out!"

Silence. Not a sound from Frósya.

"There's a woman for you, devil take it!" He pushed Frósya with his left hand, and they both went into the room.

I went back to the Karétnikovs'. I dressed and put on my boots. I started to climb down into the cellar, but Kláva took fright and said: "They may come here; they would find you and arrest me for hiding you." I climbed up into the attic, which served several communal apartments. An air hole had been cut in the ceiling of my apartment for ventilation. It had a big wooden pipe, which at that time happened to be open, and through it I could not only hear everything but also get a fairly good view of what was going on in the room. I sat down beside the air hole and looked and listened. The NKVDs kept quiet, smoking and resting after their "work." Only Álik moaned and cried pitiably. These men had dislocated his arm.

"Now then, listen to this," one of them said. "If you are not going to tell us where your husband is, then get dressed: we will arrest you in his place!"

Not a word or a movement from Frósya. Now I had made up my mind: if they started dragging Frósya out of the house, I would climb down and give myself up.

But life is full of such puzzling, incomprehensible oddities that I can never explain. Instead of my coming to Frósya's rescue, it was her own poor brother Mísha Katrúkha who did. Ordinarily after the nightly round-up, Mísha would not come home to us until dawn, knowing that the round-ups and arrests took place only at night. But this time, as if on purpose, at four o'clock in the morning, when everything had quieted down in the room, I suddenly heard steps in the vestibule. The door opened—and in came Mísha. He tried to turn back, but the men who called themselves the NKVD rushed up and seized him.

"What is your name?" they shouted menacingly.

"Why do you want my name? I am a man. Tell me, what do you need from me?"

They took Mísha to the vestibule, put him into a cold, empty pantry, threw him down on the floor, sat on his arms and legs, and one of them started beating him on the head and face with a shoemaker's wooden last, and kept asking his name.

They beat and tormented Mísha for a long time, but Mísha kept silent.

I was shaking from the horror of what I had seen and heard, and the air vent sticking through from the room to the attic began swinging and creaking. They heard it and rushed up to the air vent, shouting: "He's there, in the attic!" One of them got up on a stool and started measuring with his head to see whether I had climbed up there from the room. When they realized that a grown man could not have climbed through there, they dashed out on the street and climbed up a ladder at the other end of the building to the attic, but I kept sitting numbly by the air vent. When their steps and voices had drawn quite near, I suddenly roused myself from the fear that had frozen me and jumped from the other end of the attic into the snow. I hid in the nearby stable and looked from a window at what was taking place in the yard.

Day was breaking. I saw them take Mísha by the arms out of my apartment and down to the sleighs in the street, which were already stacked high with our commune members, big and little, like firewood. I kept waiting for them to bring or carry Frósya out. No, evidently they had left her. That meant I would remain sitting in the stable with the horses, who were peacefully munching their hay, knowing nothing about the unreasonable deeds of those intelligent creatures of the earth—men.

From the stable window I could see a part of the street. Suddenly several sleighs piled high with people started out of the settlement. A great crowd of women and children were following them. I came out of the stable and went home. The room was in ruins. Frósya, Lyúba, Dúnya, and little Álik sat pale and silent. They seemed neither surprised nor overjoyed that I had come, and that I was still free and alive. They knew I would be taken away sooner or later.

In Happy Valley, Fédya Katrúkha and Anatóly Fomín were rounded up on that same night. Afterwards one of the participants in that savage arrest, the ringleader Kolódin, told about it, not with regret but with a sneer:

"Anatóly Ivánovich agreed to go by himself, but Fédya refused. We wrapped him naked in a blanket, tied his legs together with a rope that we fastened to the tail of a horse, and dragged him all the way to the road through snow two meters deep, taking turns sitting on him and beating him."

The commune was deserted, having lost almost all its men, and the nightly raids and round-ups gradually died down. Indeed, there was no longer anyone left to arrest. We shut up our apartment and stopped living in it, since the hunt for me quite possibly had not yet ended, and the nightly harassment could very well continue. Frósya and Álik moved in with Shúra and Tánya Alekséyev. Lyúba would spend the night with one of her women friends, and I continued as before to spend the night wherever I happened to be.

Álik had begun to scream at night and cling to his mother in terror. His arm had been reset and gradually healed. In the daytime, whenever he saw a militiaman on the street, he would cling to Mama Frósya in fright.

Fearing that Frósya might be arrested in my place, leaving Álik orphaned and crippled, we decided that Frósya and Álik should go to Ukraine to her sister Sásha and live there for the time being. Ványa Shálin and I saw them off. When we were saying goodbye in the railway car at Stálinsk just before the train left, two men in civilian clothes came up to Shálin and me and asked: "Are you going too?" We said we were seeing them off. They looked at us attentively and then left. We expected them to arrest us, but we got back home safely.

I continued living alone on the run. I managed to get to Happy Valley on skis and settled down in Fédya's empty hut. I would sleep during the day and keep a sharp watch all night, holding my skis in readiness. Just the same, I now felt calmer: they would not torment Frósya and Álik on account of me; and if they did catch me, it would be me alone.

During the first five days of my solitary life in the forest, I voluntarily fasted, even though I had some dried crusts with me, and there were some vegetables in Fédya's cellar. I read the New Testament, which I had brought along from home, and I would often repeat the passage from it: "Father, forgive them, for they know not what they do." On the eighth day of solitary life in the forest, I suddenly heard voices not far from the hut. I went out and heard the familiar merry voices of our commune young people. My sister Lyúba, Shúra Shílov, and others came up to the hut on skis. I felt relieved. They told me everything was quiet in the commune. We all went home together.

The spring of 1938 arrived. The raids and arrests had ended. After all, who was there to arrest? Out of all the free hand-farmers in the beautiful but now quiet and sad Happy Valley, I was the only one left, having escaped arrest so far by a miracle. I had sown a little plot of ground with sunflowers and wheat, but I was not able to harvest them. Frósya gathered in the harvest alone; and what she harvested and threshed with her own calloused hands was all taken away from her by the village soviet.

At the end of April I went to Stálinsk to buy some clothes. After pushing my way through the enormous lines and buying very little, I went off to spend the night in the communal hut that stood near the town on the left bank of the Tom, where we would bring vegetables every summer in our flat-bottomed boats for the inhabitants of the town. In the hut I found only Mísha Barbashóv, who lived there as a watchman and stable man. The handful of other commune members who had gone shopping in the city had not yet returned. Barbashóv went out to the stable to clean out manure, and I lay down on a bunk to get a nap.

Soon Andréy Sóvin came from town. A few minutes later, he and I saw a big crowd of militiamen coming straight toward our communal hut. Andréy and I shuddered.

"Come on, Ványa, let's unfasten a boat and get away," Andréy proposed. But we did not do that. After all, we did not know why they were coming to our hut. When the militiamen got there, they ordered us into the hut and started making a search. They ransacked the hut, the attic, and the stable, but found nothing but a pile of letters on the table that we had brought with us from the commune and forgotten to put in the mailbox. They took all those letters with them.

At that time the other commune members who had been in the city were approaching the hut. When they all got back, a two-horse wagon was hitched up and loaded with the women and children, and we men set out on foot for Stálinsk under the guard of the militia. There were twelve of us commune members in all. Late that night we were put into a cellar—the women and children in one cell and the men in another. The next day, the women and children were allowed to go home, but we men were kept there—Andréy Sóvin, Nikoláy Slabínsky, Alekséy Shipílov, Sergéy Yúdin, Mikhaíl Barbashóv, and I.

As usual, we were interrogated at night. I was asked to sign some papers written in ink, and also some blank sheets of paper. I refused to sign. The interrogator (or whatever he called himself) waved a pistol in front of my nose and shouted:

"I'll let you rot in the cellar if you don't sign!"

"Well, so what?" I answered. "I'll have to die sometime in any case, and so will you, but I'm not going to sign your paper."

"All right, then, we'll sign it without you."

They produced Article 58, Paragraph 10, the most fashionable article of that time. It could be used to prosecute anybody—which is just what was done in our poor old Russia. In their indictment they charged that I had allegedly propagandized somebody against the Soviet government, that I had not paid my taxes and had propagandized other commune members not to do so, that I had conducted agitation against turning over horses to the Red Army and against handing over animals to the slaughterhouses, that I had supposedly written an essay against the Soviet government and sent it all over the country, that I myself had traveled all over the country and engaged in agitation, and so on.

Among the letters taken from the commune hut was one I had written to Frósya in Ukraine, in which I had set forth my view of any earthly government as unnecessary violence which should not exist in a rational society. This letter was presented as evidence against me. The young investigator Nikoláyev behaved in various ways: sometimes quietly, but more often coarsely, insolently, using unprintable expressions. He called me a fanatic. He asked about life in the commune, for example: "And what do you think of your smart-aleck Mazúrin?" I said I looked on him as a regular member of the commune, and if he was more intelligent than some people, that was not his fault.

In July Andréy Sóvin, Alekséy Shílov, Nikoláy Slabínsky, and Sergéy Yúdin were released, and Mísha Barbashóv was sent to a mental hospital. I was the only commune member kept in prison. How painful it was for Frósya and Álik when they came back from Ukraine to their empty home.

I sweated out the whole hot summer of 1938 in the Starokuznétsk prison. In the autumn, when snow was falling on the street and it was a little easier to breathe in the cell, I was taken to another cell, where I found Gítya Tyurk, a teacher in our communal school, a man of high principles and noble spirit. What joy it was for us to meet! While we were living in freedom, in the commune, we never experienced such joy in all our meetings.

Soon I was taken to the First Building of the NKVD for trial, which was private. It was the same courtroom and the same Judge Tármyshev who had tried my father and the other commune members in 1936. The trial was short: no questions, no final word. I said to Judge Tármyshev:

"What a strange fate. Two years ago you tried my father, and now you try me, his son. Why are you trying us?"

"You committed a crime, so we're trying you," he answered dryly without raising his head.

The witnesses to the indictment were Iván Ivánovich Andréyev, Sergéy Yúdin, Vasíly Chekmenyóv, and Onúfry Chevnováty. They were not present at the trial. There were only the investigator's papers that the witnesses had signed (under the threat of consequences, as it turned out later).

I felt no ill will toward those poor men for having put their signatures to a lie under the threat of violence.

The sentence of the court was read out: "Ten years of imprisonment."

I went out with the guards into the corridor. There stood Frósya with our newborn daughter, Natásha, but there were no tears in her eyes, and that cheered me up. We walked with the guard to the cell for pretrial imprisonment. Frósya walked beside us. The guard turned out to be a decent fellow, of whom, fortunately, there are many on this earth; but along with his kindly feelings and perhaps also his pity for me, his mind had been stupefied by government hypnosis. He had sworn an oath to the authorities, so he now blindly carried out any irrational orders he received from other mistaken people.

He walked slowly, without hurrying me and without keeping me from talking with Frósya. I pulled back the little blanket and got my first look at our daughter Natásha. She was fast asleep. I longed to kiss those rosy, chubby little cheeks and lips, but I was afraid to wake her from her pure, untroubled sleep. No! let her sleep rather than open her eyes to a reality that is so unnatural, so sad.

The next day, I was taken to the Starokuznétsk prison, and a few days later a big convoy of prisoners was loaded into the railway cars and taken to the Novosibírsk transit prison. Soon we were loaded into freight cars and taken from the Novosibírsk prison to Tomsk. In the cars we were fed only bread and salt fish and were given no water. People would lick the icy walls of the cars, and the bolts and iron handles of the cars.

When we arrived in Tomsk, we marched in an enormous column through the snow-covered streets of the city with its little old-fashioned wooden houses. We came to Cheremóshniki, and from there we went to Timiryázevka for timber cutting—places so well known to the many commune members who spent long years there and to other people who are still among the living. I wrote an appeal to Krúpskaya and Kalínin, even though I had no hope that it would ever reach those good, humane people. Soon there were rumors that Yezhóv had been dismissed from his post, and life was supposedly going to get "easier" in the country.[1] Hopes arose for liberation from "captivity."

---

1. As Commissar of Internal Affairs from 1936 until December 1938, Nikoláy Yezhóv pre-

As a result of loading heavy logs onto the platforms of railway cars, I became seriously ill with radiculitis. I could walk only in a bent-over position, moving my legs only with great difficulty. The medical assistant (a prisoner) would not release me from work because my temperature was almost normal. I showed him my swollen, inflamed loins. He was convinced that I was sick, but he said: "I can't give you a medical certificate. I would be punished for it myself." I was locked up in an ice-cold cell for refusing to work. The next day, I was forced to walk eight kilometers to work in the forest, held up by the arms of friends. I was given a shovel so that I could work without bending my sore back, and I cleared the snow off a railway line. After work, my prisoner friends again led me back, supporting me with their arms, while the guards kept pushing me on from behind and the guard dogs kept snarling. If you stopped or fell, they would tear you to pieces.

That continued for a whole week, until the illness finally died down by itself. I am grateful to my comrades in misfortune who supported me under my arms. Evidently, no cruelty or heartlessness by the authorities or suffering endured by people can extinguish the kindness and compassion in the souls of human beings for one another. That is where the unity of life is visible.

There I met our commune member Alekséy Shipílov, who had been arrested again and sentenced under some other article. But we did not remain together long, because I and a few others were labeled "up for retrial" and sent to Iskitím, where I had to work another half-year at hard labor: at a limestone quarry, loading quicklime into railway cars. After loading quicklime, we all coughed up blood.

In the summer of 1939 I was taken to the Starokuznétsk prison. The retrial here lasted a month, during which all the witnesses retracted their earlier false testimony and I was set free after being required to give my word that I would tell nobody about anything I saw or heard in the prisons and the camps.

By some miracle, my complaint reached Krúpskaya[2] and Kalínin; it got to those sympathetic souls who never believed the tales about "enemies of the people" and who had saved many human lives—for example, the Alekséyev brothers in our commune and many others—and who for this very kindness may have paid with their own lives and departed early from this world.

sided over the secret police during what was possibly the worst period of terror in Soviet history. He was arrested in 1939 and shot some time later. He was succeeded by Lavrénty Béria, who in turn was arrested in 1953, three months after the death of Stálin, and executed shortly afterward.

2. Nadézhda Konstantínovna Krúpskaya (1869–1939), the revolutionary co-worker and wife of Lénin, had some acquaintances among the Tolstoyans, notably Iván Gorbunóv-Posádov and his wife, Yeléna, the parents of one of the contributors to this book, who published a number of Krúpskaya's prerevolutionary articles on pedagogy in their journal *Svobódnoye vospitániye* (Liberal Education). After Lénin's death, Krúpskaya had no real power in Soviet affairs, but the Tolstoyans tended to have faith in her humanity and her willingness to intercede for them when she could during their persecution.

INDEX

WILLIAM EDGERTON is Professor Emeritus of Slavic Languages and Literatures at Indiana University. He is known in Russia and the West as a specialist on the nineteenth-century writer Nikolai Leskov and on the worldwide religious and social influence of Leo Tolstoy. He is translator and editor of *Satirical Stories of Nikolai Leskov*.